Pens and Needles

MATERIAL TEXTS

Series Editors

A complete list of books in the series is available from the publisher.

Pens and Needles

Women's Textualities in Early Modern England

Susan Frye

PENN

University of Pennsylvania Press

Philadelphia · Oxford

LIBRARY

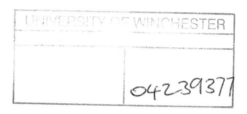
Copyright © 2010 University of Pennsylvania Press

Published by
University of Pennsylvania Press
Philadelphia, Pennsylvania 19104-4112

Printed in the United States of America on acid-free paper

10 9 8 7 6 5 4 3 2 1

Library of Congress Cataloging-in-Publication Data
Frye, Susan, 1952–
    Pens and needles : women's textualities in early modern England / Susan Frye.
        p.   cm. — (Material texts)
    Includes bibliographical references and index.
    ISBN 978-0-8122-4238-6 (hardcover : alk. paper)
    1. Arts, English—16th century.   2. Arts, English—17th century.   3. Material
culture—Social aspects—England.   4. Women—England—Social conditions.   5. Art and
society—England—History—16th century.   6. Art and society—England—History—17th
century.   I. Title.
NX543.F79   2010
704'.0420942—dc22
                                                                                    2010004563

For Lizzie

Contents

Illustrations

~

Figures

Plates

Following page 140

Note on Spelling

To make this work more accessible for the nonspecialist,
I have silently modernized the early modern spelling
and capitalization of nonliterary texts only. I have also
modernized u/v, i/j, and i/y, while replacing long s with
the modern s and completing abbreviations.

Preface

⌒

Decades of scholarly work on early modern English women have expanded our sense of their lives and of the media that they used to express those lives, media that I call *women's textualities*. Early modern modes of perception made women's verbal and visual textualities seem closely related, even versions of one another. As a result, this book considers women's writing alongside their paintings and embroidery. Through their multiple textualities, I argue, women from about 1540 to 1700 expressed themselves in several media that also record the ongoing redefinition of the feminine.

Women's textualities took many forms in early modern England. As activities, they may be placed along a continuum, from those that provide very little information about their producers to those that provide a great deal of information. Surviving forms of women's textualities include notes in samplers, alphabets both stitched and penned, initials, ciphers, wise sayings, and embroidery patterns, all of which offer glimpses of women's activities and perceptions. Still other textualities, including calligraphic manuscripts with embroidered covers and needlework pictures, pamphlets, as well as the texts now classified as literature, offer more substantive information about the connections that women saw between themselves and their texts. Whether providing only traces or whole treatises of information, women's textualities materialize their creators' identities as situated within familial, intellectual, religious, and historical traditions, even as they used those traditions to redefine themselves.

To some producers of early modern texts we can attach names, including privileged women like Elizabeth Tudor, Mary Stuart, Bess of Hardwick, Anne Clifford, Margaret Hoby, Mary Sidney Herbert, and Mary Sidney Wroth. Other women who wrote, painted, or worked textiles include those more at the periphery of power, like Levina Teerlinc, Jane Segar, Esther Inglis, and Amelia Lanyer. Still other women's names are largely unknown, their existence registered only by the needlework that they left behind and by their choice of narratives. Both the nameable and the anonymous women who produced a variety of texts led lives that were engaged with economic, political, religious, and material changes within their society—changes that encouraged both literacy and needle-work among members of the middling classes. The objects that register their subjectivities—whether the products of educated, literate women or the products of the less privileged—offer the rare opportunity to access lives that might otherwise be lost. At the same time, attending to the products of both pens and needles presents an alternative way to read the canonical literature of the period, including William Shakespeare's *Othello* and *Cymbeline*, and Mary Sidney Wroth's *Urania*.

The Introduction opens with the evidence that early modern people often saw the products of women's pens and needles as interrelated, a way of conceptualizing the combined media present in epitaphs, dedications, diaries, educational treatises, and commonplace books. Although it is widely assumed that women held the needle and men held the pen, early modern people themselves as well as contemporary scholars have worked to dispel this simplistic binary. A painting, *Alice Barnham and Her Sons Martin and Steven*, featuring a woman in the act of writing, together with Anne Bradstreet's "The Prologue" and Margaret Cavendish's dedications to *Poems and Fancies*, demonstrates the intensity and wit with which women presented themselves in relation to pens and needles. In addition to considering contemporary perceptions of pens and needles and the array of texts produced by them, the Introduction discusses key terms used throughout the book, including *early modern*, *women*, *identity*, and *agency*. The Introduction closes with a discussion about relations between the subject and the object, including the subject living in the twenty-first century and the object that has survived, however altered, from four hundred years ago. As different as the women in the past were from women of today, interpreting the objects that they used and created offers ways to recover who they thought they were and where they thought they were going.

Following the Introduction, three chapters consider the intersections among historical women's verbal and visual textualities, from those of three titled women in Chapter 1, to the production of professional artisans in Chapter 2, to the needlework of women from many different backgrounds in Chapter 3. The final two chapters continue to examine historical practice while considering the literary use of women's textualities, by William Shakespeare in Chapter 4 and by Mary Sidney Wroth in Chapter 5.

Chapter 1, "Political Designs: Elizabeth Tudor, Mary Stuart, and Bess of Hardwick," considers the relations among three privileged women who combined textualities for their public political advancement. In the process, all three women created objects resembling those that anthropologist Annette Weiner has called "inalienable possessions." These objects were produced as gifts but even more as treasures that assert the political prerogatives of their makers by connecting them to familial pasts and futures. The young Elizabeth Tudor used her needlework-covered translations to assert her familial and political identity to her father, Henry VIII, and her stepmother, Katherine Parr. She also used her portrait to declare her intellect and kinship to her brother, Edward VI. Mary Stuart, Queen of Scots, Dauphine, Queen of France, and Dowager Queen of France, lived out the iconography assigned to her until the deaths of her mother, father-in-law, and husband. At that point she seized the self-representation available in her portraits in white mourning through her poetry, her commissioned portraiture, and her needlework. In France, in Scotland, and finally in England, imprisoned at the houses of the Earl and Countess of Shrewsbury, Mary used her pen and needle to address her family, supporters, and detractors, even as she influenced Bess of Hardwick in the creation of her tapestry-sized hangings of the *Noble Women of the Ancient World* series, which include a heretofore unrecognized portrait of Mary, Queen of Scots.

I begin the book by considering these three well-known women because they had the means and the need to express themselves through writing, portraiture, and needlework to a variety of audiences. The verbal and visual textualities that they practiced were in turn adapted by women from the gentry, merchant, artisan, and middling classes for their own purposes. By the seventeenth century, as more women were learning to write as well as to read, print shops provided access to designs for needlework of the kind that had earlier been available only to queens and aristocrats. Elizabeth Tudor, Mary Stuart, and Bess of Hardwick stood at the forefront of textual practices that would become ever more widely emulated, even as they demonstrate how these elite women combined initials and ciphers, translation and calligraphy, portrait composition and interior design, to assert their intertwined political ambitions.

Chapter 2, "Miniatures and Manuscripts: Levina Teerlinc, Jane Segar, and Esther Inglis as Professional Artisans," focuses on three lesser-known but no less ambitious women than those addressed in Chapter 1. Although Teerlinc, Segar, and Inglis have not been discussed together before, as artisans all three were among England's first professional women; all three practiced their combined verbal and visual skills to recommend themselves to powerful patrons. Levina Teerlinc was a painter, scrivener, miniaturist, and designer who successfully served at the courts of Henry VIII, Mary Tudor, and Elizabeth I. Jane Segar assembled a calligraphic manuscript with painted covers dedicated to Elizabeth that included an original poem as well as ten poems translated from a Latin original and adapted to the queen's iconography. Esther Inglis received the support of kings, queens, and courtiers for the production of her renowned manuscript books. The works of these three artisans demonstrate that a space existed for skilled women to make a career by combining transcriptions of court ritual, translation, dedications, poetry, calligraphy, drawing, painting, self-portraiture, and embroidery.

Chapter 3, "Sewing Connections: Narratives of Agency in Women's Domestic Needlework," discusses how and why girls and women pursued three needlework genres: the spot sampler, a kind of visual commonplace book; the band sampler, a formal genre that nevertheless allowed sometimes inspired variation; and the needlework picture, at that time considered a "sampler" because it featured "exemplars," whether embroidered on book covers, bed valances, cushions, cabinets, hangings, or mirrors. When it came to needleworking pictures, women chose the narratives that they sewed by adapting masculine print traditions. The stories of Bathsheba and Susanna addressed voyeurism, sexual harassment (although that term did not yet exist), rape, and false witness, although in adapting northern European prints needleworkers also engaged the triumphant aspects of these Old Testament stories. Other common subjects for needlework pictures like Sarah and Hagar or the Judgment of Solomon addressed the complex status of wives and children. Choosing to work Esther, Deborah, or Judith meant representing divinely sanctioned women who took bold, even violent political action accompanied by prayers, petition, and psalms. The biblical worthies of needlework pictures appear as well in the printed texts debating the nature of womankind (the *querelle des femmes*), including Esther Sowernam's *Esther Hath Hang'd Haman* and Amelia Lanyer's *Salve Deus Rex Judaeorum*, suggesting that at least some of the women who worked these narratives were exploring active, even outspoken definitions of the feminine. As I completed this chapter, I was able to add the words of Elizabeth Isham, whose lifewriting largely confirmed my sense that women were conscious of exercising agency as they performed embroidery. In their biblical pictures, early modern English women, while living the burden imposed by concepts of the virtuous woman, pictured this ideal as beautiful but also active; sexually desirable but also chaste; submissive but also violent; quiet but outspoken to the point of presenting petitions or declaiming psalms in public; and used, even abused, by men and yet triumphant over them.

Overall, the first three chapters of *Pens and Needles: Women's Textualities in Early Modern England* examine the products of early modern English women's pens and needles, which express their changing political, personal, and professional identities, in the process creating art, literature, and exquisitely crafted objects. The two concluding chapters continue to elucidate women's historical relations to texts and textiles, while demonstrating how an awareness of women's textualities alters the readings of three canonical works of literature: *Othello*, *Cymbeline*, and *The Countess of Montgomery's Urania*.

Chapter 4, "Staging Women's Relations to Textiles in Shakespeare's *Othello* and *Cymbeline*," uses the study of women's textualities to reexamine *Othello* and *Cymbeline*. This chapter begins with an overview of women's everyday labor that produced textiles, from the most basic carding and spinning to common needlework, where the ubiquitous patterns of the peasecod, the grapevine, and the strawberry situated women within life stories of production and reproduction. Working from such textualities, I argue that while these plays acknowledge women's everyday relations to textiles, they also conflate women's hands in the act of sewing with their sexuality and their bodies with cloth. Such erotic conflations, whether present in Dutch genre paintings of the period or on the English stage, enabled the fantasy that women—or the boys who played them— were accessible and possessable. In Shakespeare's plays, this fantasy produces violence: Othello not only murders Desdemona and Emilia but also explains the handkerchief's origin, revealing his changing view of himself as a racialized, Muslim outsider, a process that culminates in his suicide. Reconfiguring women's relations to textiles by associating the handkerchiefs, sheets, and bedchambers of Desdemona and Innogen with their bodies, leads to the physical threats against them. Shakespeare's manipulation of women's relations to cloth necessarily inflects and is inflected by the genres in which he is working. And genre has consequences for female characters. Both tragedy and dramatic romance equate cloth with the female body, but the extension of time in *Cymbeline* allows cloth to be translated into Innogen's bedroom emblematic of royal feminine agency and Posthumus Leonatus's bloody cloth, as well as into disguises and a lost baby's mantle, with their promise of resurrection and reunion.

Chapter 5, "Mary Sidney Wroth: Clothing Romance," concludes *Pens and Needles* by considering how textiles are integral to Wroth's authorship of this first-known example of a prose romance written by an English woman. Instead of describing everyday practices associated with needlework, Wroth uses luxurious textiles and rhetorical practices associated with cloth to dilate her narrative. Although the world of *Urania* is located far from the everyday women's work of carding, spinning, mending, and sewing, its courtly, pastoral, and enchanted settings emphasize early modern women's use of language, including their orality, literacy, and authorship, often positing that language is inseparable from embroidery, clothing, and political textiles of state. In *Urania*, Wroth creates her leisurely, internested narratives of female desire by drawing on her Sidneyan awareness of rhetoric and aristocratic practice, making women's textual production into a narrative in which textiles enact early modern women's identity and agency. Reading Wroth with the historical relations between women's texts and textiles in mind allows us to see how she generated romance by bringing together rhetoric, anagram and cipher, dilated narrative and familial practice to register the range and reach of women's textualities.

In *Pens and Needles*, I bring together early modern women's verbal and visual texts, reading them as objects that expand our sense of women's participation in redefining the feminine from within its lived practice. In my earlier study of Queen Elizabeth I, I focused on how she rewrote early modern attempts to define and limit the feminine, using her iconography to articulate the political choices that she made and had then to fight for as her represented body. This study of women named and anonymous, historical and fictional, includes but also moves beyond the court in order to demonstrate that women from a variety of backgrounds possessed related forms of verbal and visual expression that began in royal, aristocratic, and artisanal practice and quickly spread to England's other classes, who altered and developed these textualities to suit their needs. As the recorded textualities of early modern English women became more diverse and more widespread, they resulted in objects that these women used and created, objects that delve the instabilities of gender difference.

Introduction

~

Intersections of Women's Verbal and Visual Textualities

George Ballard, the eighteenth-century tailor and antiquarian turned recorder of women's lives, provides the epitaph for Elizabeth Lucar, wife of a wealthy London merchant who died in 1537 at the age of twenty-seven. The monument raised to her in the parish church of St. Michael in Crooked Lane included an inscription that read in part:

> She wrote all Needle-workes that women exercise
> With Pen, Frame, or Stoole, all Pictures artificiall.
> Curious Knots, or Trailes, what fancie could devise,
> Beasts, Birds, or Flowers, even as things natural:
> Three manner Hands could she write them faire all.
> To speak of algorisme, or accounts in every fashion,
> Of women, few like (I thinke) in all this Nation.[1]

The epitaph's praise of Lucar's needlework, her ability to write "Three manner Hands"—secretary, Roman, and italic[2]—together with her skills in accounting and languages, demonstrates that needlework and writing, while heading the list of accomplishments attained by women of the middling classes[3] in early modern London, could be described as forms of one another. The phrase "She wrote all Needle-workes" plays with "wrote" and "wrought" as the past tense of both "to write" and "to work" (meaning "to needlework"). The epitaph also juxtaposes the objects that Lucar used to create her texts, emphasizing their interaction: To make her "Pictures artificiall" she used her "Pen, Frame" and "Stoole," when her "Pen" could have been used for several purposes: to design needlework patterns by using the pen as a writing implement or to prick the designs on cloth by using the pen as a stylus, to perform arithmetic, or to paint—because "pen" also meant "paintbrush."[4] Lucar's "Frame" could have been either a loom for weaving or a device to hold embroidery taut; her "Stoole" also held cloth for working. Her "Curious Knots, or Trailes, what fancie could devise" could refer to carefully worked embroidery designs and ink-drawn "knots," in the sense of "a design or figure formed of crossing lines; an intricate flourish of the pen" (OED). What Elizabeth Lucar "wrote" and "wrought" connected her with her privileged contemporaries similarly engaged not only in the work of furnishing their homes but also in the work of performing the feminine as domestically, financially, and intellectually capable. In noting Lucar's abilities as exceptional—"Of women, few (I thinke) in all this Nation"—the author of the epitaph acknowledges them as an integral part of English nationhood.[5] As her epitaph goes on to say, Lucar was also musical and able to speak, write, and read "Latine and Spanish, and also Italian," while "for the English, she the Garland wan, / In Dame Prudence Schoole"—a record of Lucar's education outside the household as well as familial pride in its domestic value.[6]

Like the author of Lucar's epitaph, Elizabeth Tudor uses "wrought" to pun on the relation between writing and embroidery. In her introduction to the needlework-covered calligraphic manuscript she gave to Queen Katherine Parr as a New Year's gift, dated December 1544, Elizabeth transmutes the volume's mental and spiritual acts of translation, writing, and sewing book covers into a metaphor of requested correction. The eleven-year-old Elizabeth says of her translation of Marguerite de Navarre's *The Glass of the Sinful Soul*, "I have wrought in it (as well spiritual as manual)," and asks Parr to "rub out, polish, and mend (or else cause to mend) the words (or rather the order of my writing), the which I know in many places to be rude and nothing done as it should be."[7] Elizabeth's request for help in perfecting what she has "wrought" both spiritually and manually as an eleven-year-old connects her to her stepmother as daughter and student.

Lady Grace Mildmay further connects writing, drawing, and needlework in her autobiographical writings from about 1617 to 1620. She describes drawing on paper and designing embroidery patterns during the years that she lived with her in-laws while her husband traveled widely on business: "Also everyday I spent some time in works of mine own invention without sample of drawing or pattern before me for carpet or Cushion work [two forms of needlework] & to draw flowers & fruits to their life with my plumett [lead pencil] upon paper."[8]

Mildmay's penned record of her engagement with a variety of text-producing tools registers the similarities that she perceived between needlework and drawing as the means to realize "mine own invention." She pointedly separates these activities from the more common act of copying drawings or patterns. In asserting her "own invention," Mildmay places herself at the learned end of the rhetorical practice of *imitatio*, in which a student begins by copying models, then composes work based on that of others, and finally "invents" her own work.[9] Like Lucar's epitaph and Elizabeth's preface, Mildmay's description of her daily activities demonstrates that for many early modern English women, writing, visual design, and needlework were not considered mutually exclusive activities; rather, they were related ways to create texts.

From about 1540 to 1700, the definition of an accomplished woman changed only slightly, and, just as in the Lucar epitaph, the interaction among her abilities created an emblem of virtue that connects artistic and domestic achievement. The biography of Elizabeth Cary, which Heather Wolfe has shown was written primarily by Elizabeth's daughter Lucy, provides an account at mid-seventeenth century of the girlhood education of her brilliant mother. According to Lucy, Elizabeth Cary's education began when she "learnt to read very soon and loved it much." Although Elizabeth's first encounter with French at "four or five year old" made her give it up, she later taught herself Latin, French, Spanish, Italian, Hebrew either "without a teacher" or "with very little teaching." She even learned "of a transilvanian, his language." After this description of language acquisition, the biography continues with a sentence about sewing: "She was skillfull and curious in working, never having bene helped by any body; those that knew her would never have beleeved she knew how to hold a needle unlesse they had seene it."[10] In juxtaposing languages and needlework, Lucy Cary is doing more than defending the femininity of her mother by emphasizing her needlework alongside her linguistic genius. For Lucy, what links the descriptions of Elizabeth Cary's learned accomplishments is the independence that she exhibited in learning them. Reading, learning languages, and creating needlework are not separate elements on a list of accomplishments as they might be in two hundred years' time. Instead, as in the Lucar epitaph and Mildmay's self-description, the naming of the woman's abilities invokes the head and hand that practiced them all.

Such descriptions of the activities of girls and women demonstrate the extent to which they were expected to contribute toward their families' well-being by practicing everyday the goodly—and godly—relations among verbal and visual texts. In their world, combining visual images and writing derived from a mode of thought charged with religious conviction, which made writing itself a visual art form; portraiture a vehicle for inscriptions; painted cloths, tapestries, and needlework the primary vehicle for translating written narratives into everyday design; and the household, market, court, inn, church, and theater into the social locations where speech connected with the signifying wealth of recorded texts. Rayna Kalas explains the early modern connection between the divine and language, whose "temporal and worldly effects" were thought to be "wrought in and through language" because "the efficacy of language was generally attributed to divine agency."[11] Connecting language to some kind of picture, even the calligraphic drawing of the words themselves, enhanced connections to the world's complex truths through the multivalent play of signifiers. As Juliet Fleming describes it, the practice of combining the verbal and visual derived from and perpetuated "an almost magical way of thinking about the physical properties of language."[12] People of many abilities and backgrounds perceived the complementary powers of the word and the picture, a way of thinking that allowed access to divine truth through everyday objects.

Thomas Elyot noted in 1531 that engraving a worthy man's "plate and vessel" with "histories, fables, or quick and wise sentences, comprehending good doctrine or counsels" meant that when he sat down to eat and drink, he was able to "sussitate"—that is, "resuscitate" or "restore to life" (OED)—"some disputation or reasoning; whereby some part of time shall be saved, which else by superfluous eating and drinking would be idly consumed."[13] Everyday objects imbued with writing and design could, in effect, save time by breathing truths into everyday actions. About fifty years later, George Puttenham offered a description of the "Device or Emblem," in which the intersections of the visual and the verbal also connect everyday activities to representation. As he explains, in both "devices of arms" and "amorous inscriptions," "short, quick, and sententious propositions" in words are "commonly accompanied with a figure or portrait of ocular representation, the words so aptly corresponding to the subtlety of the figure, that as well the eye is therewith recreated as the ear or the mind." Noting that these "ocular" representations with their "corresponding" words delight the eye, ear, and mind, Puttenham moves easily from combined written and visual forms to embroidered textiles: for a man may "put [such combinations] into letters of gold and send to his mistresses for a token" or "cause [them] to be embroidered in escutcheons of arms, or in any border of a rich garment to give by his novelty marvel to the beholder."[14] The visual and verbal combinations that privileged people commissioned as impresas and coats of arms, engraved within rings, and had embroidered on their clothing demonstrate the allure that multivalent expression had for the culture that Elyot and Puttenham were describing. Combining words and images made the best possible use of time, brought great truths into human reach, recreated the senses, and stimulated the beholder to "marvel."

Early modern domestic interiors depended on these suggestive intersections of the verbal and visual. Pictures like *The Family of Henry VIII* (1545) demonstrate that the presentation rooms of the Tudors were composed of intersecting texts, including the cloth of estate with its royal coat of arms, its inscription,

Introduction

Dieu et Mon Droit; the classical pillars ornamented with gold; the wooden ceiling of carved Tudor roses; and the oriental, or "table," carpet ostentatiously underfoot, a reminder of England's importation of luxury goods from the Middle East. The aristocracy practiced similar interlocking media in their interior decoration. Elyot urged the suitable "decking in the house of a noble man or man of honour" with "ornaments of hall and chambers, in Arras, painted tables, and images containing histories, wherein is represented some monument of virtue, most cunningly wrought, with the circumstance of the matter briefly declared" for the edification of the beholder.[15]

The domestic interiors of the gentry and lower middling classes were as saturated with signifying images and writing as the interiors of the royals, aristocrats, and powerful merchants. Rather than the soberly whitewashed walls of the early modern houses that we visit as museums, as Fleming points out, the early modern interior was packed with words and images. Household decoration took the form of writings and pictures painted, tacked, or hung on all available spaces, including along beams and on window glass.[16] The few remaining merchant-class houses from this period suggest the signifying exuberance within early modern walls, from imposing merchant houses like Packwood House in Warwickshire to the handful of tiny but elegant surviving row houses in Great Yarmouth, as narrow as their Dutch counterparts across the Channel. Houses both large and small contain elaborate plasterwork ceilings, furniture, and the occasional surviving needle- or bead-worked piece. As architectural artifacts, these houses demonstrate how, by the turn of the seventeenth century, merchant- and middling-class families of varying degrees of wealth increasingly appropriated sixteenth-century forms of royal and aristocratic interior decoration. In the second edition of *The Description of England* (1587), William Harrison describes how such sumptuous and decorative forms had moved from the aristocracy to merchants and then to artisans and farmers. In the "houses of knights gentlemen, merchantmen, and some other wealthy citizens" are found "provision of tapestry, Turkey work, pewter, brass, fine linen, and thereto costly cupboards of plate." Such furnishings have "descended yet lower," "even unto the inferior artificers and many farmers." Harrison describes how these artisans and farmers, displaying plate, joined beds with hangings, table carpets and "fine napery" or household linens, also decorated their walls, either with paneling or "hanged with tapestry, arras work, or painted cloths, wherein either diverse histories, or herbs, beasts, knots, and suchlike are stained."[17] Even in single-room, single-story dwellings, Tessa Watt asks us to imagine printed pictures, while at "public inns and alehouses," the places that she terms "nodal points of communication," people of many walks of life, including the laborer, were "likely to come into some contact with printed or painted 'stories.'"[18] With writing and design moving without copyright interruption from engraved print to cheap printed picture to embroidery, or from cheap picture to painted cloth and wall, narratives from religious history, as well as proverbs, emblems, and images celebrating fertile and productive country life, filled domestic interiors.

In households that expected a mix of verbal and visual media, women's verbal and visual textualities were increasingly welcome. Writing at the beginning of the sixteenth century, Juan Vives set out what proved to be an enduringly popular expression of the relations between textile work and women's literacy in *The Instruction of a Christian Woman*, first published in Latin in 1529 and dedicated to Catherine of Aragon for the education of Mary Tudor. Vives defines the feminine through needlework across class, in the words of Richard Hyrde's translation of 1540: "I hold in no wise that a woman should be ignorant of those feats, that must be done by hand: no not though she be a princess or a queen" (Sig. K1(r)).[19] Needlework is appropriate for all classes of women because, exercised as Vives imagines in quiet and confined domestic spaces, it underlies the female virtue so central to his fantasy of a secure home. Such passages also reveal his fear about the degree to which domestic security rests on the appropriate activity of women. In the context of his anxiety about the connection between female chastity and domestic order, Vives closely connects literacy and women's textile work, counseling that a girl should "both learn her book" and "handle wool and flax." Reading and textile work "are two crafts yet left of the old innocent world, both profitable and keepers of temperance: which thing specially women ought to have in price" (Sig. C4(r)). For Vives, the virtuous woman had been defined in terms of her textile labor since the time of Proverbs' worthy wife, as well as Ancient Greece's Penelope and Rome's Lucretia, "whom kings' sons found watching and working upon wool among her maids" (Sig. K1(r)).

In *The Instruction of a Christian Woman*, textile work forms part of an education that includes not only reading but also writing, with a brief mention of painting. Vives approves of writing as copying and memorizing "some sad sentence prudent and chaste taken out of holy scripture or the sayings of philosophers" (E2); that is, he approves the writing of the sayings increasingly kept in commonplace books and eventually in band samplers, or that might have been written on walls, beams, and ceilings.[20] He also encourages the already-existing tradition in 1529 of literate women keeping a family receipt book, or "little book," containing recipes for both food and medicine "diligently written" (K3). In addition, although "painting" late in *The Instruction* refers to the abhorrent practice of face-painting,[21] earlier Vives cites with approval Queen Isabella of Spain's having taught her daughters, who included Catherine of Aragon, "to spin, sew and paint" (D1). Vives authorizes women's multiple textualities because his immediate audience is Catherine of Aragon and Mary Tudor, even within a text that constantly seeks to silence and isolate women as a group. In appealing to this aristocratic female audience and in describing existing courtly and household practice, he espouses verbal and visual literacies for daughters of the gentry and middling classes as well.

At the other end of the sixteenth century, Richard Mulcaster set forth his ideal of English education in his *Positions* (1581), with its forty-five chapters on male education and one chapter on the education of girls. Whereas Vives addresses Catherine of Aragon as the most prominent member of his audience, Mulcaster addresses Elizabeth I, as well as her female courtiers, the "undershining stars, many singular ladies and gentlewomen, so skillful in all cunning, of the most laudable and loveworthy qualities of learning."[22] Even as Mulcaster is aware of his well-educated audience, when he wrote *Positions* Mulcaster was headmaster at the Merchant Taylor's School where he was, famously, Edmund Spenser's teacher. As a result, Mulcaster's writing epitomizes the ambitions and anxieties of London's middling classes even as it addresses queen and court. His interest in discussing the curriculum of city children is therefore inflected by an awareness that "*how much* a woman ought to learn" depends entirely on what "shall be needful," according to her social class or her parents' ambitions (140). Mulcaster's text outlines and reinforces the severe limitations placed on girls' education during this period, as he denies girls any school beyond the "elementary," including universities, while refusing them the study of geometry, as well as occupations with intellectual status, such as physicians or preachers (126, 141–43). Nevertheless, reading and writing have their household applications. Because the majority of women "are to be the principal pillars in the upholding of households, and so they are likely to prove if they prove well in training," Mulcaster argues that girls should be taught to read and, in most cases, to write as well, given that "many good occasions are often times offered, where it were better for them to have the use of their pen, for the good that comes by it" (137). They should also be taught music, and, though Mulcaster at one point asserts that "I meddle not with needles nor yet with *housewifery*," he eventually deals with both, writing, "I think it and know it to be a principal commendation in a woman to govern and direct her household; to look to her house and family; to provide and keep necessaries, though the goodman pay." Like Vives, Mulcaster acknowledges the woman's value as food provider and healer, for she must "know the force of her kitchen, for sickness and health in herself and her charge" (138). When Mulcaster considers the subject of needlework for girls, he connects it to their drawing and writing in the now-familiar early modern connection among women's writing, drawing, and embroidery: "If I should allow them the *pencil* to draw, as the pen to write, and thereby entitle them to all my elementary principles, I might have reason for me. For it neither requireth any great labor to free young maidens from it, and it would help their needle to beautify their works; and it is maintainable by very good examples even of their own kind" (142). As he considers the interconnections among the skills taught to girls, Mulcaster pauses on the verge of allowing them all the "elementary principles" that make up the education that he espouses for boys.[23]

Mulcaster's articulation of a girl's education based on the interconnections among writing, drawing, and needlework as well as music and languages finds expression on the early modern stage as well. In Shakespeare's *Pericles* the lost princess Marina stays out of the brothel by teaching her female pupils the skills learned all too well at the court of Crecopia, including, as Gower describes them, both oratory and needlework as composition: "Deep clerks she dumbs and with her nee'le composes / Nature's own shape of bud, bird, branch, or berry," abilities that Marina adds to dancing and music. Sixty years later, as household skills were moving down the social hierarchy, the exiled queen Eulalia in Richard Brome's *The Queen and Concubine* (1659) pledges to earn her living by teaching the daughters of country people "the Needle, Loome, / The Wheel, the Frame, the Net-Pin" together with reading, "literature," and "divers Instruments, Songs and measures." When Eulalia is restored to her rightful throne, she teaches a "servant" to read in ten days and promises her that she will write "joyn-hand" once she knows her "letters" and her "minums."[24] The educational—and pedagogical—accomplishments of such female characters reiterate the influential educational treatises of Vives and Mulcaster, with their affirmation that accomplished women must display interactive, interconnected verbal and visual skills. Moreover, in the course of the early modern period, these expected accomplishments extended across social class, from princesses like Mary Stuart and Elizabeth Tudor or the represented Marina and Eulalia, to Elizabeth Lucar of the merchant class and, by mid-seventeenth century, to girls of the middling classes, country girls, and lower servants.

Women continued to record their own strong sense of the intersection of drawing or painting, writing, and sewing in the books that they created. Constance Aston Fowler's commonplace book dating from the 1630s and 1640s is a quarto volume of 200 leaves housed at the Huntingdon Library.[25] Her book features both religious and secular drawings, many of which resemble embroidery patterns. Esther Inglis, whose manuscript books are discussed in Chapter 2, produced nearly sixty known miniature books, from *A small book containing diverse sorts of letters* in 1586 to *Fifty Christian emblems after Georgette de Montenay* and *The Booke of the Psalmes of Davide in Prose* in 1624.[26] Inglis's books, sometimes bound within needleworked covers, feature her extraordinary command of numerous calligraphic scripts, miniature drawings and paintings, and designs resembling those for needlework penned, like Fowler's, in black ink. Inglis frequently includes among her scripts or "hands" one in which each letter is composed of a series of dashes so that the writing appears to be stitched to the page.

These early modern women worked at the intersections of visual and verbal texts in different ways and with different audiences in mind, but they saw the needle, the pen, and the pencil or brush as interrelated tools because women for the most part perceived their products—writing and needlework, designing and painting—as separate but related forms of expression. This was true as well for other producers of calligraphic manuscripts, including not only Elizabeth Tudor and Mary Stuart (Chapter 1) but also Levina Teerlinc, Jane Segar, and Esther Inglis (Chapter 2), and for those women who encoded messages in their needlework (Chapter 3) and in architectural and interior design (Chapters 1 and 4). Elizabeth Lucar, Elizabeth Tudor, Grace Mildmay, Elizabeth Cary, Constance Fowler, Esther Inglis, Levina Teerlinc, and Jane Segar all exercised their pens and needles as related endeavors.

Early Modern Women: Defining Terms

As can be seen from these examples, learning about women's lives and women's textualities requires embracing a broader sense of text than the literary. This is why I argue that in recovering early modern women's textualities—their many forms of expression—we need to consider their verbal and visual texts, as well as the texts created by the intersection of the two. Adding visual texts like drawings, paintings, and needlework as well as expanding the written to include words painted and sewn expands our ability to study women of the middling classes. The rich mix of the verbal and visual in early modern life also provides access to once ubiquitous media, media to which women were valued contributors and through which women simultaneously asserted and explored their identities. Women's textualities record these assertions and explorations, as women worked within and altered definitions of the feminine. By bringing more women into view and into relation with one another, studying women's texts both on and off the page sheds light on historical women's lives, on the objects that they produced with pens and needles, and on how literary texts by and about women represented these textualities.

Because *Pens and Needles: Women's Textualities in Early Modern England* examines *early modern women* and the variety of texts that they produced, I acknowledge from the first that its analytical categories are unstable. I have chosen *early modern* because during the sixteenth and seventeenth centuries conceptual and material changes occurred that helped to form our current and always-evolving frames of reference. In England, humanist reevaluations of the Catholic Church and the subsequent Reformation changed the ways in which Protestants, Catholics, and those in between valued literacy, the vernacular, and publication in manuscript and print, at the same time that they retained the conviction that the intersections of language and pictures allowed access to truth. During this same period, the rise of the nation-state, the exploration, exploitation, and seizure of the New World and other points around the globe in the name of empire, together with England's increasing participation in global trade and industrialization, help to explain why profound shifts occurred in how people conceived of religion, politics, race, class, and gender.

Like the term *early modern*, the definition of *women* is complicated by the discourses of religion, nationalism, trade, race, and class and the changing material culture of the everyday, as well as by the inherent instability of language as constituted through cultural categories. A person born with female genitalia encountered a world with certain expectations about her behavior; about the categories of daughter, wife, mother, and widow; about what she was supposed to do and not to do as she traversed these categories during the course of her life—if in fact her life conformed to them. Within her circumstances and her ability to navigate the instabilities inherent in these categories and the conflicting cultural narratives that sought to articulate them, she necessarily created an always-changing identity.[27] She might be Elizabeth Tudor or she might be Moll Frith, exploiting the instabilities of gender to assert male prerogatives; she might attend the theater where cross-dressed males portrayed the limits but also the possibilities of the feminine as literate, witty, vengeful, articulate, sexual, and desired. She might produce a cordial for the bloody flux from her aunt's recipe, work the Vindication of Susanna in a pictorial "sampler," or like Mary Sidney Herbert turn her hand to innovative translation, like Anne Bradstreet to heroic poetry, like Elizabeth Cary to drama or history, or like Mary Sidney Wroth to prose romance. She might be married or she might not; she might have children or she might not; she might run a large household or she might spend her life either running a smaller household or in service, in either case caught up in carding, spinning, cooking, nursing, and cleaning, as part of a household or for wages. Regardless of her class or the choices made from the range available to her, she was located in and contributing to a world composed of texts—to stories, songs, conversation, and argument; to cheap printed pictures pinned to the walls of the local inn and dwellings;[28] to opulent tapestries or to the more intimate, domestically produced needlework pictures wrought in bright silks. To the extent that we can recover these texts, either through objects or verbal descriptions, we can recover what some women chose to record about themselves and their lives, whether they made their choices consciously or unconsciously. Within these texts, we may read how a few women openly questioned the roles assigned to *women* in their society, while the majority both embraced these roles and still subtly redefined them. Whether or not people were conscious of the instabilities of gender, they necessarily constructed their lives in response to the opportunities as well as the limits residing within those instabilities. As a result, the instability of the category of *women* lies at the heart of this study.

Still other terms appear throughout this work. Some terms central to my discussion spring from the theoretical questions surrounding subjectivity, especially the ongoing attempt to describe how the individual subject works to define a "self." Philip Sidney's haunting phrase, "I am not I, pity the tale of me,"[29] resounds not only as the literary and political problem of constructing a poem's speaker as a courtly lover performing within narrative but also as the problems of discovering, expressing, exploring, performing, and disguising interiority. As a result, I use the term *identity* to refer to the ever-becoming sense of a stable "self" that individual subjects attempted to generate through their relations to space, time, and discourse. *Identity* in this sense emerges as *agency* when the individual subject seeks expression, whether in everyday actions, however humble or domestic, or in the variety of texts and objects that women produced. Barbara Gamage Sidney's interactions with her doctor when she gave birth while infected with measles—although unrecoverable—were in this sense as much an expression of her agency as her activities in administering the Sidney estate at Penshurst.[30] Moreover, as these examples illustrate, these definitions of *identity* and *agency* require an awareness of the subject's multiple social relations. In the course of writing this book, Michel de Certeau's description of the "individual" as a "locus in which an incoherent (and often contradictory) plurality of such relational determinations interact"[31] has been especially useful in conceptualizing the identities of women as situated in an everyday world that was always under construction.

The problem of how to define and use effectively the objects from the past or "material culture" also raises insistent theoretical and methodological questions, including the study of the "everyday." Patricia Fumerton usefully summarizes Michel de Certeau's conception of how "everyday life" proceeds as, in "daily practices," the "common person tactically and almost invisibly transforms from within the social structures she or he inhabits."[32] Or, as de Certeau himself describes the practice of everyday life, "users make (*bricolent*) innumerable and infinitesimal transformations of and within the dominant cultural economy in order to adapt it to their own interests and their own rules."[33] By thinking about—but also beyond—privileged and literary women, I argue that thousands of early modern English women, regardless of their degree of lettered literacy,[34] exercised textualities that changed the everyday even as they lived it.

The importance of the term *everyday* joins that of the term *domestic* throughout this book. Whenever my discussion moves to the household, the institution central to early modern English life, I have very much in mind Wendy Wall's discussion of the "disorienting character" of the domestic, considered as both "a reassuringly 'common' sphere in which people immersed themselves in familiar rhythms, and as a profoundly alienating site that could never be fully inhabited or comprehended." In drama, writes Wall, the "disorienting character" of domesticity "paradoxically enabled people to imagine new identities and subject positions."[35] Wall's discussion, like my own, acknowledges the extent to which the boundaries between household and public space were permeable. Both inside and outside the home, women's verbal and visual textualities—and the ways these textualities are represented in texts that we now consider literary—form crucial sites for exploring the instabilities of early modern life that women variously accepted, confronted, and mediated. On rare occasions, women produced material evidence of these interactions that has survived the centuries, from mere traces to entire oeuvres, texts in which the "common" and the "alienating" qualities of their lives may be seen as versions of one another.

The texts that early modern women left behind I have classified as being produced by pens, needles, and combinations of the two. In a book about the blurring of textual categories, it may come as no surprise that these categories are themselves unstable and overlapping, despite the fact that much of the scholarship of the past two centuries has insisted on their separation. To the extent that pens reference writing, I mean not just the composition of literature but all the forms of writing exercised by early modern women. Women's writing varied widely in complexity and purpose, while often requiring only a limited degree of lettered literacy. As a result, for the purposes of this book, writing encompasses a continuum from embroidered alphabets to the 590,000 words of Mary Sidney Wroth's *Urania*.[36] I take into account a range of work by women that appeared in print, in manuscript, and in writing that falls into both categories, like Elizabeth's translation of *The Glass of the Sinful Soul*, first circulated as a presentation manuscript for her father and later published, or Wroth's romance, whose first volume was published while the second was not. For both printed books and manuscripts, I have kept in mind Peter Beal's useful questions, "What is this manuscript trying to tell us? Why is it constituted the way it is? What can we understand from it about the circumstances of, and reasons for, its production? And how should we be dealing with this evidence?"[37] Moreover, as Juliet Fleming has made us aware, letters on a piece of paper were once the least common form of writing. This book considers, among other written forms, inscriptions in painted pictures and textiles, alphabets and verse in samplers, as well as the classical and biblical narratives that inspired interior design, including needlework.

As mentioned in the discussion of Lucar's epitaph, the word *pen* once referred not only to pens and pencils but also to paintbrushes for drawing, design, and portraiture. Thomas Elyot, for example, advised boys who were so "inclined" to "paint with a penne."[38] Pens were implements not only for writing but also for sketching, drawing, and applying paint to a surface. In this sense, pens could be commissioned for *portraiture*, a category that I employ to describe pictures of women, whether commissioned or created by their own hand. When women like Mary Tudor, Elizabeth Tudor, Mary Stuart, and Anne Clifford paid for their portraits, they were able to collaborate with the artist in assembling the texts and objects with which they surrounded themselves. When women themselves created portraits, like the tapestry self-portrait of Bess of Hardwick made from appliquéd textiles or Esther Inglis's self-portraits in miniature drawn in ink or painted in jeweled colors, they assembled texts and objects as expressions of identity. As Andrea Pearson has recently pointed out, studying early modern portraiture allows consideration of "a new model for male artists and female sitters as agents" because "portraits more than any other form of pictorial expression immediately lend themselves to the study of identity and agency."[39] *Portraiture* also describes the ways in which women pictured themselves in the texts that they produced, including autobiographical forms of "life writing," as well as paintings commissioned as life records, or needlework featuring portraits of female exemplars as exercising female speech, political participation, and military action. In addition, I include women's building activities as a kind of self-portraiture because domestic architecture, from arranging rooms to planning and building country houses, articulates identity by writing it large in space and time.

Through the term *needles*, I wish to evoke the entire continuum of early modern women's relations to textiles, from the most basic carding and spinning of thread, laundering, mending, and sewing, to the complex textile production embodied in skilled needlework. Women were valued for these skills because they contributed to the health and welfare of household members and to the "household store." In addition to needlework's position within the early modern gift economy used to construct or affirm social affiliation,[40] needlework was prized for its ability to add to the sum of goods owned by a family at a time when the majority of people possessed few material goods. Families assembled their "store"—the accumulation of possessions demonstrating social rank and household sufficiency—in the face of the relative scarcity and expense in

England of plate, precious metals and jewels, embroidery, and other textiles like the "household stuff" of linens and clothing. Juan Vives promises that the virtuous wife's "diligence shall increase much her household store," and in a statement that shares the fantasy that women will be quiet as they sew, a hundred years later John Taylor in "The Praise of the Needle," promises that for women, needlework "will increase their peace, enlarge their store, / To sue their tongues lesse, and their Needles more." In a broadside ballad, "Salomon's good housewife, in the 31 of his Proverbs" (1607), Thomas Deloney's paraphrase of Proverbs 31 describes the ideal wife as one whose "wit a common wealth maintains / Of needments for her household store."[41]

Whether given as gifts or treasured as part of the household, early modern women's needlework included texts that deserve to be read with a full sense of how and why they were wrought. Textiles and the social practices surrounding them are evidence of the materiality of women's agency. In their textile work, early modern English women represented themselves through narrative pictures and patterns, locations of their expressed identity. Jane Schneider and Annette Weiner observe in *Cloth and Human Experience* that cloth "lends itself to an extraordinary range of decorative variation" whether through "patterned weaving" or "through the embroidery, staining, painting, or dyeing of the whole." Its "broad possibilities" for variation "give cloth an almost limitless potential for communication."[42] In Western culture, as in many other cultures around the globe, there exists an implicit connection between textiles and verbal texts because women have traditionally told stories aloud as well as in domestic design. Texts and textiles are connected not only through the stories that both tell but also through an underlying philology that describes the ways in which texts are rooted in material production. Linda Woodbridge points out that in English "'text' and 'textile' derive from the Latin *textus*, from texēre, to weave, meaning that which is woven."[43] Traditionally, women wove or embroidered cloth to communicate a story, as in the tradition of the raped Philomela who made her story into "a tedious sampler" (*Titus Andronicus*, 2.4.39);[44] that is, a piece of elaborately wrought needlework. In England from the medieval period through the eighteenth century, thousands of women worked designs and narratives in cloth. From the perspective of women's lives, embroidered work and, to a less obvious extent, the knots and patterns of sewing, weaving, and knitting, placed their workers within narratives of fertility and continuity. As the artist Manuel Vega commented about Yoruba beadwork, "nothing is decorative" because "everything" is a "coded language."[45] In the early modern period, women's domestic needlework, like Yoruba beadwork, Gee's Bend quilts,[46] or the patterns woven within Iranian carpets, encoded ways of seeing the world.

Although this analysis of verbal and visual media requires a reliance on textual and material forms of evidence that can never be complete, I have known since the afternoon when I first walked through New Hardwick Hall that to study early modern English women means considering the sheer variety of texts that women produced. Hardwick Hall was built in the 1590s by the woman now known rather casually as Bess of Hardwick but who lived the last forty-one years of her life as Elizabeth Talbot, Countess of Shrewsbury. That she exalted in this aristocratic identity can be seen in her use of the initials ES, which are prominent at several points on the roof of New Hardwick Hall as well as in her needlework pieces. During her long lifetime, Bess of Hardwick became one of the most formidable women in England, the wealthiest woman after Queen Elizabeth I, a founder of both the Cavendish and the Talbot dynasties, as well as a needleworker and what we might today call a conceptual artist. She designed New Hardwick's spaces in the 1590s, working with the finest architect of the time, Robert Smythson; oversaw its construction to the penny; and then filled it with purchased paintings, tapestries, plasterworks, and furnishings, as well as dozens of large and small needlework pieces that had been designed and worked in her household since at least the 1570s (Chapters 1, 4, and 5).

By making visible the relations among women's forms of expression, New Hardwick Hall convinced me that there had to be ways to think about Elizabeth Tudor, Mary Sidney Herbert, Amelia Lanyer, and Anne Clifford, with Bess of Hardwick as producers of expressive media through which they asserted and explored their identities in relation to agency. Furthermore, as I pursued women's verbal expressions and visual design across the shifting lines of social class, I realized that studying women's combined textualities would allow a discussion of privileged women like Bess and Mary Queen of Scots, alongside professional artisans and domestic needleworkers from the aristocracy, gentry, and middling classes, as well as writers like William Shakespeare and Mary Sidney Wroth, whose works chart the early modern insistence on these intersections. As a result, this book assembles information about many women to approach an understanding of the connections they themselves saw between their verbal and visual texts, from narratives that encoded ways of seeing themselves in the world, to ciphers of identity, from initials on a sampler to Bess's New Hardwick Hall.

Of Pens and Needles: The *Alice Barnham* Portrait

The more I viewed the objects produced by hundreds of women who wrote and wrought, the more I realized that in order to expand the definition of women's textualities I would have to address two common misconceptions that have blocked the realization that women's verbal and visual texts were once intimately related. The first misconception is that only women were associated with the needle and only men with the pen—a misconception held despite repeated attempts to complicate this binary by scholars as well as by early modern people themselves. The second misconception is that the needle was only associated with drudgery, while the pen was only associated with intellectual work. To a certain extent the needle represented women's obedience to a rigid insistence on sexual difference, but it is an unstable signifier and, as an object, it is small but phallic, penetrating as well as penetrable, conveying activity, even violence, as well as creativity.[47] The needle conveys the potential for the active, thinking feminine, without precluding women's use of the pen in paintings like *Alice Barnham and her Sons Martin and Steven* (Figure 1).[48]

I turn now to this remarkable painting dated 1557, featuring a woman with pen in hand flanked by two boys. This portrait exemplifies a woman who used the intersections of verbal and visual media to represent a sense of self. Lena Cowen Orlin has persuasively argued that the woman is Alice Barnham, raised in a prominent Chichester family and married to Francis Barnham, member of the Draper's Company in London, sixteen years before the portrait was painted. Alice and Francis Barnham and their three surviving sons composed an upwardly mobile family with extensive investment in joint stock companies and land holdings, as well as other family business.[49] Alice Barnham's portrait is of particular interest not simply because its central female figure holds a pen but because her act of writing takes place within a represented world that she has arranged. Within this world, the physical bodies of three family members interact with one another and with written texts and objects that produce and record written texts—the pen, the paper, and the writing desk containing ink wells, as well as a drawer for family documents, a manuscript book, together with inset inscriptions. The woman stands between the two boys, the elder, labeled "Martin," on the right; the younger, labeled "Steve," on the left. An open writing desk rests on the low table around which the three of them stand. The woman is using its contents, for she holds a pen and is in the act of writing, "That we all shall receive the same." This affirmation is in part a quotation from Edward VI's First Book of Common Prayer, specifically, the communion service, a short part of the book that uses some form of the verb "receive" twenty-six times in emphasizing the reception of God's bounty, and uses Barnham's phrase, "receive" or "receiving the same" five times.[50]

Although the Book of Common Prayer itself does not elaborate on what "receiving" means, to sixteenth-century Protestants at mid-century, teaching and learning the word of God were considered forms of communion. Anne Askew's *The Lattre Examinatyon*, printed in 1547, ten years before the date on the *Alice Barnham* picture, notes that Christ "minded" the Apostles "in a perfect

Figure 1. Artist unknown, *Alice Barnham and her Sons Martin and Steven*, c. 1557. Oil on panel, 38 x 33 in. Berger Collection at the Denver Art Museum. Photograph courtesy of the Denver Art Museum.

belief to *receive* that body of his which should die for the people, or to think the death thereof, the only health and salvation of their souls." John Bale glosses this passage by equating communion with the process of religious instruction: The receiving of "Christes owne instructions and meaning" is part of communion because "Required is it there, that the true *receivers* thereof, be taught of God, and learned of the heavenly father" (my emphasis).[51]

Through the verb *receive*, the *Alice Barnham* painting connects the writing of Alice Barnham with the reading of her son Martin as a pedagogical form of communion because he is holding a small book labeled "The Proverbs of Solomon"—the book of the Bible dedicated to the teaching of God's word. After this English title, a single line is painted in this book: "my son, receive ye these my words, the which shall be right wise." This is a quotation from John Hall's metrical version of Proverbs (1549–50), a paraphrase of the translation produced in the 1530s by Miles Coverdale that by 1540 became the Great Bible.[52] "My son, receive ye these my words," is a sentiment repeated in Proverbs in order to underscore the book's process of moral instruction, at chapter 1, verse 2, and again at chapter 4, verse 10: "Heare my sonne, and receave my wordes: and the yeares of thy lyfe shalbe many."

With its references to both the Book of Common Prayer and Proverbs, the painting emphasizes the reciprocal nature of what the woman writes—"That we all shall receive the same"—and what the boy reads—"My son, receive ye these my words." In its opening and closing verses, Proverbs affirms that the teaching by the mother is as important as that by the father. Hall's metrical Proverbs actually begins with this instruction: "My son thi father harke unto / & to hys lore encline. / forsake ye not thy mothers law / but sure let it be Thine," a paraphrase of chapter 1, verse 8, "My sonne, heare thy fathers doctrine: and forsake not the lawe of thy mother." As the first chapter of Proverbs ends, the speaker becomes Wisdom, personified as female; then the speaker shifts to the father, and, as the book continues, the speaker often sounds like Solomon or God, or, again, Wisdom. The audience of Proverbs, "My sonne," varies from a particular son to all sons, and so, by extension, to all readers or listeners. Amid the positive female images of mother and Wisdom, the picture of the wicked female recurs, but so does the verse "My sonne, kepe thy fathers commande-ment, and forsake not the lawe of thy mother" (6.20).

As a result, Martin's book of Proverbs and its brief sentence invoke not only the process of religious instruction as a form of communion but also the mater-nal wisdom exemplified in Western culture in Proverbs' last chapter, titled, "The wordes of Kyng Lamuell and the lesson that his mother taught hym." The "lesson that his mother taught hym," the wisdom that passes from mother to son, provides the verses describing the "Aishet Khyil" or "worthy wife," a description quoted throughout the early modern period and into the present as a feminine ideal. Just as Alice Barnham's picture represents the mother as both central for her household's affairs and the likely embroiderer of the blackwork visible at the throats and wrists of its three figures, so the wife of Proverbs performs textile work in the context of managing a household, acquiring land, and participating in trade: "She occupyeth woll and flaxe, and laboureth gladly with her handes" (31.13); "She laieth her fingers to the spindle: and her hande

Introduction

taketh holde of the distaffe (31.19); "al her householde folkes are clothed with scarlet. She maketh herself fayre ornamentes, her clothyng is white silke & purple" (31.21, 22). She is not only a hardworking producer of cloth, clothing, and textile "ornaments," but also, like elite women of the early modern period, a vigilant businesswoman and supervisor of her household: "She is lyke a marchauntes ship, that bringeth her vitailes from a far. She is up in the nyghte season, to provide meate for her householde, and foode for her maidens." The virtuous wife of Proverbs is a landholder as well: "She considreth lande, and bieth it, and wyth the fruite of her handes she planteth a vineyard." More than a century later, in *An Essay to Revive the Antient Education of Gentlewomen* (1673), Bathsua Makin uses this virtuous-wife passage to demonstrate that the ideal wife must be well-educated,[53] and references to Proverbs in needlework make similar claims about the ideal wife's abilities. The final lines of Proverbs chapter 31 demonstrate that the virtuous wife receives recognition from her husband, children, and God: "Her children shal arise, and cal her blessed: and her houseband shall make much of her. Many daughters ther be that gather riches together, but thou gooeste above them al. . . . A woman that feareth the Lord, she is worthy to bee praysed. Geve her of the fruyte of her handes and lette her owne woorckes praise her in the gates" (31.14–18, 27–31). Martin's holding of the metrical book of Proverbs invokes not only his own role as student but also his mother's instructional role as teacher of the word of God, part of her role as wife, whether at home or "in the gates"—that is, in the public part of town, the location of oratory and the market.

The painting of Alice Barnham and two of her sons not only emphasizes that God sanctions what she "receives" from him and transmits to her sons but also declares its subject's adherence to the Protestantism of Edward VI in 1557, when Mary Tudor had been on the throne for two years. The painting's references to two Protestant books—the Second Book of Common Prayer and an English version of Proverbs—are also references to two books produced under Edward VI. The Second Book of Common Prayer, based on collaboration among Thomas Cranmer, Nicholas Ridley, Henry Holbeach, and Thomas Goodrich, was debated and passed in Edward's Parliament. John Hall's metrical version of Proverbs is connected to Edward VI through its dedication by John Case to Sir Thomas Spek, "one of the gentilmen, of the king's majesty's most honourable privy chamber" (Sig. Aii(r)).

In addition to the religious and political statements made by Alice Barnham's just-written phrase and her son's book of Proverbs, the painting provides inscriptions near each of the three heads. The question of written messages in early paintings is usually vexed because such messages could have been added at any time in the painting's history and so are difficult to date. The portrait of

Bess of Hardwick labeled "Mary Queen of Scots" at New Hardwick Hall provides one egregious example. Fortunately, Alice Barnham's inscriptions are set within the design of tiles forming the backdrop of the three figures, an architectural assertion of the connection between inscription and portrait. The inscriptions on this wall also contain contemporary particulars that indicate that they are original to the painting. Above Martin's head, the text reads, "Martin was borned the 26 / of Marche at 9 of the / cloke before Norne in A Dni 1548"; above Steven's head, we read, "Steve was borne the 21. / Juli on Sunday / at night at ten of the cloke / A. Dni 1549." In addition to the records of the boys' births, above the woman's head a text appears in the first person: "I was borne the 30 September / On a Sunday 1523. Tornid / fro that I was unto that / ye se A. Dni 1557." The woman's inscription indicates her identity in terms of her birth date and her sense of transition at the age of thirty-four as mother and wife.

Husbands authorized at least four early modern paintings of women and children that can help us to appreciate how clearly Alice Barnham constructs herself as the assembler of this painting. In Hans Holbein's *Portrait of His Own Wife and Two Children* (1528), the artist paints his wife as frail and strained and her children as doubtful. In England at the end of the century, Marcus Gheeraerts painted two group portraits of a pregnant wife and Anne Pope's children that emphasize the wife's fertility, degree of privilege, and status as wife and mother: the first, *Anne, Lady Pope with Her Children* (1596), commemorates her advanced pregnancy by her second husband, Sir William Pope of Wroxton, later first Earl of Downe; the second, *Barbara Gamage with Six Children* (1590s), shows the prolific Gamage, wife of Sir Robert Sidney, later Earl of Leicester, with their oldest daughter, Mary (later Wroth), second from the left.[54]

Although the care on the face of Holbein's wife may portray the effect of his long absences from home during the period when he painted her, the open stances and confident expressions of the mothers in the Gheeraerts paintings imply husbands more immediately in the wings. In the portrait of Alice Barnham, the text in the first person emphasizing her changed state, together with the act and the objects of her writing, prominently identify her as taking an active part in her family's affairs and the pictured boys' education. In addition, the rest of her inscription, which may be paraphrased as "Turned from what I was into what you see in this picture in 1557," emphasizes some kind of personal change. Lena Cowen Orlin considers three possible changes to which this inscription might refer: the death of Barnham's third son, the religious persecution of her relatives in Chichester under Mary I, and Barnham's own sense of her passage through the stages of life.[55] Perhaps all three reasons helped to produce her sense of change in 1557. Although the nature of this change is difficult or impossible to know, the "I" of the inscription conveys key information. In particular, like the labels that identify the boys' names and ages, the text centered over the writing woman suggests that she commissioned this portrait or, at the least, was active in its composition. This painting may well be directed at her family because it memorializes a moment of transition in her life that she wished to preserve.

Such memorialization makes this painting a visual form of women's "life writing." As Michelle Dowd and Julie Eckerle describe it, "life writing" consists not only of "diaries, letters, and memoirs" or "religious treatises, fictional romances, and even cookbooks" but also of "combined" forms that "produced rhetorically sophisticated discourses of the self and demonstrated how textual form and the subjectivity it produces are mutually constitutive."[56] Alice Barnham, like Anne Clifford, Dowager Duchess of Dorset, Pembroke, and Montgomery, in her *Great Picture* (1646–47) of nearly a century later (Figure 2), is participating in yet another genre of "life writing" by representing her life as a whole, as well as a particular moment in that life. Anne Clifford's triptych represents her as a young woman on the left and a widow on the right. These younger and older selves in turn embrace the center painting of her father, the Earl of Cumberland and queen's champion; her mother the countess, pregnant with Anne; and her two young brothers. The triptych juxtaposes these figures with written genealogies, objects, and texts, including stacks of carefully titled books, a lute denoting not only music but song, a youthful embroidery in the form of a border, and inset portraits of family members, her tutor, Samuel Daniel, and her governess, Mrs. Anne Taylor.[57] We know that Clifford was memorializing her inheritance of the family titles and lands denied her for decades by situating herself as an unborn child, then as a younger and an older woman within a matrix of genealogical connection and personal accomplishment. Clifford's portrait is both conservative in its appeal to the medieval past and radical in its assemblage of texts, objects, and likenesses. A century before, Alice Barnham created her own emblem of identity, with herself at its verbal and visual center, although some aspects of her situation may remain unrecoverable.

Meanwhile, because Barnham's activities required writing and maintaining key family papers, this painting disrupts the neat distinction between male and female roles seemingly summarized by the split between pen and needle.[58] Like all binaries, the pen-needle opposition comes apart amid the details of everyday life. We know that men were active in the world of textiles, from the boys and old men who assisted women at carding and spinning, to skilled artisans who wove, dyed, or tailored cloth, to the wealthy traders of finished and unfinished wool. Male embroiderers like Guilliam Brallot, William Middleton, David Smith, John Witton, and John Parr, employed by Katherine Parr, Mary Tudor,

Figure 2. Attributed to Jan van Belkamp, *The Great Picture of the Clifford Family*, c. 1649. Reproduced courtesy of Abbot Hall Art Gallery, Kendal, Cumbria, England.

and Elizabeth, and Edmund Harrison, embroiderer to James I and Charles I,[59] made their living through the needle. Both male and female tapestry weavers and entrepreneurs in foreign and domestic guilds enjoyed the profits made from textiles produced on a larger scale. From 1667 until 1703, for example, Lady Daniel Harvey was the director of the Mortlake Tapestry Works.[60] Although men routinely engaged in many forms of textile work, Alice Barnham's portrait, with Barnham's pictured pen stroke, dispels the assumption that pens were only associated with men, while declaring the increasing importance of women's writing to the household.

Of Pens and Needles: Anne Bradstreet, Margaret Cavendish

The second misconception about pens and needles, that the early modern pen was associated with all things intellectual and the needle with enforced drudgery, derives from simplified readings of early modern English practice and the witty repartee surrounding the anxiety of women who wrote texts that circulated beyond the household. Early modern usage often suggests that women who wished to express themselves could choose between the pen and the needle. In *Gallathea* (1583), John Lyly's Diana upbraids her nymphs that they "should now become prentices to idleness, and use the pen for sonnets, not the needle for samplers."[61] Lyly's distinction is not between men and women, pens and needles but, betraying the period's anxiety about women's leisure, about women who can choose between the needle and the pen. Especially by the middle of the seventeenth century, as women began to write, preach, and publish in far greater numbers, early modern women themselves raised the question of whether the needle, in the words of Anne Bradstreet, "better fits" a woman's hand than a pen. The answers that they penned defend the act of writing without, however, throwing away the needle.

Anne Bradstreet confronted the interrelations among writing, textile work, and gender in the first book of poetry written in the American colonies. *The Tenth Muse* was seen through the press by her brother-in-law, John Woodbridge, during a stay in England in 1650. His "Epistle to the Kind Reader" expresses the sense of exposure that Bradstreet was bound to feel on publication, for he had "presumed to bring to publick view what she resolved should never in such a manner see the Sun."[62] Yet Bradstreet had prepared her ambitious manuscript of poems in a variety of adapted classical genres for a large circulation, if not for publication. She had also written "The Prologue" in anticipation of a negative reaction (McElrath and Robb, 6–8), positioning her rationale for writing in the domestic tasks of cooking and sewing. Her well-known protest may at first glance suggest that the female poet must choose either the needle or the pen:

> I am obnoxious to each carping tongue,
> Who sayes, my hand a needle better fits
> A Poets Pen, all scorne, I should thus wrong;
> For such despight they cast on female wits:
> If what I doe prove well, it won't advance,
> They'l say its stolne, or else, it was by chance.[63]

In being "obnoxious to each carping tongue," Bradstreet's speaker is "exposed" as well as "answerable" to criticism (OED). Bradstreet is anticipating that there will be criticism of her poetry because she is a woman, that her critics, like Lyly's Diana, might argue that she should spend her time sewing, to which she adds two other accusations that could be raised against her, that she has either stolen her verses or written them by chance. Although her imagined detractors might think that her hand should hold the needle, as Margaret Ferguson points out, Bradstreet answers them simply by writing.[64] In the concluding stanza of her "Prologue," Bradstreet reasserts the early modern sense that the pen may be—and should be—used by the same female hand that sews. Instead of renouncing the household work that defines her as a virtuous woman, she summons its imagery as her vehicle to enter the competitive, phallic realm of male poets. To represent this realm, Bradstreet adapts the quill imagery with which Philip Sidney represented an Astrophil who, having soared aloft on the wings of his writing, ends up plucked by his failure in love.[65] Bradstreet pictures poets metonymically soaring the skies of discourse on the feathers they use to write, acquiring "prey" or "praise" by destroying reputations:

> And oh, ye high flown quils, that soare the skies,
> And ever with your prey, still catch your praise,
> If e're you daigne these lowly lines, your eyes
> Give wholesome Parsley wreath, I aske no Bayes:
> This meane and unrefined stuffe of mine,
> Will make your glistering gold but more to shine.[66]

If the "quils" cast their eyes earthward to read her poetry, they will find it, as domestic as a "wholesome Parsley wreath," "meane and unrefined stuffe" that sets off their own "glistering gold." But Bradstreet's homely metaphors only gesture at appeasement, since the volume that follows contains an elegy on

Sidney, as well as historical and heroic poems in genres unattempted yet by women publishing in English.

Writing also at mid-seventeenth century, Margaret Cavendish addresses the question of whether textile production is more appropriate for women than writing. In the dedication of *Poems and Fancies* (1653) to her brother-in-law, Sir Charles Cavendish, she begins by noting that "Spinning with the fingers is more proper to our Sexe, then studying or writing Poetry, which is the Spinning with the braine." Regardless of what is "more proper," Cavendish extends her spinning metaphor to make her poetry a "web" that is only "a Course piece," an image resembling Bradstreet's "unrefined stuffe." Having noted—and crossed—the supposed boundary between men's and women's forms of "spinning," she goes on to make Charles Cavendish the spinner of her fate. As holder of "the Distaffe, from whence Fate hath Spun the thread of this part of my life," she turns her brother-in-law into one of the female fates so that he, too, crosses and so confuses gender lines. In another dedication to *Poems and Fancies*, "To All Noble, and Worthy Ladies," she connects "Poetry, which is built upon Fancy" as "a worke belonging most properly" to women, in terms reminiscent of Elizabeth Lucar's epitaph praising her "Curious Knots, or Trailes, what fancie could devise." Cavendish writes that women's domestic labor requires fancy, as "in their Wrought workes, and divers sorts of Stitches they imploy their Needle, and many Curious things they make." In effect, she acknowledges how the composing of words resembles the artful composing of patterns and stitches to create needlework.[67] Although both Bradstreet and Cavendish sought to deflect the discrediting effects of making work public through print—discredit from which men were not immune—the growing attempts to stabilize the categories of male and female textuality provoked their witty resistance.

If the easy split between pens and needles fails to hold, how and why did many scholars come to rely on it?[68] The pen-needle dichotomy was important to the work of some second-wave feminists, informed by both their resolve to rebalance entirely masculinist views of literature, history, and society, and by an understandable outrage at how completely the study of women had been ignored. Unfortunately, this sense of outrage in part stemmed from the view that women, with the exception of queens and other privileged women, had been largely victimized by the patriarchy—a view that erased the complexities of everyday practice as well as many of the contributions of women to early modern society. Scholars from Kate Millett, who first used the term *patriarchy*, to Gerda Lerner, who traced the descent of patriarchy from ancient times, called important scholarly attention to the misogyny of the West, but in so doing assumed that gender distinctions between men and women were largely stable. In her pathbreaking feminist discussion of needlework, *The Subversive Stitch*,

Rozsika Parker so depended on the stable difference between men and women, the pen and the needle, that she found in Renaissance gender debates that "it was almost axiomatic that a woman wanting to enter a supposedly 'masculine' sphere of activity repudiated femininity in the form of embroidery." My own study of needlework began with Parker's analysis, but departs from her second-wave feminist assumptions: first, that women's relation to the needle and the pen was constructed along binary oppositions and, second, that women's relations to these objects remained little changed from the sixteenth century to the present.[69]

Mary Lamb's assertion in her essay, "On Needle-work," that "Needlework and intellectual improvement are naturally in a state of warfare," resonated all-too-easily with the mood of second-wave feminists. Yet Lamb's essay was published April 1, 1815, in the *British Lady's Magazine and Monthly Miscellany*, more than a hundred years after the period that this book considers. "On Needle-work" is a remarkable essay, containing a precise analysis of women's household labor, the meager wages paid to seamstresses, and how women's lack of household leisure interferes with their intellectual growth. However, Lamb's statement about the division between needlework and intellectual work is complicated by the fact that she labored for years as a "mantua maker," a seamstress of ladies' outer apparel. She escaped this life only when she attacked and killed her mother with a carving knife, and was subsequently remanded to the care of her brother, Charles Lamb. Mary Lamb's "On Needle-work" obscures her background as a seamstress, a time of her life when she must have had to mix reading and writing with sewing. This obfuscation of her background, understandable because she had endured the frustration of working hard for minimal wages when she must have wanted to pursue intellectual endeavors, explains why Lamb so absolutely declared the separation of needlework and "intellectual improvement."[70]

As it turns out, the insistence on an absolute split between the pen and the needle does not hold in the nineteenth and twentieth centuries any more than it does in the early modern period. Many if not most women writers and artists, from the Brontë sisters to Gertrude Stein, Sylvia Plath, Alice Walker, and Judy Chicago, have embraced the association of verbal and visual textualities that includes several forms of textile work, even as many nineteenth-century authors chafed at the undervalued drudgery of piecework. In her journal, Louisa May Alcott records in 1856 after sewing "a dozen pillow-cases, one dozen sheets, six fine cambric neckties, and two dozen handkerchiefs" for "only $4," that "Sewing won't make my fortune, but I can plan my stories while I work, and then scribble 'em down on Sundays." Alcott's five volumes of short stories with the prefatory title *Aunt Jo's Scrapbag* (1871–79) preserve the connections that Alcott lived between text and textile. Also writing in 1856, Elizabeth Barrett Browning acknowledges in *Aura Leigh* that "the works of women are symbolical," while describing how little the men who receive the embroidered "slippers" or "cushion" value the time and skill that went into the gift. Gertrude Stein, from the vantage of time and privilege both asks and states, "What is the difference between a sentence and a sewn. . . . What is the difference between a sentence and a picture."[71] The conviction that Stein challenges, that the sentence and the sewn, the sentence and the picture are entirely separate, is the result of the value placed on writing on paper and painting on canvas as art over needlework as craft.[72] A more inclusive view of the material objects surrounding early modern women, objects that they used and that in many cases they created, offers ways to study the connections among women, pens, and needles in ways that their own textual production asks us to reexamine.

The Subject Is Objects

Throughout this project, in attempting to heed Margaret Ezell's request that scholars consider women's texts as "more chaotic and diverse than we have previously implied in our literary histories,"[73] I have benefited from many scholars' work in the areas of feminist and queer theory, which have so altered the interpretation of both the established editions of early modern texts and the less familiar material found in archives and early printed works. I was also fortunate that as I began this study a decade ago, a number of scholars had already turned their attention to material culture. The revisioning of the early modern period by Stephen Orgel, Maureen Quilligan, Ann Rosalind Jones, Peter Stallybrass, Margreta de Grazia, Patricia Fumerton, Wendy Wall, Tessa Watt, Juliet Fleming, Jonathan Goldberg, Heather Wolfe, and Will Fisher, among many others, has lighted my way as I came to include in my own practice of feminist historicism what Bruce Smith has called "historical phenomenology."[74]

Historical phenomenology provides a method to connect the poststructural analysis of the subject located in cultural discourse with the phenomenological analysis of the subject located in the physical body and its material circumstances. In considering the relations between subject and object, I have used the principles informing historical phenomenology to bring the evidence of material culture—pens and needles; pencils and brushes; and the manuscripts, books, textiles, miniatures, and portraits they produced—to the task of elucidating the lives of early modern women. All of these objects have been torn from their original contexts, have been moved, overpainted, rearranged, or otherwise meddled with. Nevertheless, they and their represented counterparts offer evidence of early modern relations between subject and object, between textual and everyday practice, that may help in recovering the significance of multiple kinds of texts in women's everyday lives—evidence that, in turn, offers ways to reread early modern literature by both men and women.

How is it possible to connect with early modern English women via the objects of their everyday lives? What happens if we study objects not only when they appear within discourse as metaphors but also as descriptions of experience that gave rise to the metaphors in the first place? Scholars have recently focused attention on the ways in which objects help in accessing early modern English culture, from feathers and sugar to the walls, bodies, costumes, and sounds of the past.[75] In their trenchant introduction to *Subject and Object in Renaissance Culture*, Margreta de Grazia, Maureen Quilligan, and Peter Stallybrass argue for the importance of objects, pointing out that students of the Renaissance, like the painters and consumers of *vanitas* paintings long ago, have "proceeded as if it were both possible and desirable for subjects to cut themselves off from objects."[76] Peter Stallybrass, in his introduction to the volume of *Shakespeare Studies* devoted to materiality, notes further that although "material culture" is a commonplace of anthropology, to literary historians, the phrase seems to be an oxymoron because, since the Renaissance, judging a text's "cultural value" has meant pitting aesthetic appreciation against the merely material quality of pen, ink, or the economic price assigned to a work.[77]

To their analysis, I find it useful to add that of the French phenomenologist, Maurice Merleau-Ponty, who comments on the relation between the physical object and the embodied subject, arguing that although we "see the things themselves, in their places, where they are," such objects are always "more than their being-perceived." That is, to extend his argument to include the study of historical objects, our perception of objects may encompass more than simply perceiving them in the present. Because our separation from the objects of the past is experienced through "the thickness of the look and of the body," a separation that is the essence of experiencing both the body and things, "this distance is not the contrary of this proximity, it is deeply consonant with it, it is synonymous with it." Viewed in this way, subject and object do not form a dichotomy but are partially integrated terms, although not terms in which the separation of the material object and the knowing body can be ignored. Instead, for Merleau-Ponty, the *separation* of subject and object is itself the *means* of experience: "the thickness of flesh between the seer and the thing is constitutive for the thing of its visibility as for the seer for her corporeity; it is not an obstacle between them, it is their means of communication."[78] In other words, the barrier between subject and object itself provides the means for two-way communication between the body and the world outside.[79]

Studying the material object offers ways in which to perceive connections between ourselves and the people of the past, as well as to access the contexts that produced the object, contexts that the object continues to recall. By embodying what folklorist Simon Bronner calls "the weave of these objects in everyday lives and communities,"[80] the object evokes the historical subjects who once used or fashioned it. De Grazia, Quilligan, and Stallybrass suggest that granting the "potential priority of the object" means that the object "renders more apparent the way material things—land, clothes, tools—might constitute subjects who in turn own, use, and transform them. . . . It is the material object that impresses its texture and contour upon the noumenal subject."[81] Gary Tomlinson, in his article in the same volume, "Unlearning the Aztec *Cantares*," elaborates on the idea that the object may redirect our thinking about historical subjects by suggesting that we remain open to the Mexican voices within *cantares* as the means to develop "a reciprocal semantics that would question western perceptual categories at the same time that it would articulate those of the remote Aztec" (9). For Bruce Smith, writing in *The Acoustic World of Early Modern England*, "the materialism of the human body, of sound waves, of plaster, lath, and thatch, of quill pens, ink, and paper, of lead type" provides access to the "people whose voice-based cultures are available to us only if we come at them by indirections."[82] This book examines the activities of early modern women by attending to the "reciprocal semantics" and "indirections" deriving from the objects that they produced and used from about 1540 to 1700, including not only their manuscripts and printed writing but also their paintings, houses, rooms, walls, drawings, and especially their textiles.

CHAPTER ONE

Political Designs: Elizabeth Tudor, Mary Stuart, and Bess of Hardwick

This chapter considers the political textualities generated by a future queen, an exiled queen, and a countess whose granddaughter might have been queen. With their pens and needles, Elizabeth Tudor, Mary Stuart, and Bess of Hardwick asserted their political prerogatives as highly placed women. As princesses, Elizabeth and Mary were educated to produce translations, prayers, letters, speeches, and poems; to use commissioned objects like portraits and clothing to further exercise their agency through self-representation; and to design and execute skilled needlework. The woman who served them both, Elizabeth, Countess of Shrewsbury, called "Bess of Hardwick,"[1] was among the most successful social climbers of her age. Although not as well educated as Elizabeth and Mary, and apparently without their literary and rhetorical ambitions, Bess received a gentlewoman's education in reading, writing, and needlework by serving in the households of Lady Zouche of Codnor Castle in Derbyshire, and then Lady Frances, the daughter of Henry VIII's younger sister, Mary.[2] Bess went on to build the Cavendish and Talbot dynasties, solidifying her political gains as a builder and interior designer, a writer of letters from within a political network of news-sharing, and the producer of needlework pictures that asserted the virtue and power of women.[3]

Political events brought the lives of these three women into close association during the sixteenth century. As their lives intertwined, so too did their textualities, as they combined visual and verbal media to create objects significant far beyond their usefulness as gifts—a category of object that anthropologist Annette Weiner has called "inalienable possessions." These objects—

manuscript books with needleworked covers, commissioned portraits, and needlework pictures—were, to use Weiner's anthropological language, created to be "historical documents that authenticate and confirm for the living the legacies and powers associated with a group's or an individual's connection to ancestors and gods"[4] (3). All three titled women expressed their dynastic identities in objects that functioned as inalienable possessions, objects making political statements that were at once carefully feminine and confirmation of their "legacies and powers."

Elizabeth Tudor: Youth and the Assertion of Prerogative

When the young Elizabeth Tudor created material expressions of her dynastic position, they passed from her head and hand to those who ruled the kingdom. Although Elizabeth's vulnerable youth was later obscured by a teleological narrative that made her queenship seem inevitable, studying Elizabeth's textual production as a girl and young woman helps to restore our sense of a life once lived at the periphery of power.

Elizabeth's first recorded gift, at the age of six, was a cambric shirt that she had sewn for her brother Edward, listed at New Year's in 1538–39 as a "shyrte of comeryke of her owne woorkynge." This would have been a fine linen undershirt, decorated with "her owne woorkynge," perhaps the embroidered blackwork designs popular for this kind of garment during the sixteenth century and suitable for girls as young as five to learn. In 1539–40, "The Ladye Elizabeth" gave Edward "A braser of nedleworke of her owne makyng."[5] This was probably a "bracer," in the sense of a "guard for the wrist, used in archery, in fencing, and in playing games at ball."[6] Because, as Annette Weiner explains, "an individual's role in social life is fragmentary unless attached to something of importance" (64), both shirt and bracer materialized Elizabeth's position as sister to her father's male heir. Although the shirt demonstrated Elizabeth's basic training in the skills of womanhood, in accordance with Vives's instructions to her half-sister Mary that women learn needlework regardless of class,[7] it was also an intimate garment of fine white linen that, worn next to her brother's skin, renewed her presence in his everyday life. The bracer acknowledged that her brother's play would turn to sport and, eventually, military prowess, while she participated in his growth from baby to boy to man.

Four years later, Elizabeth expressed her dynastic identity in more ingenious objects that combined needlework, visual design, calligraphy, and translation. In December 1544 and again in December 1545, Elizabeth assembled her accomplishments on the brink of womanhood for her father, Henry VIII, and for her educated, devoutly Protestant stepmother, Katherine Parr, in matched sets of needlework-covered calligraphic manuscripts for the New Year. By presenting her eleven- and twelve-year-old skills in needlework and in writing different versions of the italic hand, she used these objects to assert her intellectual and religious connection to the reigning couple and their court. The three extant volumes contain ambitious translations: in 1544, for her stepmother, Elizabeth translated Marguerite de Navarre's *Glass of the Sinful Soul*, a Protestant text that John Bale published on the continent in 1548. In this way, her manuscript became Elizabeth's first published work, one that, as Maureen Quilligan points out, she published three more times after becoming queen.[8] The volume for Henry VIII that may well have matched Parr's in 1544 is now lost, but I will argue that it is probably a translation of Erasmus's *Diologus Fidei*.[9] In 1545, again for Parr, Elizabeth translated a section of Calvin's *Institutes*. The matching volume of 1545 that Elizabeth dedicated to Henry VIII was a translation into Italian, Latin, and French of prayers that Katherine Parr had written.

New Year's gifts at the Tudor court carried immense significance, and Lisa M. Klein has ably discussed Elizabeth's manuscript books as gifts. Since Marcel Mauss's foundational discussion, gift-giving has explained the ways in which the proper gift creates reciprocal relations between the giver and the receiver. Klein expanded the concept of reciprocal giving to show "women as active participants in cultural exchange," a description of women's agency that is lacking from most discussions of the gift.[10] Once given, as Maureen Quilligan has further discussed, they became inalienable possessions, in the sense that their families deliberately kept them out of circulation, retaining them for generations as markers of dynastic relationship.[11] Thinking of Elizabeth's manuscript books as inalienable possessions helps us to understand them as designed to be more than gifts designed for the single moment of exchange. Instead, they were also treasures "imbued with the intrinsic and ineffable identities of their owners."[12] Elizabeth's manuscript books transcended the moment of their giving to become family heirlooms, since the two dedicated to Henry VIII were reported on display at Whitehall Palace in the seventeenth century and have continued to command considerable attention.

Elizabeth's manuscript books announce their importance as treasures that connected her to her father and stepmother, while evoking a range of familial presents, pasts, and futures. To her father, Elizabeth's texts recalled her upbringing as the daughter of a superbly educated humanist prince, an education that shaped her inborn suitability to inherit the throne, should future events require it. This demonstration was particularly appropriate in 1544, the year that Henry restored her and her half-sister Mary to the succession, an event that Mary marked by commissioning a portrait of herself inscribed, "Anno Domini 1544 / Lady Mary Doughter to / the most Vertuous Prince / King Henry the Eight /

The Age of XXVIII Years."[13] Combining needlework design, sewing, and writing with the intellectual work of translation, Elizabeth created manuscript volumes that inscribed her familial, intellectual, and religious connections.

The two volumes that Elizabeth directed to her stepmother demonstrate Elizabeth's commitment to a recently formed alliance that offered her more intellectual and emotional nurturance than her dynastic ties to her father, however central those ties were to her identity. Through her works for Parr, Elizabeth articulates her attachment to a woman who had helped to reconnect her father with his children, a woman who took a strong interest in Elizabeth's education, and a woman who was, as Elizabeth's translations of Parr's prayers for Henry demonstrate, the author of significant Protestant writing in the 1530s and 1540s.[14] Through the association of the discourses of Protestant humanism, female authorship, and ciphered needlework emphasizing kinship, Elizabeth reached out to her stepmother. In her "Epistle Dedicatory" to *The Glass of the Sinful Soul* Elizabeth connects herself symbolically to Parr's body, writing that the work comes from her "humble daughter," who "knowing the affectuous will and fervent zeal which your highness hath toward all godly learning, as also my duty toward you . . . hath moved so small a portion as God hath lent me to prove what I could do." Proving what Elizabeth can *do* will, in effect, articulate who Elizabeth *is*, even as she asks Parr to help her "rub out, polish, and mend" her work. In her preface to Parr, Elizabeth is able to acknowledge that she herself, like her needlework, writing, and translation, is under construction.[15]

Elizabeth's gifts to Parr bring together the memories and activities of six different women: Elizabeth herself, Marguerite de Navarre, Katherine Parr, Anne Boleyn, and Lady Margaret Beaufort, the Lancastrian mother of Henry VII. In his introduction to *The Glass of the Sinful Soul*, Mark Shell speculates that Marguerite de Navarre may have presented Elizabeth's mother, Anne Boleyn, with a copy of her work when they renewed their acquaintance in 1534–35.[16] In addition to recalling her mother's connection with Marguerite, Elizabeth's title, *The Glass of the Sinful Soul*, echoes the choice that her great-grandmother Beaufort made when she translated *The Mirror of Gold for the Sinful Soul* from the French, a translation that Richard Pynson printed in an edition of 1506, with decorated margins and miniature illustrations suggesting an illuminated manuscript.[17] Elizabeth's manuscript book associates her with accomplished, royal women from mother and great-grandmother to stepmother and the Queen of Navarre through a carefully chosen display.[18]

For the cover of *The Glass of the Sinful Soul* (Figure 3), Elizabeth executed an elaborate needlework design with Parr's initials at the center. "KP" was Parr's cipher, as she signed her letters after becoming Henry's wife, "Kateryn, the Queen KP." Parr also ordered that her rooms at Hampton Court be deco-

Figure 3. Elizabeth Tudor, embroidered binding for Katherine Parr, *The Glass of the Sinful Soul*, 1544. MS Cherry 36. The Bodleian Library, University of Oxford.

rated with "KP," and "KP" heads the burial inscription on her lead coffin. Perhaps, as Bruce Barker Benfield suggested, Parr retained the rather simple "KP" as her cipher because it connoted "capio," "I take in hand," a statement of Katherine Parr's well-known competence.[19] Because "KP" stands at the center of Elizabeth's cover surrounded by lovers' knots and four pansies, with their

Figure 4. Hans Holbein, "HISA" cipher for "H [Henry] I [perhaps, *Indiuspute* or *Inimitable*] S [Serviteur] A [Anne]," c. 1533–35. Light brown wash over pen and ink. Sloane bequest, 1753, 5303-3. Department of Prints and Drawings. © The Trustees of the British Museum.

play on "pensé," suggesting thought and remembrance, the cover memorializes her alliance with her stepmother and, through her, the religious, intellectual, writerly, and (more recently) Protestant women of her family. Textile historian Margaret Swain concluded that the knots of the "KP" cover were formed from pieces of thin braid wound around one another and stitched into place.[20] Although "braid" was not a textile term until the seventeenth century, this would have been a thin woven band called a *passement* because it contained silver thread, which would have made the cover less arduous to embroider than it appears. Elizabeth might herself have woven the braid, a skill that some girls and women apparently enjoyed practicing in the seventeenth century, or it was made by a silk woman in her household. Elizabeth almost certainly sewed it into place.[21]

Elizabeth's two surviving volumes from 1545, while repeating the four pansies of 1544, complicate the "KP" design with an ambitious embroidered cipher probably modeled on Hans Holbein's cipher designs. Holbein had served Henry VIII as a "painter, draughtsman, and designer" at his court in 1526–28, and again from 1528 until his death in 1543. Holbein's "HISA" cipher (Figure 4), for example, combines Henry's initials with Anne Boleyn's. Elizabeth would have seen Holbein's ciphers as either drawings or objects—the "HISA" cipher, for example, was carved twice in stone in the choir stalls at the King's College Chapel, Cambridge, while still other Holbein designs combine as many as ten initials.[22] Like Holbein's cipher, Elizabeth's cipher uses the letter "H" as its base, while the "H," "K," "P," "E," and "R"—for Henry, Katherine, Parr, Elizabeth, Edward, Rex, and Regina—are entwined closely, a physical insistence on the kinship connecting them all (Figure 5). An initial "M" for Mary is also arguably

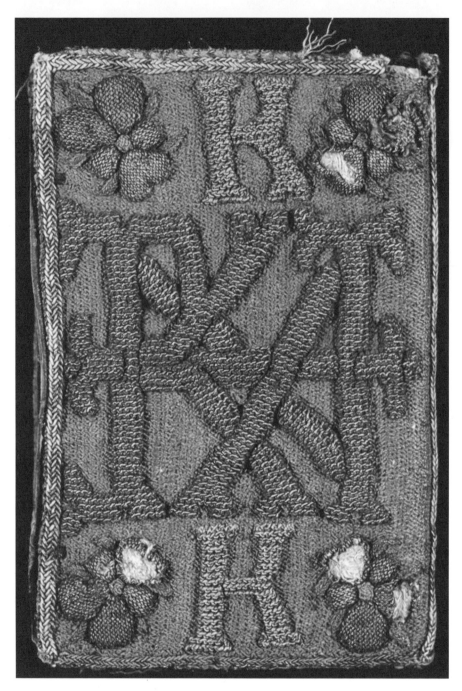

Figure 5. Elizabeth Tudor, embroidered binding for Katherine Parr with initial cipher. Elizabeth's English translation of John Calvin's *Institution Chrétienne*. 1545. MS #R.H. 13/78. ScotlandsImages.com/Crown Copyright 2009. The National Trust for Scotland AAA00482.

present. Besides Elizabeth's use of the "H," her "A," for Anne Boleyn, is identical to the "A" in the Holbein cipher; both Holbein's "A" and Elizabeth's are formed from the right side of the "H," the "H" crossbar, and a diagonal line branching to the left. Elizabeth's cipher also picks up Holbein's cross-bar ending in finials of blunted fleurs de lis and the slight flare at the tops and bottoms of the letters.

The letters forming the earlier, simpler "KP" design and the H, K, P, E, R, M, and A design are connected by "knots,"[23] the places where the letters composing each cipher are stitched to overlap one another. Whether sewn in embroidery, penned with ink, or planted in gardens, "curious knots"[24] are more than interconnected lines. In ciphers, they form patterns that connect letters to particular meanings, designs that celebrate the tension between separation and joining, like the letters forming Elizabeth's and Holbein's ciphers that are individually distinguishable and bound together. The "KP" cover's looping lines, originally silver and blue thread on blue canvas, surround the central initials with lovers' knots, forming a cross with six groups of four rings each. The four rings themselves form a particular kind of knot that appears in many cultures, one that the Vikings called "Frode" or "happiness." In addition to embroidering Frode knots, Elizabeth also penned this knot on at least one occasion, turned 90 degrees from the angle of the cover to make a kind of knotted "H." In a letter to her brother Edward after he became king, Elizabeth wrote about a portrait that accompanied this letter (Figure 6).[25] Because the letter presented the portrait, Elizabeth made the letter itself a kind of presentation piece, adding several flourishes to her increasingly accomplished italic hand. She included sixteen ornamental capitals, which usually emphasize the noun "Majesty" and the pronoun "I," as well as several small penned knots, ornamenting the letter's first word, "Like," as well as the phrases "My picture" and "For the face." She also ornamented with small knots the "A" in "And further" and the "F" of her concluding quotation from Horace. Several penned knots also underlie her signature, with a Frode knot included as a small, ink-drawn part of her signature, just to the right of her name at the bottom of the page, an imitation of the way that her father also concluded his signature.[26]

Whether penned or embroidered, the four-ringed knot of the "KP" cover and Elizabeth's signature declare the connections of kinship. Knots also represent human connection in terms of cyclic time, since they are usually formed from circles. In another hundred years, the relation between knots and time would become part of mathematics, when two intersecting rings became the symbol for infinity. Called in mathematics the lemniscate, it derives from "lemniscus," the Latin word for "ribbon," a name that preserves the derivation of the infinity sign from textile design."[27] Like the Frode knot and the lemniscate,

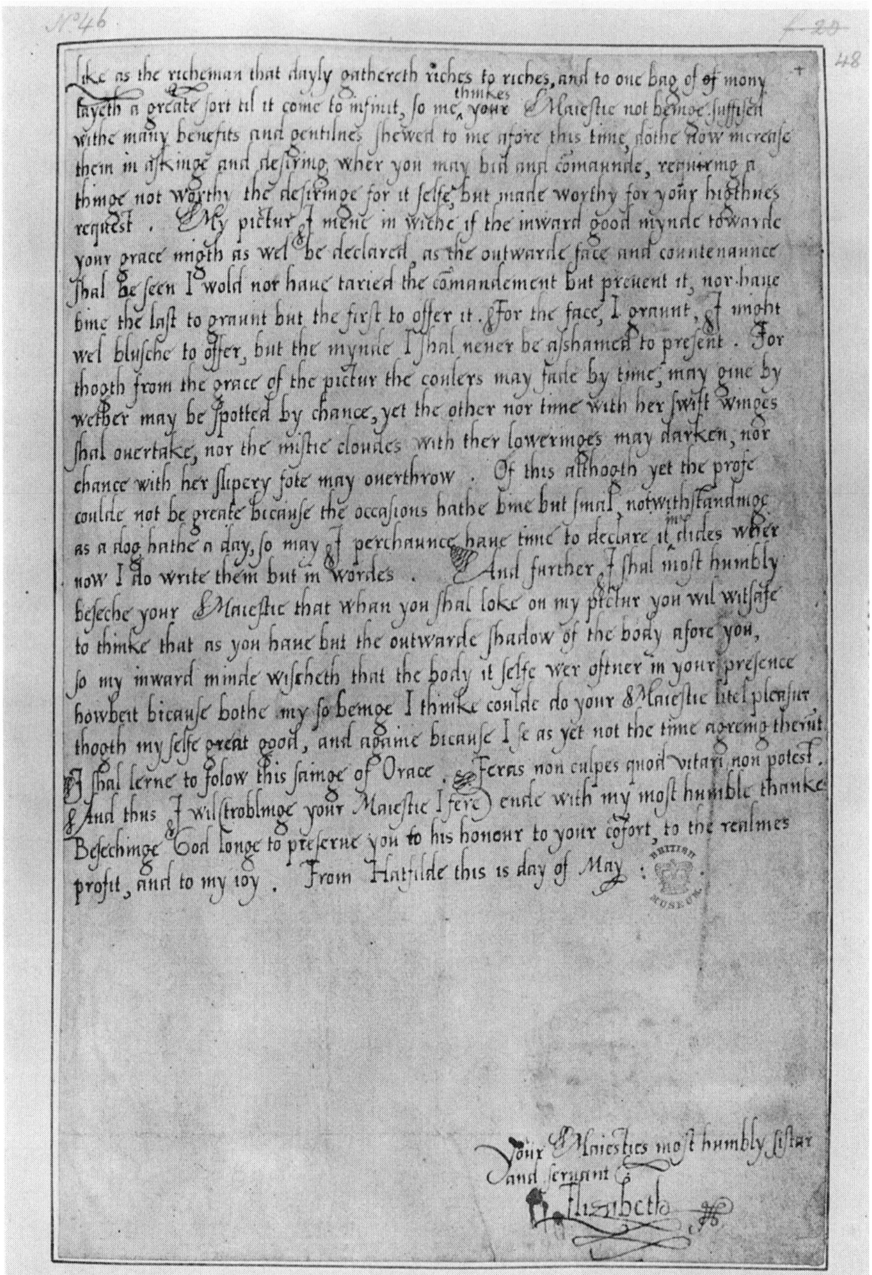

Like as the richeman that dayly gathereth riches to riches, and to one bag of mony layeth a greate sort til it come to infinit, so me thinkes, your Maiestie not beinge suffised withe many benefits and gentilnes shewed to me afore this time, dothe now increase them in askinge and desiring, wher you may bid and comaunde, requiring a thinge not worthy the desiringe for it selfe, but made worthy for your highnes request. My pictur I mene in wiche if the inward good mynde towarde your grace migth as wel be declared as the outwarde face and countenaunce shal be seen I wold nor haue taried the comandement but preuent it, nor haue bine the last to graunt but the first to offer it. For the face, I graunt, I might wel blusche to offer, but the mynde I shal neuer be ashamed to present. For thogth from the grace of the pictur the coulers may fade by time, may giue by wether may be spotted by chance, yet the other nor time with her swift winges shal ouertake, nor the mistie cloudes with ther lowringes may darken, nor chance with her slipery fote may ouerthrow. Of this althogth yet the profe coulde not be greate bicause the occasions hathe bine but smal, notwithstandinge as a dog hathe a day, so may I perchaunce haue time to declare it in dides wher now I do write them but in wordes. And further I shal most humbly beseche your Maiestie that whan you shal loke on my pictur you wil witsafe to thinke that as you haue but the outwarde shadow of the body afore you, so my inward minde wischeth that the body it selfe wer oftner in your presence howbeit bicause bothe my so beinge I thinke coulde do your Maiestie litel plesur thogth my selfe great good, and againe bicause I se as yet not the time agreing therunto I shal lerne to folow this sainge of Orace, Feras non culpes quod vitari non potest. And thus I wil (troblinge your Maiestie I fere) ende with my most humble thankes Besechinge God longe to preserue you to his honour to your cofort, to the realmes profit, and to my ioy. From Hatfilde this 15 day of May.

Your Maiesties most humbly sistar and seruant
Elizabeth

Figure 6. Elizabeth Tudor to Edward VI, autograph letter dated only Hatfield 15 May. MS Cotton Vespasian F.III, fol. 48. © British Library.

Elizabeth's knots on the "KP" cover inscribe the temporal, genealogical aspect of kinship she used to make her manuscript transcend the moment of its giving, extending its significance into the past and future.

Elizabeth's two 1545 covers featuring her complex familial cipher are identical in design, except that the single "H" at the top and bottom of Henry's book is slightly reshaped to form an "R" for Regina at the top and bottom of Katherine's (Figure 5). Katherine Parr's book of 1545 is embroidered in red and silver thread on blue canvas; Henry VIII's book of 1545 is executed in the reverse scheme of blue and silver thread on red. These paired manuscripts of 1545 strongly suggest that in 1544 Elizabeth had also created a matching gift for Henry VIII, in the reverse color scheme of blue on silver.

What has not been recognized before is that three foreign visitors to Whitehall Palace probably describe this missing book. In 1600 Baron von Waldstein reports seeing two manuscript books that the young Elizabeth gave her father in a room at Whitehall Palace in which the queen "keeps her books, some of which she wrote herself." The first book the baron saw was the 1545 translation of "some prayers of Queen Catherine" dedicated to Henry VIII, and the second had the title that translates as Erasmus's "Colloquium on Faith" or "Concerning Faith" from his *Familiar Colloquies*. John Ernest, Duke of Saxe-Weimar, observed in 1613 that among the queen's books at Whitehall there "is a little volume on parchment which Queen Elizabeth wrote in French with her own hand for her father King Henry VIII. It was the *Dialogus fidei* of Erasmus of Rotterdam." Peter Eisenberg, a Dane who visited in 1614, noted that in addition to two other small books of Elizabeth's on view at Whitehall, he saw "a little book in French, written by Queen Elizabeth with her own hand, and dedicated to her father; it is the '*Dialogus Fidei ex Erasmo Roterodamo.*'"[28] These tourist accounts suggest that the fourth, missing volume for Henry VIII in 1544 was Elizabeth's translation of Erasmus's dialogue from Latin into French, presented to her father as the companion volume for Parr, *The Glass of the Sinful Soul*, translated from French into English, and very likely with a matching cover—perhaps "HR" at the center of lovers' knots and pansies.

Using her needleworked covers to evoke familial connection was only the beginning of the visual and verbal performances that these volumes include, as Elizabeth herself points out. In her volume for Parr in 1545, her introduction, first written in Italian and then in English, shows her thinking about the relation of visual and verbal texts as she argues for the primacy of writing over the visual arts, though her manuscript volume exhibits both:

Since the creation of the world . . . by succession of time the mind of man is more ingenious and inventive, more adorned and polished, than it formerly was. And therefore some have invented sculpting in the round, casting or engraving in gold, silver, copper . . . yet others in stone, marble, wood, wax, clay, or other materials. . . . excellent painters do not deserve less praise. But all of these together never could and cannot yet represent or reveal by their works the mind or wit, the speech or understanding of any person. (1:11)

The twelve-year-old Elizabeth reasons that "the invention of letters seems to me the most clever, excellent, and ingenious" of all inventions, the means to know "perfectly" "the image of the mind, wiles, and understanding . . . of the man" in the way that the word of God allows people to perceive religious truth (1:11–12). For Elizabeth, "letters" reveal the "image" of man, a logic that connects the verbal and visual but still privileges the word. When she is in control of her portraiture, Elizabeth attempts to use her commissioned image to "reveal" her "mind or wit," as she wrote of a portrait sent to her brother, but her early enthusiasm for the truth gained through language is a theme to which she returns in letters and speeches throughout her life. Her preference for writing over visual expression helps to explain not only the limits of her needlework designs and penned flourishes but also her focus on the verbal once she became queen.[29]

The only existing letter that Elizabeth wrote her father appears as the Latin preface to her 1545 translations of Parr's Latin prayers into French, Italian, and English. The tone of that letter is more anxious than her two prefaces to Parr, with their confident affirmation of kinship, her willingness to admit that she still has much to learn, and her speculation on the development of the arts. When writing to her king and father, Elizabeth betrays her anxiety by attempting to shape his response. Regarding her choice of religious subject, Elizabeth suggests that "nothing ought to be more acceptable to a king, whom philosophers regard as a god on earth, than this labor of the soul." She asks for his approval regardless of whether she deserves it because she needs his praise as part of her moral instruction: "If it is mediocre, even if it is worthy of no praise at all, nevertheless if it is well received, it will incite me earnestly so that, however much I grow in years, so much will I grow in knowledge and the fear of God and thus devote myself to Him more religiously and respect your majesty more dutifully." She concludes by linking the value of her translation to their relationship as royal father and daughter, asserting that her work is to be "esteemed because it has been composed by the most serene queen, your spouse, and is to be held in slightly greater worth because it has been translated by your daughter" (1:9–10). When Elizabeth addresses her father, she claims their association on the basis of a hierarchical rather than an intimate sense of kinship. Elizabeth finds it far easier to address her stepmother, whose reciprocal affection she felt that she deserved. As she wrote Parr in a letter of 1548, "If your grace had not a good opinion of me, you would not have offered friendship to me" (1:18–19).

The visual and verbal strategies that Elizabeth developed through these manuscript volumes benefited her later in her political career. In presenting such elaborate books from her head and hand, proving her intellectual and household competence, Elizabeth represented herself as an educated, pious young woman. Her judgment of what would attract the attention of her parents and their courts demonstrated her education in writing more than one form of italic, in translating—and composing—in Latin, Italian, French, and English. She then presented these accomplishments in books bound with her needlework that made clear her awareness of how identity could be asserted as the nexus of verbal and visual textualities. These volumes, although in some respects the work of the eleven- and twelve-year-old girl that she was, serve notice that she was capable of combining strategies that moved beyond accepted gender roles into the world of decision makers, whose minds were trained in humanist and religious discourse.[30]

The preservation of three of the four fragile manuscripts and the later display of the two volumes dedicated to Henry VIII at Whitehall Palace demonstrate that they were valued long after they served their initial purpose. As inalienable possessions produced by a woman who became queen, these volumes continued to connect the past, present, and future through kinship. They also reminded viewers of Elizabeth's lifelong work as an author. As she lived up to the conviction expressed in her 1544 dedication to Katherine Parr, that "the wit of a man or a woman" should "be always occupied upon some manner of study" (1:6–7), Elizabeth would go on to translate Petrarch, Horace, Seneca, and, in her sixties, Boethius's *Consolation of Philosophy*, write significant prayers, poetry, and even more renowned speeches, while leaving her needlework behind with her disempowered youth. But at the ages of eleven and twelve, while first exploring how to represent herself to a courtly audience, Elizabeth used her volumes to signify the humanist education of a prince within an explicitly feminine object valued for generations.

Elizabeth and Edward VI: Portraying "the Inward Good Mind"

As she grew older, Elizabeth, like her half-sister, Mary, before her, became involved in the visual medium of portraiture, a textuality that created still another kind of family treasure asserting her royal gifts and prerogatives. The

Figure 7. Artist unknown, *Elizabeth When a Princess*. Portrait of the Lady Elizabeth Tudor, 1546 or 1547. Windsor Castle. The Royal Collection. © 2009 Her Majesty Queen Elizabeth II.

portrait called *Elizabeth When a Princess* was painted when Elizabeth was fourteen years old (Figure 7). The portrait, which appears in the inventory taken after Edward VI's accession in January 1547, is described as "A table with the picture of the lady Elizabeth her grace with a book in her hand her gown like crimson cloth of gold with works"; it was completed by September 1547 and was then in her brother's possession, although it may have been begun while their father was still alive.[31] The portrait is an important visual document of Elizabeth's self-representation only two years after she presented her father and stepmother with the surviving set of calligraphic manuscripts. As Andrea Pearson points out, even if the female subject of a portrait has not paid for the painting, the "sitter" may contribute "to the crafting of her own image."[32] Elizabeth was aware of the importance of her portrait's impact. As she later wrote to her brother about another portrait of herself, she hoped that her "inward good mind toward your Grace might as well be declared as the outward face and countenance shall be seen."[33] In other words, she hoped that the painting would communicate her interior goodwill toward him, and so profoundly connect sister and brother.

Like the needlework-covered translations through which Elizabeth substantiated her bond with her father and stepmother, she used *Elizabeth When a Princess* to affirm her bond with the new king. Once her brother ascended the throne, much was at stake in reminding him of his beloved older sister. Above all, Elizabeth wished to be invited to the court more often, where, in the physical presence of the king, she would have a chance to influence decisions concerning her allowance and estate management, as well as her future husband, during the years when talks were being conducted about her possible marriage with Prince Frederick of Denmark or the brother of the king of Navarre or a brother of the Duke of Guise. After 1553, as doubts about Edward's health deepened, being at court might even have had an impact on the succession.

If, as I think probable, this is a portrait of Elizabeth in the apparel that she wore for her brother's coronation, then this portrait would have been painted to remind the new king of his sister's claim to his regard. As Ann Rosalind Jones and Peter Stallybrass have summarized this practice, "Many Renaissance portraits were supplements to rites of passage in which large sums of money had been spent on clothing and jewels."[34] Because large or expensive gifts of clothing were unusual enough to appear in accounts or be acknowledged in grateful letters, we can track such finery. The portrait of the Lady Elizabeth corresponds with a sudden improvement in her finances following her father's death. At this time, she received a substantial inheritance, although payment of the revenues from her lands was delayed. The Privy Council also recorded payments "To my Lady Elizabeth's taylour 25 pounds 10 shillings 7 pence; for a bill of her embroiderers, 41 pounds 5 shillings; for a bill of her robes, 73 pounds 12 shillings and 4 pence."[35] Considering that her brother's entire coronation cost £442,[36] Elizabeth's funding of more than £170 may well not only mark a new regime but also provide an appropriate occasion to inscribe this new beginning in a technically meticulous painting. The portrait's jewels, embroidery, and rich textiles are so carefully rendered that they become a major focus of the portrait. The care that the painter took in reproducing Elizabeth's embellished clothing recalls the cost of the embroidery and robes, as do the woven stuffs making up her dress of which, writes Janet Arnold, the red cloth is either "cut velvet" or "silk." Arnold continues, "The undersleeves and matching forepart are in a very rich material with a white satin ground and raised looped pile of gold thread."[37]

Elizabeth may well have required the unknown painter to give her the direct gaze that Holbein had given her father and brother. Nicholas Hilliard, writing later in the century about "drawing after the life," argues that it is best for sitters to decide how to stand and look: "I would wish any body to be well resolved with themselves before hand, with what grace they would stand, and seem," in order to avoid appearing with "unnatural or affected grace." Indeed, Hilliard recounts how the older Elizabeth decided to have her portrait made "in the open ally of a goodly garden, where no tree was neere, nor anye shadowe at all." Perhaps, like Mary in 1544 or Katherine Parr when she was queen,[38] Elizabeth not only composed but also commissioned this portrait.

Elizabeth When a Princess is reminiscent of Annunciation paintings featuring the Virgin and the Bible. Elizabeth stands between two books—the folio in the background on a lectern, suggesting the Old Testament, and the smaller quarto held with her left hand, the New Testament. Books, as testaments and books held by female subjects are common elements in portraits of this period in part because the books invite their audience to read the sitter's character as well as argue for her pious literacy. In particular, the books in this portrait imply Elizabeth's caution about religion in the opening days of her brother's reign because, unlike the English translation of Proverbs that the son holds in the Barnham family portrait (see Figure 1), the pages in the large book are left cautiously blank; the small book may be Latin or English or Greek, but it is closed. The *Alice Barnham* painting's staging of the central woman, like Anne Clifford's *Great Picture* and Mary Tudor's portrait of 1544, juxtaposes her portrait with several written inscriptions. *Elizabeth When a Princess* provides two books without visible text and only one short inscription, visible on infrared, that may well date from its composition: "*soror regis*," "sister of the king," which at least means that the inscription was added after King Henry VIII's death.[39]

The artist represents his sitter as someone with whom one must reckon. The direct, firm, and intelligent gaze of this fourteen-year-old replicates the authoritative gaze of Holbein's *Henry VIII*. Elizabeth's intelligence is also confirmed by the gesture of holding the small book in her hand, her index finger marking her place. Moreover, the smaller book both covers and reminds the onlooker of Elizabeth's female sexuality. Unlike the more reticent, circuitously worded letter that she later wrote to her brother about another portrait, in

Elizabeth When a Princess this sitter frankly asserts her position in the social hierarchy: She displays her finery, looks directly at her audience, and holds the book above the pubic bone in a gesture that simultaneously evokes her ability to have children in the line of succession and asserts her chaste, scholarly turn of mind. As Elizabeth's reign progresses, it becomes increasingly difficult to discern whether she paid for artists' "pens" and "pencils," collaborating with the artists who painted her portraits. But Elizabeth's clothing, gaze, and books in this portrait from about 1547 suggest what was at stake at the time it was painted, even as it is a remarkable statement of her early political acumen.

Mary Stuart in White Mourning

To examine Elizabeth's needlework-covered calligraphic manuscripts and her early portrait is to consider the work of a vulnerable young woman for whom the English throne was in sight but whose richest and most complex iconography still lay in her future. When Mary Stuart, Queen of Scots and Dowager Queen of France, arrived in England in the vain hope that her cousin Elizabeth would come to her aid in the civil war dividing Scotland, the glory of Mary's queenships and their attendant iconography lay suddenly in her past. Once she arrived in England, her visual and verbal attempts at defense failed to save her from imprisonment in the wake of her husband Darnley's murder. Her marriage to James Hepburn, Earl of Bothwell, and the ensuing Scottish civil war led to her eighteen-year imprisonment and her execution in 1587.

But in France, as Queen of Scotland and the betrothed of the dauphin, son of Henry II, Mary Stuart was brought up at the center of one of the most sophisticated courts in Europe. In addition to learning languages, including Greek, German, and Italian, before she turned thirteen, Mary declaimed a Latin oration to a royal audience that defended the education of women by emphasizing the accomplishments of female exemplars. Mary also participated in the courtly arts of dancing, needlework, hunting, and hawking. As a girl and young woman, she discussed drawing with the court's primary painter, François Clouet, and poetry with Pierre de Ronsard, who had served her father, James V, at his Scottish court.[40] Ronsard, together with Joachim du Bellay, Jacques Tahureau, Jacques de la Taille, Réné Guillon, and Melin de Saint-Gelais, wrote poetry and entertainments for her as dauphine-reine, as queen consort, as patron of the arts, and as the young woman whose royal body linked France to the thrones of Scotland and England.

Shortly after Mary's marriage, her father-in-law, Henry II, died suddenly when a lance pierced his eye during a court tournament in June 1559. Francis II and Mary were subsequently crowned King and Queen Consort of France in

Rheims on September 15. The attendant entries and celebrations were marked by iterations of their earlier political iconography, while Ronsard wrote a sonnet in which Jupiter decreed that Mary would rule England for three months, Scotland for three months, and France for six.[41] Unfortunately for Mary, this kind of statement, together with the fact that the French began joining the arms of England, Scotland, and France in their heraldry, produced an alarm in England that influenced foreign policy toward Scotland throughout the 1560s and solidified William Cecil's suspicion of Mary.[42] Unlike Elizabeth's conscious development of her iconography with her ciphered manuscripts at eleven and twelve years of age and her portrait at fourteen, Mary took control of her iconography later in her young life, when she was seventeen or eighteen, and only after the deaths of her mother, father-in-law, and husband made it both necessary and possible for her to control her own image. The most famous of her representations, the image that would dominate her portraiture throughout her life and after it, was her portrait in white mourning, or *deuil blanc*, an image that Clouet painted in the first *deuil blanc* portrait of 1559–60, for which we seem to have a preliminary drawing (Figure 8).

The most complete surviving description of French white mourning as ritual dress is Roger Ascham's description of Queen Eleanor, widow of Francis I, in 1550. Mary, who was then eight years old, may have seen the effect that the queen's appearance created and later called upon that memory. Eleanor attended Mass, wrote Ascham, "clad very solemnly all in white cameric, a robe gathered in pleats wrought very fair as need be with white needle work, as white as a dove." Eleanor was attended by her ladies, clothed in the striking black and white palette in which Mary would later dress her own attendants. Eleanor's ladies, who were richly attired, seemed to Ascham "boys rather than ladies, excellent to have played in tragedies,"[43] a comment that responds to both the theatricality of the women's appearance at Mass and the gender bending practiced at the French court. The Dowager Queen Eleanor's *deuil blanc*, like that of Mary Stuart's a decade later, is typified by the combination of a white veil attached to a *barbe*, or white collar, tied up to the hairline at the nape of the neck, together with "a gauze cap finely gathered to a wire edging covered with white stitchery," to which a white veil in lawn is pinned.[44]

It remains unclear whether Mary first wore white mourning to commemorate the death of her father-in-law, Henry II, in July 1559 or the death of her mother, Mary of Guise, in June 1560. She also wore it when her husband, Francis II, died in December 1560. At some point during this painful period, Mary became aware not only of the impact of wearing *deuil blanc* but of the impact that Clouet's portrait had on its beholders and of its ability to represent her to political sympathizers, to potential suitors, and to her English cousin, Elizabeth.

Figure 8. After François Clouet, *Mary Queen of Scots in White Mourning*, 1560. Pen and ink on paper, black and white photo. Bibliothèque Nationale, Paris, France / Giraudon / The Bridgeman Art Library Nationality. Copyright status: French / out of copyright.

In August 1560, the English ambassador to France, Sir Nicholas Throckmorton, reported that Mary talked to him about her portrait in *deuil blanc*. According to Throckmorton, Mary responded to Elizabeth's praise of Mary's portrait: "Quoth she, 'I perceive you like me better when I look sadly than when I look merrily, for it is told me that you desired to have me pictured when I wore the deuil.'" Increasingly aware of the impact of this mourning attire, Mary must have had duplicates available for presentation, as useful for impressing the English queen as for representing her on the international marriage market. If she had not already sent Elizabeth a copy, she must soon have done so.[45]

Contemporary versions of Clouet's much-copied portrait include the drawing at the Bibliothèque Nationale attributed to Clouet (see Figure 8), and paintings now at Holyrood, Turin, the English National Portrait Gallery, Hampton Court, and in the Wallace Collection, while at least two other examples of Mary in three-quarter profile survive. The appeal of Mary's portrait in white mourning long outlived her, becoming the template for many posthumous portraits. Her ill-fated grandson, Charles I, owned two copies.[46] In all these versions of Clouet's original, Mary is wearing the royal mourning traditional to French queens, its ritual white setting off the pale, grave face, an icon of youthful vulnerability as well as of the chaste daughter, daughter-in-law, and widow. In the Clouet drawing, the gaze of Mary's almond eyes rests to the left of the viewer, a less direct statement than Elizabeth's gaze in *Elizabeth When a Princess*. In that portrait, Elizabeth's gaze; her books; and the vibrant reds, whites, and golds of her apparel outlining her slim young body represent her status, intellect, and sexuality. Mary's portrait depends on a far simpler composition and palette as the portrait's presentation of her fine features swathed within layers of white embroidery, lace, and linen displays the sitter's youthful fertility within the parentheses of royal loss.

Mary's poem on her husband's death on 5 December 1560 is evidence of her awareness of the impact of this portrait. In a passage about her portrait in *deuil blanc*, Mary meditates on its likeness of her, concentrating on her own feelings of loss rather than on eulogizing her husband. In French, the language in which she wrote most of her poetry and nearly all her correspondence, the verse reads:

> J'ai au coeur et à l'oeil
> Un portrait et image
> Qui figure mon deuil
> Et mon pâle visage
> De violettes teint [éteintes]
> Qui est l'amoureux teint.[47]

Translated literally, Mary wrote, "I have in the heart and in the eye / A portrait and likeness / that figures my *deuil* [grief; mourning clothes; the period of mourning] / and my pale face / of violets fading [so tinted] / which is the complexion [tint] of loving." In Mary's verse, her portrait is located both inside and outside the speaker, in her heart and eye; that is, in her body but also in her painted portrait, as well as in the heart and eye of its viewer. The stanza's final play on "teint," meaning "color" or "tint" but also "complexion," makes it clear that it is not just her face but the *appearance* of her face—pale against the white clothing, a representation of love and loss—that is important to the poem's speaker.

Mary's poem on herself in her ritual clothing may precede or be a response to Ronsard's "poem Eligie a Marie Stuart," written when she sailed for Scotland. Ronsard wrote, "Although the beauty of your face is forever imprinted on my heart and does not fade with the passing of the years . . . the ornament of my studies and looks is that portrait which hallows the place like a sacred image enshrined in the temple of a great god." For Ronsard, her mourning clothes create a sensual portrait of transition, "Swathing your body from head to waist, your long fine mourning veil, billows fold upon fold like a sail in the breeze," as "you prepared to leave the fair country of which you held the crown."[48] Pierre de Bourdeille, Abbé de Brantôme, the historian who accompanied Mary to Scotland, also composed a poem on the queen in white mourning, in which he notes the effect of white on white: "la blancheur de son visage contendoit avec la blancheur de son voile,"[49] "the white of her face contending with the white of her veil." Like Mary's own poem, the poems of Ronsard and Brantôme animate Mary's portrait in white mourning, bringing it to life in order to acknowledge her loss of mother, father-in-law, and husband within two years, as well as the fact that these losses precipitated Mary's new, vulnerable, yet autonomous political state. The many versions of this portrait, whether in pencil, paint, or words, function as forms of inalienable possession constructed as treasured statements of Mary's past, present, and future selves.

Mary's subsequent portraiture, including the textile portrait at New Hardwick Hall that I discuss later in the chapter, demonstrates that the vision of a Mary dressed to evoke both royalty and loss became central to her later iconography. Her biographers point out that the Scottish inventories of her elaborate clothing, much of it imported from France in 1561, are far more colorful than most extant portraits of her suggest. This Scottish inventory, while listing the clothes of white mourning, also describes the sixty gowns she wore of "silk, satin, velvet, cloth of gold and cloth of silver" and mantles of "purple velvet" and "ermine."[50] This wardrobe, brought from France and regularly updated, is more in tune with a Mary renowned for her dancing, hunting, and hawking, a

Mary fearful that John Knox will find out that she played cards all night, a Mary eager for a husband and children.

But the *deuil blanc* was apparently never far from Mary's thoughts, even after four years of sumptuous attire at her Scottish court. Mourning continued to represent her position as Dowager Queen of France and Queen of Scotland in her own right, a queen whose chastity was inseparable from the loss of her husband-king, Francis II. According to the firsthand account that Elizabeth's ambassador, Thomas Randolph, wrote to the Earl of Leicester, at her wedding to Henry Stuart, Lord Darnley, in July 1565, she dressed in mourning. Afterward, she invited her husband and the wedding guests to undo the mourning garb pin by pin: "She suffreth them that stood by, every man, that could approach to take out a pin, and so being committed unto her ladies, changed her garments."[51] At this point, Mary's use of her mourning clothes transcends portraiture to become court entertainment, an unclothing before an intimate audience. As part of her wedding day, the ritualized undoing of her *deuil* returned her to familiar symbolic ground, to images of herself as queen that in the end she preferred not to shed. For Mary did not abandon her mourning after her marriage to Darnley. Instead, in her later portraiture, she adapted the costume of the white mourning portraits to create the Mary Queen of Scots signature look, characterized by a cap of white gauze shaped by a wire, to which is pinned a white, transparent veil covering a black gown. Although the shape of the cap announcing her ties to French fashion and to the French court changes from portrait to portrait and the fabric in the later portraits may be gauze or lace, hung in folds or drawn tight to form a V over her forehead, Mary in cap and veil, usually in a three-quarters pose, centers the composition of nearly every extant portrait of this queen.[52] Mary left France, but she refused to leave the most flattering, poignant, and suggestive of her representations behind.

English Imprisonment and the Creation of Inalienable Possessions

A series of dramatic events led to Mary's fleeing Scotland for England in July 1568. These events included the murder of her second husband, Darnley, when his residence was blown up with gunpowder and he was found stabbed outside it; her scandalous third marriage to the Earl of Bothwell; the rebellion of the Scottish Confederate Lords against her; and her defeat and imprisonment for nearly a year at Lochleven Castle after her forced abdication in favor of her son, James VI (later James I of England). When she managed to escape from Lochleven, she endured a second Scottish defeat at the Battle of Langside. Once Mary escaped the Confederate Lords and crossed Solway Firth to arrive in England,

William Cecil ordered her lodged in Carlisle Castle and kept there. As her confinement more clearly became an imprisonment and Mary realized that Elizabeth might very well imprison her indefinitely, she began exercising her verbal and visual textualities for different audiences, with very different political goals in mind. First, through intermediaries and her own letters, needlework, and other gifts, Mary pleaded for Elizabeth to release her or, at the very least, to see her. Second, Mary needed to rally support from sympathizers and kin in Scotland, England, France, and Spain, although, by the time she left Scotland, the rumors of her misdeeds, coupled with her actions, had alienated many former friends. Third, Mary wished to communicate with her son, James, who was being raised without her perspective on his political and familial relations or her sense of the comportment of a ruler. In addition to these external audiences, Mary Stuart surrounded herself and her comparatively small court-in-exile, which varied from thirty to sixty followers, with the visual expressions of her multinational and royal identities, a way of affirming them regardless of her circumstances. And finally, Mary combined commissioned portraits, needlework, letters, and poetry to express her frustration that her life's promise had been so thwarted.

Mary's many attempts to reach Elizabeth were all marked by gifts, and all ended in disappointment. One example may stand for many: John Leslie, Bishop of Ross, who was Mary's advocate, describes his meeting with Elizabeth to ask her to meet with her cousin. He presented Elizabeth with "tokens" of Mary's needlework and a standish, or inkstand, with a cipher on its lock. In response, Elizabeth was appreciative but cagey. She praised Mary's needlework "principally that a great part thereof was wrought with her own hands" and promised that the standish "should remain continually in her sight in her study." The cipher engraved on its lock was probably the intertwined initials of both queens, because Elizabeth said that she wished "all things were in the same state they were into when this cipher was made between us." When Elizabeth offered to reciprocate with a ring, Ross answered that "we required not to have the ring, but . . . her aid and support," to which Elizabeth responded that she would "give it gladly as honour and conscience would permit."[53]

Although this gift of needlework to Elizabeth, and subsequent gifts of "a skirt of crimson satin lined with taffeta and worked with silver thread," as well as "three nightcaps,"[54] did not produce the desired meeting, Mary's needlework became a principle means through which she asserted her royal identities and her position as heir-in-waiting to the English throne. Famously, she and Bess of Hardwick collaborated from about 1569 through the 1570s on several dozen extant cushions, rectangular emblems, and some forty surviving octagon-shaped pictures in tent stitch.[55] This body of needlework includes many emblems of Mary's political identity and ambition. One rectangular piece worked in tent stitch on linen canvas in silver, gold, and colored silk thread (Plate 1) features an armillary sphere floating over a treacherous seascape surrounding a lone ship, and bordered by the arms of France, Spain, England, and Scotland, amid other emblematic pictures. Its motto in Spanish, "Las pennas passan y queda la speranza," "Sorrows pass but hope survives," suggests that Mary is the intrepid ship sailing through a sea of monsters, while she marked it as her work with the emblem of the marigold turning with the sun and the Order of the Thistle encircled by the Scottish royal arms. Mary's octagon with the embroidered word "delphine" features a leaping dolphin. Since her coat of arms had once displayed a leaping dolphin, in this piece Mary plays on the association in both French and English with the words "dauphin" and "dauphine" as a reminder of her marriage to the future Francis II, a marriage that had sent her Guise relatives into ascendance. Another octagon shows a ginger cat, whose red hair recalls Elizabeth, hunting a small but nimble mouse. Although pictured as the mouse in this embroidery, Mary refused to see herself as completely helpless. She wrote to Elizabeth in 1571 in words that epitomize her stance as resourceful victim. Mary describes herself as being in an "extremity" because of the actions of those who, while having no "occasion" to hate her, "have for a long while given proof of their inclination by injuring me in your opinion and that of all others." Nevertheless, Mary resolutely affirms that "I have acquitted myself according to my power."[56]

One way that Mary "acquitted" herself "according to her power" in 1569–71 was to discuss marriage with the Duke of Norfolk. A cushion now at Oxburgh Hall (Plate 2) is either a second version or the original of a rectangular embroidery piece that played a political role when Mary gave it to the duke during their illicit courtship. The design, of a hand clipping off a barren vine so that the fruitful vine may flourish, is surmounted by the same motto as Mary's signet ring, "Virescit Vulnere Virtus." One translation of the Latin is "Virtue flourishes by wounding," and another, "Courage grows strong at the wound." The message may have been meant to communicate Mary's patience in captivity, but it was also open to a treasonous interpretation, that the barren stalk of Elizabeth should be cut away with the pictured pruning hook so that the fruitful branch of Mary might grow. Regardless of Mary's intentions, this interpretation must have been the reason that this piece was introduced as evidence against the Duke of Norfolk at his trial for treason, apparent proof of his conspiracy to marry the Queen of Scotland, for which he lost his head.[57]

At the same time that Mary, working with Bess of Hardwick and their households, stitched such emblems expressing her political perspective, she also managed to send a series of gifts to her son, James. Because he was being raised by her enemies, Mary wanted to participate in his education. Her gifts show a desire to help him to learn to read, to learn the proper behavior of a prince, and to understand the political affiliations that he inherited through his mother. As she wrote to the French ambassador, M. de la Mothe Fenelon, she longed to communicate with her son in order to "admonish him of his duty." She managed to send James embroidered riding reins, some clothes, and a book from which to learn his ABC. In January 1569/1570, she sent messengers to James with another, unnamed book for him from "a loving mother that wishes you to learn in time to love, know and fear God: and next that you conform to God's command and good nature to remember your duty [toward] her that has born you in her sides." Perhaps the unnamed book was the "verse treatise on the 'institution' of a prince," a calligraphic manuscript covered in needlework that Mary produced for James about this time. In 1616, Bishop Montague of Winchester noted, "The Queen his Majesty's Mother wrote a book of verses in French of the Institution of a Prince, all with her own hand, wrought a cover of it with a needle, and is now of his Majesty esteemed as a precious jewel."[58] Although no description of the manuscript's needlework cover exists, embroidery in silver or gold thread was a common feature of book bindings like those that Elizabeth had worked. Perhaps, given the description of the volume as "a precious jewel," Mary also worked seed pearls or small gems into an emblematic design for her son.

Mary embroidered still another set of political emblems from 1569 through the 1570s, when Bess of Hardwick and Mary sewed frequently together. These were produced for the state bed that she created for herself and that she left to James in her will. In fact James received this bed after Mary's death in 1587, but it went missing in the mid-seventeenth century.[59] After embroidering the individual emblems, very likely a combination of octagons and rectangles, she would have appliquéd these individual pieces onto its long velvet curtains, its three valances, and the bed's ceiler, or canopy. Mary seems to have conceived the idea for it in the 1570s, in part to assert her royal identity to herself and her remaining court, who attended her in the rooms that she called her privy chamber and bedchamber, as if she were still living in a royal palace. In part this bed allowed her to lie each night surrounded by her identity as instantiated in heraldry and emblems. She probably derived comfort from the idea that her son would one day receive it and would be able to read in it not only her struggle to maintain her political identities but also her struggle to pass them on to her child, the King of Scotland and heir to Elizabeth's throne.

According to the description of the state bed's emblems that William Drummond sent to Ben Jonson in 1619, Mary's needlework—completed with the help of her professional embroiderer, her painter or tapissier, attendants, and perhaps Bess and her retainers as well—recorded her genealogy and familial alliances as well as her frustration at imprisonment.[60] The emblem most overtly about Mary and James, Drummond describes as "for herself and her Son, a big *Lyon*, and young Whelp beside her, the word, *Unum quidem, sed Leonem*," "only one [cub], but a lion." Most pieces that Drummond describes register the kinship affiliations that Mary wanted to emphasize, including the arms of Scotland, France, and England, embroidered both separately and quartered throughout the hangings. The anagram of "Marie Stewart" with which Mary had signed a poem on the Bishop of Ross's release from prison in 1574, "*sa virtu m'attire*," "its virtue attracts me" (Bell, 80), was also the motto of an embroidered emblem for this state bed that included a "Loadstone turning towards the pole," implying that virtue like Mary's attracts as inevitably as a magnet. Other kinship associations in Mary's needlework include the rendering of her mother's impresa of a phoenix in flames—of which another example from this period is extant—with the motto "*en ma fin git mon commencement*," "in my end is my beginning."[61] Mary Stuart also worked the impresas of Francis I; of Henry II, her Guise uncle the Cardinal of Lorraine; and of the Duke of Savoy, who had married Marguerite, daughter of Henry II and Catherine de Medici. Mary's embroidered emblem of the impresa of Henry VIII recalls Mary's and Darnley's double descent from Henry's sister, Margaret.[62]

As Michael Bath has recently discovered, Drummond's description is one of four surviving descriptions of Mary's bed of state. The most complete of these descriptions, which Bath calls "Hawthornden Anonymous," was written by an informer who saw the bed when it was fully assembled, most probably in Mary's bedchamber. In addition to noting the embroidered emblems covering the bed, this observer reported that on "the roof of the bed" he saw a "painted" device of "the queen's majesty portrayed kneeling before the cross and her crown and her scepter laying at her feet and holding her hands to heaven." In other words, the canopy of Mary's bed of state featured a portrait of her praying with the icons of her monarchy at her feet, in the tradition of the portrait of her grandfather, James IV, in the *Book of Hours of James IV and Margaret Tudor* (1503). The observer also saw that this portrait of Mary painted on the bed's canopy had a motto ending with the word *Undique*. The complete motto must have read "*Angustiae Undique*," "through the narrows or difficulties," a motto appropriate for her imprisonment that was also incorporated in the full-length portrait of her at New Hardwick Hall painted on wooden panel.[63]

According to Michael Bath, these descriptions of Mary's lost emblems probably derive from intelligence reports sent to Walsingham, who wanted to keep track of Mary's visual self-representations in the interests of security (*Emblems for a Queen*, 19). The English had been aware that, from the beginning of Mary's captivity, her needlework had political significance. In 1569, when Nicholas White visited Mary at Tutbury, he wrote William Cecil of his unease about Mary's needlework as well as her personal charm. When White asked her what she did when the weather precluded outdoor exercise, she answered that "all that Day she wrought with her Needle, and the Diversity of the Colors made the Work seem less tedious, and continued so long at it till very Pain made her to give over." When she opened the seemingly innocuous subject of which was the superior art form, carving, painting, or working with the needle, they quickly were at loggerheads: Mary thought painting the most commendable, but White reports that he responded with the iconoclastic suspicion that pictures present a false truth. Mary's cloth of estate under which she sat also made White suspicious: "I noted this Sentence embroidered, *En ma fin est mon commencement*; which is a Riddle, I understand not."[64] The "sentence" that provoked White's suspicions—"in my end is my beginning"—in fact formed part of her mother's impresa of the phoenix, which Mary later worked for her state bed hangings as well as for the hangings left with Bess of Hardwick. White's report of this motto strongly suggests that this cloth of state had once belonged to Mary of Guise. It was probably delivered to her daughter among the several cartloads of her goods sent from Scotland, with which she worked to transform her rooms into some semblance of court chambers even before she could add her own needlework to the mix.

In this often-quoted description of his encounter with Mary, White is prescient in discerning that Mary's embroidery, like all her trappings of state, was inherently political. White's description also tells us about Mary's preference for visual forms of representation. When Mary brought up the question of which art form is superior, she limited herself to visual forms—carving, painting, or working with the needle. When Elizabeth had turned to the question of the superiority of art forms, in her letter to Parr beginning Calvin's *Institutes*, she asked whether sculpting, casting, carving, painting, or *writing* was most dependable, and argued for the primacy of language over visual image, a choice consistent with Elizabeth's verbal gifts. Mary, whose own rhetorical and literary skills had been polished at the French court, nevertheless seems to have preferred the visual to the verbal, which would explain her comments to White. It also seems possible that Mary had a rather wicked sense of humor and might have been baiting White, a Protestant whose iconoclasm she could have predicted.

Women like Elizabeth Tudor, Mary Stuart, and Bess of Hardwick expected to orchestrate the intersecting codes through which they articulated their evolving identities, even if they risked being misread. For early modern people, the intersection of the visual and verbal created powerful signifiers that could be used for good or ill. "Device" could mean not only a needleworked emblem, an allegorical entertainment, a harmless plan for the future but also a secret plot; a "knot" could be a beautiful design but also a conspiracy. "Cipher" could mean what the OED calls "an intertexture of letters," a monogram in which connection takes on visual dimensions, as when Elizabeth Tudor's intertwined initials signify familial and political links. In the context of letter-writing, "cipher" also meant, as it does today, a code for secret writing. Mary Stuart learned to correspond with her mother using ciphers in order to hide politically significant proper nouns. Elizabeth also used this strategy, as when she signed a letter written in cipher to Mary's half-brother James Stewart, Earl of Moray.[65] For us, "cipher" also retains its earlier meaning of a "symbolic figure, a hiero-glyph," often one with unknown signification. Although some of these defini-tions are still in use, the early modern words used to describe codes demonstrate a tendency to see the visual and verbal as inherently related. For example, "deci-phering" could mean creating the code in the first place rather than figuring it out, while the "illustration" of an emblem signified the accompanying verse rather than its picture. The slippage between a picture and a motto or verse seems to have been the point, as early modern people valued the wealth of possible interpretations residing in juxtapositions of word and image. They also appreciated the compact significance of forms like pictures with verses, emblems, coats of arms, and posies. Even the young Elizabeth, who preferred writing to any visual form, attempted to harness the power of the verbal-visual connection. Mary embraced the emblem and the cipher at the moment when she was in her most personal and political distress, finding there the means to express the compound identities that had led to her imprisonment and that she refused to relinquish because in them resided her only hope for her restoration to power.[66]

Although both men and women used a variety of codes in this period, wom-en's codes derived their significance from particularly gendered situations and found expression in particularly gendered ways, whether in needlework, com-missioned portraits, or writing. In very different times and places, women have developed coded texts for their communications. During the English Civil War, Lady Brilliana Harley, under siege by the forces of the Crown, sent secret mes-sages written on cloth so that they could be concealed by her messengers, and wrote coded communications by using a key of paper. This key was cut into a pattern that, laid over an otherwise ordinary family letter, exposed the words of a secret message.[67] As I discuss in Chapter 3, in the seventeenth century, English women of the gentry and middling classes increasingly joined royal and aristo-cratic women in producing coded forms of communication in embroidery, joining initials and names to carefully chosen pictures, often of Old Testament women.

Mary Stuart's ciphers were often decoded by a sympathetic audience that included Bess of Hardwick; her attendant, Mary Seton; the Duke of Norfolk; and her son James; however, their meanings remained suspicious to viewers representing the English government, such as Nicholas White, William Cecil, and Francis Walsingham. Mary had no choice but to bet her life that her most dangerous codes would be available only to sympathizers.[68] In 1586, when Cecil's intelligence network was able to decode the full extent of Mary's treason against Elizabeth through her ciphered messages to Anthony Babington, her crime was so apparent that Elizabeth acquiesced to her death, even as she tried to obscure her role in the execution of an anointed queen and kinswoman. Mary used all the forms of pen and needle available to her in order to assert her identities, which also meant subverting Elizabeth's power. As a result, Elizabeth is necessarily present in all of Mary's work. She is the force to be outlived, the curtailer of Mary's liberty, the cat to her mouse, the obstacle between Mary and her son, the barren vine to be cut off if she and her son are to flourish.

Mary Stuart and Bess of Hardwick: Sewing Connections

Mary Stuart's companion and jailer, Elizabeth Talbot, Countess of Shrewsbury, came from a very different background than that of her royal prisoner. She was born Elizabeth Hardwick, the daughter of a family of impoverished gentry in Derbyshire. Three marriages in ascending order of social importance and a stint as Elizabeth's lady-in-waiting led her to her wealthy, well-born, and contentious fourth husband, George Talbot, Earl of Shrewsbury. In her devotion to her own and her offspring's social mobility, the Countess of Shrewsbury was just as committed to dynastic ambition as her impressive prisoner was to hers.

Bess of Hardwick's needlework must be read in the context of her decades spent remodeling and building the country houses of Chatsworth, Hardwick Hall, and New Hardwick Hall, as she balanced princely display with the financial management that would underwrite both the Cavendish and Talbot dynasties. During the first years of Mary's imprisonment, Bess focused on Chatsworth, a joint purchase with her second husband, Sir Thomas Cavendish—a purchase that he seems to have memorialized with a jewel-studded book containing both their portraits. While occupying the existing house, the Cavendishes built a new, impressively situated building.[69] After Thomas Cavendish's death, Bess held Chatsworth until their oldest son, Henry, was twenty-one. In the meantime, she continued to update Chatsworth with tapestries, plasterwork, carpets, and portraiture, together with worked cushions, bed hangings, and wall coverings. In 1569, when Mary Queen of Scots came into the Shrewsburys' custody soon after their marriage, Bess drew on Mary's expertise and that of her household to help her with her interior furnishings, an influence visible in the production of the five remarkable needlework hangings that Santina Levey calls the *Noble Women of the Ancient World*.[70]

During this period, when Mary's political fate in Scotland was still being decided, a number of letters from 1569 until about 1577 report that Bess and Mary were relatively intimate. As Ralph Sadler wrote to Cecil, "The Countess of Shrewsbury is seldom from her," even as Mary kept to her rooms. Elizabeth wrote to the countess thanking her for her service regarding Mary, and the two are described engaged in working together during the first years of Mary's forced stay in Shrewsbury properties. In 1569, Shrewsbury reported to Cecil that "Mary daily resorts to my wife's chamber, where with Lady Leviston and Mistress Seton, she sits devising works." Although these letters assured Cecil that they spoke of nothing of consequence, Bess was expected to spy on Mary for Cecil and Elizabeth, a fact that reinforces the likelihood that Mary and Bess frequently talked politics.[71] Likewise, their needlework, drawn from a variety of sources, but especially from illustrated books of emblems, herbals, and natural history owned by Mary,[72] articulates their very different identities in terms of their political and social ambitions.

Neither Mary nor Bess seems to have had much patience for intricate or tiny stitches. Instead, nearly all of their surviving work demonstrates that they were caught up in the design and meaning of each piece, as well as in the ways in which the different pieces related to one another. As a result, most of their work was produced in relatively coarse loops of tent stitch, also known as petit point, which Mary learned along with many others as a girl at the French court.[73] Although tent stitch executed in tiny stitches creates vivid detail, in larger stitches it allows maximum coverage of space in a minimum amount of time. Nevertheless, each emblem they made represents many hours of work. The dozens of octagonal pieces that they produced together—Mary often working her cipher of an upright "M" on top of an upside-down "M" or the cipher of Francis II into those that were her own—were designed to be appliquéd onto larger pieces of luxurious material to assemble bed or wall hangings. This appliqué process enabled a number of relatively small needlework pieces to clothe the entire bed of state hangings destined for James, or the wall hangings now on view at Oxburgh Hall in Norfolk. Mary's apartments never lacked for tapestries: Bess's inventories reveal that there were over forty tapestries at Chatsworth alone. Elizabeth sent still other tapestries from the Tower to provide Mary's rooms with both insulation and decoration as she moved with her exiled court from one Shrewsbury property to another.[74] But both Mary and Bess became intensely involved in creating textile works that embodied more personal expressions of identity than tapestries produced in professional workshops. The desire of both women to embroider their history and ambitions motivated them to work together, to spend years adopting the engravings from illustrated books, many owned by Mary, to have artisans transfer these designs to canvas, and then to stitch their trademark octagons and emblematic rectangular pieces.

The two women became used to collaborating. Bess used Mary's overseer of her dowry in France, James Beaton, Archbishop of Glasgow, to obtain silk; Mary took Elizabeth Pierrepont, Bess's granddaughter, into her retinue from the age of four as a mark of favor;[75] while Bess knew throughout Mary's imprisonment that her captive might readily become her queen. Moreover, Bess soon used Mary's relations with her in-laws, the Lennox family, to contrive the marriage of her daughter, Elizabeth Cavendish, to Lord Darnley's younger brother, Charles Stuart. Their daughter, Arbella Stuart, King James's only first cousin, was born in 1575. As the great-granddaughter of the sister of Henry VIII, Margaret Tudor, through the Lennox line, Arbella's claim to the English throne threatened James enough that he had her imprisoned in the Tower in 1611, after her sensational, cross-dressed attempt to free her husband, William Seymour, and to flee to France. Thanks to Arbella's help, Seymour escaped, but Arbella, who in part financed her escape by selling some of Mary Stuart's needlework to Bess's daughter, Mary Talbot, died four years later, still imprisoned by James.[76]

In the mid-1570s, the first open split between Mary Queen of Scots and Bess of Hardwick came in the wake of this ambitious marriage. Although Queen Elizabeth was displeased by the match and the birth of another claimant to her throne and sent Margaret, Countess of Lennox, to the Tower as a result, Shrewsbury continued as warden of the Queen of Scots—an expression of Elizabeth's continued confidence in the earl and countess,[77] despite the dynastic move that the marriage represented. But as bad feeling among Mary, the earl, and the countess grew, rumors spread that one or the other of her jailers was engaged in treasonous activity with Mary. The rumors flourished for a decade, becoming especially vicious in the mid-1580s as they became entangled in the marital discord between the Shrewsburys. In 1584, Bess and the earl decided to live permanently apart and the earl moved to take over his wife's rents and revenues. At this time, Mary suggested in letters to her sympathizers that Bess was actively treasonous against Elizabeth. She also wrote to Elizabeth, repeating unflattering gossip about her court that she had supposedly heard from Bess and offering her more information if they could meet. Mary also charged that Bess was responsible for starting the rumors that she and the earl were romantically and politically involved with one another.[78]

In the end, the queen and Privy Council acted on the countess's behalf, restoring Bess's revenues and eventually relieving her and her husband of the care of Mary Stuart, with the result that Sir Ralph Sadler assumed her charge in 1584.[79] Although she supported her former lady-in-waiting in her suit against her husband, Queen Elizabeth was careful not to promote Bess's granddaughter Arbella too much. The crown seized Arbella's English lands and revenues when she was two years old, as James VI had earlier seized her Scottish title and inheritance.[80] Arbella's lack of funds guaranteed her dependence on her queen and her grandmother. Although Mary and Elizabeth never met, and Elizabeth never visited Bess's houses in Derbyshire, Queen Elizabeth was an ever-present factor in Bess of Hardwick's political life, just as she was in Mary Stuart's, as the three formed a triangle of alliance and conflict for over fifteen years.

Bess of Hardwick: Embroiderer and Builder

Before the rift with Mary, from 1569 through the 1570s, Bess of Hardwick continued to improve Chatsworth, in the process creating the most ambitious known artwork produced by an English woman in the early modern period. Mary, who stayed at Chatsworth for periods during the 1570s,[81] seems to have been the catalyst for Bess's transformation from a skilled needleworker, who already employed a professional embroiderer and draughtsman, into what we today would call a textile artist. Because Mary's extended household often included portrait artists and tapissiers like Florens Broshere,[82] artisans with a talent for both transferring prints to cloth and drawing freehand, for the first time Bess had access to a continental level of expertise in design. Bess used both silk from abroad and the materials that she had at hand, including, for her largest hangings, the priests' copes acquired by her third husband, Sir William St. Loe. After being tailored to form a larger picture, these vestments were appliquéd to rich background materials using embroidering stitches.[83] This appliqué technique, in France called *taillure*, was in widespread use in both England and France as a way to translate used but still sumptuous textiles into other forms, including campaign tents, horse trappings, large cushion covers, and wall hangings. Margaret Swain observes that Mary had already used this technique to recycle priests' vestments into bed hangings for her two Scottish husbands, Darnley and Bothwell.[84]

To fashion her *Noble Women of the Ancient World* series and related works, Bess had to organize the collaborative effort necessary to create these impressive, tapestry-sized hangings, which measure about nine by eleven feet each. There was much to be done, from deciding on a narrative featuring a central female figure, to drawing the cartoon, transferring it to cloth, setting it in a frame, and then embroidering the pieces of it to the background material, while also stitching braid or cord to the background to further embellish the design. So much labor was involved that Bess's production of large textiles in the 1570s must have amounted to a small home industry at Chatsworth, a domestic workshop for interior design.

The best-known products of this Chatsworth workshop are the *Noble Women of the Ancient World* hangings. The principal figures in this series included the chaste Penelope (Plate 3), the armored Zenobia, the stalwart widow Arthemesia, the raped but actively honorable Lucrecia (Plate 4), and the politically sexual Cleopatra. These strong female figures from the historical mythology of womankind are named in both Christine de Pizan's *City of Ladies* and Petrarch's *Triumphs*,[85] where they function as female exemplars, countering the misogynist accounts of women so prevalent in medieval and early modern Europe. Long before she produced these hangings, Bess had anticipated the names of two of her figures by christening one daughter Temperance (a figure in her later virtues and vices series) in 1549 and, in 1557, naming her eighth child Lucrezia. She clearly had a long-standing interest in at least some of these female exemplars. Still others may have come to her attention because of the books and education of Mary Stuart.[86] Bess's workshop also created more than forty "portal" female figures as well, each of them a female personification standing in an arched doorway, including a *Liberal Arts* series and a *Cardinal Virtues* series.[87] When Bess fashioned her iconography of Women Worthies, virtues, and female personifications, she had more choices for creating her own set of inalienable possessions than the two queens whom she served. Elizabeth and Mary found themselves in the middle of national and international disputes about the relations among their female bodies, their divine connections, and their ability to govern. As a wealthy countess rather than a queen, Bess used her Chatsworth workshop to assert her identities as the powerful, chaste, and resourceful wife to her several husbands, as well as the founder of dynasties. Bess represents these identities in her *Notable Women* series. Still another series of three large appliquéd hangings featuring a virtue and its opposite were begun about the same time, although completed a decade or two later. In them, Bess paired Hope with Judas, Temperance with the immoderate Assyrian Sardanapalus, and she placed Faith—depicted as Elizabeth I in a textile portrait of the queen—opposite Mohamet.

The tapestry of Penelope, with her attending figures, Patience and Perseverance, now greets the visitor to New Hardwick's Great Hall. Bess's Penelope is pictured as a virtuous producer of textiles, with her hand resting on her weaving, which is the upright roll in the hanging's lower right. With her other hand raised as if she is about to issue a command, this Penelope is an authoritative

Figure 9. *Countess of Shrewsbury*. English School, Hardwick Hall, after 1569. The Devonshire Collection (acquired through the National Land Fund and transferred to The National Trust in 1959). © NTPL/Graham Challifour.

figure. In this hanging, Bess used Penelope to figure herself as the chaste, textile-producing wife during her husband's absence, the head of her household, and producer of her own woven text. This Penelope resembles a younger version of the portrait of Bess painted at age forty, with her largish nose and small mouth and her countess's coronet (Figure 9). Through this Chatsworth Penelope Bess also connects ancient virtues to herself because she is dressed in an antique flowing gown, overdress, and mantle, but she wears sixteenth-century lace at her wrists and a ruff framing her face, while a crown—suggesting the coronet of a countess—sits on her head.

The Earl of Shrewsbury admired these hangings enough to quarrel with his wife about their ownership in the 1580s. As a result, we have conflicting accounts of the collaboration that produced them. George Talbot claimed the "rich hangings made by Thomas Lane, Ambrose, William Barlow, and Henry, Mr Cavendish's man" because he had paid, housed, and fed them to make works composed of "copes of tissue, cloth of gold." Bess responded to her husband by noting that the "copes" were acquired by her third husband, St. Loe, and that the hangings were in fact worked by her "grooms, women, and some boys I kept." She wrote that she "never had but one embroiderer at one time that wrought on them. His Lordship never gave the worth of 5l. towards the making of them."[88] In the end, Bess kept her impressive hangings and eventually used them to furnish her final building project, New Hardwick Hall, which was largely completed by 1597.

Apart from her series *Noble Women of the Ancient World*, in the 1570s Bess of Hardwick also produced several other large embroidered pieces. One long cushion cover, *Diana and Actaeon* (Plate 5), provides an example of some of her most remarkable embroidered compositions, the source of which were often Mary's books. In this case, Bess freely adapted an engraving by Virgil Solis from Ovid's *Metamorphoses* printed in 1563 (Figure 10). By the time Bess took an inventory of New Hardwick's possessions in 1601, the cushion was situated in the Long Gallery in a place of honor,[89] alongside Bess's portraits of Elizabeth and other members of the royal family. A panel of embroidery on linen canvas rather than appliqué work, the cushion cover would still have been a collaborative piece, in that it was drawn by one of the professional embroiderers, or tapissiers, in her own employ or that of Mary Stuart, and worked by members of Bess's household as well as Bess herself. The panel alters Virgil Solis's engraved illustration of Diana and Actaeon by making Diana's power absolute and her revenge more violent. In the process, Bess's needlework exceeds Solis's visualization of the story, which may be why Solis has not previously been recognized as its source.[90] Although Solis's engraving concentrates on the single moment when Diana splashes water on Actaeon, transforming him into a stag, Bess's version splits the story into two parts, each with its own Diana and its own Actaeon. In the first part, Diana sits naked but with legs decorously together in the middle of a stream, holding a mirror in order to complete her toilette. Before she can do so, however, she has become aware of Actaeon's intrusion. The embroidery shows her frozen in this moment of realization as she looks over her shoulder at him. The first Actaeon stands at the center of the panel in Elizabethan dress, right hand arrogantly on his hip, left hand holding a lance. A ribbon in large letters encircles him, a caption announcing, "*Actaeon ego sum*": "I am Actaeon," a male hunter, certain of my identity, unblinkingly observing the goddess bathing—although in Ovid the only time that *Actaeon ego sum*

Figure 10. Virgil Solis, *Diana and Actaeon*. From Ovid's *Metamorphoses*, Augsburg. 1563. From the *Illustrated Bartsch*. Published by courteous permission of Abaris Books.

appears in Book 3 is after Actaeon, changed into a stag, silently shouts his identity to the human beings who no longer recognize him.

The second part of the story captured in this cushion cover is Diana's active response, a version of Solis's engraving because, as in Figure 10, she splashes Actaeon with water, turning him into a stag. Bess chose a faster transformation than the engraving's, in which the man with a stag's head still stands upright, with his spear in his hand. Although only his head, like Bottom's, is metamorphosed in both versions, in Bess's adaptation, his dogs have already turned on him and begun to devour him as he falls to the ground. Bess altered the engraving in other ways that emphasize Diana's power and ensuing triumph, as the goddess effects Actaeon's transition from man to beast and has the satisfaction of watching him being eaten alive. Part of Diana's power in the needlework picture is that, once angered, she loses all sense of feminine modesty as she wreaks her revenge on Actaeon. In the engraving, Diana covers her vulva with her hand, whereas in the embroidered picture Diana is more bent over, her legs wide apart. She ignores the towel that her attendant holds out as she splashes Actaeon. Ovid's splashes and Solis's lines become rainbows of power in Bess's needlework, arcing from Diana's upturned hands across the first, confident Actaeon, to reach and transform the body of the second Actaeon, who is falling helplessly amid his dogs. By emphasizing Diana's feminine strength rather than her shame, the needlework panel asserts the perspective of an active, powerful woman over the confident pleasures of the male voyeur. In its revision of its source, then, this cushion cover illustrates the triumph of Bess's identity over a masculine perspective, an assertion also illustrated by her large cipher, the initial "S" intertwined with "E," embroidered in the lower right-hand corner. In her *Diana and Actaeon*, Bess's gaze provides her take on a familiar classical subject, just as, in the 1590s, it would guide her in creating her most remarkable text of all, New Hardwick Hall.

The countess's life underwent several radical changes during the 1580s, as her husband's estrangement, complicated by rumors of his infidelity with Mary Stuart, took on national significance. In 1582, Arbella's mother died, and the young girl began living with her grandmother from time to time. In 1584, Mary was removed to the care of Sir Ralph Sadler, and subsequently became the responsibility of Sir Amias Paulet, who repeatedly took down her cloth of state in order to discourage her few remaining pretenses of a court-in-exile, although Mary's followers just as often reinstalled it.[91] About the same time, as the Shrewsburys separated and her son took possession of Chatsworth, Bess moved to her birthplace, Old Hardwick Hall. She began renovating Hardwick and added a wing in an attempt to make it fit for her needs and those of her granddaughter, Arbella. Three years later, Mary was executed at Fatheringhay for treason. At the elaborate funeral that cost Elizabeth over £3,000, Bess was among Mary's chief mourners.[92] Meanwhile, the Earl of Shrewsbury maintained his personal and financial separation from his wife, with only a couple of forced reunions. His death in 1590 meant that she received a substantial increase in income from her jointure, which included profits from Shrewsbury lands during her lifetime.

At this point, Bess turned from the rather awkward rebuilding of Hardwick Hall to creating New Hardwick Hall from scratch. It would seem that with Chatsworth and Hardwick behind her, she had had enough of haphazard planning. As when she produced her *Noble Women of the Ancient World* series in the 1570s, collaborating with professional designers and artisans to create forms of expression that were very much her own, in the 1590s she made the most of working with the noted architect, Robert Smythson. The result is what Mark Girouard calls "the supreme triumph of Elizabethan architecture." For Alice T. Friedman, New Hardwick "represents a watershed in English architecture, not only because its patron was a woman, but because it radically altered the typology of the English country house."[93] The extant structure that is Hardwick Hall has been remodeled over time, and its surviving objects have been moved, but because the Dukes of Devonshire preferred to spend money on the resplendent

Chatsworth, New Hardwick Hall is a partially preserved time capsule of the status and ambitions of Bess of Hardwick at the turn of the seventeenth century.

As architectural historians, Mark Girouard and Alice Friedman emphasize Bess's innovation of creating a house with the great hall at its symmetrical center, part of a ground floor that includes kitchens, sleeping quarters for servants, servant access to the chapel, and other utilitarian spaces. The second floor contains her chapel as well as the sleeping, living, and dining quarters for Bess and Arbella, and many of the women who served her. The third floor, reached by an impressive limestone staircase, houses Hardwick's most magnificent rooms for public reception, including the High Great Chamber, the Long Gallery, and Bess's Withdrawing Chamber.[94] The house as a whole, while built to provide comfort, privacy, and views of the Derbyshire countryside over which it towers, enshrines the Countess of Shrewsbury's position in the social hierarchy and her ambition that her granddaughter, Arbella Stuart, be recognized as heir to the English throne.

In part because she must have hoped for a visit from Queen Elizabeth to this end, Bess supervised interior design work, representing her proximity to the throne by combining designs in plasterwork, stone carving, tapestry, painting, and needlework. The grand third floor's High Great Chamber (Figure 11) features large plasterworks centered around the monumental painted frieze of Queen Elizabeth enthroned as Diana. Bess did not give precedence entirely to her monarch because just across the corner formed by their adjoining walls, the plasterwork shows that Elizabeth is being watched, Actaeon-like, by a man partially hidden from her sight behind a tree. Below the plasterwork still hangs the suite of tapestries featuring the story of Ulysses and Penelope that evokes Bess's self-representation as this faithful and productive wife. Above the imposing fireplace in this same Great Chamber stands Elizabeth's motto, "Dieu et Mon Droit"; but the word "et" is spelled "EST," with the "E" and the "S" superimposed on one another as in the cipher of the *Diana and Actaeon* panel, a cipher that connects Bess's initials with Elizabeth's motto, true, but that also insinuates its appropriation.[95] Such in situ design elements connect thematically with the many other pictures of Women Worthies throughout the house, like the *Noble Women* series and the *Diana and Actaeon* panel. The suite of tapestries featuring Ulysses and Penelope also interacts with the painting of Penelope working at her loom as Ulysses returns home, which in 1601 was located in her Withdrawing Chamber.[96] Overall, the integration of architectural and interior design at Bess's New Hardwick Hall united the gaze of the powerful females pictured in her textile productions with the pleasures of designing a house for her combined political and personal needs.

Figure 11. High Great Chamber, Hardwick Hall, with pastoral frieze, Diana as Elizabeth / Elizabeth as Diana, tapestries of Ulysses, and Elizabeth's motto over the fireplace, 1590s. © National Trust Photo Library / Nick Guttridge.

A Textile Portrait of Mary Queen of Scots

A portrait of Mary Queen of Scots among Bess's large, appliquéd hangings has been overlooked, perhaps because of her well-known preference for female figures from either classical myth or the tradition of feminine personification. But Mary's portrait hangs in plain sight, a reminder of her involvement with the other hangings that now greet the visitor to New Hardwick Hall. Originally produced for Chatsworth in the 1570s, each hanging features one central, commanding female figure attended by two smaller figures. The Penelope hanging that I have already discussed includes the smaller figures of Perseverance on her left and Patience on her right (see Plate 3). Zenobia in armor has Magnanimitas, also in armor, and Prudentia on either side; Arthemisia, sceptered and crowned, is framed by Constans and Pietas. The hanging of Cleopatra with Fortitude and Justice has been lost, but Lucrecia, flanked by Chastity and Liberality, is pictured at the moment when her muscular right arm drives the dagger into her breast (see Plate 4).

The figure of Chastity to the left of Lucrecia is in fact a full-length portrait of Mary Queen of Scots (Figure 12), in the traditional three-quarter view, attired in the *barbe*, cap, and veil that typified white mourning at the French court. Although the expected elements of Mary's *deuil blanc* iconography are all present in this textile portrait, the veil of this full-length figure flows in two long pieces from her cap to the left. In the usual *deuil blanc* picture, only Mary's head and chest are visible, while her veil simply falls from her head, framing her upper body. In the *Chastity* hanging, which, like all of those in the series features a full-length figure, the movement of her veil suggests the classical training of the tappissier/artist who produced its cartoon, someone probably in Mary's employ. Like Ronsard's description of the movement of Mary's white mourning in which "your long fine mourning veil, billows fold upon fold like a sail in the breeze," this version of Mary also depends on her flowing veil for its effect. As Aby Warburg showed, one of the most formative influences of classical artwork on Renaissance Italian painters was the movement of garments and hair. Warburg quotes Leon Battista Alberti on the importance of the fold, in whose "gentle, moderate movements," "folds should follow every movement, rippling, so that no part of the garment is still."[97] The elegant ripple of Mary's veil testifies to the draughtsman's continental background, a ripple echoed in the form of the prancing unicorn standing behind Mary, with its tail also in motion and its lifted front hoof.

The unicorn signifying chastity is an addition to the usual *deuil blanc* painting of Mary Stuart, if a predictable one for a portrait of the Queen of Scotland, because two unicorns flank the Scottish royal coat of arms. As a result, Mary was

Figure 12. Bess of Hardwick, *Chastity as Mary Queen of Scots*, 1570s. Appliquéd hanging. Hardwick Hall. © National Trust Photo Library/John Hammond.

frequently associated with unicorns, like those that pulled her and her mother's carriage during the pageantry celebrating Mary of Guise's visit to France. Mary herself embroidered a panel, *An Unicorne*, with her cipher (Figure 13). After her execution, her hearse was decorated in part with unicorns, and the standard in her funeral procession featured "an Unicorne Argent in a field of Guiles, a poesie written, *In my defence God me defend*," an elaboration of James IV's royal motto, *In my defens*.[98]

Figure 13. Mary Queen of Scots, *An Unicorne*, 1570s. From the Oxburgh Hangings. Linen canvas embroidered with gold, silver, and silk in tent stitch. Victoria and Albert Museum, London / The Bridgeman Art Library. Copyright status: English / out of copyright.

More viewers would have made the connection of this *Chastity* figure with Mary Queen of Scots if it still hung in its first location at New Hardwick Hall. According to the inventory of 1601, it was hung as part of the Lucrecia group in "the withdrawing chamber" on the third floor. At that time, Bess's Withdrawing Chamber was a large but still intimate closet, opening from the Long Gallery on the third floor. In this chamber, she chose to place her hangings of Penelope, Zenobia, Arthemesia, Lucrecia, and Cleopatra produced twenty years earlier under her supervision at Chatsworth, when she and Mary were still often in one another's company. Bess had also gathered together a number of paintings and textile works related to Mary Queen of Scots in this room. The paintings adjacent to these textiles, which may have been mounted on the hangings themselves, are probably listed together in the 1601 inventory because they hung together. The listed paintings include portraits of Mary, Mary and Darnley as royal couple, and Mary's parents. Mary commissioned at least one of her portraits during her imprisonment in Derbyshire, and she probably had the portraits of herself and Darnley and of her parents sent to her along with the cartloads of possessions that followed her to England. All of the Stuart family portraits are still at New Hardwick.[99] In the context of this Withdrawing Chamber—in part a shrine to Bess's connections with the Scottish queen—the female figure to the left of Lucrecia labeled "Chastity" would have been readily identified as still another portrait of Mary Stuart.

Why would Bess have dedicated a large portion of her Withdrawing Chamber to Mary in her New Hardwick Hall of 1597? Although Bess and Mary had fallen out about fifteen years before, Bess combined these images in her extraordinary room that was at once on display and for "withdrawing." The reason is that besides her marriage to the late earl, Bess's claim to an exalted social position lay in her former intimacy with Mary and the fact that Mary had become a member of Bess's family through the Lennox marriage, a kinswoman who connected Bess to both the Scottish and the English royal families. The same Bess who placed her granddaughter, Elizabeth Pierrepont, in Mary's retinue and who was one of Mary's principal mourners, assembled in this room a theater of identity populated with notable female figures that included other portraits both painted and embroidered. Bess might have taken comfort in memorializing the Queen of Scotland and Dowager Queen of France, albeit in a figure that is much smaller than the more commanding figures of Lucrecia and Penelope, who represent the countess's own virtuous, feminine authority.

This portrait of Mary in textile work may have been overlooked because the value of paint on canvas has to some extent blinded us to the widespread existence of portraits in textiles. Contemporary portraits in other textile media existed, like the portrait of Mary as Queen of Scotland praying on the ceiling of her state bed and the portrait of Catherine de Medici in black mourning that survives in a tapestry series of 1582–85. Seventeenth-century domestic needlework includes a number of examples of stitched portraits of Charles I, Charles II, and their queens, as well as one example of Mary Queen of Scots "entering Paradise" dated 1680.[100] The tapestry-makers and professional embroiderers employed by Mary and Bess were artisans who may well have been portrait painters also. In *The Art of Limning,* Nicholas Hilliard attempts to distinguish between the "gentill painting" involved in "limning" and the "*Painting or drawing*" for "common men's use, whether for furnishing of Houses, or any patterns for tapestries,"[101] but in the sixteenth century, the lines between different kinds of design work and painting were still less distinct.

This textile portrait of Mary may also have been overlooked simply because the figure is labeled *Chastity.* The English view of history that stresses Mary's alleged adultery with the Earl of Bothwell, complicity in the murder of Darnley, and subsequent seduction of the Duke of Norfolk hardly encourages one to look to Mary Stuart as the personification of chastity. Attacks on Mary, like the placard posted at the market cross in Edinburgh after Mary's marriage to Bothwell, which represents Mary as a mermaid preening herself above Bothwell's crest of the hare, depict her not as merely vain but as a whore. Elizabeth wrote to her on 25 June 1567, underscoring the English point of view of her marriage to Bothwell: "For how could a worse choice be made for your honor than in such haste to marry such a subject, who besides other and notorious lacks, public fame hath charged with the murder of your late husband. . . . And with what peril have you married him that hath another lawful wife alive" (1:118). George Buchanan, once a poet at Mary's Scottish court, elided her political errors with her unchaste body in *Ane Detection of the Doings of Mary Queen of Scots* (1571), when he called her murder of Darnley and adultery with Bothwell the actions of "a woman raging without measure and modesty," deprived by the rebellion against her "not of liberty, but of unbridled licentiousness of evil doing." Mary's religion made it inevitable that in England she would be connected to the Protestant figuration of the Catholic Church as the Whore of Babylon. The play *Horestes* portrays Mary as a whore, while in Book V of *The Faerie Queene,* written after 1590, Edmund Spenser summarizes the case against her in allegorical terms, with Murder, Sedition, and Incontinence prosecuting Duessa as the Mary figure, joined by "foule *Adulterie* her face before, / And lewd *Impietie,* that her accused sore." Although Spenser's poem, to which Mary's son James strenuously objected, makes it clear that Mary's highest crime is treason,[102] from the English point of view, conspiring to murder her husband, marrying Bothwell, and, later, conspiring to overthrow Elizabeth were considered inextricable from her sexual incontinence.

Mary's defenders, like the Bishop of Ross, found it necessary to frame their response to such attacks as "the defence of her honour," which is also the title of his pro-Marian tract of 1569. Mary herself insisted on her unsullied chastity, praying in a meditation of 1573, "Let chastity and perseverance / Live in my heart with all obedience" (Bell 75). In a sonnet also dated 1573, she writes that God desires "un corps chaste," "a chaste body," which she asks to be allowed to bear "pour toujours"—"forever" (Bell 78–79). Within this discourse of the attack and defense of Mary's honor, when the "honor" of a queen referred simultaneously to her chastity and to her sound political judgment, Bess's *Chastity* panel with Mary in white mourning defends her by framing her with emblems of purity, on the left by her flowing veil echoed in the unicorn's tail, and on the right by the unicorn's head, horn, raised hoof, and the sprig of myrtle that she holds aloft. By presenting her as the personification of chastity with the Scottish unicorn as a reminder of her royal lineage, the panel confronts Mary's detractors with the dominant image of her iconography, the queen attired in *deuil blanc*, her royal statement of marital fidelity and familial loss. Nevertheless, this version of Mary created by Bess of Hardwick and housed within the very latest of country houses stands in attendance on the central figure of Lucrecia, one of the countess's self-representations as virtuous wife. In the end, this appliquéd panel may seem to defend Mary Queen of Scots, but it is at least as much about Bess of Hardwick, Countess of Shrewsbury, as it is about Mary, even as it provides a new—and four-hundred-year-old—portrait of the imprisoned queen.

Elizabeth Tudor, Mary Stuart, and Bess of Hardwick each participated fully in their culture's expectation that privileged women would produce both written and visual texts, creating inalienable possessions of treasured value that continue to articulate their political identities as dynastic connection. In sewing together a family through needlework-covered manuscripts, Elizabeth sought—and received—the support of Katherine Parr, abandoning such projects when as queen she concentrated on prayers, poetry, translations, and public speeches. When relatively powerless and often absent from court, Elizabeth used her texts and portraits to serve notice to her immediate family, as well as to supporters and detractors alike, that hers was a presence with which to reckon. Mary Stuart's control of her iconography began with her portrait in white mourning, to which she returned throughout her life. During her imprisonment in England, she wrote and sewed herself into a web of referents to her rank; to her familial connection; and to her situation as mother, prisoner, and devout Catholic. At the close of the sixteenth century, after Mary Stuart and the Earl of Shrewsbury were in their graves, Bess of Hardwick assembled a Withdrawing Chamber constructed from the figures of her iconography, including her *Notable Women* series, among whom were portraits of herself and Mary, juxtaposed with painted portraits of Mary Queen of Scots and her family. In marshaling these images, Bess paid tribute to the queen whom she had known best, in whose everyday life she had once participated, and whose Stuart alliances she had appropriated for her own dynastic ambition. In her elaborately decorated Withdrawing Chamber, Bess of Hardwick could contemplate the identities that the squire's daughter had acquired, with their promise of power and wealth for her progeny.

Chapter One

Miniatures and Manuscripts:
Levina Teerlinc, Jane Segar, and Esther Inglis
as Professional Artisans

Even as Elizabeth Tudor, Mary Stuart, and Bess of Hardwick materialized their dynastic identities in their textualities, during this same period a few women who lived at the periphery of power created their own verbal and visual texts in order to attract patronage. The women who are the subject of this chapter were upwardly mobile members of the artisan class,[1] among the first women who might be considered early modern professionals. Endowed with abilities that were cultivated in family workshops run along continental models, they enjoyed connections to the court conducted in part through male relations eager to profit from their abilities. All three interacted with rulers by combining media within religious and heraldic manuscript traditions, traditions associated since the Middle Ages with the social and financial rewards of sustained patronage.

Levina Teerlinc, Jane Segar, and Esther Inglis negotiated the paths to patronage in distinct ways at different points in the early modern period. Teerlinc served as court miniaturist and artisan to Henry VIII, Edward VI, Mary I, and Elizabeth I, while producing illuminated manuscripts for the political and religious use of Mary Tudor. As was then common, Teerlinc did not sign her miniatures, manuscripts, or designs, which makes attribution a matter of ongoing debate. Nevertheless, art historians have come to agree on a core of works attributed to her on the basis of court documents describing gifts of extant paintings and manuscripts, as well as on the basis of stylistic resemblance. Of the miniaturist-scriveners discussed in this chapter, Teerlinc enjoyed the longest and most successful career. She served an apprenticeship in Italy with Giulio Clovio,[2] but her career becomes most visible after her success as an artist attracted the patronage of Henry VIII. At his court, she achieved the status of gentlewoman while her husband was made a Gentleman Pensioner.

Of Jane Segar we know little more than that she was the sister of William Segar, the scrivener and painter who rose to prominence under Elizabeth and James I to become Garter Knight at Arms. Jane Segar produced an eye-catching calligraphic manuscript, dedicated to Elizabeth I. *The Prophecies of the Ten Sibills upon the Birth of Christ* (1589) consists of ten poems translated from a Latin original first circulated in the fourteenth century[3] as well as a prose dedication and final poem of her own composition. This handwritten text is bound within two jewel-like *verre églomisé* covers that she painted. Unlike the decades-long production of Teerlinc and Inglis, Segar's elaborate manuscript seems to have been a one-shot attempt to attract the patronage of Elizabeth through its elaborate compliment to her as virginal head of the Church of England.[4]

Esther Inglis, like Jane Segar, signed her work, often including self-portraits of herself in the act of writing. This able artisan, descended from Huguenots who had settled in Scotland, produced at least sixty miniature books that juxtapose an astonishing calligraphic skill with miniature paintings, self-portraits, and embroidered or embossed leather covers. Inglis dedicated her books to a range of powerful people during the reigns of Elizabeth I and James VI and I, including to the monarchs themselves.

Although we do not know a great deal about these women, we do know that they produced miniatures and manuscripts for very different reasons and that all three produced exquisite objects that have survived the centuries. These objects make visible the agency of their producers, who knowingly or unknowingly followed a female tradition of artful book production that had begun in the Early Christian era, when nuns trained in both the writing and illumination of manuscripts. By the twelfth century, Hildegard von Bingen and Herrade von Landesberg were creating calligraphic manuscripts that included self-portraits from within monastic workshops. In the fourteenth century, Christine de Pizan collaborated in producing illuminated manuscripts with several portraits of herself, at a time when manuscript production was migrating from religious houses to family workshops in France and the Netherlands.[5] Levina Teerlinc, Jane Segar, and Esther Inglis, working in England and Scotland from the early sixteenth through the early seventeenth century, were their heirs, even as their illuminated manuscripts met new demands for political and religious expression.

Levina Teerlinc, Miniaturist and
Member of Royal Households

Levina Teerlinc is one of a handful of women so far identified as working artists at court in sixteenth-century England. Each of these artists was associated with a painting family, which means that she grew up in a studio or workshop in which work was completed in a collaborative fashion.[6] In such an environment, artistic ability and a willingness to contribute to the group enterprise would have been highly desirable traits in both male and female offspring. Toward the end of the sixteenth century, Alice, the widow of William Herne, who was "Serjeante Painter to the Quenes Majesty," assisted George Gower, also the painter of the best known of the Armada Portraits of Elizabeth, with painting and gilding bedsteads for Elizabeth's household—a reminder of how varied the duties of a "painter" could be.[7] Hans Holbein produced portraits, but he also illuminated manuscripts and designed prints and printer's impresae, as well as loving cups, jewelry, and interior furnishings like an elaborate chimneypiece.[8] As Roy Strong points out, artists during this period were versed in many artisanal skills, including the ability to "paint panel portraits, design and often make jewels and plate, execute designs for tapestries and stained glass, supervise the décor and costumes for court fêtes" and "provide drawings for engravers of illuminated official documents."[9] To this list, which includes "designs for tapestries," should be added designs for courtly needlework. Although sixteenth-century court embroidery has rarely survived, and needlework has since been demoted from an art to a craft, embroidered work as well as magnificent tapestries are recorded among Henry VIII's possessions in the Royal Inventory of 1547.

This inventory lists embroidered pictures alongside paintings, statues, and luxurious furnishings as equally valuable. At Westminster, for example, a room also filled with tapestries included a "Table of our lady and saint Anne with their husbands and kindred embroidered with venice gold and silk," a "Table of the Salutation of our lady embroidered with venice gold and silk with a curtain of red sarcenet," and a "Table having in it the five wounds [of Jesus] embroidered upon black satin." These embroidered pictures stood alongside paintings of Saint Jerome pointing to a dead man's skull, the three children of the King of Denmark, a pieta, the prodigal son, and a portrait of the young Henry VIII "wearing his hair with a flower of silver upon the lock." The embroidered "Salutation" had a curtain hung before it, as did many of the paintings, to preserve its colors.[10] At a time when ornate textiles formed much of the king's wealth, embroidered work in all its variety was considered a serious art form. It was also the one art form that many women at court produced.

Courtly needleworkers would have required a steady supply of designs for their works, whether these were original "patterns" or adapted from other media. As discussed in Chapter 1, Elizabeth probably adapted Hans Holbein's ciphers for her needlework, while Mary Stuart and Bess of Hardwick collaborated with a group of artisans who transferred designs to cloth. It makes sense that Levina Teerlinc, a "gentlewoman of the court," whose design work included coins, documents, woodcut book illustrations, and the royal seal, as well as portraits and illuminated manuscripts, would have turned her hand to designs for needlework, one of the court's most ubiquitous activities. The ongoing work of Tudor artisans to meet this demand explains why the Inventory of 1547 twice lists gatherings of "diverse patterns" together with needlework supplies.[11]

The history of the first woman artist who served the Tudors, Susanna Hornebout or Horenbout, active in the 1520s to the 1540s, suggests that she was involved in a variety of artisanal activities that sheds light on Teerlinc as well.[12] The Horenbouts had been long associated with the Ghent-Bruges school of manuscript production. Henry VIII imported the entire Horenbout family from the Netherlands to meet his need for portrait miniatures, as well as to record his ritualized activities in illuminated manuscripts. The Horenbout workshop's *Liber Niger* of the Order of the Garter, which includes limned portraits and rituals like *Henry VIII Enthroned Flanked by Knights of the Garter* (c. 1534),[13] serves as a reminder that court miniatures developed from the tradition of religious manuscript illumination, a tradition that Henry VIII used to represent God's approval of the Tudors as England's ruling family. In addition to offering symbolic authorization, as Jessica Wolfe points out, the "detail-oriented arts of limning and goldsmithing" bears out "Renaissance culture's fascination with the inscrutable" and its "frequent invocations of *multum in parvo*, or much in little, which posits that the smallest spaces are more replete, and thus symbolically larger, than more expansive ones." The miniature, whether within or outside the illuminated manuscript, was valuable because it invited the reading of its "densely packed spaces."[14]

Situated in a family that produced such markedly sacred objects, Susanna Horenbout enjoyed the favor of Henry VIII, Anne of Cleves, and Katherine Parr, which enabled her to make a good match in her first husband, John Parker, from a propertied family in Fulham. Parker served as Yeoman of the Robes and Keeper of the Palace at Westminster, and Henry VIII marked the couple's social position by giving them New Year's gifts. In 1532, when Susanna is listed as a "gentlewoman" of the court, Henry VIII gave them a "gilt cup with a cover, weighing 22 ½ ounces" and in 1533, "xii gilt spoons." Susanna was widowed in 1537 and, in 1539, she married John Gilman, a gentleman vintner who was later

Sergeant of the King's Woodyard. In that same year, Henry sent her to accompany Anne of Cleves to England, providing the impressive sum of £40 toward her expenses. Anne of Cleves "made her the first of her gentlewomen," and Horenbout served her during her brief reign as queen. Later, Horenbout also served Katherine Parr and, apparently, Mary Tudor, "from whom she received two yards of black satin." She may have lived into the early 1550s; she was dead by 1554 (Campbell and Foister, 726).

Following the path paved by Susanna Horenbout, Levina Teerlinc became a member of Henry VIII's court upon arriving in England around 1545. Teerlinc's activities may be traced through a handful of surviving documents, including her annuity payments, as well as records of New Year's gifts listing Teerlinc as a "gentlewoman" of the Privy Chamber, like Horenbout before her. Teerlinc enjoyed the favor not only of Henry VIII but also of Katherine Parr, Anne Parr Herbert, Countess of Pembroke, Queen Mary I, and Queen Elizabeth I, in recognition not only of Teerlinc's skills as an artisan but also, quite probably, of the personal qualities that she brought to her attendance at court.

Teerlinc's roots in her family's workshop provided her with abilities steeped in a particularly royal sanctity.[15] Like Horenbout, she derived from a family famous for its illuminated manuscripts. Teerlinc was the oldest of five daughters born to Katharina Scroo and Simon Bening (also spelled Benninck or Benig). Bening and his father, Sander or Alexander Bening, was, like Lucas Horenbout, associated with the Ghent-Bruges school known for its illuminated manuscripts as well as for the art form that derived from illumination, the miniature. The Horenbouts and Benings had in fact collaborated in producing such masterpieces as the *Book of Hours of James IV and Margaret Tudor* (1503), which contained 250 pages, including nineteen miniatures.[16] As the miniature genre, and the portrait miniature in particular, became increasingly separate from the illuminated book, it retained a sense of its origins in a religious tradition appropriate for the portraits of quasi-divine rulers.

Like her father and grandfather, Teerlinc was an illuminator of manuscripts and painter of miniatures, who had trained as a scrivener and calligrapher as well.[17] She apprenticed with the Croatian miniaturist working in Italy, Giulio Clovio, whom Giorgio Vasari called the "little Michelangelo." Clovio is famous for miniature portraits, medallions, and illuminated manuscripts like the *Farnese Book of Hours* (1546), which includes a painting that records the Corpus Christi procession in Rome. Perhaps, like his contemporary Perino del Vaga, Clovio also designed copes and tapestries; on occasion he incorporated tapestry designs into his paintings.[18] Taking into account the years during which Teerlinc trained in her family workshop and then with Clovio, she must have been born by at least 1520, so she was in her twenties or thirties when she and George

Teerlinc arrived in England. In November 1546, Henry VIII granted them an annuity of £40 "during the King's pleasure"—an amount that exceeded the £33 6s. a year paid to Lucas Horenbout as well as Holbein's £30 a year.[19]

Like all the women artists examined in this chapter, men as teachers and go-betweens formed an integral part of Teerlinc's success. Not only did her father and Clovio train her as a miniaturist and an illuminator; her husband, George Teerlinc, was, like his wife, in time well-placed at court. Queen Katherine Parr's brother, William, captain of Henry VIII's Gentlemen Pensioners, apparently helped place George Teerlinc in this elite band of one hundred members of whom about half served at any given time in the King's Presence Chamber.[20] George is listed among the Gentlemen Pensioners in the order for the king's funeral procession, when he "received 9 yards of black cloth for his livery and an additional 9 yards for his 3 servants." On his wife's death in 1576, George Teerlinc is again mentioned as "one of our Gentlemen Pensioners." Although Katherine and Anne Parr patronized Levina for her portraiture[21] and, doubtless, for her other design work, what George did outside his ceremonial role at court is less certain. He may have acted as a dealer in tapestries, textiles, and artwork produced in the Netherlands. He seems to have been an agent for his wife, as the *Acts of the Privy Council* of 1550–52 record, during the reign of Edward VI, "A warrant to ——— to pay unto George Tarling [Teerlinc], in way of the King's reward, being sent with his wife to the Lady Elizabeth's Grace to draw out her picture, ten pounds." Because the usual payment for a miniature ranged between £1 and £3, this notation of an unusually large payment of £10 may acknowledge George's services as his wife's traveling companion as well as his usefulness as her agent. This warrant may also describe the missing portrait that Elizabeth sent to her brother from Hatfield.[22]

Like John Parker and Susanna Horenbout, the Teerlincs together made serving the Tudors a family enterprise. They applied for a grant of denization in 1566 in order to make themselves and their son English subjects, while that same year George leased land in Stepney and built a house for the large sum of "five hundred pounds." Teerlinc's annual stipend of £40 was paid quarterly, sometimes to her and sometimes to her husband, throughout the reigns of Edward VI and Mary I. In 1559, the first full year of her reign, Elizabeth made Teerlinc's £40 an annuity for life, with her typical failure to account for the effects of inflation on salaries. Although the annuity was paid to both Teerlincs, it was clearly in recompense for Levina's skills and court attendance, as at Levina's death in 1576 a document dated 11 August "given by the queen under her privy seal" records that "the said Levina died the xxiiith of June last past." Although Levina died just before her £10 was to be paid, Elizabeth is nevertheless "pleased that the said George shall have payment of the said ten pounds . . . as our gift."[23]

Susanna Horenbout had served in the households of Henry VIII, Anne of Cleves, and Katherine Parr. Levina Teerlinc was made similarly welcome in the households of Henry VIII, Edward VI, Mary I, and Elizabeth I. Both Horenbout and Teerlinc provided the court with a variety of design skills, from painting and drawing to interior design work and, quite probably, designs for needlework. When Horenbout was included in royal households, however, there were several of them in which to find employment, including those of the king, his queens, and his offspring. Far fewer court placements were available under Edward VI, Mary, or Elizabeth. As Charlotte Merton points out, when Elizabeth succeeded to the throne in 1558, she came under tremendous pressure to provide places for "the throng of loyal servants and political allies" she had acquired during the years in which she was heir-in-waiting. At the same time, she "had a far greater number of relatives to satisfy than Mary."[24] Amid this press for preferment, Teerlinc was important enough to the new queen for her to grant the artist a lifelong annuity, while her husband continued his appointment as a Gentleman Pensioner. Undoubtedly Teerlinc offered Elizabeth a sense of connection to the courts of her late father, brother, sister, and stepmother through her services as an artist and a designer. Perhaps Elizabeth was also rewarding one or both Teerlincs for their loyalty to her during Mary's reign.

Because Teerlinc received an annuity and was listed among the gentlewomen of the Privy Chamber, it was appropriate for her to present miniatures as New Year's gifts. In 1556, Teerlinc presented Mary with "a small picture of the Trinity." The 1559 gift to the new queen, Elizabeth, was of "the Queen's picture finely painted upon a card." In 1562, the New Year's Gift Roll begins recording gifts that suggest how interested Teerlinc, together with the new queen Elizabeth and her court became in scenes of court ritual that featured the queen. The annotation in 1562 that describes Teerlinc's painting of "the Queen's person and other personages in a box finely painted," suggested to both Auerbach and Strong the Maundy Thursday miniature (Figure 14). This small painting shows Elizabeth in the middle of the ceremony that included washing the feet of poor women in imitation of Jesus. The description of this gift notes further that the painting is currently "With her said majestie," implying that the miniature had found favor with Elizabeth and that she chose to keep it among her intimate possessions. In 1563, the roll lists "a card with the Queen's Majesty and many other personages"; in 1564, "a certain journey of the Queen's Majesty and the train finely wrought upon a card," recording an unnamed but choreographed procession; and, in 1567, "the picture of the Queen her Majesty's whole stature drawn upon a card painted." The 1568 roll lists "a paper painted with the

Figure 14. Attributed to Levina Teerlinc, *An Elizabethan Maundy*, c. 1565. Vellum on card, 2 3/4 x 2 1/4 in. (enlarged). Trustees of the Countess Beauchamp, Madresfield Estate.

Queen's Majesty and the knights of the order," an entry that confirms that Teerlinc worked on paper or vellum in something more like a manuscript format as well as on the "cards"—prepared vellum tablets mounted on playing cards—on which miniaturists painted works meant for boxes or other jeweled settings. Teerlinc's painting of Elizabeth and "the knights of the order" also makes visible the intersection of two traditions, that of the increasingly secular miniaturist and illuminated manuscript, and the heraldic tradition of illumination that memorialized dynastic connection. In 1575, Teerlinc produced a courtly scene "painted upon a card of her Majesty and diverse other personages"—again, quite probably the record of a court ceremony—while the next year, that of her death, she produced "the Queen's picture upon a card."[25] Aside from these miniatures, the extent of Teerlinc's oeuvre is difficult to ascertain, not only because she did not sign her work but also because so few miniatures from this period are extant.[26] But using the Maundy Thursday miniature as a starting point, both Auerbach and Strong attribute several other works to Teerlinc, including the royal seals of Mary and Elizabeth, as well as legal documents in which Elizabeth is represented in miniature, like the "Indenture for the establishment of the Poor Knights of Windsor" of 1559. Strong finds that Teerlinc is responsible, too, for designs turned into a woodcut of Elizabeth at prayer in 1569 and the title page of Elizabeth's first Great Bible.[27] In this period before painting portraits became a specialized activity, Teerlinc must have performed a range of activities, from portrait painting and manuscript illumination to creating heraldic and legal documents as well as designs for seals, coins, and needlework.

In addition to participating in her political and religious painting activities, like many early modern painters, including her father, Levina Teerlinc also produced at least one self-portrait. Gillian Perry notes, "In about 1561 the Roman manuscript illuminator Giulio Clovio," with whom Teerlinc had earlier trained, wrote to her "thanking her for the gift of her self-portrait." That portrait, "which has not so far been identified" was among Clovio's possessions when he died in 1578.[28] Liana De Girolami Cheney, Alicia Craig Faxon, and Kathleen Lucey Russo print a miniature titled *Self-Portrait at Age 50* (1546) as a possible Teerlinc self-portrait, but the size and complexity of the pictured woman's ruff date the picture from the 1580s.[29] Carole Levin notes that Teerlinc may have left a self-portrait in the otherwise unidentified portrait of a lady in which "the sitter is wearing ornamental dice," because "the word for 'dice' in Flemish is *Teerlinc*."[30] At present, however, a Teerlinc self-portrait has not been found.

Given Teerlinc's training in the Ghent-Bruges school of manuscript illumination and her style of modeling the human body in the miniatures, manuscripts, and other designs attributed to her, art historians have agreed with Roy Strong that she produced the illuminated manuscript *Queen Mary's Manual for blessing cramp rings and touching for the evil: the rituals of the royal healing ceremonies*. In addition to the blessing for the cramp rings, which were distributed to women against the pain associated with menstruation and childbirth, this manuscript includes "The Ceremony for the healing of them that be diseased with the king's Evil," an account of the service accompanying the Royal Touch. This service begins, as inscribed in the calligraphy of Plate 6, "First the king kneling upon his knees shall begin and saie In nomine deus et filii, et spiritus sancti Amen. And so sone as he hathe saide that he shall saie. Benedicite. The Chaplin kneling before the king havying a Stole abowte his neck shall answer."[31] As this excerpt indicates, the manuscript is a liturgy of courtly ritual that was both political and religious. Although the manuscript describes what King Henry and his chaplain said and did, its two most significant illuminations feature Queen Mary I. Indeed, the illumination opposite the page quoted here is a detailed miniature portrait of Mary in the act of practicing the royal touch to alleviate the "king's evil," the skin disease scrofula (Plate 6). The written pages, then, work with Teerlinc's miniatures of Mary to connect her father's reported ritual with its adaptation for the new queen. Mary's need to authorize her religious and political identity by connecting with the practices of her father and his royal, male predecessors required the creation of an apparently seamless connection between her Catholicism and her father's court rituals. In the process, she had to overlook his cruelty toward her and her mother, Catherine of Aragon, in the name of church reform. This text overlooks as well the quarrel between Mary and her brother when, as Edward VI, he had intensified their father's reforms.

Who better to address Mary I's need for religious and political continuity than Levina Teerlinc, who as a member of the court had witnessed such ceremonies when Henry VIII performed them and so could record them for Mary's appropriation? The Heralds of the College of Arms recorded orders of ceremony in illuminated manuscripts with their own religious and political overtones. But unlike Teerlinc, who on occasion crossed over to produce heraldic illumination, the heralds did not record such intimately religious ceremonies featuring the monarch. Mary must have turned to Teerlinc as liturgist and illuminator to help in composing and recording the ceremonies that, performed for packed audiences at court, confirmed her intimate connection with God as England's monarch, together with her claim to a religious continuity that denied that the Reformation had ever taken place.

The several blank pages that conclude this manuscript also argue for Teerlinc as its author instead of some more itinerant manuscript illuminator and calligrapher. Although the extra pages may be there as a result of carelessness, it seems likely that Mary and Teerlinc had plans to add to the manuscript, but those plans were never realized because Mary died in only the fifth year of her reign. Elizabeth, its next owner, did not add to it but may well have used it. Elizabeth chose not to bless the cramp rings. But she did perform the Maundy rituals each year, as well as touching for the king's evil in a highly dramatic and public ceremony, as Carole Levin has discussed in appreciable detail.[32] Both the Maundy and Royal Touch are important practices to weigh in the ongoing discussion of the medieval or Catholic elements of Elizabeth's self-representation.

Teerlinc's *Queen Mary's Manual for blessing cramp rings and touching for the evil: the rituals of the royal healing ceremonies* may also provide a context for understanding her miniature of Elizabeth's Maundy Thursday ceremony (see Figure 14). Because it seems that Elizabeth chose to keep the Maundy picture close at hand, it may well record one particular instance of an annual ceremony in the combined medieval and Tudor traditions, which included the adaptation of washing women's feet initiated by Catherine of Aragon and followed by Mary.[33] It may even be that this Maundy miniature records not so much an event as another collaboration, this time between Queen Elizabeth and Teerlinc, to create this new queen's own practice of the Maundy rituals. Teerlinc's miniature, which shows Elizabeth prominent in the foreground in a red dress but with her back to the viewer, is hardly a portrait. Rather, it is a record in the tradition of manuscript illumination of the piety of a royal female in the middle of devotional activity. It is also a detailed record of the event itself, in the tradition of Clovio's recording of the Corpus Christi day procession through Rome in the *Farnese Book of Hours* and the Horenbouts' recording of Henry VIII and the assembled Knights of the Garter in the *Liber Niger*. Teerlinc's Maundy miniature may have once formed part of more documentation of the ritual that did not survive,[34] perhaps including a calligraphic manuscript in which Teerlinc preserved the order of events, the prayers, the pronouncements, and the songs that formed Elizabeth's ceremony.

In 1572–73, William Lambarde reported in detail "the Order of the *Maundy*" as he saw it performed at Greenwich Palace. His verbal description and the painted version (c. 1562) seem on the whole to portray the same ceremony. As Lambarde makes clear, by the time Elizabeth entered the Hall, the foot-washing had already begun because the Yeomen of the laundry, followed by the queen's Sub-Almoner and her Almoner, had all washed the women's feet before she arrived. Once "Her Majesty came into the Hall," writes Lambarde, the religious service began: "some singing and prayers made, and the Gospel of Christ's washing his disciples feet read." At that point, the "ladies and gentlewomen" "addressed themselves with aprons and towels to wait upon her Majesty, and she, kneeling upon the cushions and carpets under the feet of the poor women, first washed the one foot of every of them in so many several basins of warm water and sweet flowers." The miniature shows Elizabeth about midway through this ritual, with roughly half of the poor women whose feet are still to be washed on one side of the Hall, and the half she has finished on the other. A lady immediately to the right of the queen is holding one of several basins that Lambarde records were used during the ceremony. After the pictured scene,

Elizabeth personally gave the women a series of gifts: cloth for a gown, shoes, wooden platters of food, and wine. The queen presented each woman with the towels and aprons worn to the ceremony by her waiting ladies and gentle-women, which are visible in the miniature already being worn by the three women to her right. She also gave each woman a purse with enough pence to equal the years of the queen's age. Elizabeth chose not to give away the gown that she was wearing to one of the poor women, as Mary had. Instead, perhaps following the custom of her brother,[35] the Treasurer of the Chamber, Thomas Heneage, ransomed it for "several red leather purses" each containing twenty shillings, which were also distributed to the women. Afterward, Elizabeth "took her ease upon the cushion of state" pictured on a raised dais at the picture's center left, and after "hearing the choir," who wear white surplices with red ruffs and foresleeves, the queen withdrew.[36] Presumably, this complex cere-mony, whose furnishings and principals differed little from 1562 to 1572–73, depended on a written and quite possibly illuminated text preserved from year to year, a text that Teerlinc would have been the logical scrivener and painter to produce.

Levina Teerlinc, trained not only within medieval manuscript traditions but also within the Italian Mannerist movement as practiced by Giulio Clovio, pro-duced and designed significant works for the Tudors and their courtiers. Although she may well have been the first miniaturist in England to paint full-length portraits in her miniatures, based on current attributions Teerlinc's painting failed to represent a high point in the long history of the Ghent-Bruges school. Instead, the value of her illuminated manuscripts and designs lay in their adaptability to Tudor politics. Teerlinc's work was especially useful for the sixteenth century's two reigning queens, Mary I and Elizabeth I, whose gender placed great pressure on the need to adapt religious iconography and ritual. Their representations on coins and royal seals, in the designs of embroidery, painted cloths, and tapestries asserted their God-approved right to rule England. Ceremonies performed for large audiences, like the Royal Touch, the Maundy Thursday rituals, and chivalric rites provided subjects with the opportunity to see the royal body performing these divine connections. Levina Teerlinc was one of several artisans who helped the Tudors to pull off these representations. For Mary I and Elizabeth I, she may well have collaborated in adapting cere-monies as well as recording them in her illuminated manuscripts.

Jane Segar, Elizabeth's Would-Be Poet

Teerlinc, like her older contemporary Susanna Horenbout, proved herself so skillful and politic an artist that she gained the patronage and even the personal trust of successive Tudor monarchs. But while Henry VIII had brought Teerlinc to England to help fill the artisanal void created by the deaths of Lucas Horenbout and Hans Holbein, at Teerlinc's death in 1576 Elizabeth made no attempt to replace her at court. Unlike her father, Elizabeth apparently had no interest in importing artists from the Netherlands, and women artists were not as prominent as they had been at the earlier Tudor courts. In the 1570s, Nicholas Hilliard, goldsmith and master miniaturist, had begun producing his miniatures but was not included in the queen's household. As a result, he often had to look outside the court for patronage, even traveling to France from 1576 to 1579 in search of commissions. He did not receive his own royal annuity of £40 until 1599,[37] when it was worth far less than Teerlinc's. Other prominent painters in England from 1570 through the turn of the century who made more than a limited stay in England include Hilliard's students Rowland Lockey and Isaac Oliver, as well as Marcus Gheeraerts the Elder, Marcus Gheeraerts the Younger, George Gower, Cornelius Ketel, Hieronimo Custodis, John Hoskins, Peter Oliver, Lucas de Heere, Francis Segar, and his brother, William Segar, who produced heraldic documents and larger portraits. These men variously produced their work as miniaturists and goldsmiths, as members of the guild of painter-stainers, as foreign visitors trained in continental workshops, and as members of the College of Heralds.

Within this context of professional miniaturists and within the context as well of women who produced calligraphic manuscripts with embellished covers, the sister of William Segar, Jane "Seagar," as she spelled her name, produced a calligraphic manuscript dedicated to Queen Elizabeth dated 1589, *The Prophecies of the Ten Sibills upon the Birth of Christ* (Plate 7). Unlike Teerlinc's work, Segar's manuscript is the product of a court outsider, a gift meant to attract royal notice that had yet to be given. But Segar faced an uphill battle for the queen's attention because after Levina Teerlinc's death Elizabeth seemed unconcerned about including women who were miniaturists or calligraphers in her household.

Jane Segar's manuscript, with two jewel-like covers of painted glass or *verre églomisé*, set within a red velvet binding edged with a silver passement, contains eleven poems. Segar begins her manuscript with a gynocentric appeal in a prose dedication to Elizabeth (Figure 15). In it, Segar explains that the poems are the "handy-worke of a mayden, your Majesties most faithfull Subiect," and thus recommends itself from a virgin to a virgin. As a gathering that begins with the physical and implied spiritual connection afforded by virginity, its eleven poems—each the prophecy of a different sibyl, except for the last poem written as Jane Segar's own prophecy—offer a look at the iconographic and rhetorical strategies that a would-be poet and secretary brought into play in producing a presentation volume for the queen.

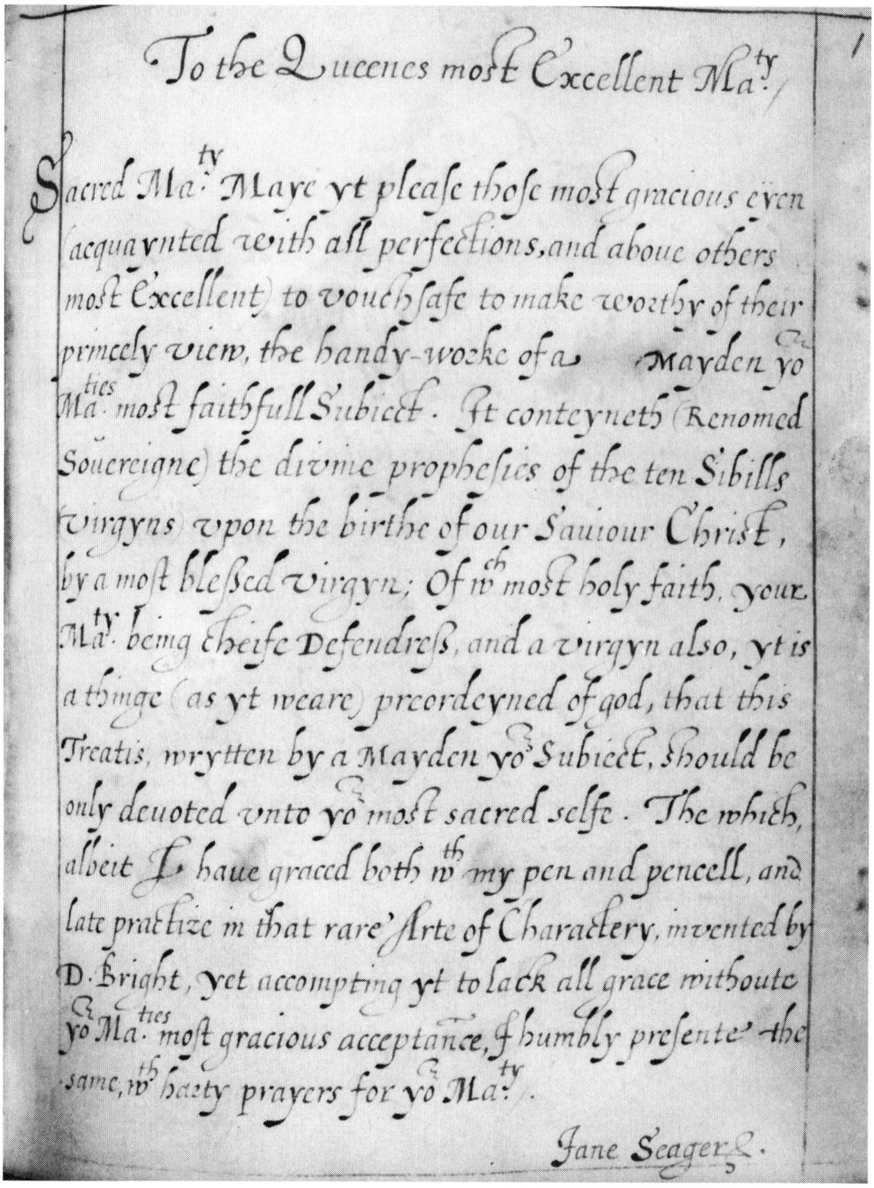

To the Queenes most Excellent Ma.ty

Sacred Ma.ty Maye yt please those most gracious even
acquaynted with all perfections, and aboue others
most Excellent, to vouchsafe to make worthy of their
princely view, the handy-wocke of a   Mayden yo
Ma.ties most faithfull Subicct. Jt conteyneth (Renomed
Souereigne) the divine prophesies of the ten Sibills
Virgyns vpon the birthe of our Sauiour Christ,
by a most blessed Virgyn; Of wch most holy faith, your
Ma.ty being theise Defendress, and a virgyn also, yt is
a thinge (as yt weare) preordeyned of god, that this
Treatis, wrytten by a Mayden yos Subicct, should be
only deuoted vnto yo most sacred selfe. The which,
albeit J haue graced both wth my pen and pencell, and
late practize in that rare Arte of Charactery, invented by
D. Bright, yet accompting yt to lack all grace withoute
yo Ma.ties most gracious acceptance, J humbly presente the
same, wth hasty prayers for yo Ma.ty.

Jane Seager.

Figure 15. Jane Segar, dedication to Elizabeth I of *The Prophecies of the Ten Sibills
upon the Birth of Christ.* 1589. British Library MS Add. 10037. © British Library.

As an object produced by intersecting visual and verbal textualities, and the
conviction that truth may be accessed at such intersections, *The Prophecies of
the Ten Sibills* is a carefully made object that represents its producer as an agent
simultaneously interested in attracting Elizabeth as a patron and in producing
a work strongly marked by personal choices. The entire volume works to connect Jane Segar with Elizabeth I through the sibyls,[38] virginal female prophets

from ancient empires who, like Virgil, were said to have predicted the birth of Christ. The manuscript displays Segar's abilities as a miniaturist, translator, and calligrapher, as well as her facility in the recently developed shorthand or "charactery" of Timothy Bright. So thoroughly does this presentation manuscript display her several skills, that it may well have functioned not just as a gift but as a solicitation of future patronage. Alan Stewart notes that Robert Beale produced a presentation copy of *Instructions for a Principall Secretaris* three years later, in 1592, in order to exhibit his "skill as a secretary," and thereby attract employment.[39] Such a practice reveals the possibility that although Segar's volume was clearly designed for presentation, it might also have served to display her abilities. The possibility of Segar's bid for patronage through her combined verbal and visual abilities recalls the difficulties that women must have encountered in attracting patronage in late sixteenth-century England. Although her brother William was increasingly well connected at court throughout her childhood and adolescence and although she was probably raised in a workshop that would have trained her in the family business of producing illuminated manuscripts and paintings, Jane Segar faced Elizabeth's unwillingness to replace the abilities of Susanna Horenbout and Levina Teerlinc.

In a College of Arms manuscript, William Segar left a draft genealogy that confirms that Jane Segar was his sister and Francis Segar his brother, although he falsely records himself as the elder brother.[40] William and Francis were both noted painters and miniaturists. In his *Palladius Tumia* (1598), Francis Meres lists as painters "William and Francis Segar, brethren," and Erna Auerbach notes a payment of forty shillings paid to an unspecified "Segar" for adorning a still extant "cover of vellom of Mr. Dr. Collette's book of ordinance wherein his own handwriting is" with the "picture of Mr. Dr. Collette upon the cover of vellom of the book or ordinaunce very fair in cullors." Auerbach concludes that, while it's not clear which Segar brother was paid, the payment points to the fact that "the best known limners of the period were sometimes asked to undertake the decoration of these modest manuscript books"[41]—in this case, adorning John Colet's manuscript with his portrait. Colet's payment to an unspecified Segar opens the possibility that Francis was a member of the family workshop, despite his appointment as Gentleman of the Bedchamber to Maurice, Landgrave of Hesse. Apparently Francis acted as Maurice's agent at the court of James I and so would have been frequently in England.[42] Despite both brothers' travels to the continent, the Segar family probably maintained a family workshop or studio, as had the Horenbout and Bening-Teerlinc families. Such a studio would have helped to train their sister Jane, and would have supported her efforts by providing the materials, design, and technical knowledge required for her remarkable volume. The existence of such a studio would also help to explain the sheer ambition that she exercised in producing the *Prophecies of the Ten Sibills*, whose miniaturist covers are not quite finished to the level of William's artistic work, but whose calligraphy is of professional quality.

In the Segar family, creating a jewel-like manuscript book for the queen would seem an appropriate attempt to gain some form of royal patronage if one were a man, and a conceivable if bold attempt if one were a woman. As in Teerlinc's manuscript setting out the ceremonies of the cramp ring and the royal touch, Segar calls attention to her combinations of verbal and visual media. The slightly thick lines of the covers' painted designs point to Jane as the artist, and in her dedication to Elizabeth (see Figure 15) she lays claim to the manuscript's art as well as its poetry when she writes that she has "graced" this work "both with my pen and pencell," where a "pencell" means "an artist's paint-brush of camel's hair . . . especially one of small and fine make, suitable for delicate work."[43] Segar's jewel-like covers signal the giver's wish to appear courtly and learned, decorative yet serviceable. Bound in red velvet like many volumes in the queen's library and edged with a silver-wound passement sewn to the velvet,[44] this is a beautiful object that, although it does not meet the exacting standards of the continent, might reasonably have attracted the queen's perusal.

Jane Segar nevertheless surpassed the usual English forms of miniature work produced for manuscripts by using the technique later called *verre églomisé* for her covers, in which the design is painted in gilt and sometimes color on the back of a piece of glass.[45] During the Renaissance, miniatures and enameled, jeweled, or *verre églomisé* pieces were classified as similar objects because gold paint and colored pigments required the use of precious metals and gems. Although painting on glass was more commonly practiced in France than in England in the 1580s, Elizabeth owned at least one object of *verre églomisé*, "Christ's passion, very beautifully painted upon glass," then on view at Whitehall.[46] Over time, the glass forming Segar's front cover has broken, but because the front and back covers were once virtually identical, it is possible to reconstruct the front. The covers are sufficiently detailed that, although the manuscript is dated 1589, it might well have taken several weeks or months to complete, depending on Segar's proficiency and her other activities.

Segar's covers present a complex design in vivid gold and jewel-derived colors of green, red, gray, and white. At their center is an oval cartouche toward which the painted figures incline. Because one Segar—or the Segar workshop—was paid to paint a miniature portrait of John Colet on the vellum cover of Colet's manuscript, Jane Segar's gift for the queen might well be expected to feature the queen's painted portrait on its cover. Instead, perhaps because she was not capable of creating a likeness, the cartouche contains a portrait in symbols, an inscription in the cipher, or *charactery*, of Timothy Bright, an innovation that I will shortly discuss. The inscription reads when deciphered, "E. R.: God and Mine Right; Glory to Her That Glory Is" (my translation).

A number of other themes resonate between the covers and the manuscript's contents. Not only does painting a miniature in jewel tones create a presentation volume that resembles a religious icon, but, in reading the covers' images from bottom to top, we pass through the natural world of leopards, tigers, or panthers, through the classical mediational figures of a nude woman on the left and satyr on the right, upward to the civilized, imperial world of Roman soldiers decked by green pavilions, to the heavens where two putti frame matching dogs of fidelity.[47] The natural world is surmounted by a tiny crescent moon at the top center of each cover, the symbol associating Elizabeth with the virginal huntress Diana. The soldiers present an imperial theme: the flame and smoke issuing from the urns set between them suggest temples, oracles, and the prophecies within, tapping into Elizabeth's imperial iconography, which had become increasingly evident from the 1580s. In the 1580s, poets and painters had begun to assert the queen's connections to the Roman Empire that had been long available in the myth that Aeneas's grandson, Brutus, left Rome to found England. This imperialist iconography situated in the body of the queen took on a particular energy after the defeat of the Spanish Armada in 1588, the year before the date of Segar's manuscript, although the English were imagining an empire that had yet to expand beyond the British isles.[48] The covers' portrayal of the natural, civilized/imperial, and heavenly realms is dominated by the encrypted portrait of Elizabeth at the cover's center, the picture that is there and not there, written in a cipher that the queen would probably not have been able to read without assistance but which nevertheless represented her within the codes of Bright's charactery.

Opening the cover reveals Elizabeth again present, this time in the English of Segar's dedication (see Figure 15), which makes several strong claims. The dedication links Elizabeth to Segar through their shared virginity and the virginity of sibyls and the Virgin Mary, even as it acknowledges Elizabeth's "Sacred Majesty." Their shared virginity, together with Elizabeth's position as "chiefe defendress" of the faith, makes the presentation of this volume a fulfillment of divine will, for, writes Segar, it "is a thinge (as yt weare) preordeyned of God, that this Treatis, wrytten by a Mayden your Subiect, should be only devoted unto your most sacred self." Finally, Segar associates her accomplishments with "pen and pencell" in creating this presentation volume with her "practize in that rare Arte of Charactery, invented by T. Bright." Segar defines her identity not only in relation to Elizabeth, queen and sacred virgin, but also in relation to the accomplishments of Timothy Bright, a professional man educated at

Cambridge who had already attracted Elizabeth's patronage and with whom the Segars may have been affiliated.

Segar's use of Bright's *Characterie: Art of Swift and Secret Writing* tells us a great deal about how Segar constructed her volume as a demonstration of her practical abilities as limner, calligrapher, and stenographer, as well as, more intimately and mystically, the conveyor of ancient prophecies affirming Elizabeth's position as Head of the Church of England. Bright, an author, a physician, and, later, a member of the clergy who produced a popular volume on melancholy, received a patent from Elizabeth in 1588 for the practice of his characterie, the first English shorthand. Bright's system was supposedly adapted from ancient language systems, being written vertically like Chinese although based on imagined Roman shorthand models, thus containing its own imperial appeal.[49] Bright's system also filled the contemporary need for a technology that could record and transmit information more quickly than longhand.

During the twentieth century the privilege once conveyed by ciphers and shorthands became obscured by their association with female secretaries, just as "secretary" itself devolved into a job that women often performed for minimal pay. But in the sixteenth century, systems of secret writing were used by males and many of the privileged females discussed in this book. Bright tapped into these political needs in ways that attracted the royal attention that Jane Segar probably never received. The queen learned of Bright's system when his mentor at Cambridge, Vincent Skinner, recommended him and his "characterie" to his friend Michael Hicke, Secretary to William Cecil, as a kind of code. When Cecil called Bright's invention to Elizabeth's notice, she awarded Bright a Bill of Privy Signet, in effect one of the first copyrights, protecting the development of his characterie and reserving its profits to Bright for fifteen years.[50]

Bright's *Characterie: An Art of Swift and Secret Writing*, published in 1588, the year in which England found itself vulnerable to the Spanish invasion, addresses Elizabeth in its dedication. Bright is concerned with the uses, both public and secret, that may be made of his work—uses that seem contradictory four hundred years later, when a published system of writing hardly seems secret. But Bright's dedication makes it clear that to himself and his contemporaries, his system suggested both the tradition and political need for secret writing on the one hand and new vistas of publicity on the other: "The uses are divers: Short, that a swifte hande may therewith write Orations, or publike actions of speach," while "Secrete, as no kinde of wryting like."[51] At its inception, shorthand was analogous to cipher, in that "characterie" meant "expression of thought, by symbols or characters," while "cipher" meant "a disguised or secret manner of writing," through "characters artificially invented" (OED). In using Bright's invented symbols to represent letters, Segar calls attention to writing as drawn

Chapter Two

symbol, especially because she uses gold ink to write the sibyls' prophecies in Bright's charactery.

Shorthand remained a technology so valuable that men attempted to control it for more than three centuries. The earliest discussion of Segar's manuscript was written by Westby Gibson for the British Shorthand Society in 1884. The society's membership was exclusively male. For Dickens's David Copperfield in 1850, learning shorthand in order to transcribe the Parliamentary debates was the beginning of a promising career in public life. For Copperfield (as once, perhaps, for Dickens), the task required a tremendous effort: learning the marks that formed an "alphabet" "was an Egyptian Temple in itself,"[52] a description that evokes the mystical association with hieroglyphics that stenography inherited from cipher, even as it recalls the difficulty of memorizing its symbols.

Segar's manuscript makes maximum use of charactery's negotiation of the relation between the public and secret needs of an emergent English empire. The manuscript claims simultaneously to be the product of Jane Segar, modest maiden and historical contemporary of Elizabeth I, and Jane Segar, visionary persona, who possesses sacred knowledge that she transmits from the ancient imperial world to a new imperium through translation. As mentioned earlier, Segar translated ten poems into English from a medieval Latin original not provided in her manuscript, and added an eleventh poem of her own composition. Instead of providing a Latin-to-English facing-page translation, she provides her English version on the left page written in black ink in an artful italic hand and a second English version on the right in gold ink, transmuted into the symbols of Bright's charactery (Figure 16). This layout of the manuscript's pages manufactures a complex relationship between Segar and the poetic prophecies of the sibyls. In early modern facing-page translations, the translation appeared on the left page and the original appeared on the right. By placing her poems in English on the left and the versions in charactery on the right, Segar suggests that each English poem is a translation of an original, ciphered prophecy written in gold. And where would this ciphered original come from but a sibyl? In this way, Segar manipulates the conventions of facing-page translation to make her English verses appear to be translations from the golden symbols of some sibylline code. Yes, her use of Bright's system of shorthand advertises the historical Segar's ability to use it as a secretary might. But Segar also manipulates the conventions of translation in ways that allow her visionary persona to claim access to the authentic speech of the sibyls. In this way, Segar uses translation to empower herself as both translator and poet, locating the gift of prophecy within herself.[53]

Segar is bold in assuming sibylline personae, but she is not alone in her attraction to these legendary mystics. In *Concerning Famous Women*, Giovanni

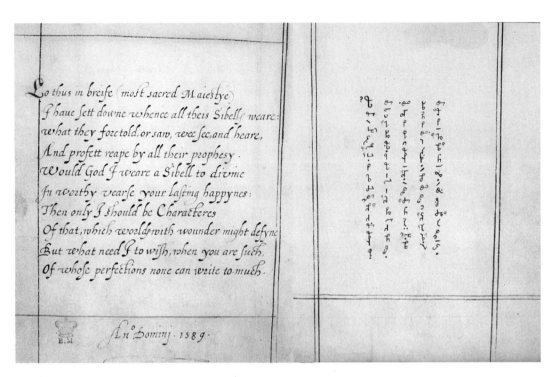

Figure 16. Jane Segar, concluding poem and facing-page transcription in Timothy Bright's charactery, *The Prophecies of the Ten Sibills upon the Birth of Christ*. 1589. British Library MS Add. 10037. © British Library.

Boccaccio describes the Sybil Erythraea in terms that equate sibyls with biblical prophets: "The power of her intellect was so great, and she was so deserving in God's eyes because of her prayer and devotion, that through her own studies, and not without divine gift . . . she gained the skill to write about the future with such clarity that it seems to be the Gospel rather than fortune-telling." For Boccaccio, the sibyls become the opportunity to berate men for not accomplishing more: "If women through genius, industry, and God's grace reach such divinity and sanctity, what must one think of men, who have greater aptitude for everything?"[54] When Christine de Pizan revises Boccaccio in *The Book of the City of Ladies*, the sibyls authorize Christine's endeavors as a female character and function as a representation of the female author. As Maureen Quilligan writes, the sibyls manifest "by their appearance to Christine the previously secret, hidden wisdom of female power in the world, putting it into a textual form by helping to build simultaneously the city and the book" (Quilligan, *The Allegory of Female Authority*, 30). As Droitture tells Christine at the beginning of Book II, God placed in sibyls "such a profound and advanced prophecy that what they said did not seem to be prognostications of the future but rather chronicles of past events which had already taken place." Moreover, "They even spoke more clearly and farther in advance of the coming of Jesus Christ, who came long afterward, than all the prophets did, just as can be seen from their writings."[55] In 1599, this tradition of the sibyls' superiority to biblical prophets survived in such works as Anthony Gibson's translation of *A Woman's Woorth*, dedicated to Elizabeth, Countess of Southampton, and Elizabeth I's maids of honour, which affirmed that "the Sibilles, all of which prophesied of the true messias the Son of God so evidently, so there is not a text in the olde Testament, more expresse then their propheticall writings were."[56]

The intellectual history of the sibyls thus had much to recommend it to a young woman writer and artisan like Jane Segar. Segar may have known *The City of Ladies*, either through the anonymously translated English version of 1521 or, more probably, in a manuscript version, although the recognition of Christine as its author had apparently been lost.[57] Regardless, Segar clearly hoped that the ways in which the sibyls embody and argue for women's intellectual connection to the divine would appeal to Elizabeth. Nevertheless, evoking sibyls was not a strategy guaranteed to attract Elizabeth's patronage, because sibyls stand above and beyond the earthly power that they serve. In 1575, Robert Dudley welcomed Elizabeth to Kenilworth through a Sibylla whose voice of prophecy first salutes Elizabeth as the Christ-like "Prince of Peace" but ends by reducing her status to that of a house-guest.[58]

Not only did Elizabeth not care for Dudley's Sibylla, she might, like her father before her, have viewed female prophets with profound suspicion. Elizabeth Barton, the Benedictine nun who prophesied the downfall of Henry VIII if he married Anne Boleyn, was pointedly executed on the day that the "citizens of London were required to take the Oath of Succession," as Diane Watt points out. Prophecy was an empowering activity for women, writes Watt, offering them "an opportunity for direct involvement in the public sphere at the national level," but its connection with political treason caused Parliament to outlaw "any fond fantastically or false Prophecy . . . to the intent thereby to make any Rebellion Insurrection Dissension loss of Life or other Disturbance." Howard Dobin notes that Elizabeth's religious establishment was beset by the "immense popularity and potency of old prophetic texts," which were widely consulted on the issue of the succession throughout her reign because of her childlessness.[59] The preacher Edward Topsell summarized the fear that prophecy was inherently political when he warned in 1599 that "first of all we must beware of false and foolish prophecies, which being the dreams of many brainsick persons, have bewitched the hearts of men that heard them . . . that princes and countries have been destroyed thereby." Segar taps a power that ventures close to treason on the one hand and witchcraft on the other. Topsell mentions the dangers of sibyls in particular: "Many of the learneder sort are much affected with the prophesies of the Sibyls, Methodious and others."[60]

In her volume Segar does not claim a divine prophetic power for herself in the way that Elizabeth Barton did, or that Eleanor Davies, Eleanor Channel, or Elizabeth Poole would in the seventeenth century.[61] She does not claim to see visions or actually to predict the future but to offer an imperial if mystical compliment to the queen through the fiction that the sibyls not only predicted the birth of Christ but also the coming of a church headed by Elizabeth. Segar actively promotes the queen's religious leadership by interpreting the fourteenth-century Latin poems to mean that Elizabeth is essential to the stability of the English church. In doing so, Segar uses the sibyls as if they could be readily assimilated into the Roman imperial iconography of Elizabeth as Vestal Virgin as well as the Marian religious iconography of Elizabeth as miraculous and sacred virgin; as if Segar could join the queen in an idealized past when women's powers were integral to church and state. Perhaps because of the dangerous associations that sibyls unleash, Segar takes pains to screen the boldness of her assumption of their voices. In her manuscript, Segar is at once the intrepid translator of the sibyls' prophecies and their cautious presenter. But that presenter's voice, however modest, inevitably reminds the reader of Segar's adventurous project, an elaborately produced manuscript combining miniaturist painting set within a luxurious textile binding, calligraphy in black and gold ink, translation, Segar's own prose and verse, and her knowledge of Bright's charactery.

The sense of secrets revealed and prophecy fulfilled, with Segar functioning as both their source and their translator, is particularly strong in the voice of the third sibyl, Libyca. This poem is the most politically suggestive in the context of the Protestant, post-Armada world of a manuscript dated 1589. In an extension of the Elizabethan iconography of empowering virginity, Libyca foretells marriage between Christ and the virginal Church. The idea of Christ marrying the Church is hardly new, as it is the allegorized reading of the Song of Songs, but here the Catholic imagery is superseded by insemination imagery, which predicts an intimate relation between Christ and "The queene his church":

Behold, Behold, the day shall come when as
A Joyfull Prince shyning upon his seed
His Churche with graces shall illummat:
And cleare the darcknes which through synne was bred.
He shall unlock the uncleane lipps of them
That guilty are, and being true and just,
He shall his people love, but for his foes

They shall not come, nor stand before his sight:
He shall indure with blessings from above,
The Queene his Churche, the more for Our behove.

Anno Mundi 2720

At the outset, the repetition of "Behold" emphasizes the sibyl's ability to see the future as she calls on the reader to share her vision. Libyca asks her audience to see God's self-insemination as illumining "His Churche with graces," so that his birth is inseparable from the church. Jesus is forceful: he will "unlock the uncleane lippes of them / That guilty are." Although loving, he opposes his foes by wiping them from existence as had recently happened during the Armada: "They shall not come, nor stand before his sight." The poem's movement from Christ's insemination of the church through the protection of his people ends with the promise of the Word made concrete. Segar's concluding couplet seems logically as well as metrically awkward until we factor in the contemporary meanings of "indure" and "behove." "He shall indure with blessings from above / The Queene his Churche, the more for Our behove," uses the more precise meaning of "indure" as "to harden" or here, perhaps, to make concrete. "Hove" meant "to lift" or "raise," so that the concluding couplet may be paraphrased, "With blessings from above, Christ will make real the queen as his church (and the church as his queen or bride), in order to raise us up."

In this way, Segar adapts her Latin original for Elizabeth's context, writing herself into Elizabeth's imperial iconography by building analogies among the Virgin Mary, the church as Christ's bride, Roman virgins, and the queen. As a result of Segar's attempts to represent her connection to Elizabeth in this volume, her imagery becomes enmeshed in the problem of Elizabeth's virginity. In 1589 lifelong virginity maintained its magical, fertile connotations through the same connection to the Virgin Mary on which Segar's poems depend. But by 1589, Elizabeth had failed to produce a direct heir, a physical and political fact raised by Libyca's ongoing comparison of the queen and the Virgin Mary. The comparison between Mary and an aging Elizabeth works best when, as in Crispin de Passe's engraving associating Elizabeth with the Marian imagery of the pelican rending her breast to feed her young,[62] the work draws on their similarities without examining too minutely the discrepancies between queen and Mary. When the analogy is carried to great lengths it is a risky one. Lines like "shee shall bring forth / the only surety of our saving health" (Segar; "Agrippa," 5–6) or "In tender years a sacred virgine myld, / Of beauty rare and perfect excellence: / Shall nourishe with the milke of her chast brest / The Lord of host, and everlasting King" ("Cimmeria," 1–4), become uncomfortable reminders that the queen in her mid-fifties could not pull off Mary's miraculous insemination. Segar's frequent use of the word "king" for Jesus also recalls the absence of a named successor and with it both the desire and fear surrounding contemporary prophecies about the royal succession.

In Segar's hands, these three religious themes celebrate virginity as proof of the word's power, in poems presented by a virgin to a virgin. If Segar's translated poems had not been dedicated to a queen from whom she hoped to elicit a response, they would read simply as religious poetry emphasizing three themes in the story of the birth of Christ. Their first theme is the value and mystery of Mary's virginity, for, as the opening lines declare, "The highest birth shalbe under the fleshe / A virgine trew without all spot, or blame" ("Agrippa," 1–2). As "a virgine most inviolate" ("Samia," 7), "In tender yeares a sacred virgine myld, / In beauty rare and perfect excellence" ("Cimmeria," 1–2), "a virgine chaste" ("Persiea," 1) gives birth to God. In keeping with the theme of Mary's powerful virginity, the poems' second theme is the power of the word to connect that virginal body to Christ. This Mary, whom "The sacred worde shall fill with heavenly grace / By the prescience of the holye spirit" ("Agrippa," 3–4) recalls pictures of the Annunciation in which the words of the angel inseminate the Virgin Mary by piercing her ear: "Th/eternall word shall come from heaven above, / And shall inspire the body of a mayd, / Conceavying by the eare a blessed babe" ("Europoea," 1–3). These associations developed among virginity, the word, and the birth take place within an emphasis on a third theme, the Virgin Mary as a Jewish woman, in ways that anticipate the racialized philosemitism of Elizabeth Cary in *The Tragedy of Mariam, Fair Queen of Jewery* (1613). Mary is "a faire virgine of the Hebrew race" ("Erythroea," 4); Christ's "mother hee shall chooze of blessed race" ("Europoea," 10), so that his birth may "remove the worldes obscurity: / Unfoulding all the Prophets prophecies / And knotty volumes of the Jewish race" ("Samia," 2–4). The reader also glimpses moments in the story of Christ in reading through the poems—the nativity, the ride into Jerusalem on Palm Sunday, the promise to redeem the sins of humanity laying the groundwork for the Church. But Segar's translation of the poems and their placement between her dedication and her final poem, both directed at Elizabeth, politicize the power of virginity, the word, and the prophecy that unites them.

Like Segar's apparently simple religious themes, the poems' apparently transparent poetic form conveys a sense of truth through repetition. Each prophecy consists of ten lines: eight lines of blank verse followed by a concluding couplet in sometimes rough iambic pentameter. Cumana's shorter prophecy is the exception, with six lines of blank verse and a concluding couplet. The dates at the bottom of each prophecy headed "An[n]o Mundi," cover the time from "Ano Mundi 2720" to A.D. 1589. Although "Agrippa," "Samia," "Libyca,"

"Persiea," and "Europoea" all appear in 2720, as if a group of five sibyls is prophesying at the same time, still other prophecies supposedly date from "Ano Mundi" 2380, 3890, and 3900, while Segar's final poem is dated Anno Domini 1589. The connected claims of virginity, the power of the word, and the fulfillment of the "Jewish race," supposedly spoken by different sibyls at both the same and different times, appear to substantiate each other and the manuscript as a whole. Like the later publications of Elizabeth Cary and Amelia Lanyer, Segar's choice of religious discourse works both to authorize her writing and to assert the importance of women's voices in the world at large.

The manuscript's final poem (Figure 16), the only poem that Segar composed rather than translated, is both modest in addressing the queen and bold in presenting itself as the pronouncement of an eleventh sibyl, the poet herself. Although this poem is the only one not to begin with the name of the sibyl who speaks it, it follows the format of the preceding ten prophecies and concludes with a date, "1589." Segar's own poem further resembles the ten preceding prophecies, because, like them, it appears in English on the left and, on the facing page, in the gilt symbols of Bright's charactery. The result is that Segar's eleventh poem presents its speaker as simultaneously a sibyl alive and prophesying in 1589 and a properly modest female who must make the most of this chance to represent herself within Elizabeth's good graces. She demurely addresses Elizabeth, "Lo thus in briefe most Sacred Maiestye, / I haue sett downe whence all theis Sibells weare: / What they foretold, or saw, we see, and heare, / And profett reape by all their prophesy." The speaker continues an ambitious expression of desire: "Would God I weare a Sibell to divine / In worthy verse your lasting happynes." But instead of predicting Elizabeth's happiness, the final lines are the most ambiguous in the manuscript, as the speaker states that if she were a sibyl able to prophecy Elizabeth's happiness,

Then only I should be Characteres
Of that, which worlds with wounder might defyne
But what need I to wish, when you are such,
Of whose perfections none can write to much.

The lines are difficult because they emphasize the gulf between Segar and Elizabeth even as they attempt to bridge that gulf. Segar wants to praise the remote and powerful queen, to predict her "lasting happyness," as one might expect at the conclusion of a volume dedicated to her. But Segar also wants to recommend her volume, her poetry, and her skills as scrivener, painter, and stenographer. As a result, when she writes that "only I should be Characteres / of that, which worlds with wounder might defyne," the phrase "only I" means both "no more than I, just I" as well as "uniquely, especially I." The word "characteres" is likewise multivalent, meaning shorthand but also, like Busirane's "vile characters" in *The Faerie Queene* (3.12.31),[63] signifying mysterious or magical writing—a cipher whose meanings shade into the obscure realms of magic and prophecy.

With these nuances of "only I" and "Characteres" in mind, I suggest two paraphrases for the lines with which Segar concludes her manuscript. The first paraphrase emphasizes Elizabeth, as is appropriate in a presentation volume but concludes that Segar alone can complete this prophecy: "If it were true that I were a sibyl able to divine your happiness, Elizabeth, in that case only I would represent in my person the characters through which others in the future will read you, to their wonder." A second paraphrase of Segar's final lines demonstrates how she uses Elizabeth to portray herself: "If I were a Sibyl, then the characters through which the future defines you would be my own—and would in some sense be *me*." Just as Elizabeth's portrait exists in charactery on the manuscript's covers, inviting decipherment, so Jane Segar's prophecy of Elizabeth's happiness forms a picture—in characters—of the poet herself: "only I should be Characteres / of that, which worlds of wounder might defyne." It is through characters that Segar represents the queen, but it is also through characters that Segar represents herself within the iconography of that queen's religious and imperial greatness. In this way, Segar's concluding poem asserts her as the queen's facing page, a translator and translation of Elizabeth's glorious present and future.

How close did this volume come to Elizabeth? Might Segar have presented it to the queen through her brother? About the life of William Segar we know only the broad outlines and a few details, but perhaps enough to suggest the fate of Jane's manuscript. We know, for example, that William was one of the age's more successful social climbers. Born of English parents but of Netherlandish descent, he began his career as a scrivener and an illuminator. With the help of Thomas Heanage, Elizabeth's treasurer of the Chamber and later vice-chamberlain, he became a member of the College of Arms as a painter and recorder of chivalric pageantry and genealogies, which in time he organized, sometimes described, and frequently illuminated. William Segar not only illuminated calligraphic manuscripts, he went on to paint full-length portraits in oils, including those of another patron, Robert Dudley, Earl of Leicester, as governor-general of the Netherlands, and Robert Devereux, Earl of Essex. Segar painted the *Ermine Portrait* of Elizabeth at Hatfield Hall with both painterly precision and emblematic suggestion. As a member of the College of Arms, which not only researches and preserves the genealogies of the armiturgical but also organizes the ceremonies surrounding the monarchy, he marshaled

Elizabeth's victory procession celebrating the defeat of the Armada from Somerset Place to St. Paul's Cathedral.[64] William Segar also published more than a dozen spectacles and overviews of chivalric deportment. In 1590, he published *The Book of Honor and Armes*, with a title page whose grotesques, imperial tents, and strapwork are similar to his sister's overall design of the covers for the *Prophecies of the Ten Sibills.*

As William Segar moved between the court and the College of Arms, he became a leader of the artisans who organized, executed, and transcribed court spectacle during the reigns of both Elizabeth and James. As a member of her brothers' household and workshop, Jane would have helped to produce a variety of illuminated manuscripts with her practiced calligraphic pen and slightly less proficient "pencell." Their workshop would have provided the often rare and expensive ingredients and family recipes needed to mix her colors and produce gilt paint and ink; in such an atmosphere writing and limning were frequently conjoined. There, like Levina Teerlinc and the young Elizabeth herself, Segar produced a manuscript meant to convey Elizabeth's political significance as religious in origin.

William Segar's duties at court may have provided the opportunity for Jane to have presented her manuscript to the queen. In a variety of capacities, he had access to the court if not directly to the queen. In his *Honors Military and Civil*, William includes an account of "Justs at the Tilt-yard, 1590," which featured a temple with a crowned pillar with a prayer printed in gold beneath. There, after a song, young women dressed as "vestal Maydens," presented Elizabeth with gifts, including "a vaile of white, exceeding rich and curiously wrought: a cloke and safeguard set with buttons of gold, and on them were graven emprezes of excellent device."[65] Such gifts were elsewhere presented to Elizabeth by young women described as virgins within court entertainments. During the entertainments in 1592 for the queen at Sudeley Castle, the figure of Daphne ran for help to Elizabeth, "the Queene of Chastity," and then presented her with "Sibylla's prophesies" in terms that suggest that Jane Segar's volume could have been the gift. As she handed over the volume, Daphne announced, "These tables, to set downe your prayses, long since, Sibylla's prophesies, I humbly present to your Majesty; not thinking that your vertues can be deciphered in so slight a volume, but noted. The whole World is drawn in a small mappe, Homer's Illiades in a nutshel, and the riches of a Monarch in a few cyphers; and so much ods, betwext explaining of your perfections and the touching, as is betwixt painting and thinking; the one, running over a little table in a day, the other over the whole world in a minute."[66] Like the "tables" synonymous here with "so slight a volume," Segar's slim manuscript within its two painted covers or "tables" offers all the great mysteries inscribed in miniatures, "running over a little table," possibly Segar's slim book.

Jane Segar's volume need not have been presented during an entertainment, because William might well have found a less public opportunity to present it to the queen. Jill Seal Millman and Gillian Wright point out that William was created Somerset Herald in 1589, which may have occasioned the book and its presentation, perhaps as a New Year's gift.[67] If the Sudeley gift was not Segar's manuscript, it demonstrates that the conceptual context within which Segar was writing around 1589 still existed at Elizabeth's court in 1592. Moreover, Daphne's speech explains why ciphered, miniature volumes, or tables, continued in demand. They were thought capable of recording the world in "a smalle mappe," the *Iliad* in a "nutshell," or the riches of a monarch "in a few ciphers," descriptions that inscribe the value of verbal messages when conveyed by visual design.

Jane Segar's subsequent anonymity suggests that her bid for patronage at most received a modest acknowledgment from the queen despite—or because of—her facility with language and charactery, her explorations of the relations between sibylline prophecy and the England of 1589, between prophecy and Elizabeth. What then became of Jane Segar? William Segar's draft of his family genealogy at the College of Arms lists after his sister Jane's name, "m[arried] Lionel Plumtree." A Lionel Plumtree makes a brief appearance in Richard Hakluyt's *Voyages* as the teller of a harrowing tale of the wool trade, the fifth voyage into Persia sponsored by the Muscovy Company in 1568–74.[68] It seems likely that this Plumtree, who could have been Jane Segar's senior by twenty years, or his relative of the same name, became her husband at a time when the Muscovy Company was both approaching Asian markets via Russia and trying to develop the Russian market itself. The Plumtree connections to the Muscovy Company would explain why, opposite the joined Segar and Plumtree coat of arms, William Segar's only comment about his sister Jane appears beside her name: "Now in Russia 1603."

Esther Inglis: Materializing Authorship

Unlike Jane Segar, whose manuscript may never have reached the queen, Esther Inglis (1571–1624) successfully built a career based on manuscript books created for royal and aristocratic patrons. Inglis, like Susanna Horenbout much earlier in the sixteenth century, was a miniaturist and, like Levina Teerlinc, combined that skill with exceptional abilities as a scrivener and calligrapher. In addition, Inglis sometimes covered her nearly sixty known calligraphic manuscripts in embroidery in a method reminiscent of the young Elizabeth Tudor's manuscript production (Plate 8). Like Elizabeth and Segar, Inglis produced translated texts as well as short prose and verse pieces of her own. Esther Inglis's books frequently consist of a central pious text placed within covers of her own making and introduced by a variety of materials, usually including a title page, self-portrait, and dedication to someone of rank. In the late sixteenth and early seventeenth centuries in England, such texts continued to circulate in manuscript precisely because print became the more available technology. So valued were elegant manuscript books at the turn of the seventeenth century that scribes were sometimes employed to copy printed books to re-create the look of less widely marketed volumes.[69]

Among these manuscript books, Esther Inglis's are significant because they are small to tiny in size, with the smallest measuring one and a half inches by two inches or two inches by three inches, like the *Argumenta Psalmoru Davidis* of Plate 8 dedicated to Henry Prince of Wales in 1608. This miniature cover features a design of flowers extending from a vase embroidered with silver and gold thread and seed pearls on a red velvet background.[70] Inglis's books are also written in dozens of different scripts accompanied by drawings and ornaments, all of which mark her gatherings as the work of her hand. The most significant aspect of her books lies in the relation between their existence as handmade objects and the ways that she uses them to represent herself as a woman author. Every material feature of Inglis's books asserts her project, to assemble and publish exquisite textual objects whose value resides in the tension between manuscript and print cultures, the hand and the machine. In creating a place for herself between these two cultures, Inglis connected the writing woman to desired political and social affiliations at the same time that her books materialized an authorial self.

The family that produced Esther Inglis's skilled hand was devout, educated, and struggling to obtain an economic and social foothold.[71] Born in 1571 in London, Inglis was the daughter of two Huguenot refugees, Nicholas Langlois and the renowned calligrapher Marie Presot. By 1574 Inglis had moved to Edinburgh with her family. There, after living on poor relief, her father became Master of the French School about 1580, after which King James paid him an annual pension of £80 to £100 Scots. Langlois taught French and writing to his pupils and is described as "forming of their hands to a perfect shape of letter." Her mother, very likely the more accomplished calligrapher, must also have been involved with the school. A page of her writing in several hands is now at the Newberry Library.[72] For this family's members, as for most humanist-educated Europeans at the turn of the seventeenth century, writing well meant living a moral life. Jonathan Goldberg points out that London's famed educator Richard Mulcaster aimed "to frame the childes hand right," an expression that joins the child's hand to the child's morality. As Goldberg summarizes this early modern conception of handwriting, "Habits of behavior begin with the control of the hand, with the formations of the hand."[73] Inglis demonstrates familiarity with a number of writing masters, including Clément Perret, Hondius, and "John de Beauchesne, a French Huguenot who became writing master to the children of James I." She was also familiar with a number of printed manuals of handwriting, including de Beauchesne's *A Booke containing divers sortes of handes* (London, 1570) (Cat., 19). But she would have learned her writing skills primarily from her mother in their Huguenot household. As a result, Esther Inglis fashioned her books within the implicit connections between her Protestant upbringing, her well-trained hand, and the dozens of "hands," or styles, of handwriting that she had learned. When Inglis dedicated the first of two known books to Elizabeth I in 1591, the *Discours de la Foy*, "Discourse of Faith," whose verses may be by Inglis or her father, she referred to her own writing "in diverse sorts of letters," describing their total effect as "a portrait of the Christian Religion, that I have drawn with the pen, which I send to your Majesty to honor the small knowledge that God has given me in the art of writing and portraying."[74] Compared to Jane Segar's manuscript, Inglis's book as a "portrait of the Christian Religion" presents a more acceptable means to authorize oneself as a skilled poet, translator, scrivener, and miniaturist. Yet Inglis's claim that handwritten letters can form a "portrait" resembles Segar's suggestion in her last poem that the poet could herself be composed of wondrous characters, signs, or letters.

In Scotland, Inglis's career was at first managed by her father, who wrote dedicatory verses for her early books, including the *Discours de la Foy*. Around 1596, Esther Inglis married Bartholomew Kello, who had probably studied theology at the University of St. Andrews, and who seems to have begun his career as a scrivener. Kello's professional relation to his wife's work is open to speculation. We know that Kello played the part of loyal helpmate, even at times managing his wife's career by acting as fundraiser, occasional deliverer of her books, sometime translator of French texts, and author of dedicatory Latin verses praising his wife and her patrons. Inglis retained her maiden name, later anglicizing Langlois to Inglis, perhaps because it was the custom of married women in Scotland or because, like her French mother, doing so indicated her desire to retain a professional identity apart from her husband.

King James VI of Scotland employed both Kello and Inglis as scriveners. An unsigned and undated warrant of this period is most likely a version drafted by Kello that he hoped the king would sign, clarifying Inglis's position as well as Kello's own at court. The warrant begins by noting that, because there is concern about the accuracy of state documents, Kello will be responsible for "all such Passports, Testimonials, Letters of commendation and recommendation,

Missives and Others alike to be granted and direct by our Sovereign Lord to foreign Princes, Personages, Estates, and Nations." Kello must either perform the writing himself or oversee such writing, as the document repeatedly asserts: "the said Barthilmo Kello" is "to write or cause all the said letters by his discretion be written BY THE MOST EXQUISITE WRITER WITHIN THIS REALM."[75] "The most exquisite writer within this realm"—a phrase repeated twice in this document and capitalized the second time—was undoubtedly Esther Inglis, whom the draft objectifies by equating her with the exquisite texts of her production, while her husband is charged with seeing that she gets the job done. Although the name "Esther Inglis" appears nowhere, the name "Bartholomew Kello," once entirely capitalized, appears four times. On the whole, the warrant says less about James's concerns and more about Kello's anxieties about how to control and profit from his wife's abilities, so its author is undoubtedly Kello.

This drafted warrant probably dates from early in the Inglis-Kello marriage, around 1596 or 1597, because we know that by 1599 James was finding Kello useful not only as a scrivener but as a messenger and spy, and that Inglis's books often featured in his activities.[76] Kello repeatedly used the presentation of Inglis's books as an excuse to journey abroad, just as he used his excursions as a messenger or information gatherer to present his wife's books and then dun his hosts for cash. As Georgianna Ziegler points out, Kello used his wife's books as the means to approach people of rank both in Scotland and in England, including the circles of the Essex and Sidney families, and those associated with the courts of Anne of Denmark and Prince Henry.[77]

Kello's management of Inglis's books resulted in benefits for them both. Following James's accession to the English throne, they moved to England, where Kello became Rector of Willingale Spain in Essex in 1607 and, in 1620, again as a result of royal patronage, Rector of Spexhall in Suffolk. Their son, Samuel—the only boy of four surviving children—succeeded him there, during his father's lifetime and perhaps against his father's will. A letter that Inglis wrote King James that same year set the wheels of this nomination in motion when she requested the preferment of her son by referring to a book that she had recently sent the king:

> Most Mighty Monarch,
>   Dare I presume upon the honor and credit that I have had at diverse times to speak your Royal Majesty, and hath ever found your Highness favour, and upon the gracious accepting of a little work by this Youth given to your Highness at Sterling called SIDUS CÆLESTE [Celestial Constellation], as to make humble suit for this one and last thing to this

my only Son, who, having past his course two years ago, would gladly follow Theology if it shall please God.[78]

In tone, this letter from Inglis to King James resembles the straightforward prose of her dedications. Moreover the letter, which she signed, speaks of her personal level of familiarity with him. James responded, although perhaps not in a way that Kello himself could have wished, by bestowing Kello's own living on his son instead of giving Samuel the next available living, as requested in the letter.

The fact that Esther Inglis rather than her husband wrote the king suggests that, despite Kello's varied career in James's service and the payments and rewards that he received, both husband and wife knew that Inglis was the person who could obtain the king's attention. Although Inglis's books constituted a family enterprise to the extent that they helped to further her husband's political activities, added to the family's income with gifts of money that ranged between £5 and £22 (Cat., 66), and, eventually, provided for Samuel, the accomplishments that they demonstrate are Esther Inglis's. Inglis's dedications are entirely about herself, her books, and her relation to her proposed patrons. Far from claiming authority from her roles as wife and mother, Inglis presents herself as the prototype of the career woman who has assumed the usually male role of scrivener as well as the function of the male activities of publishing a text. Although her mother's example must have enabled her appropriation of this role and Inglis herself may have trained at least one talented child, Inglis's dedicatory material and artwork convey only a limited sense of community with other women writers.

The exception is her sense of connection to Georgette de Montenay, French author of a volume of Christian emblems first published in 1571 in Lyons. Long before Inglis dedicated her ambitious book, *The Emblemes Chrestiens of Georgette de Montenay*, to Prince Charles in 1624—in which the dedication declares that the book is the product of "two yeeres labours of the small cunning" (Cat., 81)—as Georgianna Ziegler points out, Inglis copied a Montenay emblem into the concluding material of a book of psalms dedicated in 1608 to Prince Henry.[79] Inglis demonstrates a further fascination with Montenay by modeling several of her own self-portraits on the Montenay portrait included in the 1619 Frankfurt edition of her work. In the book of Inglis's emblems dated 1624, the year that she died at the age of fifty-three at Leith, she copied this portrait of the French author into her book of Montenay's emblems (Cat. no. 54, 81). For this book, Inglis selected fifty of Montenay's emblems and drew two original emblems, one for Prince Charles and one for the Duke of Buckingham (Cat., 81). Her title translates in full as "This Book Containing Fifty Christian Emblems First

Invented by the noble damoiselle Georgette de Montenay in France, very pleasant and delectable to read and see, these are at present written, traced stroke by stroke, and drawn, by the hand and pen of me Esther Inglis in the year of my age fifty-three: at Edinburgh in Scotland."[80] The *Emblemes Chrestiens*, like the *Livret des Pseaumes* dedicated to Elizabeth, is constructed to represent a printed book measuring about seven by five inches.[81] As Inglis writes in her dedication to Charles, although producing this book means that she has "transcended the bounds of modestie, where with our Sexe is commanlie adorned," she has produced these emblems, "the fruits of my pen (but the invention of a noble Lady of France whose portraict is in the forfront heerof)."[82] Apart from her admiration for Montenay, Inglis reaches out to strong female patrons—to Elizabeth I, to Lucy, Countess of Bedford, and to Lady Susannah Herbert and other members of the Sidney Circle—but never attempts to bridge the social divide between them as Amelia Lanyer's poetry attempts to do.[83]

Rather than seek authorization from her husband, from her position as wife and mother, or from a sense of intellectual community with other educated women—all strategies used by women authors, especially the few who published their work at the turn of the seventeenth century—Inglis martials her Huguenot religious principles to authorize herself as a woman who steps over "the bounds of modestie, where with our Sexe is commanlie adorned." These principles inform her choice of moralistic or religious texts—the Psalms, a popular choice among women writers like Ane Locke and Mary Sidney Herbert; selections from Ecclesiastes or the Proverbs of Solomon; and the emblems of Georgette de Montenay.

Her principles serve her well, allowing her to exert her energies in directions both sanctioned and unusual, in language both modestly feminine and fierce. In the dedication of Montenay's emblems to Charles, Inglis writes that "remembering your Highness douce and sweet inclination I recovered again the Spirit of an Amazon lady" (Cat., 81). Although it is Charles who supposedly allows Inglis to recover the "Amazon" spirit that she first mentions in her dedication to Prince Maurice of Nassau, the force of her image derives from herself rather than from him and once again runs up against the bounds of the female "shamefastness" that, as she reminds her dedicatees, fail to control her even as they remain somehow in place. To Sir Thomas Hayes, later Lord Mayor of London, she writes "avec la hardiesse plus que feminine," "with a more than feminine courage" (Cat. no. 31, 60); and to Susanna, Lady Herbert, Inglis declares that she has not worked all these years to hide her abilities: "No more have I payned myself many yearis to burie the talent god has geven me in oblivion" (Cat., 26). She also excuses her boldness in religious terms in a dedication addressed to Elizabeth in 1599, where she writes in one of the few French verses that she herself authored that "God's sacred spirit" "steadies, opens, redresses, illuminates, governs / My heart, my eye, my foot, my soul, and my hand."[84]

Inglis's principles, at once so modest and so supportive of her authority to produce her books, also inform the motto that accompanies her self-portraits (Figure 17): "De l'Eternal le bien, de Moi le mal ou rien"; "From the eternal [comes] goodness; from me, either evil or nothing." Frequently placed within her self-portrait as the text that the represented Inglis is writing, the motto becomes inextricable from the picture of herself seated or sometimes standing at a table with her pen in hand, an inkpot nearby. In the context of these emblematic self-portraits, her motto does not so much efface her agency as claim her central relation to God, a relation that is meant to explain how she comes to be sitting in a self-portrait, looking out from a book that she has fashioned with her own hands. That her religious motto exists to authorize her writing rather than the other way around became evident to me when, holding her books in my hands, I noticed that it is necessary to turn the book upside down in order to read the motto that she is writing. The viewer necessarily focuses first on Inglis's face surmounted by her hat and her hand holding the pen before turning the book in order to read her motto.

With its sheet music and lute back added to the pen and inkpot, this particular self-portrait, which appears with only slight variations in seven of her books,[85] places Inglis, consciously or unconsciously, in the tradition of those continental artists who used their self-portraits to emphasize their cultivated attainments in addition to painting and drawing. In this sense, Inglis's inclusion of music in her self-portraits claims the kind of well-rounded humanist education as the left side of Anne Clifford's commissioned *Great Picture*, with her young figure surrounded by sheet music, a lute, and her embroidery (see Figure 2). On the continent, Catherina van Hemessen's *Self-Portrait at the Spinet* (1548), Sofonisba Anguissola's *Self-Portrait at the Spinet with a Friend* (1563), and Lavinia Fontana's *Self-Portrait at the Spinet* (1579)[86] make similar claims, although each self-portrait's symbolism varies with its painter. Inglis does not possess the painterly technique and sophistication of these more eminent artists, but she is eager to place in circulation a complex representation of her identity as writer, artist, and woman. For her, the music and lute may be a reminder of the connection between her writing and her religious convictions, as in Puritan households, singing adaptations of Inglis's favorite text, the Psalms, was an everyday activity.

Inglis needed divine authorization of her female authorship not only because she had crossed traditional gender lines to act as a career scrivener and artist but also because her calligraphic speciality became the imitation of print,

Figure 17. Esther Inglis, self-portrait with motto "De l'Eternal le bien, de Moi le mal ou rien." Ink on paper. From *Le Livre de l'Ecclesiaste*. Add. MS 27927, f. 2, 1599. © British Library.

as her tiny books evolved into downscaled versions of the larger printed books produced by men working in collaboration with one another. By "tracing" the letters onto the page herself, as she herself described the act of writing, Inglis took over for the printing press. As Margreta de Grazia discusses, the early modern press was conceptualized as inherently masculine, possessing, for example, "a *Groove* . . . made to receive the *Tongue* of the *Male-Block.*"[87] Such sexualized language suggests ways to understand how printing as reproduction required a machine "made to function as a generational or reproductive system: made up of sexualized parts, it performed virtual copulative acts." Like the printing press, writes de Grazia, the parts of typefaces reveal an anthropomorphic vocabulary, with letters having "feet," "shoulders," and even a "face" and "body."[88] In copying and miniaturizing typefaces, often in a hand whose letters are less than a millimeter high (Cat., 55), Inglis adapted and used these forms of male textual reproduction. The first typefaces were copies of written hands,[89] and Inglis returns to print as her copy source not only to craft a book more valued because more preciously jeweled and miniature than a printed one but also to make print culture yet another aspect of the textual world with which she collaborates. In appropriating the masculine making of the book as object, Inglis had particular reason to articulate her position as woman writer both to herself and to her limited but influential audience of patrons.

Inglis's willingness to take on all aspects of the production of books for presentation—which may have sprung simply from her need to economize—amounts to a profound disruption of the usual male-controlled forms of textual production at the turn of the seventeenth century. Coterie manuscripts for the most part circulated in holographic form, often copied by a scrivener. Presentation books designed to elicit patronage were frequently the result of workshops, in which the labor was divided along the model of medieval book production, with calligraphers, limners, binders, and cover specialists. Similarly print culture divided the labor of textual production among writers, compositors, printers, engravers, and binder-booksellers. Although there were women printers and women from printing families, most women were widely separated from the production of books precisely because women were allowed—and in elite homes, encouraged—to study calligraphy or the writing of "hands." But "copying" as Inglis "copied" print by shrinking it, suggests the extent to which women's copying of texts and textiles mapped out new areas of agency within controlled norms. Inglis and other women calligraphers, embroiderers, translators, and poets who copied the work of males and also of one another, worked outward from approved domestic arts to the nonthreatening copying of others' texts through translation and calligraphy, toward seeking wider recognition for their work.

Figure 18. Esther Inglis, *Vive la Plume*. Ink drawing at the conclusion of calligraphic manuscript *Cinquante Octonaires sur la vanite et inconstance du monde*, dedicated to Henry, Prince of Wales, 1607. Windsor Castle, Royal Library. © 2009 Her Majesty Queen Elizabeth II.

As Inglis took upon herself the production of letters and the pages themselves, she entered the gendered territory of book production with a courage that becomes visible when she cheers herself on. She developed two emblems that read as both self-display and self-encouragement: "Vive la plume!" (Figure 18) shows the words beneath crossed pens, feathered and jeweled, encircled by a laurel wreath and surmounted by a crown, and "Nil Penna Sed Usus" ("Not the pen but the skill") runs on either side of crossed quill pens within a similar wreath and crown design.[90] These triumphant emblems not only serve as expressions of Inglis's facility with the pen and the skilled hand that holds it but also flout the gender conventions of pen, press, type, and the page itself. Wendy Wall points out that because pages are "pressed"—the term used to describe women during sexual intercourse—"Published texts are thus already gendered: The printed page is always a fallen woman because it is, by definition, highly public and common."[91] Inglis took control of masculinized type and feminized page alike, developing the iconography of her authorized subjectivity in self-portraits that feature herself holding a pen and writing as well as in her emblems of the pen. Through these drawings she claims both letter and page as a different kind of feminine territory—not weighed upon or pressed, but moral, readable, and bold.

Inglis did not stop at replicating and miniaturizing books and typeface, but at times she compounded her plays on print culture by heralding her books' titles within elaborate frames adapted from actual printed title pages. Inglis's able bibliographers, A. H. Scott-Elliot and Elspeth Yeo, explain that the title page of the *Livre des Pseaumes* "is a close copy of the title-page of Hero of

Alexandria's *De gli Automati* (Venice, 1589), published by Girolamo Porro" except that "the printer's rebus of the leek has been replaced by a Tudor rose" (Cat., 33); the title page for her *Emblemes* is a copy of the same Venetian title page. Following the title page is a half-length portrait of Inglis seated before an open book, a pen in her right hand, and herself writing her motto. Inglis's juxtaposition of a title page in ink made to replicate a printed title page followed by an "engraved" self-portrait, together with various commendatory verses of the author, reveals her using the visual effects of print culture to announce her own form of authorship. Of these visual effects Wendy Wall explains, "At the end of the [sixteenth] century, engraved title pages became more common. . . . During the medieval period, portraits of authors were placed on presentation copies, but in print these portraits were presented in the form of the title page, a feature that arose to accommodate the new desire to identify the text for a larger public" (*Imprint of Gender*, 73–74). Wall's example of the title pages of Samuel Daniel's *Delia and Rosamond* bears out her assertion—as does the Shakespeare First Folio—that although title pages could function as author portraits, they did not necessarily preclude a portrait printed in addition to a title page. Inglis appropriates this more elaborate convention of expensive printed books.

Not all of Inglis's self-portraits have this engraved appearance because few of her manuscripts strive to be entirely print-like. Many self-portraits following the title page in her tiniest manuscripts were executed in paints mixed in the jewel-like miniature style. David Laing, Inglis's primary nineteenth-century bibliographer, although very much her admirer, saw these self-portraits as betokening "no small degree of vanity"—"but," he points out, this was fruitless, for "it has happened in many instances that the metallic colours have turned black."[92] Actually, very few of the painted self-portraits have turned black. But the most elaborate of the portraits appear in the manuscripts that most closely approximate printed books, books executed in black ink, including the *Pseaumes* dedicated to Elizabeth in 1599 and the *Emblemes* dedicated to Prince Charles in 1624. Like the published male authors for whom the title page, writes Wendy Wall, "certainly demanded that the reader acknowledge the writer as a presence when mentally cataloging the text" (*Imprint of Gender*, 87), Inglis's title page and accompanying self-portrait and verses in praise of her pen required the recipients of her manuscripts to acknowledge their source. Her print-like title pages and self-portraits also serve the interests of manuscript patronage because reminding the dedicatee of the author's identity and authority amounts to a bill for services rendered.

Inglis asserts her authorship in its most material sense in her claim that her books should be placed among miniatures, those other small, richly produced

Chapter Two

objects so valued at court. She makes this claim because, unlike printed books, Inglis's books were classed—or she wished them to be classed—with miniature portraits and emblematic jewels, as tiny treasures to be kept in the possessor's inner sanctum. In her dedication to Elizabeth of *Le Livre des Pseaumes*, Inglis expresses the hope that "this little present, written by my hand, in a foreign land, might obtain a place in some retired corner of your cabinet,"[93] the realm of miniatures. She tells Charles that she hopes her book is destined for "sum retired place in your Highnesse Cabinet" (Cat. no. 36, my transcription). Miniatures, as Patricia Fumerton has pointed out, tended to be "love tokens—presented as gifts to cherished intimates" and therefore conventionally kept in a cabinet located in the closet or bedchamber, in the most private of rooms but also the most political.[94] Inglis's expressed desire to have her jewel-like, miniature volumes included among the precious objects to be found in Elizabeth's and Charles's cabinets asks her royal dedicatees to treat her presentation volumes as one would an intimate gift. This request was not entirely out of line, as other objects that passed from artisan to patron, like the subsidized "gifts" of Levina Teerlinc, found a place among Elizabeth's private possessions.

The small size of Inglis's books was only part of their claim to the status of miniature and precious object. Inglis produced their jewel-like covers, for royals usually embroidered with seed pearls, and gold and silver thread on red velvet like the cover design of flowers in a vase of Plate 8. Inglis's covers complement her books' interior display of elaborate calligraphic hands, title pages, self-portraits, limned ornaments, ink drawings resembling blackwork, and emblems. Still another, larger embroidered cover, Inglis's translation of the psalms dedicated to Elizabeth, features an elaborately embroidered cover on crimson velvet. A Tudor rose and crown are decorated with pearls as well as silver and gilt thread, with much of the pattern "couched," or padded beneath, to create a raised effect on which her designs rest, worked in elongated satin stitch, so called because its use allowed the silk thread to shine. Through these devices, the book announces itself as the gift to and possession of a sovereign, a one-of-a-kind jewel that anticipates the rage for embroidered "raised work" later in the seventeenth century. In still other Inglis books that include colored miniatures of King David, for example, jewels had to be ground to produce the colors. Ann Rosalind Jones and Peter Stallybrass point out in *Renaissance Clothing and the Materials of Memory* that because of this practice, "A miniature was simultaneously a painting and a jewel."[95] Inglis's assemblies of written and visual texts present themselves as miniatures meant to be treasured as jewels, books with an elaborate form that qualifies them for patronage by resembling courtly gifts. On the outside, they glitter with small seed pearls and embroidery in gold, silver, and colored silk; on the inside, they are miniature inked drawings resembling blackwork embroidery patterns, colored drawings of flowers or limnings, and Inglis's perfectly even and varied calligraphic texts. As a publishing author in her own particular sense, Inglis capitalized on the tension between manuscript and print conventions, calling attention to the small spaces occupied by her miniature versions of the book.

The particulars of Inglis's books as manuscripts and as appropriations of print culture reveal a woman who not only used her skills to make the books that could ensure her family's social position but also augured the extent to which a few women in the late sixteenth century and hundreds of women in the seventeenth century undertook to commodify their writing. Aside from the notable exceptions of Isabella Whitney and Elizabeth I, Ane Locke and Anne Dowriche, few English or Scottish women saw their poetry in print before the seventeenth century. In a society in which acceptable women's endeavors involved the collaborative yet creative work called copying, Inglis carefully but nevertheless radically rewrote the activities of female copyist to become a self-published author. Within her books the interplay of borrowed materials and invented forms lays claim to her authority as author, from her title pages copied from printed books to her willingness to transcend the boundaries of "shame-fastness" in order to re-form her culture's masculinized press. In Inglis's books, the feminized page becomes infused with her Amazonian spirit. Her dedications, her self-portraits, and her emblems celebrating both her pen and her skill assert her awareness that she challenged normative conceptions of the feminine and further suggest that she enjoyed her self-conceived role.

Inglis inhabited a space in the system of patronage that had been occupied in Western Europe by a few women writers, scriveners, and artists like Christine de Pizan and Levina Teerlinc, as well as Inglis's own mother. Compared to her mother and to many of the women involved professionally in calligraphy and its associated forms of pen-and-ink drawing, Esther Inglis moved in higher circles and created a public role for herself as a writer of her own books. These books were cherished and passed on to us in large numbers despite the ease with which these small objects might have been misplaced, a tribute to the fact that many of them have been treasured in safe and private places for centuries. Inglis did not achieve Christine's move beyond the mechanics of writing to intellectual engagement with male authors of the caliber of Boccaccio, Jean de Meun, or Dante;[96] nor did she attain fame as an inventive translator and poet as Jane Segar strove to do. Inglis also failed to achieve Susanna Horenbout's or Levina Teerlinc's social mobility within the structure of the court. As a scrivener for James VI, Inglis doubtless received undocumented forms of support, including court lodging, wages, clothing, or other items either useable or saleable. But on the whole she occupied a more tenuous position at the periphery of the courts of James, Anne of Denmark, and Prince Henry and in the Essex and Sidney circles than did her artisan predecessors.

In many ways isolated from other writing women, Esther Inglis is nevertheless part of a tradition of women who created calligraphic manuscripts within carefully produced covers, including Christine de Pizan, the young Elizabeth Tudor, Mary Stuart, Levina Teerlinc, and Jane Segar. Moreover, in seeking to authorize herself as a writer within developing print conventions, Inglis's self-assertion corresponds to the growing sense among the women who followed, such as Mary Sidney Wroth, Elizabeth Cary, Amelia Lanyer, Bathsua Makin, Anne Bradstreet, Aphra Behn, Katherine Phillips, Margaret Cavendish, and Anne Finch, that writing was a reasonable and therefore defensible female activity. As Inglis's miniature manuscripts reassign masculine forms of textual reproduction to her own forms of book publication and authorship, they make a compelling verbal and visual argument that women should be able to make a living by wielding the power of brush, needle, and pen.

CHAPTER THREE

Sewing Connections: Narratives of Agency
in Women's Domestic Needlework

Levina Teerlinc, Jane Segar, and Esther Inglis simultaneously lived within and altered their society's expectations of women's roles as they used their rare abilities to make objects for powerful patrons. This chapter on domestic needlework[1] and its related texts describes how women in the household continuously shaped their environment by creating objects that expressed their always-evolving identities. To adapt what Michel de Certeau writes of the colonized, women were able to use "the dominant social order" in ways that "deflected its power, which they lacked the means to challenge." By engaging in expected practices that nevertheless explored and partially reset the parameters of their existence, "they escaped it without leaving it."[2] From maintaining a commonplace set of patterns called a *spot sampler*, to using new genres of needlework that altered masculinist print culture, English domestic needleworkers challenged the "dominant social order" even as they obeyed the injunction to sew.

Women from a variety of backgrounds created needlework pieces that placed accepted subjects in every room, that helped to clothe themselves and their families, and that declared the family's social status, even as they may be read as personal and political expressions. Far from being merely decorative, even the simplest needlework patterns, like that of the ubiquitous strawberry, embodied ways of seeing the world, as I discuss in Chapter 4 on textiles in *Othello* and *Cymbeline*. Women's needlework transported the narratives of women from the classical and biblical past into the early modern household, and women from their households into the mix of contemporary events. Throughout the sixteenth century, royal women and members of the aristocracy and upper merchant classes embroidered the Women Worthies who captured their imagination, usually with the help of retainers who transferred engravings to cloth. We have also seen that still other privileged women, like Lady Grace Mildmay, drew their own designs.[3] The inhabitants of the seventeenth century witnessed profound economic and material changes that encouraged the spread of skilled needlework. As economic historian Keith Wrightson points out, early modern people themselves noted "major changes in the structures of economic life."[4] These enabled a rapid rise in printshop sales of books, ballads, and printed pictures of the sort that draftsmen could transfer to cloth for domestic needleworkers. Women of the middling classes began seizing the opportunity to create objects emulating the professional needlework, lace, and carpets of the more privileged, adding to their family's household store while exploring the same narratives that titled women like Mary Stuart and Bess of Hardwick had worked in the second half of the sixteenth century.

In order to examine women's domestic embroidery in this chapter, I discuss the three forms of needlework that the early modern English called *samplers*: the spot sampler, the band sampler, and the needlework picture. The first section of this chapter introduces the personal and political relations between the sampler and women's agency. The next section locates embroidery within everyday household practice, in which the spot sampler's scattered patterns and stitches were acquired from relatives, as well as mistresses, skilled serving women, and other members of one's circle. The third section focuses on the emergence and practice of a new genre of needlework, the band sampler. The band sampler is the most familiar, formalized genre of needlework, one that remained current for at least three hundred years. Its conventions date from the 1630s and 1640s,[5] the same period when the publication of prints, pamphlets, and books was rapidly increasing. The majority of this chapter examines the third type of needlework that in the early modern period was also called *samplers*, embroidered pictures usually deriving from prints but turned into an expressive art form through the choices that women made. To discuss embroidered pictures I consider first how the choice of working David and Bathsheba, Susannah and the Elders, Sarah and Hagar, and the Judgment of Solomon registers contemporary questions concerning marriage, jointure, and childbearing. Second, I discuss the most popular subject for needlework pictures, Queen Esther, as an authorizing exemplar for women in both thread and print. As needleworkers selected the subjects and narratives of their embroidery, they chose the same biblical women that authors evoked as exemplars in the ongoing debate on the nature of women, also known as the *querelle des femmes*.

Considering the ways in which Esther's speech is necessary to redeem the Jewish people leads me to examine the extent to which Esther, Deborah, and

Judith authorized not only needleworkers but also psalmists from Elizabeth I to Anne Finch. In the final section I examine what appears to have been the second-most popular needlework subject, the beautiful and violent Judith, who, like Deborah in the canonical Bible, composes and declaims a psalm of victory, and who—together with her fellow headhunter, Jael—typifies a resolute, active female will.

In *Renaissance Clothing and the Materials of Memory*, Ann Rosalind Jones and Peter Stallybrass demonstrate that through needlework, women "could record and commemorate their participation not in reclusive domestic activity but in the larger public world."[6] By crediting needlework as a category of evidence beyond the binaries of public and private, they invite us to read needlework pictures not only as a practice in the home but also as one that opens outward to other connections. In this chapter, I build on this insight by considering the extent to which needlework, so often signed, initialed, or otherwise distinguished as the work of a particular hand, registers the subjectivity of individual women within local and familial systems, as well as within national contexts.[7] Most of these contexts tended to limit women's education and ability to take action, but within these limits, women chose to work an Esther, a Charles I or II, a Henrietta Maria, a Catherine of Braganza, or a Judith, and those decisions record the agency of an individual subject as well as those of a group. A woman's embroidery of biblical Women Worthies allowed her to express connections with female exemplars known for their personal virtue and beauty, as well as for adventures marked by eroticism and violence, all within the socially sanctioned activity of sewing.

Samplers and Women's Agencies

Although the scholarship on samplers focuses on the spot and band sampler, the word *sampler* was used during the early modern period to refer to any needleworked picture, usually with the understanding that its embroiderer had chosen its subject for a reason. The first recognized use of the word *sampler* in English occurs in John Skelton's description of an embroidered Phyllyp Sparowe. At times an overtly erotic poem, "Phyllyp Sparowe" (1505? first printed 1545) also suggests how a sampler at the beginning of the sixteenth century offered a way for the poem's speaker, Jane Scrope, to memorialize the dead:

> I toke my sampler ones
> Of purpose, for the nones,
> To sowe with stytchis of sylke
> My sparow whyte as mylke,

That by representacyon
Of his image and facyon,
To me it myght importe
Some pleasure and comforte.[8]

Although this literary example must be read with care, connecting as it does the sparrow, the needle, and Jane Scrope's female body, Skelton's use of the term "sampler" acknowledges needlework's memorializing function as well as its intimate connections with the emotions of the embroiderer who seeks "Some pleasure and comforte." The second act of Shakespeare's *Titus Andronicus* makes similar claims about the ability of women to sew emotion and narrative into their samplers. When Lavinia enters with her tongue and hands cut off, her Uncle Marcus compares her to "Fair Philomel" who "but lost her tongue" but still "in a tedious [i.e., carefully wrought] sampler sewed her mind." Although the modern audience member may concentrate on Lavinia's inability to *write* "her mind," compared to her predecessor, Philomel, the horror of Lavinia's amputated hands is that she cannot *sew* her narrative.[9] As I discuss further in the next chapter, in masculinist literary and visual traditions, sewing tends to be conflated with women's sexuality. Nevertheless, as in these passages from Skelton and Shakespeare from either end of the sixteenth century, it is possible to glimpse the early modern perception that a woman used her sampler to tell stories of explicitly personal relevance—that "by representacyon" she "sewed her mind."

Using *sampler* to denote a "needlework picture" continued in the seventeenth century. Elizabeth Isham, a writer, artist, herbalist, and head of household in Northamptonshire, left two detailed descriptions of her childhood education, which featured a mix of reading, writing, and needlework. Isham wrote of her activities at four or five years of age, about 1614, that she was already making samplers in the sense of needlework pictures: "I wrought two samplers" after finishing "another sampler of trutsch [true stitch] one which I took out [i.e., copied] myself."[10] True stitch is a kind of embroidery exactly alike on both sides of the backing, exercised with a moral sense that it is "true" because there is no rough, hidden underside of the embroidery. Working an entire sampler in this single stitch would have been a demanding project even for an experienced needleworker, but Isham's account suggests that even as a young girl she was an accomplished embroiderer. In 1631, Henry Chettle's description of his character Lucibella in *The Tragedy of Hoffman* includes a picture sampler of an emblem worked "All true stitch by my troth," of "heart in hand, and true loves knots" with the posy, "No flight dear love but death, shall sever us." At mid-seventeenth century, Nicholas Hookes memorialized

Mrs. A. Mors of Kings Lynn using the word *samplers* to connect a variety of needlework pictures that she had worked. According to Hookes, in addition to classical subjects, she "did make all *beasts fowle fish* and *men*, / As though she'd *work* th'Creation o're agen." She even "*wrought* the starres into a *Canopie* / And in her *Samplers* taught *Astrologie* [Astronomy]" where "*Tycho* might have read new *Lectures* there."[11] Hookes's description reveals another aspect of needlework valued beyond its economic importance: its ability to miniaturize the larger world, to "*work* th'Creation o're agen," and, in doing so, to contain a scientific lecture on astronomy, presumably on the alignment of the planets. As Jessica Wolfe points out, the fascinations of miniaturization are related to early scientific ways of measuring and perceiving data, especially to miniature machines such as watches. Like them, Mrs. Mors's samplers were capable of "condensing the text into a smaller physical space in order to allow it to occupy a larger symbolic space."[12]

How might needleworkers themselves have conceptualized what they were doing when they worked a pictorial sampler? One answer lies in the word *sampler* itself, because its root, *exemplaris*, is the same as "examplar," "exemplum," and "example" (OED). Randle Cotgrave's *Dictionarie of the French and English Tongues* (1611) defines an "exemplaire" in terms that show how "sampler" was still a synonym for "exemplar" in the early modern period: "A patterne, sample, or sampler," "an example" "for others to follow, or to take heed by" as well as "the copie, or counterpane of a writing."[13] To work a sampler in the sense of a needlework picture was to experience the narrative as an example, not simply but complexly, in the tradition of Boccaccio's use of the exemplum as an opportunity for "moral reflection."[14]

Jasper Mayne's *The City Match* (1639) lightly mocks a particular genre of the pictorial sampler, the biblical picture adapted from print sources. This kind of sampler became popular in the 1630s and remained so until about 1690. In *The City Match*, Mayne's witty, duel-fighting heroine, Aurelia, calls such pictures "Hebrew samplers."[15] In the sixteenth century, royal and aristocratic women had worked pictures with Old Testament themes, such as the *Sacrifice of Isaac* long cushion at New Hardwick Hall. What was new was the number of girls and women of the middling classes who adapted engravings and woodcuts for their needlework. Seventeenth-century needleworkers embroidered their Hebrew samplers for some of the same purposes that courtiers and professional embroiderers had, to make bed testers and cushion covers. But in large numbers they further adapted biblical subjects for book covers, small cabinets, and mirror frames for middling-class households. These Hebrew samplers offer the opportunity to consider how early modern women may have experienced the

Chapter Three

narratives of female agency available to them in the scriptures.[16] By embroidering Jewish female figures whom they simultaneously considered to be historical women and representatives of themselves, early modern needleworkers found reservoirs of significance within even brief biblical passages that they had read or heard read repeatedly, that were enlarged on in sermons, and that they discussed among themselves.

In the seventeenth century, many English women, whether royalists or nonconformists, followed the religious practice that N. H. Keeble describes of taking biblical narratives "as symbolic anticipations of the individual's personal experience" as well as "allegorical representations of the general experience of saints, sinners and nations. It had happened to *Israel* as it happens to Christianity, and to all Christians."[17] Elizabeth Isham recorded in her *Book of Remembrance*, how, raised in a family that owned religious books with generations of annotation, she became fascinated with the history of the Jews. About 1620, Isham asked her grandmother "whether we were Jews or not." Her grandmother answered by quoting "the 11 Chapter to the Romans where is showed" that "we are the Israel of God, gal [Galicians] 6.16." Although Isham only reports working one biblical subject, "my silken Adam and Eve," she went on to study the Jews, noting that "after I stitched a handkerchief I read in a book of diverse nations especially of the Jews," and that she read a book of "the Jews' customs."[18] Through the genre of the Hebrew sampler, whose specific narratives I discuss later in this chapter, seventeenth-century needleworkers brought Jewish historical women into their own time and place through the immediacy of embroidered pictures.

Needleworkers embroidered cloth with designs drawn on them that usually derived from prints. The most popular source for Hebrew samplers was the prints designed by Gerard de Jode,[19] but the basic composition of the story was only the beginning. Needleworkers often changed these prints by dressing their figures in contemporary clothes or by changing their hairstyles for a more contemporary look. Sometimes only props, like exotic umbrellas, suggest the Middle East, while a Solomon or an Ahasueras may be worked to resemble a Stuart king, identifiable through the wig and facial hair.[20] In first choosing and then updating such biblical narratives, needleworkers crossed their society's always permeable line between historical Jew and contemporary Christian to create representations of their lives and their engagement with politics. Before I discuss the possible significance of the most popular needlework pictures for their makers, however, it would be useful to situate their creation within the everyday practice of needlework and that most essential of needlework genres, the spot sampler.

In order to prepare to work the varied stitches required for both repeated patterns and embroidered pictures, early modern needleworkers maintained a spot sampler, a kind of visual commonplace book.[21] As an example "for others to follow" (Cotgrave's *Dictionarie*), this kind of sampler functioned as a reminder of how to perform the stitches needed to create complex patterns, from the ubiquitous fertile vine patterns of the strawberry, grape, and peasecod, to more particularly familial designs, like an animal associated with the family name. Some women, like Grace Mildmay and Elizabeth Isham, who enjoyed drawing and counting out their own designs, could have used the spot sampler as a testing ground for a new design that would then cover an entire cushion, a linen shirt, a bed cap, a waistcoat, or a jacket.

The oldest known English spot sampler demonstrates how it recorded stitches and patterns that could be used throughout a lifetime and then passed to female kin. This sampler, embroidered in a variety of stitches, including buttonhole, detached buttonhole, chain, satin, ladder, back stitch, and cross stitch, with beadwork and French knots contains the brief written message "JANE BOSTOCKE 1598 / ALICE LEE WAS BORNE THE 23 OF NOVEMBER: BE / ING TUESDAY IN THE AFTERNOONE: 1596" (Plate 9). This message links Jane Bostocke's claim to her identity[22] as a distinct and single subject with her identity as related to Alice Lee, especially since "Jane Bostocke" is partially outlined in seed pearls, suggesting that the sampler was a gift. Pamela Clabburn reports the recent finding that Jane Bostocke and Alice Lee were distantly related, being third- and fourth-generation descendants of Robert Corbet and Elisabeth Vernon of Shropshire. Jane Bostocke, who never married, lived a distant fifty miles from Alice Lee. But because Jane Bostocke was buried in Alice's village, it seems probable that Bostocke visited the Lee family, perhaps more than once. Some of the designs in the Bostocke sampler have been unpicked, and those, Clabburn notes, "appear to be of a castle on an elephant, a squirrel cracking a nut and a raven"—designs relating only to Bostocke's side of the family. The designs left intact are crests of the Lee and Corbet families that Jane and Alice had in common: "a talbot, a deer and a lion." Jane Bostocke's legacy to Alice Lee, then, was a spot sampler that included badges of familial connection as well as patterns in blackwork and colored silks, including two strawberry patterns and lovers' knots that may also have been part of family tradition. In passing on her spot sampler to the next generation, Bostocke passed on examples for Alice's own needlework, a register of female alliance.[23] Only a few early modern spot samplers survive from the British Isles, but these ubiquitous objects were once the principle means to remember not only the most practical elements of embroidery but also the tiny stitches and larger patterns that located girls and women within extended networks of affiliation. Because of their value to successive generations, spot samplers were often included in wills.[24] The *Oxford English Dictionary*'s entry for *sampler* dated 1546 is from a will whose wording suggests a spot sampler: "I give to Alyson Pynchebeck my sampler with seams"; that is, my sampler with examples of patterns.[25]

The finished needlework pieces that spot samplers made possible were usually performed with other women. John Skelton's "XXI Garlande or Chapelet of Laurell" describes the women who make his "cronell of lawrell" as talking among themselves as they "enbrowder" it, "With, 'Reche me that skane of tewly sylk'; / And, 'Wynde me that botowme of such an hew', / Grene, rede, tawny, whyte, purpill, and blew."[26] Women's life writing a century later does not provide detailed conversations, but Margaret Hoby, Anne Clifford, and Elizabeth Isham are still the best sources for descriptions that help us to envision the domestic context of early modern English needlework. Lady Hoby, a wealthy landholder and head of household who was also the widow of the Earl of Essex's younger brother, records in her diary from the turn of the seventeenth century that she performed needlework nearly every day. One day she "wrought til 6"; another, after eating breakfast, "I wrought and read of the bible til dinner time: after, I wrought, and did my duty in the house." Hoby must usually have worked with her maids, even though she notes only twice that "I went and wrought with my Maids til almost night." While she sewed, she often listened to books read aloud to her. Although Hoby is not often given to detail, she records being read to while she embroiders in over twenty entries of her diary, with readings from Fox's *Book of Martyrs*, Timothy Bright's *Melancholy*, Hugh Latimer's *Sermons*, and, a particular favorite, Richard Greenham's *Workes*, four volumes of Puritan sermons.[27]

In her Knole diary of 1603–19, Anne Clifford records frequently performing needlework, which she embroidered in the company of both kinswomen and maids. Usually, like Hoby, she assumes the presence of those working with her, but in writing with relief at having finished "the long cushion of Irish stitch which my Coz. Cecily Nevil began when she went with me to the Bath,"[28] Clifford recalls sewing with a favorite cousin, daughter of her aunt Elizabeth, Countess of Bath, with whom she and her mother had frequently stayed when she was growing up.[29] The cushion that Clifford finished was probably multicolored, because "Irish stitch," later called *flame stitch*, a variant of Florentine work or Bargello, uses a series of straight stitches to produce a geometric pattern of zigzags in colored silks that shade into one another, as in the example of a seventeenth-century pincushion in Figure 19. Although geometric, the stitch has its associations with the natural world because of its gradations of color. At the

Figure 19. Martha Edin, pincushion in Irish stitch (also called *flame stitch*) from the contents of her embroidered cabinet, c. 1670–80. T. 446-1990. © the Board of Trustees of the Victoria and Albert Museum.

end of the seventeenth century, John Aubrey described the overview of the Bacons' garden at Gorhamby as "resembling the works in Irish-stitch."[30] Clifford may have been particularly fond of the look that it produced and was probably working a set of matching cushions, as another entry, made when her husband had sent her down to Knole, explains that in her grief and anger "at this time I wrought very hard & made an end of one of my cushions of Irish stitch work." For the formidable Lady Anne Clifford, needlework was clearly not so much about the pictures, as it had been for Bess of Hardwick and Mary

Chapter Three

Queen of Scots in the generation before her. Instead, she seems to have executed a repeated needlework pattern in order to produce matching cushions, at the beginning of the rage for "unified suites of furnishings" for domestic interiors. Like Hoby, Clifford sometimes specifies what was read to the needleworkers, from a more worldly library than Hoby's: "Montaigne's Essays," for example, "the Fairy Queene," "the History of the Netherlands" or "Ovid's *Metamorphoses.*"[31]

Elizabeth Isham, living in Northamptonshire, the daughter of a Justice of the Peace knighted by James I and later made first baronet, listened to both religious and more secular books while working, including "Ovid's *Metamorphoses,*" "Sandys travels of the holy land," and "God's revenge against Murther" as well as the Bible and religious works.[32] She worked in company with the household's maids as well as with her beloved sister, Judith, who disliked needlework and was only willing to learn it from Elizabeth (Isham, 10, 24, 36). Isham also mentions how the girls and women of her household "used to repeat one to another as we sat at work, those things which we can remember that was remarkable or might edify" (60). From her self-description, Elizabeth Isham was a gifted artist, who later painted watercolors and portraits, "pictures of some folks whom I loved" (39, 74), noting at one point in her *Remembrance* that she preferred visual media to verbal, since "I have ever found the golden chain of Eloquence to be more attractive to draw" (93). Isham enjoyed inventing her own designs for needlework, so much so that she questioned whether she should feel guilty about the pleasure she took in her ability (57, 78, 83) and upbraids herself because her "working" often keeps her from visiting neighbors or family as she ought (61, 73). She records "inventing" and working designs on handkerchiefs, a coit (head covering), and other clothing, a purse for her brother and a purse, cap, and watchcase for her father (29, 46, 78). She also spun wool and flax, mended, knitted gloves and hose, and made cutwork and other forms of lace as well as the complexly knotted and braided cording that she called "breadwork" (braidwork) and "bandstring," used for purse strings, to lace up clothing, tie back curtains, and suspend bed testers.[33] She gave to the poor what she saved by working, and took comfort that "I could diverse ways work to get by and I thought to keep me or give me content" (64).

Isham's most ambitious needlework project, described at several points in her *Remembrance*, was a series of flowers and herbs that she drew from samples she had gathered, a precursor of her interest in practicing medicine as an herbalist. She justified this work, which consumed her, by noting that "as Solomon made for his delight gardens or orchards eccl 2.5, so in my work I made the shadow of these things & I diverse times thought to make my heart rejoice in the things which I had made" (83). She "delighted" in them because "I had devised such verity in little things that I might long look & still entertain my eyes with new objects which I did near to the life neither had I ever seen the like" (83). She found justification for her pleasure in Solomon's gardens as well as in the virtue of God's own "works": "I thought there was not true beauty which did not foreshow some virtue in it" (74). Isham began this journey into the visual arts when she learned "my work being taught by my mother's waiting woman" (18). She took to it quickly, learning all her teacher's stitches and designs. Her explanation, that "I know not what genius led me to love it so well that I took forth patterns of all" (18), strongly suggests that her lifelong interest in needlework began as she recorded all of her teacher's patterns in her first spot sampler.

Without spot samplers, supplemented by needlework patterns in print and manuscript, and manuscripts like Thomas Trevelyon's miscellany that copied printed sources,[34] these intense sessions of needlework would have been impossible. Even for talented artists like Elizabeth Isham, spot samplers provided the stitches and patterns that women shared with the relatives and other household members who wrought with her. As a result, spot samplers, together with the skilled objects that they helped make possible, manifest lifetimes of connection among women.

Band Samplers

The carefully organized work that we usually connect with the term *sampler*, the band sampler, with its alphabet, stitches, and patterns proving a young girl's proficiency in the basics of needlework, first appears in the 1630s and 1640s, becoming common by mid-century.[35] The rise of the band sampler occurred as more families engaged in what Keith Wrightson calls "the multifarious activities spawned by London's role as England's leading centre of manufactures, premier trading city, largest consumer market, and the hub of internal commerce."[36] During this time, pressure was growing for women in ambitious households to furnish their homes in ways that imitated the interiors of the elite. Living lives at once more luxurious and more self-consciously Protestant also meant that more members of the household needed to read and, very often, to write as well. As Catherine Richardson summarizes the shift in household practice that accompanied these seventeenth-century changes, "Social transformation was given a dynamic energy amongst those who filled the wide space between the landed elite and the poor, and this focused attention on the extent to which they attempted to emulate the cultural practices of their superiors."[37] At a time when textiles were the principle markers of class, upwardly mobile families in particular required contributions to the family store that skilled forms of domestic needlework could help provide, accompanied by a correspondent accumulation of plate, joined furniture, linens, clothing, perhaps some tapestries but certainly painted cloths, and a variety of accessories.

Skilled needleworkers were valued at this time, when luxury goods were not only expensive but difficult to find. At the end of Elizabeth's reign, Robert Sidney, then Governor of Flushing, had to employ an agent on the continent to hunt down lace and tapestries for purchase. For the middling-class household of the seventeenth century, women's domestic needlework supplied basics like hemmed sheets, clothing for children, and the smocks and shirts that doubled as underclothing and nightwear, while their finer knotting and needlework approximated rare, professionally produced turkey carpets, tapestries, embroidered clothing, gloves, book covers, and the hangings required for walls and beds. At the beginning of the century, cushions for benches and stools were a necessity before upholstered furniture became common.[38] The textiles that clothed the early modern interior, like the clothing and accessories people wore in the exterior world, demonstrated family status. During the seventeenth century, the greater number of families seeking social mobility translated into an urgent need to produce markers of privilege. As a result, the woman who could turn out luxury items for the price of a piece of linen and a quantity of silk thread was a valued member of her family and community.

Until the end of the seventeenth century, performing fine needlework was far more than a decorative act used to fill idle hours. Although privileged women had leisure time that they filled with a variety of pursuits, including reading, writing, teaching, religious practice, gardening, preserving, riding in coaches, playing cards and gambling, as well as walking, playing musical instruments, singing, and dancing, the fear of women's idleness, with its resulting temptations, haunts writings by and about women throughout the early modern period. This deep anxiety about women's leisure, which many people in the twenty-first century have inherited, has obscured the recognition that early modern embroiderers were producers of texts and artwork, even as textiles around the globe, including the American quilt, have been widely affirmed as complex artistic expressions. To some extent, the tendency to equate early modern needlework with the "leisure" of privileged women is a holdover—and a misreading—of Thorsten Veblen's popular analysis of leisure in *The Theory of the Leisure Class* (1899). Veblen, like Friedrich Engels before him, argued for the importance of women's work but objected to the upper-class "household cares" of a "ceremonial character" because "the pervading principle and abiding test of good breeding is the requirement of a substantial and patent waste of time."[39] Veblen's critique of elite Americans at the turn of the twentieth century not only gained currency but, curiously, continues to exist alongside the more recent recognition that ceremonial activity is socially significant. Household needlework in the early modern period was not a mark of leisure but was accepted proof that hands were not up to mischief, a fear expressed by Margaret Hoby, who noted in 1600 that "I was busy about needful things as prevented temptation, yet was not Curious, til Mr Hoby Came home, I was not Idle." In 1677–78, Anne Halkett remembered of her childhood education that, in addition to retaining masters to teach her reading, writing, French, music, and dancing, her mother "kept a Gentlewoman to teach us all kinds of Needlework, which shows I was not brought up in an Idle Life."[40]

The period when fine domestic needlework was central to a family's worth did eventually come to an end. By the mid- to late seventeenth century, an influx of relatively cheap luxury textiles from Europe, India, and the Middle East resulted in a gradual decrease in the demand for domestic needlework.[41] As the demand for needlework decreased, so too did its value. As increasing numbers of families readily purchased the items that women had once produced with skill and effort, the memory of *why* women had filled their homes with needlework faded, even as skilled sewing continued to be equated with the feminine. Once the economic and social motivations for domestic embroidery were forgotten, the hard work of previous generations became a way to criticize the habits of eighteenth-century women. Looking back from 1716 to that earlier time, Thomas Tickell assumed the nostalgic voice of an "elderly aunt" in *The Spectator* (No. 606). This "aunt" bemoans the shift from her generation's virtuous habits to the pleasure-seeking of her young nieces: "Those hours which in this age are thrown away in Dress, Play, Visits and the like, were employed in my time, in writing out Receipts, working Beds, Chairs and Hangings for the Family." As a result, "It grieves my Heart to see a couple of idle flirts sipping their Tea, for a whole Afternoon, in a Room hung round with the Industry of their Grandmother."[42]

But a hundred years earlier than this lament, English families felt the need for domestically produced, highly finished needlework. As a result, the demand for printed advice on how to produce it grew steadily, and girls included patterns from these sources in their band samplers. The earliest pattern book in English was published in 1530 in Antwerp as W. Vosterman's *A new treatise as concerning the excellency of the needle work spanishe stitches and weaving in the frame*. These and other books remained rare in the British Isles until the seventeenth century. With the development of print culture and the economic shift that supported the increase in numbers of pattern books, writes Liz Arthur, "In England between the 1620s and the end of the century more than 150 books of needlework patterns were published."[43]

One pattern book that went through three editions, John Taylor's *The Nee-*

dles Excellency (1631, 1634, 1640),[44] was published to take economic advantage of the fact that although women had no choice but to sew, within that cultural imperative, they could make many choices. Books like this purveyed novel patterns to supplement household traditions, as well as offering upstart households a way to enter established networks of production. Like the receipt books whose titles offered to transfer domestic knowledge from some privileged cabinet to one's own, including *The Queens Closet Opened: Incomparable Secrets in Physick, Chirurgery, Preserving, Candying, and Cookery* (1655),[45] *The Needles Excellency* offered women access to an expertise they could share with the titled needleworkers of previous generations. Taylor's introductory sonnets on the needlework of Catherine of Aragon, Mary and Elizabeth Tudor, Mary Sidney Herbert, and the less well known Lady Elizabeth Dormer[46] offer an imaginary connection to the opulent world of royals and their courtiers afforded by skilled needlework. This fantasy of connection to elite needleworkers was marketed to women despite the fact that during the seventeenth century fine needlework was moving down the social scale instead of up, as the wealthiest women increasingly paid embroidery professionals to create gifts, clothing, and larger household items.

Social mobility was only one of the possibilities that Taylor was selling in his pattern book. Even as he suggests that sewing makes women less likely to talk—when in fact sewing offered groups of women the opportunity to talk, sing, and tell stories—Taylor inserts himself into the community of women who pass knowledge among themselves, claiming that his pattern book participates in the female alliances through which needlework patterns were exchanged and sewing produced. His prefatory materials include a poem, "The Praise of the Needle," which catalogs the various stitches, including "Tent-worke[,] Raisd-worke, Laid worke, Frost-worke, Net-worke" (A4), although his book offers patterns, not individual stitches, which his readers would have had to learn from another woman. Yet Taylor claims that learning patterns from his book is like learning them in a household:

So Maids may (from their Mistresse, or their Mother)
Learne to leave one worke, and to learne another.
For here they may make choyce of which is which,
And skip from worke to worke, from stitch to stitch. (A2(v))

Taylor emphasizes women's choice of tasks, and that movement from one to the next made them seem lighter. As he continues, in needlework "Practice and Invention may be free, / And as a Squirrel, skips from tree to tree" (A2(v)). Although Taylor's book could not begin to replace the expertise of a mother, mistress, or skilled serving woman, his emphasis on the ways in which pattern books expanded the needleworker's "choyce" was valid. His emphasis on "Invention" is echoed in Elizabeth Isham's language from the same period, as when she thanks God "for thy unspeakable gift concerning my desire inventing things to work" (Isham, 85).

In making available a variety of needlework patterns, books like Taylor's supplemented the spot and band sampler while making possible another form of intergenerational alliance among women through the ownership of pattern books. Like published and manuscript receipt books, pattern books acquired by one generation were used two and even three generations later. This intragenerational ownership of books explains why so few printed pattern books are extant and why those that remain are heavily cut up, like those in Britain's National Art Library. Rozsika Parker demonstrates that Sarah Wilkinson's sampler of 1699 incorporates the stock male and female couple that derive from Richard Shorleyker's *Scholehouse of the Needle*, first published in 1624, seventy-five years earlier.[47] In spite of—and perhaps because of—the religious, economic, and political volatility of this period, women's needlework remained a continuous, culturally centralized tradition that proceeded by folding new households into its practice. New developments did spread, including techniques like raised work,[48] and crewel patterns worked in chain stitch. The flame stitch, or "Irish stitch," worked by Anne Clifford, Countess of Dorset, in the first decade of the seventeenth century was being used by middling-class women to cover fire screens in the first half of the eighteenth century.[49]

As part of its movement across class, needlework was increasingly touted as the means to earn a living for the woman without other financial resources. A verse frequently reproduced in band samplers announced as early as the late seventeenth century that its maker learns "both art and skill / To Get my Living with My Hands / That so I might be free from Band / And My Own Dame that I may be / And free from all such slavery." One hundred and fifty years later— and in spite of Mary Lamb's essay "On Needle-work," published in 1815, pointing out the low wages paid to women—this same verse appears in Jane Curtis's sampler of 1827, demonstrating how enduring was the hope of economic independence through "art and skill."[50] Unfortunately, the verse remained optimistic in the face of the low sums paid women who sewed for wages as their principal means of support. Women might well have earned a better living if they had followed the advice of the pamphlet addressed *To the Women and Maidens of London* (1678) to give up "their Needlework, point laces, &c. and if they come to poverty" in favor of learning accounting, so that they could better support themselves.[51]

In the 1630s and 1640s, the expectation of the gentry and middling classes that their girls learn the advanced skills necessary to produce embroidered objects and clothing gave rise to a new genre of needlework, the band sampler. The band sampler formalized the process of learning basic and more complex stitches and a girl's first patterns. From the first, it offered the possibility of innovation even as girls learned the rudiments of the skilled needlework necessary to help clothe themselves and their homes. The band sampler is organized in rows but with no requirement for their order, content, or number. What each girl included in her four to twenty rows varies,[52] but usually she included an alphabet or saying, a variety of stitches and patterns in colored threads and white work, and a larger statement in the form of a picture or longer verse. As a result, the band sampler not only registers the basic elements of female deportment but also, like the dominant culture itself, allows the possibility of individual variation.

With their alphabets, proverbs, and short verses, samplers also offer evidence of what Heidi Hackel calls an "abecedarian literacy." Based in the early modern practice of learning to read by spelling out words, "abecedarian literacy," writes Hackel, "resists the definitional categories of literacy and illiteracy, emphasizing the continuum of competencies of reading and writing."[53] As worked into the fabric of a sampler, even limited literacies served their maker. As Michel de Certeau writes of proverbs, samplers are "*marked* by uses; they offer to analysis the *imprints of acts* of processes of enunciation." Such "processes of enunciation," he continues, indicate "a social *historicity* in which systems of representation or processes of fabrication no longer appear only as normative frameworks but also as tools *manipulated by users*" (Certeau's emphasis).[54] The girls who completed samplers conformed to the "normative framework" of their social milieu in a genre that produced a visual framework. They simultaneously manipulated the conceptual and visual framework of the band sampler, transforming a requirement into work whose content was simultaneously expressive and useful.

The band sampler articulated identity through the choices that girls and their teachers made among visual patterns and written texts. Although at first band samplers may look alike, the hundreds of surviving samplers are actually built on the importance of varying the sampler's requirements. As in highly structured verbal forms like the sonnet, the formalism of the band sampler invited divergence. Aided by older relatives, skilled maids, and other teachers, girls wrought samplers with sometimes inspired variation. One unfinished sampler dated 1660 and signed Margret Mason (Plate 10) begins with two people in the midst of three geometric patterns, a pattern of alternating lovers' knots and flowers, a band of strawberries and blossoms, a knot and gillyflower-carnation design, two alphabets, Mason's signature, and two incomplete patterns. In the middle of these rows stands a miniature house with its adjacent knot garden on the right. A tiny path formed from unstitched cloth leads from the house to the bordered garden, its four squares, each stitched with a flower to represent its knot pattern, surround a fountain. Like the title of André Mollet's gardening handbook, *The garden of pleasure containing several draughts of gardens, both embroyder'd-ground-works, knot-works of grass* (1670), Mason designed her sampler to play on the implicit relation between designs for embroidery and knot gardens in this period.[55]

Looking through the hundreds of seventeenth-century samplers in the collections of the Victoria and Albert Museum reveals large differences in the level of girls' expertise, differences that signal variations in age and manual dexterity, as well as in the degree of willingness each brought to her assigned task. Some girls demonstrate a remarkable aptitude for precision and design, even as more awkward samplers suggest work completed under duress. As Lucy Hutchinson declared of her childhood education at the end of the sixteenth century, "For my needle, I absolutely hated it," while Elizabeth Isham writes of her sister that she "willingly would not learn her work" (24).[56] Not every girl who completed a band sampler saw it as a means of self-expression.

Still other differences among the samplers depend on location and class. In the American colonies, linen and silk thread were difficult to come by, so they were usually replaced by wool backing and wool thread, or wool thread on velvet. For the most part, girls in England seemed to have had access to linen for their sampler backings, although it may be that wool samplers were once plentiful but failed to survive the damage caused by moths. In extant English samplers the type of thread registers differences in financial status that allow us to trace the spread of this household textuality through the social hierarchy. The band samplers produced in wealthier households—or, perhaps, households with fewer daughters—were completed in the shiny silk threads increasingly available in a range of vivid colors, while the more common but still colorful samplers were produced in the cheaper green and red thread purchased by less wealthy households. As Caroline Bowles wrote in 1836 of these green and red samplers, for girls, "the sampler's task" was "less distasteful" than simple hemming: "There green and scarlet vied, and fanc[y] claimed / Her privilege to crowd the canvass field / With hearts and zigzags, strawberries and leaves, / And many a quaint device; some moral verse / Or Scripture text enwrought; and last of all, / Last, though not least, the self-pleased artist's name."[57]

Despite differences of age, willingness, privilege, and location, most young needleworkers who embroidered their initials or names used the letters of the alphabet to claim their affiliation with the work of their hands and minds. In the general absence of information about the initials or names in most needlework pieces, these extant objects provide a rare physical record of their makers' existence. From the perspective of women's lives, such work embodies both the process of sewing within a network of household and community connections and a representation of each woman's self-perceived location inside that community, an identity encoded within shared patterns of meaning. Girls' inclusion of their initials or names further inscribed the expectation that these would change when they married, while married women who combined first and marital names in embroidered initials could signal in two letters a vast, often traumatic, personal change.[58] The initials and names, the sewn alphabets, sayings and verses, a note left signed and unsigned in worked cabinets—many of which were writing boxes with drawers and dividers for ink bottles, blank paper, letters, penned or penciled designs—constitute texts produced in households where combining visual and verbal media sustained and enriched everyday lives. In some cases, the notes tucked into the small drawers of cabinets constitute the only life-writing we have from otherwise unknown English women. Hannah Smith's message (Figure 20) accompanying her "cabinet" (Plates 11 and 12) is dated 1657. She notes that if she ever wants to remember the time when she went to Oxford, "I may Look in this paper and find it." Having moved to Oxford in 1654 and left in 1656 when she "was almost 12 years of age," "I made an end of my cabinet; at Oxford, & my quenest^{c}h [Queen Esther?]; & my cabinet was made up in the year 1656 at London. I have written this to satisfy my self; & those that shall inquire about it. Hannah Smith." Smith's sense of her achievement includes her having traversed the genres of needlework expected of middling-class girls by mid-century. Beginning with one or more band samplers, she had progressed to pictures, including the frontispiece of her cabinet assembled in London, with Barak and Deborah on the left and Jael and Sisera on the right, and her picture of Queen Esther. Her embroidery demonstrates a brilliant command of stitches, including tent stitch, queenstitch, stem stitch, long and short satin stitch, with seed pearls and spangles. The lions just above the biblical figures on the doors are raised padded work. The interior of Smith's "cabinet," like those of her contemporaries, includes small drawers, holders to tuck bottles of ink and other liquids, and a secure place to place a message about its maker.

The colonial American band samplers of sisters Alice and Margrett Hemmings of 1692 and 1695 not only articulate sororal connection but also show how one needleworker would pick up as well as alter ideas for texts, stitches, and organization from another needleworker. The older sister, Alice, worked the alphabet and the injunctions "Love thou the Lord and he will be a tender father unto thee" and "Dear Child delay no time but wit / h all speed amend the looser tho / u dost live the hearer to the / end yesterday is gone to morrow /

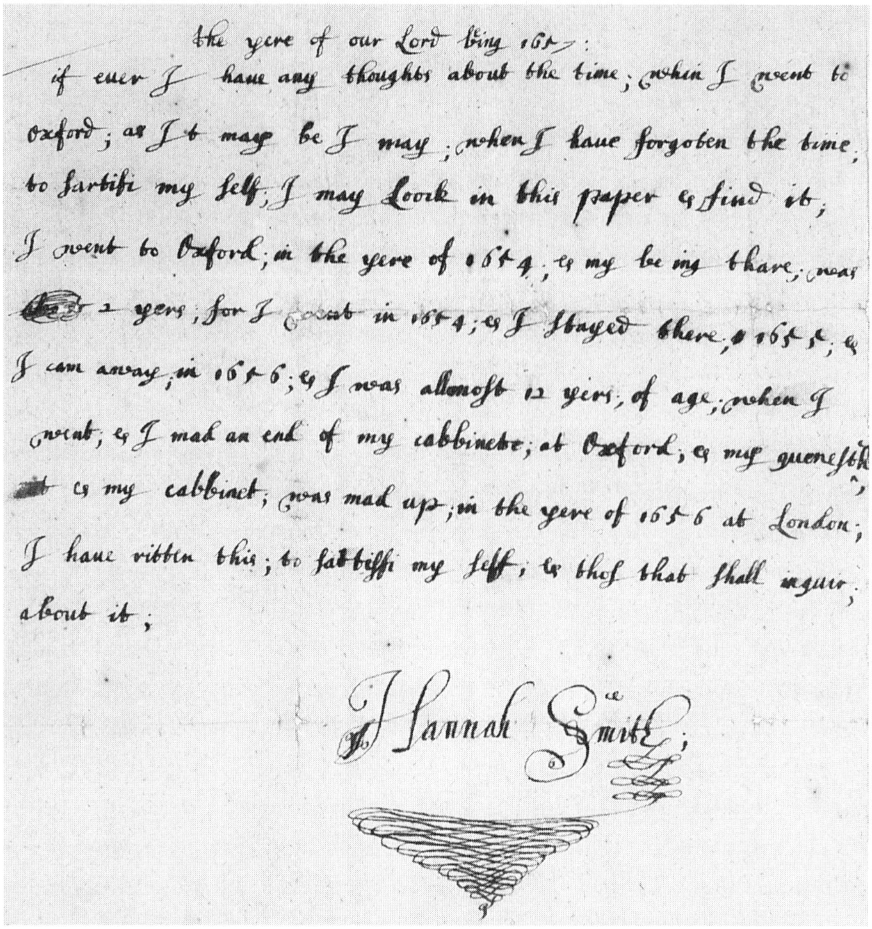

the yere of our Lord bing 1657 :
if ever J have any thoughts about the time ; when J went to
Oxford ; as It may be J may ; when J have forgoten the time,
to sartifi my self, J may loock in this paper & find it ;
J went to Oxford ; in the yere of 1654, & my being thare ; near
2 yers ; for J goabt in 1654 ; & J stayed there, 1655, &
J cam away, in 1656 ; & J was allmost 12 yers, of age ; when J
went ; & J mad an end of my cabbinete ; at Oxford, & my quenesh
& my cabbinet ; was mad up ; in the yere of 1656 at London ;
J have ritten this ; to satisfi my self ; & thes that shall inquir ;
about it ;

Hannah Smith ;

Figure 20. Hannah Smith, message placed in her embroidered cabinet, 1657. The Whitworth Art Gallery, The University of Manchester.

is non of thine this day the lif / e to vertuous acts incline." Margrett copied all of her sister's needlework designs with only slight variations in length, but she altered Alice's choice of sayings. Margrett kept one text of her sister, "Love thou the Lord and he will / be a tender father unto thee," but replaced Alice's alphabet with another text entirely, the conclusion of the Worthy Wife passage of Proverbs 31, stopping in mid-sentence when she came to the end of her linen backing: "Faume is deceitfull and beauty is vai / n but a woman that feareth the Lord / shee shall be praised give her of the fruit of her hands and let her own."[59] Reading samplers requires looking past the language of the commonplace to recall that people who deployed biblical quotations and other wise sayings were using them as tools to express and explore identity.

In choosing the conclusion of Proverbs for her own sampler, Margrett Hem-

Chapter Three

mings, like the woman of the *Alice Barnham* painting that references Proverbs, or Anne Brontë, who stitched the entire Worthy Wife passage in a sampler dated 23 January 1830,[60] was aligning herself with a biblical verse that defines the ideal woman by stressing the wife's hard work and attention to textiles. As the Authorized Version of the Bible stresses, "She maketh herself coverings of tapestrie." The passage further commends her supervision of the household, her ownership of land, her entrepreneurship, her physical stamina, and her kindness to the less fortunate. Finally, the verses promise, her husband and community will praise her. Margrett stitched a definition of the feminine that called on her family and neighbors to recognize her, to "give her of the fruit of her hands."[61] A slightly earlier band sampler worked in Massachusetts about 1640–50 by Loara Standish also calls attention to her sampler as the work of her hands. Among lovers' knots, flowers, and patterns, Standish ends with a short verse whose meter is slightly awkward, suggesting that she or someone close to her composed it: "Lorde guide my hart that / I may doe thy will also fill / my hands with such / convenient skill as may / conduce to vertue void of / shame and I will give / the glory to thy name." In Hemmings's "hands" filled with the fruit of their labor and Standish's "hands" filled with "convenient skill," both girls call attention to the physical act of sewing their band samplers, the hours they spent in the hands of the girls who worked them, and the virtue thought to accompany such knowledge.

During the seventeenth century, reading and writing became more widespread among girls, while needlework was increasingly taught by schoolmistresses. As a result, not just alphabets but verses and other written statements become more prominent in band samplers,[62] a trend that moves beyond sampler alphabets to make samplers an important medium for commonplace verse. From the alphabets and initials of the first seventeenth-century band samplers that record the cultural capital of girls' knowing their letters, to more ambitious pictures, longer verses, names, and stated aspirations, samplers demonstrate the mingling of verbal and visual texts as part of household work, forms of intersecting textuality that expressed not only selves who were appropriately educated but also selves who actively explored where that education led them.

The Male Gaze and the Female Search for Justice: David and Bathsheba, Susanna and the Elders, and the Judgment of Solomon

The rise of the band sampler and needlework picture in the 1630s and 1640s coincides with a sharp rise in print production and sales, as well as with the increased publication of works written by women.[63] Many, if not most, of the people buying books, pamphlets, sermons, ballads, and printed pictures lived in the same households where advanced needlework skills were most prized. So it is that patternbooks took off as a genre, and print shops catered to the women who wanted prints transferred to cloth for needlework. Although, as Kathleen Staples points out, Lady Brilliana Harley used "a pattern drawer named Mr. Nelham" who sent her thread and cloth with designs for needlework from London, the domestic embroiderer who lived in a city could go to a print shop, leaf through books and loose engravings, choose the print or prints she wanted to work, and have a pattern transferred to cloth then and there.[64] Peter Stent, whose print shop flourished from around 1642 to 1665, advertised and sold a variety of prints. Included in a broadside of 1653 advertising Stent's wares are a variety of prints suitable for transfer to cloth, as well as books of "Birds, Beasts, Flowers, Fruits, Flyes, Fishes, etc." These books were one source for the embroidery designs called *slips*, individual designs of animals and plants such as butterflies, lions, birds, insects, carnations, or sprigs of herbs.[65] Women often worked a series of slips individually and then mounted them, as Mary Queen of Scots did her octagons, on a velvet backing for cushion covers or bedhangings. Needleworkers also added slips of birds, beasts, and flowers to their pictures deriving from the classics or the Bible so that a picture of the Three Graces or a Queen Esther often includes a surprisingly large lion, dragonfly, or flower, or a smaller jumping hare. Stent sold royal portraits as well as a list of religious subjects, consisting of "Abraham offering Isaac," "Adam and Eve" (both fairly frequent choices for band samplers and other needlework), the "Apostles of Christ," "David killing the bear," "Deborah" (another popular choice), "Genesis" in "40 plates," the "Lord's Prayer," "Moses lifting the serpent in the wilderness," "Peter," "Pharaoh drowning in the Red Sea," the "Prophecy of Christ's Second Coming," "Psalms of David with music," "Susanna and the elders" (frequently chosen), and the "Ten commandments."[66] A folded sheet advertising Arthur Tooker's list of available single sheets and books of prints is tipped into a copy of Alexander Browne's *Ars Pictoria* (1675) at the British Museum's Department of Prints and Drawings. Tooker's "Catalogue of Plates" notes that they are "useful for Gentlemen, Artists, and Gentlewomen, and School-mistresses Works." It lists "Plates of Arnold de Jode," "One Plate containing 7 of the Nobilities Heads," "several Stories of the beginning of the Bible," and "Sixty Stories . . . of Landskip & Ovals with neat borders, and variety of Beast, Birds, Hunting, Trees, Worms, Fruit, Flowers, Fishes, &c. Coloured fit for Cabinets, Dressing boxes, Powder-boxes, Baskets, Skreens, &c."[67] On the basis of the few such lists of available prints that survive, it is clear that women were discriminating customers, selecting narratives and slips to work according to religiously approved subject, individual desire, and, doubtless, popularity. In addition, the cost of acquiring fabric and thread, the sheer number of hours required to produce an embroidered picture and the fact that the picture might be on display, meant that women selected their subjects with care.[68]

The genre that I call, after Jasper Mayne, *Hebrew samplers*, with its Protestant avoidance of potentially idolatrous images from the New Testament, was the clear favorite.[69] In addition, for many of the most compelling gynocentric narratives, including Susanna and the Elders, parts of Esther's story, and the entire book of Judeth (so spelled from the Great Bible of 1540 through the Authorized Version of the Bible of 1611), early modern people frequently looked beyond the Old Testament to the apocryphal books that Jerome had first included among biblical texts in his Vulgate. The Apocrypha were printed between the Old Testament and the New Testament in both the Geneva and King James bibles, a placement that encouraged readers to assume their authority, even though *apocrypha* meant both "hidden" and "spurious." Like the needleworkers, William Shakespeare and Anne Hathaway found meaning in the names of female figures from the Apocrypha, naming their first daughter Susanna, baptized in 1582 six months after their marriage, and, in 1585, naming Hamnet's twin Judith.

After a woman selected her biblical subject from the Old Testament or Apocrypha, she might purchase it already drawn on a silk or linen backing, might draw it herself, or might have it transferred. Prints were transferred with a technique called *pouncing*, the same method used to transfer cartoons to walls for the painting of frescoes. Pins were used to prick the engraving, then charcoal or similar material was dusted through the holes to create points on the fabric, and finally these points were connected to form the design for embroidery. When raised work became popular around 1650, consumers could purchase pre-drawn patterns and kits that included tiny wooden arms and hands ready to be sewn into the appropriate place. Sometimes bits of mica were included for the windows.[70] Purchasing cloth with the transferred print of an engraved story was only the beginning of choice, however, as many needleworkers decided to work compositions that combined prints telling different parts of a story into a single embroidered picture. They also chose the colors of the thread and added slips to personalize their work. As the catalog of the Goodhart Samplers Exhibit notes, "The pattern-drawer and the printed source could only provide a simple outline of a design for the embroiderer's use—it was left to her to devise a satisfying technical interpretation." Or, as Jones and Stallybrass describe the creativity of the individual embroiderer, needlework "meant creating new objects through subtle forms of imitation and putting them on display: it approached other kinds of public artistry."[71] The relatively small size of such pictures for cushions, cabinets, mirror frames, book covers, and other accessories allowed women the pleasure of creating miniature worlds whose small spaces they suffused with meaning.

Women may not always have chosen to perform needlework, but in compiling the subject, colors, and additional decorative elements necessary for a picture, they exercised a distinct, if limited, agency. That hundreds of women chose to work the same prints suggests not only that they had a limited choice but also that they experienced personal engagement with certain popular figures. As in discussing literary texts, we cannot know what a needleworker *intended* consciously when she chose a particular subject. But our understanding of the significance of seventeenth-century needlework can be enhanced by analyzing the details in the pictures and by reading embroidered subjects in the light of scriptural narrative and the meanings that early modern people assigned them in poetry and prose. The female figures within Hebrew samplers faced difficulties with a courage backed by divine approval, suggesting that many women who chose to work them formed an imaginative alliance with their goodness and beauty, as well as their violence, power, and erotic appeal.

Four surviving examples of David and Bathsheba, including Plate 13, combine different prints from Gerard de Jode's series from the life of David. The survival of these and other versions of David's story suggests that many needleworkers were drawn to this subject.[72] Like many pictures worked for domestic interiors, this panel contains several parts of the biblical story all at once. Needleworkers were creating the world in little, and, as members of a culture that found "densely packed spaces"[73] rife with significance, they often preferred that their embroidery design present several parts of the same story at once. The overall composition features the erotic appeal of Bathsheba bathing at the center of the picture, observed by David. In Plate 13 he is a small figure looking on from his balcony at the far upper left, but in other, related versions of this picture, David is represented by an oversized head peering over the palace walls at the upper right. Besides David's voyeurism, there are other elements of secrecy. In the lower right-hand corner, at another moment in the story, King David plots the death in battle of Bathsheba's husband, Uriah the Hittite, with a kneeling soldier who speaks from behind his hand. At the center of the composition, a serving woman holds out a letter to Bathsheba, although it is unclear whether the letter is from David arranging an adulterous assignation or whether it contains the news of her husband's death. David's exploits, sins, and forgiveness were of great interest to early modern people, in part expressed through the cultural focus on his psalms, as I discuss later. But the several needleworkers who chose this particular version of David and Bathsheba may also have been interested in Bathsheba.

The narratives associated with Bathsheba offer at least two potential interpretations for the women who embroidered it, one distinctly negative, focusing on David's fall from grace and Bathsheba's passivity. According to this first reading, the choice of David and Bathsheba as a domestically worked picture registers the tension created by the intrusion of the male gaze into the private moment when Bathsheba bathes naked and unashamed. For viewers attracted to the vulnerability of her female body, the needlework picture of Bathsheba offers the possibility of what Mary Garrard calls "legitimized voyeurism."[74] The picture exposes the secretive male gaze that could well have represented the needleworker's sense of the sexual pressure, abuse, and rape that took place in many households. Because the picture is a version of an engraved print, it derives from a masculinist tradition that featured bathing women like Bathsheba, Susanna, and Diana, a tradition that allows the viewer to enjoy their exposure.

However, the needleworker's version of this story presents not only David's voyeurism but also David's plotting with the soldier and the delivery of a letter to Bathsheba. As Svetlana Alpers points out, within the Dutch tradition from which Rembrandt's *David and Bathsheba* of 1654 derives, such letters signify not a fragment of the story but the story as a whole.[75] The de Jode workshop in Antwerp would have worked within this tradition of referencing the entire story with the letter extended to Bathsheba. "Bathsheba's bath exists in the midst of the rest of the things that happen in the Book of Samuel," writes Alpers of a narrative that includes not only Bathsheba's seduction but also her giving birth to Solomon, David's heir as King of Israel. According to Alpers, Rembrandt attempts "to describe (or illustrate) everything that goes on rather than trying to narrate in depth a few significant events," a way of perceiving narrative as signifying more than a single voyeuristic moment: "While in the Italian tradition artists assume that there are certain significant moments that call for representation, the northern artist assumes that the number of possible illustrations for any text is infinite" (Alpers, 212).

In discussing this attention to the larger narrative within northern European paintings, Alpers also describes the rationale of English needlework pictures, which derive from but also revise the prints produced in northern Europe available to embroiderers. In needlework pictures, Bathsheba's story is not simply one of voyeurism and subsequent adultery. The letter's suggestion of Bathsheba's extended narrative could allow a needleworker to try on a striking identity as the star of a tale featuring adultery, plotting, and murder, who becomes the wife of King David and genetrix of a dynasty. Consciously or unconsciously, she might also find in Bathsheba a figure who offers an escape from the everyday pursuit of virtue. When the man is King David, swept away by a woman's beauty, the picture's force might lie in the appeal of her unguarded sexuality framed by the fountain, the focus of a narrative at once royal, sensual, violent, and generative.

The narrative of Susanna and the Elders again features the intrusive male gaze, one that proves nearly fatal to the bathing woman, although she triumphs against false witness. In this story, the bathing woman is spied on by a group of respected men who, first, conspire to force her to have sex with them, and, second, bear false witness against her when she refuses, which places her on trial for her life. Many if not most English domestic needleworkers may well have experienced the sexual harassment that Susanna and the Elders makes visible, represented in Plate 14 in a needlework piece also deriving from four different engravings by Gerard de Jode.[76] But retelling the full complexities of Susanna's story in engraving, thread, or paint afforded the exploration of how a woman exposed to voyeurism, blackmail, slander, and threatened execution legally proved the unprovable, that despite accusations of infidelity, she had remained a chaste wife. "The History of Susanna," part of the Book of Daniel continued in the Apocrypha, provides justice for her when the youthful Daniel intervenes at her trial, as she is about to be put to death for infidelity. When Daniel interviews the elders separately, he discovers that they fail to agree on the kind of tree under which they supposedly found Susanna "companying together" with a young man. Because Daniel discerns this slight discrepancy in the testimony against her, the elders' attempt to humiliate and execute Susanna fails, and she is vindicated.

Throughout the early modern period, Susanna was an archetype of the good wife whose refusal to be blackmailed into the elders' rape puts her life in danger.[77] Before her story was widely available to middling-class women for their embroidery, it held appeal for Mary Queen of Scots. While imprisoned, a portrait, perhaps by Nicholas Hilliard, was painted of her wearing her rosary and a crucifix. Within the crucifix was a miniature of Susanna and the Elders. With the motto "Angustiae Undique," "through the narrows or difficulties," the miniature suggests the extent to which Mary viewed her own imperiled situation as an analog of Susanna's and hoped for similar vindication.[78] Mary's choice of this miniature could refer to her possible rape by the Earl of Bothwell, as recounted in the sonnets about their relationship, whose authorship remains in question.[79] She may also have used it to refer to false witnesses like George Buchanan or to William Cecil, who resolutely kept her from seeing Elizabeth. The Susanna narrative held out all of these interpretations to Mary Stuart during her eighteen-year imprisonment in England.

Susanna continued to be an important exemplar for women nearly a century after Mary Stuart commissioned her portrait. Susanna Parr's self-defense, published in England when needlework pictures were at their height, suggests what

Plate 1. Mary Queen of Scots, possibly with Bess of Hardwick, needlework panel, part of the Oxburgh Hangings, "Las Pennas Passan y Queda La Speranza," 1570s. Tent stitch on canvas. T. 33-1955. © the Board of Trustees of the Victoria and Albert Museum.

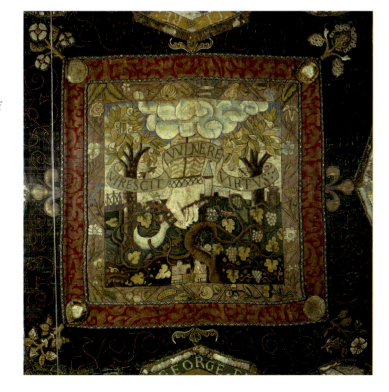

Plate 2. Mary Queen of Scots, needlework panel, part of the Oxburgh Hangings, "Virescit Vulnere Virtus," 1569–71. Tent stitch on canvas. © National Trust Photo Library / Mark Fiennes.

Plate 3. Bess of Hardwick, *Penelope Flanked by Perseverans and Paciens*, 1570s. Appliquéd hanging, Hardwick Hall. © National Trust Photo Library / Brenda Norrish.

Plate 4. Bess of Hardwick, *Lucrecia Flanked by Chasteti and Liberaliter*, 1570s. Appliquéd hanging, Hardwick Hall. © National Trust Photo Library / Brenda Norrish.

Plate 5. Bess of Hardwick, *Diana and Actaeon*, 1570s. Embroidered long cushion cover freely adapting Virgil Solis's engraving, Hardwick Hall. © National Trust Photo Library / John Hammond.

Plate 6. Attributed to Levina Teerlinc, "The Ceremonye for the heling of them that be diseased with the kyngs Evill" (recto), with facing-page miniature of Mary I applying the royal touch. *Queen Mary's Manual for blessing cramp rings and touching for the evil: the rituals of the royal healing ceremonies*, c. 1553–58. Westminster Cathedral Library.

Plate 7. Jane Segar, *The Prophecies of the Ten Sibills upon the Birth of Christ*, 1589. Calligraphic manuscript dedicated to Elizabeth I, back cover, verre églomisé. British Library, MS Add. 10037. © British Library.

Plate 8. Esther Inglis, *Argumenta Psalmoru Davidis*, 1608. 1.8 x 2.8 in. By permission of the Folger Shakespeare Library.

Plate 9. Jane Bostocke, earliest known English spot sampler, 1598. 16.8 x 14.3 in. T. 190-1960. © the Board of Trustees of the Victoria and Albert Museum.

Plate 10. Margret Mason, band sampler featuring embroidered knots and knot garden, 1660. T. 182-1987. © the Board of Trustees of the Victoria and Albert Museum.

Plate 11. Hannah Smith, *Deborah and Barak; Jael and Sisera.* Detail of Plate 12. Cabinet doors in silk, 1654–56. T. 8237. The Whitworth Art Gallery, The University of Manchester.

Plate 12. Hannah Smith, open embroidered cabinet, 1654–56. 12 x 10 x 7.5 in.
T. 8237. The Whitworth Art Gallery, The University of Manchester.

Plate 13. Maker's initials S C, *David and Bathsheba*, 1661 or 1681. Tent stitch on linen. WA 1947.191.310 Ashmolean Museum, University of Oxford.

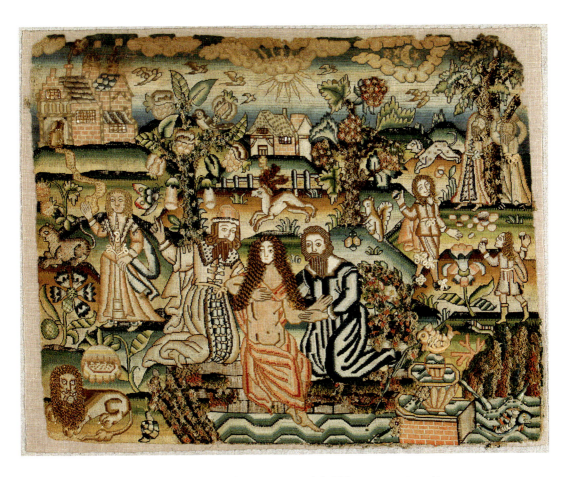

Plate 14. Domestic needleworker, *Susanna and the Elders*, c. 1630–60. 29/62
Glasgow Museums, The Burrell Collection, Culture and Sport Glasgow
(Museums).

Plate 15. Domestic needleworker, *Abraham Casting Out Hagar and Ishmael*, c. 1650. 29/45, Glasgow Museums, The Burrell Collection, Culture and Sport Glasgow (Museums).

Plate 16. Book cover, *Abraham Banishes Hagar and Ishmael*, 1652. Silk on satin, 5 x 9 x 1.6 in. T. 44&A-1954. © the Board of Trustees of the Victoria and Albert Museum.

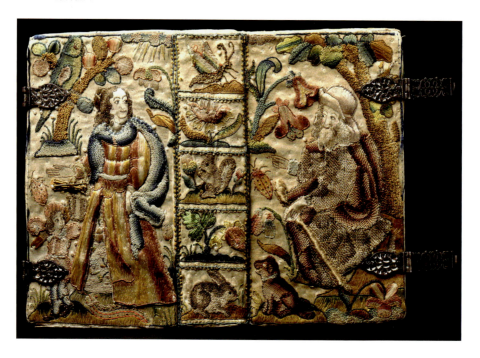

Plate 17. Mirror frame, *Abraham Banishes Hagar and Ishmael*, 1660–80. Unfinished embroidery showing transferred design, silk on linen, 30 x 22 in. T. 247-1896. © the Board of Trustees of the Victoria and Albert Museum.

Plate 18. Maker's initials I H, *Esther and Ahasueras*, 1652. Glasgow Museums, The Burrell Collection, Culture and Sport Glasgow (Museums).

Plate 19. English mirror frame showing King Charles II, Queen Catherine of Braganza, Judith, and Jael, c. 1665. Silk; warp-float faced 7:1 satin weave; embroidered with silk floss and yarns, gilt-metal-strip-wrapped silk, gilt metal purl and cardboard in brick, overcast, running, satin, and split stitches; couching, padded couching and laid work; French knots, braided pom-poms and seed pearls; in tortoise-shell frame, 101.9 x 74.1 cm (40 1/8 x 29 ¼ in.). Gift of Mrs. Laurance H. Armour Sr. in memory of her mother, Mrs. Henry Malcom Withers, 1963.746. Art Institute of Chicago.

Plate 20. Linen purse embroidered with grapes, vines, flowers, and small animals, c. 1600–1650. T. 87-1935. © the Board of Trustees of the Victoria and Albert Museum.

Plate 21. Tapestry with the arms of Robert Dudley, Earl of Leicester, probably Sheldon Tapestry Workshops, Warwickshire, c. 1585. T. 320-1977. © the Board of Trustees of the Victoria and Albert Museum.

Susanna could mean to early modern women. Parr uses the figure of Susanna to argue that she has been both unjustly accused and resoundingly vindicated. The title *Susanna's Apologie Against the Elders: Or a Vindication of Susanna Parr; one of those two Women lately Excommunicated by Mr Leis Stuckley, and his Church in Exeter* (1659) connects the biblical narrative with the author's name, Susanna, to signify Susanna Parr's veracity in the face of her minister's persecution. Reading the six pamphlets related to this case, Patricia Crawford shows how the controversy to which the title refers began in 1657, when a minister, Lewis Stucley, excommunicated two women, Susanna Parr and Mary Allein, the wife of a prosperous serge maker, who were members of an independent congregation in Exeter. Stucley and his associate, Thomas Mall, sought to punish the two women for speaking out in church, for interpreting the deaths of their children according to their own religious views, and for attending the sermons of other ministers. Attacked as unchaste and even incestuous, shunned by the community, the "forged accusations" that Parr and Mrs. Allein were "indeed children of hell" compelled Parr to publish her pamphlet, asking "the Ministers of Christ in this Nation" to "call Mr Stucley to an account, for his smiting his fellow-servants." What was at stake for Susanna Parr in the Susanna narrative was men's misuse of their power, specifically in bearing false witness, with the suggestion of sexual harassment haunting the case.[80] The anonymous needleworker of *Susanna and the Elders* in Plate 14 chose the subject of Susanna, like Mary Stuart and Susanna Parr, in connection with concerns about abuse and slander that women shared through such female worthies. By melding several moments in Susanna's story together, this needleworker makes it clear that, like Susanna Parr, what appealed to her was Susanna's story as a whole, complete with triumphant conclusion.

Some needlework subjects, like that of Bathsheba, produce pictures that can be read in more than one way; still others, like Susanna, express a clearer sense of right and wrong. The subject of Sarah and Hagar is another that produced multiple interpretations, observable in three different versions of a single print by Gerard de Jode (Figure 21). In sum these three different embroidered versions of de Jode's print of Abraham and Hagar demonstrate how women across the middle decades of the seventeenth century adapted different elements of this complicated family of two women, two sons, and one patriarch to meet the needs of a particular time and place. If the point of view is that of Sarah, rightful wife and mother of Abraham's son, Isaac, then what matters most is Abraham's willingness to cast out his handmaid, Hagar, and their child, Ishmael, at the behest of his wife, Sarah, and so ensure her legitimate son, Isaac, as heir. The version pictured in Plate 15 from the Burrell Collection in Glasgow emphasizes the narrative from this point of view in a mid-seventeenth-century needlework picture featuring raised work emphasized by "carved pieces of silk-covered wood" for the hands, padded faces, and different kinds of cloth used to form the characters' clothing, including lace (Arthur, 39). Unusually, this picture includes a written text encircling the figures of Abraham, Hagar, and Ishmael: "SARAH UNTO ABRHAM DOTH COMPLAINE THAT ISHMAEL NO LONGER SHOULD REMAIN / AN HEIR WITH HER SON ISAACK FOR TO BE / CAST OUT THEREFORE BONDWOMAN SHE." This text is a vivid example of what Svetlana Alpers calls a "caption," an embroidered version of the Northern European tendency to reproduce "conversation" within a work of art (Alpers, 207–12). The stitched caption in Sarah's voice, a rhyming paraphrase of Genesis 21, is present in a more passive form in the Latin at the bottom of the de Jode print, *Abraham's Dismissal of Hagar* (Figure 21): "Hagar, whom Sarah was unwilling to have continue as Abraham's concubine, must go far away with her son, Ishmael."[81] The print's caption is not as forceful as the worked caption with Sarah's direct speech, although, like the print, the embroidered picture shows the conversation between Abraham and Hagar instead of the conversation between Abraham and Sarah that is quoted in the caption. The caption particularly exalts in Sarah's triumph over Hagar, and the resulting recognition of her son, Isaac, as Abraham's heir, suggesting that the needleworker was more on Sarah's side. Nevertheless, following de Jode, the picture's emphasis is on the plight of Hagar, whose upraised eyebrows give her a look of surprise as she holds the hand of her son, Ishmael, while Abraham gestures toward them, forcing them into the wilderness.

Two other versions of this same print in the Victoria and Albert Collections (Plates 16 and 17) provide two other reworkings of de Jode's composition. In both, the figures of Abraham and Hagar are decoupled and reversed from how they appear in the original. The woman who worked Plate 16, Abraham and Hagar as a book cover, focuses on the lovers, updating Hagar's hair but keeping Abraham's hat and beard from the print, adding Abraham's dog as well as slips of insects, a squirrel, a bird, a hare, and an owl among flowering plants and trees along the spine. This joyous picture covers two books often bound together, a Holy Bible of 1651 and *The Whole Book of Psalms, Collected unto English Meeter* of 1652.[82] Its beautifully finished embroidery of silk on satin suggests a gift, perhaps worked by a betrothed woman or a young bride. The plight of Hagar is here transformed into a straightforward love story, in which a man and woman exchange loving looks across the book's spine. In everyday use, the book would be closed and it would not be obvious that the lovers are gazing at one another. It would be necessary to open the book wide in order to see that their eyes meet; having to do so created a rather clever game, in which the Bible and Psalms seem to be beautifully covered in appropriate needlework, but the man

Cum puero Ismaële procul, dimittitur Hagar, Quem Sara hæredem noluit eße suum   Genes . 21.

Figure 21. Gerard de Jode, *Abraham's Dismissal of Hagar*. From *Thesaurus Sacrarum Historiarum Veteris Testamenti*, Antwerp, 1585. Reproduced by permission of The Huntington Library, San Marino, California.

and woman seen on its front and back covers are more intimately connected than it first appears.

The needleworker who chose several of the parts of the Hagar story for a mirror frame (see Plate 17) also seems to have been interested in Abraham and Hagar as an amorous couple because they are duplicated in the contemporary couple partly worked at the bottom of the frame. Mirror glass was sufficiently rare in the seventeenth century that its value was frequently emphasized with an embroidered setting, and many such mirror frames have survived. This one adds several elements not included in the Burrell Collection picture or the book cover but that are in the de Jode print (see Figure 21), including the frame's Hagar in the top left corner, lost on her way back to Egypt, speaking to the angel who responds to her prayer while her son lies dying of thirst in the corner at top right. The angel promises Hagar that God will "multiply thy seede exceedingly," creating a great nation from her son (chapters 16 and 21). The mirror also adds two elements not in de Jode's print, Sarah with Isaac in their traditional tent at the top, and the unworked fountain at the bottom produced by the angel to save Hagar and Ishmael from thirst. The mirror frame version of Abraham and Hagar, like the book cover, emphasizes their amorous looks. But by representing Hagar's conversation with the angel, Ishmael near death in the wilderness, as well as Sarah and Isaac in their opulent tent created from small pieces of fringe and contemporary fabric, this needleworker allows the larger story to filter through the four courting figures, an acknowledgment of the issues of infertility, inheritance, and a wife's influence over her husband that are present in the larger narrative.

As complicated as the status of Ishmael is in the Abraham-Sarah-Hagar triangle, the status of the baby brought before Solomon is resoundingly clear. The Judgment of Solomon, in which Solomon finds the true mother of the disputed child, presented an emblem of justice for medieval and early modern Europe. For early modern women, at least some of whom were embroiled in the legalities of marriage, childbearing, and jointure, the choice of this picture could be a telling one. Anne Clifford's diary records her decades-long battle to gain the inheritance that her father had sought to deny her, which included a period when her husband, the Earl of Dorset, separated her from her first daughter, Margaret, in order to persuade her to give up the suit. Suzanne Gossett has described how children were frequently abducted or forcibly taken from their mothers. Landed widows might be forced to give up their children to those who bought their wardship, as Mary Sidney Wroth feared, while Anne of Denmark's first known falling out with James VI was over her enforced separation from her first son, Henry, whom James wanted the Earl of Mar to raise.[83]

Chapter Three

These high profile cases point to the extent that women could not be certain that their maternity would be recognized.

Anxiety about the rights of mothers may explain in part the popularity of needlework pictures of the Judgment of Solomon (Figure 22). These pictures air the question of women's control of their children by presenting Solomon's ability to discern the real mother of the disputed child. In the story, the true mother prevails, and the child returns to her, a conclusion that becomes an emblem of justice centered in the recognition of the unshakeable bond between mother and child. This white lace picture punctuated with seed pearls and glass beads charmingly gathers this story of a public trial of maternal rights into the world of domestic needlework. Charming or not, the baby lies naked on the ground before Solomon's throne, and a soldier holds it upside down while threatening to cut it in half.[84] Still other Hebrew samplers evoke themes related to parents' relation to children, including Abraham and Isaac or Jeptha's Daughter, which convey the necessity for absolute obedience to God, even if it means the death of a child. Another popularly embroidered picture, Moses in the Bulrushes, rehearses a different outcome. Moses's mother must give him up to be raised in safety by Pharaoh's daughter as the sons born to Hebrew women were being killed (Exodus 2:1–10), but his sister, Miriam, the prophetess and poet, finds a way for his own mother to nurse him in the palace. Miriam's power as a Woman Worthy is later undermined in Numbers 12, when she joins her other brother, Aaron, in rebelling against Moses and suffers leprosy as a result. But for many early modern people, Miriam remained a noteworthy figure of a female poet and prophet.

Choosing Esther

If the point of spot and band samplers was to provide not just stitches but a pattern of familial and cultural connection, the point of many picture samplers was to provide not just decorative textiles but exemplars of human, often female, behavior. As a result, the genre of Hebrew samplers may have provided women with a chance to portray alternative selves, springing from divinely approved narratives. Embroidered pictures of Bathsheba, Susanna, Sarah and Hagar, the Judgment of Solomon, and Moses in the Bulrushes demonstrate that the moments pictured in needlework are embedded in larger biblical narratives, as well as within the lives and desires of the needleworkers themselves. The most commonly worked picture in the seventeenth century was Esther, whose narrative offered women several explicit scenes when a woman's actions and words carried vast political significance.[85] The women who worked the story of Queen Esther and her husband, the Persian Emperor Ahasueras, might well

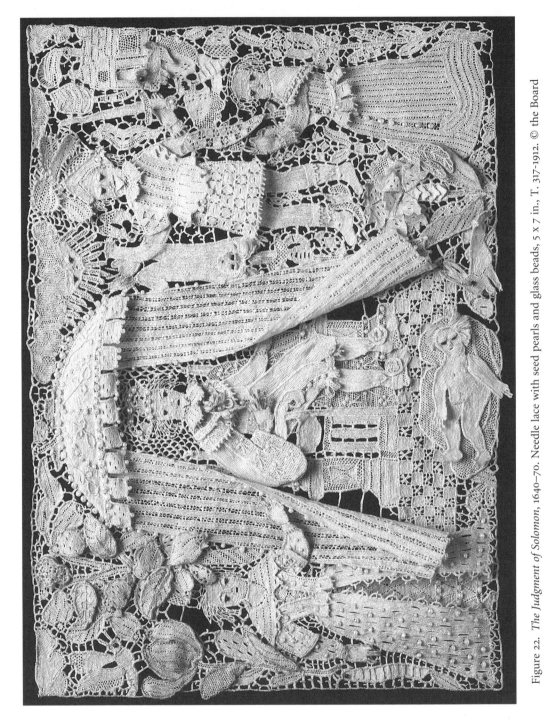

Figure 22. *The Judgment of Solomon*, 1640–70. Needle lace with seed pearls and glass beads, 5 x 7 in., T. 317-1912. © the Board of Trustees of the Victoria and Albert Museum.

have been reaching out to a female figure of undeniable authority from the religious past in order to explore a personal relationship with scriptural narrative.

The needlework pictures of Queen Esther and Ahasueras are not simply fantasies of liberation from the constraints of female gender roles. As described in the Old Testament Book of Esther and the apocryphal continuation,[86] Esther is herself caught within legal and narratival systems that deny women public speech and public action. She is a married woman who has been warned not to reveal that she is a Jew when brought to her husband's palace. When Haman plans to kill all the Jews, in the apocryphal addition, she fasts and prays for three days until she is on the point of fainting when she requests her husband's permission to speak. This request violates the law that only those summoned before the emperor may appear in his court, for "who is not called, there is one lawe of his to put him to death, except for such to whom the King shall hold the golden scepter, that he may live" (Esther 3:11). Unlike the tapestry suites of Esther that feature her at her toilette or banqueting, or Artemesia Gentileschi's choice to paint Esther fainting before Ahasueras,[87] the embroidered versions of Esther from England and New England focus on the moment when Ahasueras extends his scepter to Esther (Figure 23 and Plate 18). This is the gesture that simultaneously allows Esther to speak publicly and commutes her execution. As Lady Anne Halkett described this moment in a meditation on the Book of Esther at the end of the seventeenth century, "with an heroicale courage she resolved contrary to custom to greet the King & said if I perish I perish." Then "The golden scepter is held out to her by which she is encouraged to make her . . . address to the King."[88] Figure 23 shows Esther holding a scroll that reads, "At my petition." Moreover, this needleworker chose to stitch her initials, MI, and the date, 1665, just below her central figure—a convenient place for this information in a crowded picture, but also a place that suggests identification with Esther. Plate 18 is dated 1652 and displays the initials IH "worked on the tablecloth at the left, on the top of the central pavilion" (Arthur, 93). Both Figure 23 and Plate 18 depict nearly all the events in Esther's triumph over Haman. When Ahasueras allows her to speak, Queen Esther responds by inviting her husband first to a feast and then to an elaborate banquet where she exposes Haman's corruption, along with his planned murder of the Jewish people. One night, Ahasueras cannot sleep and is reminded that Mordecai once saved his life. As a result of Esther's entertaining and Ahasueras's insomnia, Haman is condemned to lead Mordecai, Esther's uncle and Haman's political rival, around the kingdom to parade his new clothes, after which Haman is hanged on the gallows intended for Mordecai (5.14). In Figure 23, which provides the more literal interpretation of the story, Haman leads two Mordecais

Figure 23. Maker's initials M I, *Esther and Ahasueras*, 1665. Silk on satin. T. 125-1937.
© the Board of Trustees of the Victoria and Albert Museum.

on horseback, one to the upper left and one to the upper right in order to show that they processed around the entire kingdom. The gallows in Figure 23 is in the upper left, supplied with a ladder that has many rungs, suggesting the impossibly tall gallows of forty cubits. Plate 18 includes the stock figure of a mermaid in the water at the lower left. Its gallows in the upper right displays a larger and so more vividly punished Haman. Both anonymous needleworkers added various flowers and animals; the worker of Figure 23 included at its bottom center the ubiquitous fountain; the worker of Plate 18 included along the bottom edge a dog chasing a hare among strawberries, peasecods, a flower, and a frog. Not pictured is the fact that Esther becomes a wealthy woman in her own right when Ahasueras rewards her with "the house of Haman, the Jewes enemy" (8.1), and that she gains a violent revenge when Haman and his ten sons are hanged.

To work the narrative of Esther, then, is to choose a narrative in which a queen leads a double life as a hidden Jew, then prays for God's help, risks death to petition her husband, entertains him and her enemy in order to present her "petition," and finally succeeds in political speech and action that saves the Jewish people from extinction. It is a narrative that sixteenth-century royal women found compelling for their own reasons. Queen Mary I commissioned a portrait of herself by Hans Eworth early in her reign in which she wears a medallion of Esther kneeling before Ahasueras. Now at the Fitzwilliam Museum in Cambridge, this portrait of Mary was probably intended for Philip of Spain, not only because it shows Mary at her most appealing but also because, within the medallion's miniature, Esther, crowned with a slightly oversized crown, kneels before Ahasueras as he extends his scepter to her in a clear gesture of submission—which does not, however, make Esther any less a queen.[89] For Mary, Esther's submission before Ahasueras would have communicated her complex proposed connection to Philip of Spain, as both his queen and his wife.

Mary Queen of Scots also turned to the Esther story; one of her embroidered pictures, now lost but listed in the Chartley Hall inventory of 1586, was *The story of Esther and Haman in a square*.[90] Mary's long history as a needleworker reveals how carefully she chose the designs and narratives of her needlework. In her captivity Mary Stuart may have found hope in Esther's triumph over Haman, an interpretation that reads the Scottish queen as a figure of Esther, and Haman, a figure of Elizabeth or William Cecil or both. As the Hebrew samplers of seventeenth-century women draw on the same set of Women Worthies as Mary Tudor and Mary Stuart, the figure of Esther comes to stand for the leader of a repressed but finally successful minority. During the English Civil War, one needleworker used Esther to express her allegiance to Charles I by adding details, like working the year before his death, "1648," in seed pearls.[91] On the side of parliament, the image of Haman occurred to Brilliana Harley, an enthusiastic needleworker, when she wrote her son Edward during the Long Parliament, "I am glad that the Bishops begin to fall, and I hope it will be with them as it was with Haman; when he began to fall, he fell indeed."[92]

In seventeenth-century England, the Esther story also held immediate meaning for readers as well as for those who wanted to embroider Esther because she was a central figure in the ongoing debate on women. To the disputed extent that Christine de Pizan's opening salvo in the debate, *The City of Ladies*, was available to early modern readers, they might have known Christine's version of Esther that credits her with saving her people. *The Monument of Matrons* (1582) includes several references to Esther's story, interspersed with references to Judith, Deborah, and Bathsheba. In 1599, Anthony Gibson's translation of Alexandre de Pontaymeri's *A Womans Woorth, defended against all the men in the world* notes that Esther, together with Deborah and Judith, "wrought marvels for conservation of their people," to the "perpetual memory of the feminine sex." On the other side of the aisle is Francis Quarles's *Hadassa: or the History of Queen Esther: with Meditations thereupon, Divine and Morall* (1621), dedicated to James I. Quarles manages to turn the story of Esther into a prince's conduct book by focusing on Ahasueras's masculine and imperial authority, a revision of Esther that demonstrates just how proto-feminist a figure she is in many other early modern texts.[93]

Two of the most proto-feminist of the works featuring Esther occur early in the seventeenth century, as the combination of James's marked misogyny and rising numbers of literate, religiously active women increased the pressure—and the market for—the debate on women. Amelia Lanyer used the figure of Esther among other biblical women to counter misogyny by remarking in her prose dedication to *Salve Deus Rex Judaeorum* (1611), "To the Vertuous Reader," that she has produced her poetry "to make knowne to the world, that all women deserve not to be blamed." For "God himselfe," she writes, "gave power to wise and virtuous women" to confront the "arrogancie" of their enemies: "As was cruell *Siserus* by the discreet counsell of noble *Deborah*, Judge and Prophetesse of Israel: and resolution of *Jael* wife of *Heber* the Kenite: wicked *Haman*, by the divine prayers and prudent proceedings of beautifull *Hester*: blasphemous *Holofernes*, by the invincible courage, rare wisdome, and confident carriage of *Judeth*: & the unjust Judges, by the innocency of chast *Susanna*: with infinite others, which for brevitie sake I omit."[94] Lanyer looks to these Worthies for the authority of "discreet counsell," their "divine prayers and prudent proceedings," and the "courage," "wisdome," and "confident carriage" of Judith. Like the needleworkers and like William Shakespeare and Anne Hathaway in naming their daughters, Lanyer is seeking to call up a host of women exemplars by naming a selected few. In the prefatory texts of *Salve Deus* these Worthies explain and anticipate Christ's special regard for women. Toward the conclusion of her poem, which acknowledges the power of the Dowager Countess of Cumberland over her pen (124–29), Lanyer returns to these Worthies—to whom she adds Cleopatra—in order to assert that the countess embodies their virtues. The twenty-six stanzas toward the end of *Salve Deus* describing these Worthies have seemed to offer little for critics to discuss.[95] But considering the importance of Women Worthies in the heated debate on women helps to explain their presence in Lanyer's extended encomium as well as in contemporary embroidery. Lanyer emphasizes Esther's virtues by describing her lengthy prayer, "That by Gods powre shee might obtaine such grace, / That shee and hers might not become a spoyle / To wicked *Hamon*, in whose crabbed face / Was seene the map of malice, envie, guile" (115–16).

The second notable text that places Esther at the fore of the debate on women is Esther Sowernam's *Esther hath hang'd Haman: or an answere to a lewd Pamphlet, entituled, The Arraignment of Women* (1617). This pamphlet is a well-known response to Thomas Swetnam's attack in *The Arraignment of Lewd, Idle, Froward, and Unconstant Women* (1615).[96] In addition to turning her opponent's last name, Swetnam, from "Sweet-nam" into "Sour-nam," to create a pseudonym, the author uses the first name, Esther, to echo the Esther of her title, a way of doubling the biblical name that Susanna Parr's *Susanna's Apologie Against the Elders* would use more than forty years later. The choice of Esther for author and title makes Esther into a defender of women, represented as the Jews, against their attacker, Thomas Swetnam, represented as Haman. Although the pamphlet is a polemic rather than a retelling of Esther's story, the title, "Esther Hath Hang'd Haman," apparently functioned as a catchphrase for women's ability to overcome attacks on their virtue, intelligence, and value, while emphasizing their ability to avenge themselves violently on their enemies with the help of God.[97]

Whether needleworkers knew of Sowernam's pamphlet, Esther represented several interrelated characteristics that sprang from her full narrative. Not surprisingly, then, in 1653, Esther also figures prominently in a petition filed in the wake of the Civil War on behalf of the political activist, John Lilburne, titled *Unto every individual Member of Parliament: The humble Representation of divers afflicted Women-Petitioners to the Parliament*. As one paragraph of this defense of Lilburne points out, "Your Honours may please to call to mind the unjust and unrighteous Acts made by King *Ahasueras* in the case of *Mordecai* and the Jews; yet *Esther* that righteous woman being encouraged by the justness of the Cause" risked "her life to petition against so unrighteous Acts obtained by *Haman* the Jews' enemy." This petition, probably written by Lilburne's wife, Elizabeth, equates Haman with the parliamentary act that denied Lilburne his freedom. The "women" hope that Parliament, like Ahasueras, "will not be worse unto us, than that Heathen King was to *Esther*, who did not only hear her Petition, but reversed that Decree or Act gone forth against the Jews, and did severely punish the obtainer thereof."[98] Esther's "petition"—the same word used three times in the book of Esther (5:6; 7:2; 9:12)—in this case authorized women's contemporary political action.

Authorizing Women's Speech, Prayers, and Psalms through Esther, Deborah, and Judith

Politically active from within her household and divinely inspired, Esther's story features her extensive speaking in prose and her apocryphal prayer, which

Lanyer seems to have found authorized her writing as one of the "wise and virtuous women" to whom "God himselfe" "gave power" (49). Poet Hester Pulter also used Esther's verbal gifts to validate her "Poems Breathed forth By The Nobel Hadassas" of the 1640s. This bound royalist manuscript, which Mark Robson found in the mid-1990s, uses "Hadassas," a version of the Hebrew name for Esther or Hester, to denote its author.[99] For Pulter, the name Esther is the starting point required for her poetry. Pulter begins her poems with a tribute to her daughter, also named Hester, who had died by the time her mother was writing. Although the biblical Esther is the most reluctant of the Women Worthies to speak up on behalf of the Jews, the Bible celebrates several other women more open about their verbal gifts. The most popular Women Worthies present in early modern written and visual culture, Deborah and Judith, join their own speeches, prayers, and psalms to Esther's prayer, petition, and private persuasion.

The Bible itself connects the prophet and judge Deborah with Jael, who helps her and the general Barak to triumph over Sisera. With the help of Barak, Deborah sings a psalm, as commemorated by Hannah Smith on the front doors of her cabinet, where she worked Deborah and Barak on the left front panel, and Jael and Sisera on the right (Plate 11).[100] Deborah's ninety-five lines of psalm begin, "Praise ye the Lord, / For the avenging of Israel," details how "I Deborah arose" as "a mother in Israel," and proceeds to describe the actions leading to their victory, in part through Jael's slaying of Sisera:

Shee put her hand to the naile,
And her right hand to the workemens hammer
And with the head of the hammer shee smote Sisera, shee smote off his
   head,
When she had pearsed and striken through his temples. (Judges 5)

Deborah's song concludes by connecting Sisera's defeat with the enemy's loss of embroidered textiles, among other spoils—including women—that a victory would have brought home. In her psalm, Deborah pictures Sisera's mother looking in vain for her son and his spoils of war "of divers colours, of needle worke, / Of divers colours of needle worke on both sides, meet for the necks of them that take the spoile" (Judges 5).

One connection that early modern women might have perceived among Esther, Deborah, Jael, and Judith was their relation through divinely authorized speech, including their prayers and psalms. As Margaret P. Hannay has discussed in detail, early modern men and women used David's Psalms for religious meditation and the expression of personal emotion: "When people meditated on the Psalms they were thus able to express their own subjectivity in sacred words." Observing that "Women were full participants in this tradition," Hannay points out that David's Psalms were adapted to express a variety of women's emotions, from fear of childbirth to the struggle with doubt in their faith, "to speak their fears and even to express their anger." Anne Askew, Ane Locke, and Mary Sidney, Countess of Pembroke, and Anne Halkett were among the authors drawn to David's Psalms for meditation and paraphrase.[101]

David's Psalms were deeply embedded in the everyday life of early modern England, but so were the biblical worthies. Lady Anne Halkett, while noting that the Holy Spirit "confines not himself to neither sexe nor condition but woman as well as men," and that "Virgins, married women, and widows have beene indued with the Spirit of Prophesy," saw Deborah as "both a Judge and a Prophetesse." Recognizing that "the Lord honoured" her "with being instrumental by her Judging and instructing to bring rest to the land forty years," Halkett prays, "What I want of her Spirit O Lord give me in humility and fervent Charity," "if I can no other way procure rest to the land I may be dayly praying for the peace of these lands where our Jerusalem is."[102] Moreover, there are other female authors of psalms and prayers in the bible. Miriam's song of triumph of forty-five lines to celebrate the escape across the Red Sea appears in Exodus (chapter 15), while the Book of Judeth includes Judith's prayer as she stands by Holofernes's bed: "O Lord God of all power, looke at this present upon the workes of mine hands for the exultation of Jerusalem." When Judith returns to the Jewish people with the head of Holofernes, signaling a Jewish victory, her fifty-three-line song of thanksgiving declares itself a psalm from the outset:

> Begin unto my God with timbrels,
> Sing unto my Lord with cymbals:
> Tune unto him a new Psalme:
> Exalt him, and cal upon his name.

Judith proclaims that God "hath delivered mee out of the hands of them that persecuted me," from the midst of "ten thousands" of the enemy. Like Deborah and Jael working together, Judith has prevented the sacking and rape of the Jews when the enemy "bragged" that he would

> kill my young men with the sword,
> And dash the sucking children against the ground,
> And make mine infants as a pray,
> And my virgins as spoile.

But the Almighty Lord hath disappointed them by the hand
of a woman.

Judith's song then describes in the third person how her own beauty weakened
Holofernes at the moment of his death: "Her beautie took his mind prisoner, /
And the fauchin [sword] passed through his necke" (Judeth 16).

Protestants of this period, who repeatedly read the Bible through, and who
could call to mind entire passages by naming only book, chapter, and verse,
noticed that Esther, Deborah, and Judith were eloquent in public speech as well
as prayer, that Esther and Deborah were holders of high public office, and that
Deborah and Judith, along with the punished but still gifted Miriam, composed
and declaimed their own psalms. Philip Sidney, in tune with his sister, Mary
Sidney Herbert, and the Elizabethan court, adds Deborah to *The Defense of
Poesy*'s list of David, Solomon, and Moses of those who "do entitle the poetical
part of the Scripture."[103] Michael Drayton's *The Harmonie of the Church* (1591),
includes his versions of the songs sung by Moses, Jonah, Nehemiah, and Solomon, as well as the song of Miriam (although she is not named) titled "The
Song of Israelites for their deliverance out of Egypt." Drayton also included
"The Song of Deborah and Barek," "The Praier of Judith," the "Song of
[H]Anna for the bringing forth of Samuel her son," "The Song of Judith, having
slaine Holophernes," as well as "The Praier of Hester, for the deliverance of her
people."[104] More than seventy-five years later, writing from a more radical point
of view, the Quaker preacher Margaret Askew Fell mounted the argument of her
title, *Women's Speaking Justified* (1667), by noting that "Hester" used "glorious
expressions" to comfort her people, when she "went and spoke to the King, in
the wisdom and fear of the Lord, by which means she saved the lives of the
People of God." In addition, writes Fell, "you may read how Judith spoke, and
what noble acts she did, and how she spoke to the Elders of Israel." Fell further
suggests that we "read also her prayer in the Book of Judith, and how the Elders
commended her, and said, 'All that thou speakest is true, and no man can
reprove thy words, pray therefore for us, for thou art an holy Woman, and
fearest God.'"[105]

Biblical women renowned for their combinations of wisdom, strength, and
verbal skill helped to authorize Elizabeth I from the time of her coronation
entry. During that procession through London, one pageant placed a queenlike
figure in a palm tree as part of the advisory pageant titled "Debora the judge
and restorer of the house of Israel." In the third of her prayers in Spanish,
published in 1569, Elizabeth asks for "strength, so that I, like another Deborah,
like another Judith, like another Esther, may free Thy people of Israel from the
hands of Thy enemies."[106] The manuscript copy of Queen Elizabeth's thanksgiv-

ing prayer on the defeat of the Armada was found among the papers of Sir Thomas Egerton, who wrote at its head, "A Godly prayer and thanksgiving, worthy the Christian Deborah and Theodosia of our days." In this prayer, Elizabeth addresses her "Everlasting and omnipotent Creator, Redeemer, and Conserver" far more humbly than either Deborah or Judith, thanking God for the four elements, which "Thou hast this year made serve for instruments both to daunt our foes and to confound their malice" (1:424 and n.1). Her "Song on the Armada Victory, December 1588," is headed, "A song made by her majesty and sung before her at her coming from Whitehall to Paul's through Fleet Street in Anno Domini 1588," a description which suggests an Old Testament procession of victory. Elizabeth's psalm begins by echoing the tone of Deborah's thanksgiving:

> Look and bow down Thine ear, O Lord.
> From Thy bright sphere behold and see
> Thy handmaid and Thy handiwork,
> Amongst Thy priests, offering to Thee
> Zeal for incense, reaching the skies;
> Myself and scepter, sacrifice. (410–11)

The poet, educator, and polemicist Bathsua Makin not only awarded Queen Elizabeth "the crown" of all learned women in *An Essay to Revive the Antient Education of Gentlewomen* (1673), she also pointed out that "*Deborah*, the Deliverer of *Israel*, was without all doubts a learned Woman, that understood the Law," while Miriam "was a great Poet, and Philosopher: For both Learning, and Religion were generally in former times wrapt up in Verse." Makin also saw in "The Women" who "met *David*, singing triumphant Songs composed (it's like by themselves)," "a great Specimen of liberal Education."[107]

Other writers of psalms and heroic poetry, including Anne Askew, Ane Locke, Mary Sidney Herbert, Anne Dowriche, An Collins, Dorothy White, and Anne Bradstreet, must in part have had the examples of Deborah and Judith in mind as they wrote. Anne Finch, Countess of Winchelsea, invokes the language of the psalm and the women who made and sang them in her often-quoted poem, "The Introduction." Published in 1710 but circulated toward the end of the seventeenth century, Finch's poem begins and ends with a strong sense of the male discouragement of a woman writing poetry, but at the center of her poem Finch places Deborah as leader and psalmist:

> A woman here, leads fainting Israel on,
> She fights, she wins, she Triumph's with a Song;

Devout, Majestick, for the Subject Fitt,
And far above her Arms, exalts her witt.[108]

When needleworkers chose these same Worthies for their pictures, their work registered visually the verbal dimensions of their chosen exemplars.

Choosing Judith

Another psalmist with her wits about her is Judith, among extant needlework pictures an extremely popular subject; according to Ruth Geuter, Judith is the most common subject after Esther and Susanna. Associated with Deborah through Judith's head-hunting counterpart, Jael, Judith, together with Deborah and Esther, are the central biblical Worthies. As Margarita Stocker has discussed in depth, Judith was an enormously popular figure in Renaissance art because she represents a radical mix of violence tinged with erotic possibility and political subversion. More conservatively, Judith also represents widowed chastity coupled with the careful observance of religious tradition.[109] Judith appears in chapter 8 of the Book of Judeth as a widow of "three yeeres, and foure monthes," living in "a tent upon the top of her house," wearing "sackcloth on her loynes" covered by "widowes apparell," fasting except on the sabbath and other appropriate festivals. She is also "of a goodly countenance, and very beautifull to behold." Like Esther following the defeat of Haman or the Worthy Wife of Proverbs 31, Judith is a woman of property, for "her husband Manasses had left her golde and silver, and men servants and maide servants, and cattell, and lands, and she remained upon them" (8:4–7). In the Book of Judeth, the plan to overcome the general Holofernes and his hordes, who like Haman intend to destroy the Jews, is entirely Judith's. The narrative uses a great deal of material detail to describe Judith's transformation into femme fatale: pulling off "the sackcloth which she had on" Judith "washed her body all over with water, and annointed herselfe with precious ointment, and braided the haire of her head, and put on a tire upon it, and put on her garments of gladness." Strapping sandals to her feet, putting on "all her ornaments," she "decked her selfe bravely to allure the eyes of all men that should see her." Taking her own food and drink (her meat bag comes in handy later to carry Holofernes's head), she proceeds to the enemy camp. She gradually gets to know Holofernes. One night, when Holofernes retires to bed, drunk, Judith prays to God forcefully and directly. Then, taking down his sword, she "approched to his bed, and tooke hold of the haire of his head, and said, Strengthen mee, O Lord God of Israel, this day. And she smote twise upon his necke with all her myght, and she tooke away his head from him" (8.4–9). Because this description is repeated in

Judith's song, the reader of Judeth gets a double description of the execution of the Jews' archenemy. Needlework pictures preserve the moment after Holofernes's death, when Judith, accompanied by her maid, holds his head up by the hair.

Like Jael, pounding the nail into Sisera's head as he sleeps in her tent, and afterward beheading him, Judith provides a deadly narrative of female violence in a domestic setting. Esther succeeds in having her enemy hanged; Deborah oversees the enemy's defeat; Jael and Judith accomplish the violence with their own hands. As a result, to choose to work the narrative of Judith to dress the walls of one's home was to choose self-abnegating chastity in a story that also sanctioned a woman murdering a powerful man as he slept in his bed. The delicate white cutwork sampler that presents Judith together with her maid, the head of Holofernes suspended between them (Figure 24), takes part in an iconographic tradition that includes Artemisia Gentileschi's five versions of "Judith and Holofernes," with their revelation of Judith's fierce determination, the unspoken teamwork between Judith and her maid, and Holofernes's blood.[110] For Amelia Lanyer, "valiant Judeth" is a figure who, like Deborah, God gave the "powre to set his people free": "Yet *Judeth* had the powre likewise to queale / Proud *Holifernes*, that the just might see / What small defence vaine pride, and greatnesse hath / Against the weapons of Gods word and faith" (114–15).[111]

As both chaste widow and resolute executioner, Judith represents the potential for female political action more forcefully than Esther. In a seventeenth-century worked mirror frame that doubles the images of Charles II and Queen Catherine of Braganza (Plate 19), two of the corners are occupied by militant, if unidentifiable, female figures, one bearing a lance and the other a scepter, while the upper left corner displays Judith, with sword in one hand and head in the other. At the lower right corner is Jael, holding her hammer and nail. This embroidered frame merges two traditions in seventeenth-century needlework: the representation of female biblical figures and the political portraits substantiating the needleworkers' engagement with contemporary politics. In the case of this mirror frame and other pictures featuring embroidered images of Stuart royalty, the needleworker used her handiwork to represent the relations that she saw between herself and her royalist support of the king and queen. She works both miniature portraits in martial helmets and standing figures, together with Judith and Jael, Worthies of gory but godly action, the two triumphant undercover agents who saved Israel. From the needleworker's point of view, stitching Judith's story or Jael's may have meant engaging a violent if divinely approved identity, a version of the self able to perform otherwise unthinkable

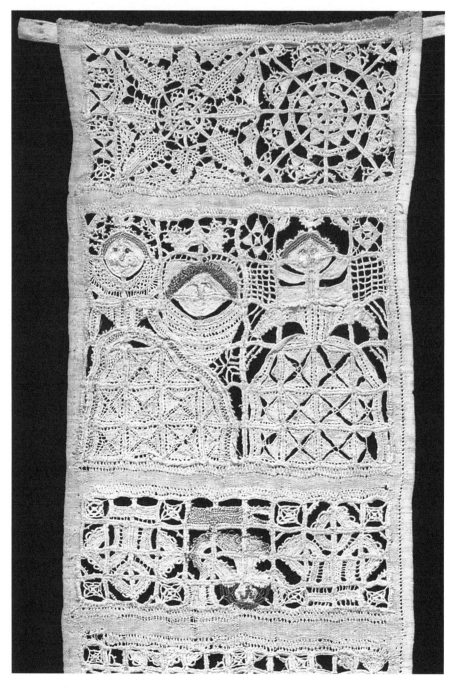

Figure 24. Judith and her maidservant with the head of Holofernes, detail. Cutwork or white work sampler, first half of the seventeenth century. Fitzwilliam Museum, Cambridge.

revenge, one who executes her resolve without fear, anger, or concern about reprisal.

Working Hebrew samplers offered thousands of women the opportunity to adapt a masculinist print tradition to express female emotions, words, and actions as divinely approved. Most early modern women would have found it difficult to imagine challenging the cultural limitations that they faced. Nevertheless, many women used the conservative traditions of the household arts and biblical texts to articulate their capacity for sexual, legal, religious, and psalmic identities, in ways that connected them to other women, past and present, as well as to the political events of their time. In the West, the imperative to perform accomplished needlework as well as basic sewing would take centuries of technological and economic change to dissipate. In the meantime, needleworkers took part in an expected activity that was always expressive and potentially proto-feminist. Except for its spread downward through the social hierarchy during the seventeenth century, there is much that appears static in the genres of early modern needlework. Nevertheless, domestic embroidery preserves the seeds of social change by recording women's increasing engagement with print culture, their advancing literacies, and their engagement with intelligent, outspoken, authorial, and divinely inspired exemplars. The seventeenth century was a time when civil war, religious ferment, and economic change left many displaced people in their wake. But this same nexus of events helped to create women who were more literate, more willing to oppose attempts to silence and ridicule them, and more politically and legally active. Many of them chose their needlework subjects accordingly.

CHAPTER FOUR

Staging Women's Relations to Textiles in Shakespeare's *Othello* and *Cymbeline*

Women's Historic Relations to Textiles: Basic Labor and Designs

Two Women Sewing (1600) by Geertruid Roghman, an artist who was a daughter and sister of artists, pictures two women communing as they work (Figure 25). This view of the associations between women working together is one of a series of engravings showing women performing domestic tasks without the erotic overtones of so many Dutch interiors.[1] The domestic culture of the Netherlands at this time closely paralleled that of England in a number of ways, as is evident in the books of needlework patterns and other self-help books that passed steadily across the channel in both English and Dutch.[2] Because the Dutch had the wealth and technical expertise to record interior domestic scenes, and the interest in doing so, they left a visual legacy that is suggestive of English domestic life as well. In Roghman's engraving, the woman on the right pauses in the act of pulling her thread to look intently at her companion. The second woman, whose elevated feet rest on a foot warmer, is bowed over her work, yet from the corner of her eye glances at the first woman, suggesting that she is aware of her companion's gaze. Their subtle interaction implies a silent interval in the middle of an ongoing if mysterious conversation, Roghman's image of a complex relationship between women enacted through their work.

Roghman's engraving could easily be a snapshot of English women sewing as well. In England, women performed a range of textile work both inside and outside the household. Women made up the bulk of the laborers who not only

Figure 25. Geertruid Roghman, *Two Women Sewing*, 1600. Engraving. Rijksmuseum, Amsterdam.

sewed but also prepared the wool that was England's primary export and internal resource.[3] Poorer women and children as well as the servants of wealthier people carded wool; children, older people, working-class women, and members of the gentry alike spun wool and flax.[4] Once a family's immediate needs were provided for, women in agricultural and other working-class households carded, spun, and wove or dyed cloth to sell or barter in order to supplement the household income, while others labored for minimal wages as seamstresses.[5]

Women also hemmed and embroidered their family garments and linens that they frequently owned, including bed ticking, napkins, pillows, and sheets, as well as embroidered accessories like handkerchiefs and purses. In the process, as Roghman's engraving illustrates, women worked together, conversing but also singing or being read to.

Not only did early modern women connect through basic textile work; the designs of their skilled needlework bear witness to women's affiliations and the desire to articulate identity. As bell hooks points out in *Art on My Mind: Visual Politics*, "Representation is a crucial location of struggle for any exploited and oppressed people asserting subjectivity and decolonization of the mind."[6] In embroidery, English women represented themselves through patterns and pictures that can be read as locations of identities lived within a network of household and community connection.

Despite the importance of embroidery in English everyday life, few historians of visual culture have paid attention to English women's domestic textiles. Between Burckhardtian humanism and Berensonian connoisseurship, not only women artists but also female textile workers and consumers have been occluded from view. For Jakob Burckhardt the study of Renaissance culture permitted the "discerning and bringing to the light the full, whole nature of man"—a perspective that included the mention of upper-class women as having the "mind and the courage of men." Although Burckhardt was paying women the highest compliment of his time, and he certainly esteemed exceptional women as worthy of study in his account of the Italian Renaissance, subsuming such women into the intellectual category of men prevents an exploration of women from within their own ways of seeing.[7] In contrast with Burckhardt, Bernard Berenson pursued the study of a specifically visual culture in the Renaissance through the conscious erasure of historical context. In developing and popularizing Giovanni Morelli's concept of "scientific connoisseurship," writes Mary Ann Calo, Berenson emphasized "the study and attribution of paintings based on careful scrutiny of morphological detail." As Berenson explained, "In every instance we shall begin with the decorative elements, and while doing so we shall ignore the other elements whether spiritual or material, social or political."[8] Burckhardt's humanism and Berenson's formalism have been critiqued by contemporary theoretical analyses, but such critiques are only now moving from the margins of art history toward the center of the discipline. The shift toward analyzing women's textiles from the sampler to the quilt began in the mid-1970s when Miriam Schapiro and Judy Chicago first produced textile pieces together with art criticism that simultaneously challenged the absence of women from art history and sought to recognize the importance of women's textiles to visual culture, both in the past and in the present.[9] Recovering women's contributions to the visual culture of everyday life allows us to reassert the feminine context in which they were produced, the associations of women that they recall, and the meanings that sewing once held for women, as represented in Roghman's engraving.

Although the analysis of women's textiles in art history began thirty years ago, the continuing search in art history for what Dinah Prentice has called the "incorruptible truth of appearances" continues to privilege the painted canvas or engraving over textiles, because those works have proved more "incorruptible" over time.[10] Cloth is, after all, woven plant material that is flexible and mobile: as clothing it folds away in a chest as easily as it takes on the shape of its wearer, a handkerchief slips up a sleeve, and tapestries roll up for transport from house to house. Because cloth incurs hard use, it is not as durable as painting or sculpture. Yet the centrality of cloth in everyday life, the fact that people produced, consumed, and actively used it—that it touched, covered, and wrapped the human body[11]—makes it of primary importance in the attempt to recover the structures of everyday life in early modern England. Annette Weiner and Jane Schneider point out, "The ritual and discourse" surrounding the making of textiles "establish cloth as a convincing analog for the regenerative and degenerative processes of life, and as a great connector, binding humans not only to each other but to the ancestors of their past and the progeny who constitute their future."[12] Women's associations with the power of cloth to connect human beings across time and to mark marriage, sex, birth, and death are very much at stake in William Shakespeare's plays *Othello* and *Cymbeline*.

Early modern drama simultaneously acknowledges and tends to eroticize and truncate women's powerful connections with and through cloth.[13] The "fictional" textiles of *Othello* and *Cymbeline*, which I term *staged*, or *represented*, are not precisely the same textiles present in the "real" world outside the playhouse, which I term *historical*, or *everyday*. Both plays demonstrate that the key difference between staged and historical textiles can be the extent to which they are interpreted and possessed by men. In the everyday world, men recognized women's textile production as work that contributed to their households. In addition, like the women themselves, men believed that such work demonstrated women's chastity. In the staged worlds of *Othello* and *Cymbeline* its represented women are for the most part stripped of their virtuous associations with cloth in favor of emphasizing the erotic associations of cloth with women's bodies. As a result, the staged women of these plays find it difficult to use textiles to prove their worth and virtue. In these plays textiles often signify the contested female body as men attempt to possess either Desdemona or Innogen by reducing her to cloth, cloth that may then be attacked. The plays' separation of textiles from the everyday world of women, from Geertruid Roghman's room in which two women sit safely and companionably sewing, redefines women's worth, speech, and association, with violent consequences for Desdemona and Emilia in the tragedy of *Othello* and with threats of violence toward Innogen in the dramatic romance *Cymbeline*.

The Erotics of Needlework

At the same time that female domestic labor provided women with the means to *prove* their chastity through purposeful activity, men's writing and painting represented as erotic both women's textile work and the very cloth that they produced and cared for. The erotic associations between women's work and their sexuality is central to plays like *The Wisdome of Doctor Dodypoll* (1600), *The Shoemaker's Holiday* (1599), and *The Queen and Concubine* (1659), as well as *Othello* (1603–4) and *Cymbeline* (1609–10), and is visible even in pattern books sold to needleworkers. The printer William Barley opens his reproduction of a Venetian pattern book, *A Book of Curious and Strange Inventions* (1596), with verses in English addressed to a female readership that quickly stray into sexualized language even as they acknowledge that the needle produces some kind of text. For the "prettie maidens" viewing "this prettie booke," the verses distinguish between the masculine studies of the "liberal arts" and those of women's needlework, which, though they require "wits most sharp and swift," "Their milke white hands the needle finer fits, / With silke & golde to prove their pregnant wits."[14] While acknowledging the implicit sharpness and swiftness of women's minds, Barley confidently asserts that "the needle finer fits" their hands, so that sewing in expensive metal thread is the true proof of "their pregnant wits"—with "pregnant" suggesting both a feminized capacity for invention and the extent to which sewing women seem inseparable from their reproductive function.

In describing the power of women's minds and hands, Barley's verses preach that women should guard their chastity. Barley's closing reminder that needleworkers should "Keepe cleane your Samplers" (Sig. A1(v)), like Eulalia's admonition to her girl pupil in Richard Brome's *The Queen and Concubine* to "Keep your work clean, and you shall be a good Maid,"[15] points to the material difficulty of keeping needlework clean but also evokes sewing as representing the eroticized, reproductive female body, as cloth that can be readily soiled. From Barley's caution about soiled samplers it is not far to Iago's disingenuous question to Othello about Desdemona, "Have you not sometimes seen a handkerchief / Spotted with strawberries in your wife's hand?" (3.3.439–40). Although the spots were put there by either Othello's mother or the Egyptian sibyl, depending on which version of the handkerchief's origin the audience may be asked to accept, by the time Othello plans Desdemona's murder, the "spots" he sees have moved, thanks to Iago's insinuations, from the handkerchief to the bedsheets, as he anticipates that with her death, their "bed, lust-stain'd, shall with lust's blood be spotted" (5.1.37). The erotic associations of women's hands, their work, and the resulting household textiles objectify women not only as sexualized but as capable of being possessed by the male voyeur.

English evocations of sewing as erotic activity emphasize a woman seen sewing through a window, while Dutch seventeenth-century genre paintings place the female body within the frame of a picture also meant for display. Thomas Dekker's *The Shoemaker's Holiday* (1599) features a voyeuristic scene when Jane must work in a shop to earn her living as her husband, Ralph Damport, fights in France. Jane's work as a seamstress makes her visible to Hammon, who has courted her before. Seeing her sewing through the shop window, he comments on how spying on her working so arouses him that it makes him "stand": "How prettily she works! Oh, pretty hand! / Oh, happy work! It doth me good to stand / Unseen to see her."[16] Jane's simple inquiry when he shows himself, "What is't you lack, sir"? (3.4.23), calls attention to both his sexual desire and her female body as able to fulfill it.[17] The conversation that follows mingles the goods that she has made—handkerchief, ruffs, and band—with her hand: "How sell you, then, this hand?" Hammon asks, where the "hand" offered or acquired through marriage is also the eroticized hand of the seamstress. When Jane answers, "My hands are not to be sold," Hammon rejoins, "Nay, faith, I come to buy" (3.4.25–29). In the end, Hammon—whose name recalls Esther's enemy, Haman—nearly succeeds in purchasing and thus possessing both her hand and handiwork.[18] Middleton and Dekker's choice for their character's name in *Roaring Girl*, Mistress Openwork, at a stroke demonstrates a similar association of her sexualized body literally displayed as "open" by her public, mercantile activities, with her needlework, because "open" or "cut work" is produced by taking out the horizontal threads in a piece of cloth and then using the needle to collect the remaining threads into lacy patterns characterized by holes in the fabric, as in Figure 24.[19]

Because the Dutch were fascinated by the inherent sensuality of the domestic world and the ways in which that sensuality raised moral questions about human behavior, they left a visual legacy that is useful in understanding the erotics of needlework across the channel in England. Gabriel Metsu's *The Huntsman's Present* offers a scene that demonstrates how needlework in Dutch painting represents the erotic (Figure 26). Metsu's central figure is a well-dressed woman, located within a domesticity framed by the room's large linen press. She turns her head toward a man gesturing with a partridge, a symbol of

Figure 26. Gabriel Metsu, *The Huntsman's Present*, 1658–60. Rijksmuseum, Amsterdam.

her sexual vulnerability. Although she reaches toward a book on the table—perhaps a Bible—her shoes are already off her feet and on the floor, a plaster Cupid presides over the scene high in the painting's background, while the linen press framing her body has one door ajar.[20] The woman's sewing rests at the center of the composition, in her lap, its intimate physical space redolent of the sensuality of female handiwork. In the Dutch emblem book tradition, sewing women are often depicted in association with Cupid, who watches or even assists. In one of Jacob Cats's emblems, for example, a Cupid watches a woman embroider. Its inscription translates her handiwork into sex in terms that confuse who penetrates whom: "Your needle bores a hole; your thread makes the stitch. Love, treat me in the same way; keep all the same strokes. You know I am wounded by your sweet mouth. Go on, heal the pain there where you gave me the wound."[21] Because the female body engaged in textile work articulates the feminine by performing it, the "prettie women" of English plays and Dutch genre paintings plying their "prettie needles" are simultaneously devalued by the possibility of selling their bodies to men and valued for their resistance, even as their resistance is also seen as erotic.

An anonymous play acted by the Children of Saint Paul's, *The Wisdome of Doctor Dodypoll* (1600), manages to combine the staged display of a woman sewing with a painting of a woman sewing. The play opens with the stage directions, "A Curtain drawne, Earle Lassingbergh is discovered (like a Painter) painting Lucilia, who sits working on a piece of Cushion,"[22] and the boy playing Lucilia continues to sew throughout the first scene. The play's erotic framing charts the ways in which gender is both constructed and complicated through the association of the female body with needlework, especially when a boy costumed as a woman performs the work. Shortly after this scene, a bawdy song reminiscent of Cat's verse, sung by another "female" character, celebrates "love" as beyond sexual difference or gender in the interrelations among a "thing"—whether male or female genitalia—and the "prick" of the needle, representing the prick of love or the penis: "What thing is love? for sure I am it is a thing, / It is a prick, it is a thing, it is a prettie, prettie thing. / It is a fire, it is a coale, whose flame creeps in at every hoale" (Sig. 4A(v)). The flame creeping in "at every hoale," like the opening scene and for that matter the entire play, suggests that the eroticism of women performing needlework may be transferred to boys. In the play's central scene, the earl's painting of the "woman" sewing becomes a prop displayed to an assembly of men gathered for a banquet. One of the men present, Alberdure, praises the disguised earl's workmanship in terms that at first sound like he is describing textiles as much as a painting. Alberdure emphasizes "the cunning strangenes of your antick worke"—when Cockeram's *Dictionarie* in 1623 defined "antick worke" as "of diverse shapes of Beast, Birds, Flowers"[23]—and points out that the painting is "sprinckled with rare flowers of Art"—like an embroidered panel. He then proceeds to describe what the picture reveals of the embroidering sitter's "livelie piercing eye" and "this lovelie hand," inquiring, suggestively, "Where are the other parts of this faire cheeke?" (Sig. B4(v)). By staging the moment in which the embroiderer becomes the object of desire in a painted portrait, *Doctor Dodypoll* acknowledges several of its own unstable distinctions—between boy actor and acting female; between artisan and aristocrat, merchant and lower gentry; between jewels and paintings, paintings and embroidery; and between represented women sewing and the behavior of living women. In this extension of the *ut pictura poesis* tradition, whose instabilities the early modern association of verbal and visual texts constantly explores, *Doctor Dodypoll* plays out the interrelations among sewing, painting, and playing at the feminine on stage. Imagining needlework as practiced within domestic spaces produces three related fantasies that register as heterosexual in conduct books and genre paintings and as transgendered on stage. The first fantasy is that "women" kept indoors and out of the public eye will somehow remain chaste. The second is that women can be isolated from the outside world and from each other; and the third, that women so isolated are sexually available to a particular man—the reader, the viewer, or the audience member.

Violated Cloth in *Othello*

This reading of *Othello* and *Cymbeline* considers the value placed on women's everyday labor as suggested by Roghman's two sewing women as well as drama and pictures that displayed such work as erotic. Although any staged representation necessarily reconfigures a great many factors present in everyday life, from time and space to speech and action, *Othello* and *Cymbeline* violently conflate women with cloth until they are perceived *as* cloth—cloth that is simultaneously metaphor and stage property, a representation and material embodiment of the female characters' suspected infidelity. This symbolic reconfiguration of women's everyday agency and identity enables a radical reduction of representation that in turn allows the plays to gain symbolic access to their staged bodies.

Women's historic relation to textiles contrasts so greatly with the staged relation that the gap between the two creates a double way of experiencing the plays. First, the staged textiles continue to materialize women's historic relations to cloth as its producers and consumers. As Marx writes with reference to art, "Production not only creates an object for the subject, but also a subject for the object."[24] When we consider objects as constituting "subjects who in turn own, use, and transform them," as Margreta de Grazia, Maureen Quilligan, and Peter Stallybrass urge us to do in their introduction to *Subject and Object in Renaissance Culture*,[25] then we can use these and other plays as part of the attempt to recover the early modern connection between women's textiles and the subjectivity that they enabled and inscribed. But at the same time that *Othello* and *Cymbeline* register women's historic connection to textiles, the plays generate their violent narratives from the disruption of the material relation between female subject and textile object. In *Othello* and *Cymbeline* women tend to *become* the cloth rather than its producers and consumers. *Othello*'s use of the purse, the wedding sheets, and, most important, the strawberry-embroidered handkerchief draws on a powerful visual semiotic of the connection textiles expressed and enforced between men and men, women and women, and women and men—categories whose maintenance required the definition and exclusion of exoticized "other" races, other customs, and other religions. Although domestic textiles formed powerful markers of these connections within English society, *Othello* sets up an implicit contrast between their everyday Englishness and the sexualized, racialized meanings with which Iago first invests them and that Othello so rapidly accepts.

If we consider the handkerchief in *Othello* as *domestic textile*—that is, as an artifact produced, worn, or used by a woman within the context of the everyday household, and which may have been used in the play precisely because it was at hand—then we can see the extent to which *Othello* alters the significance of the handkerchief. To a large extent, the sexual aspects of the handkerchief are implicit in everyday use. As Peter Stallybrass has pointed out, the handkerchief's touch on body apertures like the nose and mouth, at a time when a woman's mouth was frequently equated with her genitalia, enables the handkerchief to become "in Othello's mind . . . metonymically associated with the operations of the body."[26] The handkerchief eventually comes to represent not only genitalia but also the sexual behavior of Emilia (who refers to it as her "thing") and of Desdemona.[27] In the world of everyday England, domestic textiles evoked a chaste if eroticized body, but the play extends their significance to represent the female body and behavior *as* a piece of cloth. The play differs from the everyday world, then, by making female identity as malleable as cloth so that it derives its shape not from women's work and everyday affiliations but from Iago and Othello.

In the longest and most problematic explanation of the handkerchief's origin and power, the Egyptian sibyl speech of act 3, scene 4, Othello momentarily restores the handkerchief's association with historical women's lives. But he does so by placing it within an exoticized Africa and by providing it with a history that reveals the extent to which the categories of domestic and public space, of husband and wife, are increasingly connected with misogyny and racism in this play. In the sibyl speech, interrupted only by Desdemona's exclamations of disbelief, Othello is making one last attempt to get Desdemona to show him the handkerchief and thus disprove Iago's allegations of adultery. In the process, Othello binds up his personal history with the handkerchief and its English embroidery pattern. The speech takes the production of the handkerchief out of the hands of the recognizably domestic women who spun, wove, and embroidered it to place it in the hands of the "Egyptian" who supposedly gave it to Othello's mother: this "handkerchief / Did an Egyptian to my mother give" (3.4.53–54). Othello's narrative, while it restores female production and the kerchief's place in the gift economy as an object exchanged between women, also recalls the fantastic tales of adventure, slavery, cannibals, and monsters that Othello told Desdemona during their secret courtship. The point of the handkerchief's tale, however, is not to charm Desdemona with foreign adventure. Instead, Othello incorporates into his newest fantastic tale the same suspicion and violence that Iago is encouraging him to incorporate into his own life story. According to Othello, the handkerchief's power lies in its ability to make his mother "amiable, and subdue my father / Entirely to her love" (3.4.57–58). In contrast with his hasty explanation in the last act that the handkerchief was "an antique token / My father gave my mother" (5.2.223–24)—which places the handkerchief in his father's hand as *his* gift to give and pass on to his son[28]—in the sibyl speech Othello puts together a series of exotic details that position the handkerchief as an artifact that is distinctly feminine but also North African, a piece of silk from "hallowed" worms, the product of a two-hundred-year-old Egyptian sibyl who reads minds.

By this point in the speech, it's my contention, the contemporary audience member would have been seeing double: On the one hand, the handkerchief is a recognizable domestic article redolent of the household and appropriate female productivity; on the other, it is everything that Iago seeks to make it, and much more. The pronoun "it" in the sibyl's warning that Othello recounts for Desdemona makes the handkerchief interchangeable with her sexuality and his honor in possessing a chaste wife. If his mother "lost it, / Or made a gift of it, my father's eye / Should hold her loathèd, and his spirits should hunt / After new fancies" (3.4.58–61). At the same time, the "it" has become magical, possessed of powers, curses, and clairvoyance. "Its" transformed nature is the source of "its" threat: "To lose't or give't away were such perdition / As nothing else could match" (3.4.65–66). When Othello attempts to warn Desdemona with this tale, she—who until now has been as much Othello's willing audience as his lover—detects the threat in the narrative. She asks, "Is't possible?" Othello's reaction is to elaborate the handkerchief's North African origin. It is a sibyl— the type of prophetess who wrote her prophecies in verse rather than worked them in patterns of strawberries, one of the few mythic women said to have produced written texts rather than textiles—who "In her prophetic fury sewed the work," "dyed in mummy which the skillfull / Conserv'd of maidens' hearts" (3.4.70–73).

As he elaborates the history of the handkerchief, Othello twists the dyeing and sewing of domestic textiles into the exoticized conflation of race, magic, and virginal sacrifice with which Brabantio first accused him when he discovered his daughter's elopement. Brabantio's charge in act 1, "Damn'd as thou art, thou hast enchanted her" (1.2.64), is his explanation for why Desdemona has "Run from her guardage to the sooty bosom / Of such a thing as thou" (1.2.71–72). In that first situation, Othello rejected Brabantio's version of his courtship to argue that his storytelling "only is the witchcraft I have us'd" (1.3.168). But when he suspects Desdemona of infidelity, Othello uses his storytelling to ascribe magical powers and an exoticized and violent history to the handkerchief—"'Tis true; there's magic in the web of it," he says (3.4.67). This shift in Othello's self-conceptualization, from the first act's insider who has crossed successfully into Venetian society to the third act's outsider intent on emphasizing his difference, is a result of Iago's work. Iago labors to make Othello certain that Desdemona, "Of her own clime, complexion, and degree," must consider marriage to a man of color "unnatural" (3.3.235, 238).[29] In order to accept the fact that Desdemona has turned from her marriage bed to Cassio's, Othello must be convinced by Iago that their marriage is itself unnatural because of their racialized difference. Othello's acceptance of himself as other makes its first appearance in the Egyptian sibyl speech and culminates in the last tale that he tells:

> in Aleppo once,
> Where a malignant and turban'd Turk
> Beat a Venetian and traduc'd the state,
> I took by th'throat the circumcised dog,
> And smote him—thus. (5.2.361–65)

When Othello kills himself on the line, "And smote him—thus," in killing what Patricia Parker calls "this narrativized other,"[30] the Turk and Muslim within, he destroys the reconceptualized identity that made possible his jealousy and murder. Othello, who in the first two acts of the play exists to perform his ability to connect the categories of Venetian and Other, in act 3 concocts the handkerchief's Egyptian etiology while performing himself as the other that the Venetian society imagines him to be,[31] the other whom he slays after murdering Desdemona.

If the handkerchief's double history as domestic and Egyptian artifact helps to mark the intersecting fault lines of sexuality and racialized other in the play, its pattern of strawberries also marks divergent ways of reading the handkerchief. The strawberry was popular as a pattern because, in the words of John Gerard's widely read *Herball* (1633), its fruit had "the taste of wine," while "the root is thready, of long continuance, sending forth many strings, which dispense themselves far abroad, whereby it greatly increaseth." Gerard's *Herball* also points out that the strawberry has medicinal qualities: "The leaves boiled and applied in manner of a poultice taketh away the burning heate in wounds"; a "decoction thereof strengtheneth the gums"; the leaves are good to put into lotions or washing waters, "for the mouth and the privy parts"; and "the distilled water drunk of white wine is good against the passion of the heart, reviving the spirits, and making the heart merry."[32] Needleworkers evoked the strawberry's reproductive and healing qualities in their many versions of the strawberry pattern alternating leaves, vines, and fruit. The grapevine is another favorite pattern representing fertility, as is the peasecod that Mall Berrie seeks to have drawn on her handkerchief in *The Fair Maid of the Exchange*.[33] Oak leaves and acorns were also turned into a fertile vine for the purposes of needlework. Like the knots and patterns of European knitters or Asian carpet-makers, such patterns conveyed narratives of connection and generation.[34] As Holland Cotter reminds us, "Ornament, usually regarded as the equivalent of background music, is essential to creating a coherent visual universe."[35] In early modern England, generative vine patterns told the story of needleworkers' connections to production and reproduction.

I have examined several dozen early modern samplers with strawberries embroidered in many different patterns in the collections of the Victoria and Albert Museum. Nearly every spot and band sampler contains at least one strawberry pattern, and sometimes there are two. The Jane Bostocke spot sampler (see Plate 9), the earliest dated English sampler, contains two different strawberry patterns—one worked in red and green in the lower right-hand corner, and the other in blackwork immediately above the grapevine pattern at the bottom center of the panel. Such patterns, kept in a spot sampler to which a woman added stitches and patterns throughout her life, could then be transferred onto such textiles as handkerchiefs, collars, or coifs as desired. Because the strawberry's process of flowering, fruiting, and swelling makes it an inevitable representation of fertility within a geometric range of design,[36] the everyday reading of the handkerchief's pattern of strawberries is the potential fruition of Othello and Desdemona's marriage, a fruition that, as in the *Herball*'s recital of the strawberry's powers, "guards against the passion of the heart, reviving the spirits," and "make the heart merry." Although many members of the audience might be able to see that the handkerchief is embroidered with strawberries or know that the strawberry is supposed to calm the very symptoms that Othello begins to display, the second reading of the pattern as representing spots of adulterous lust begins to emerge when Iago first mentions this pattern. After Iago recounts how Cassio, when asleep, threw his leg over him, while calling him "Sweet Desdemona," he shifts gears to torment Othello by emphasizing the patterned handkerchief's domestic significance while insinuating that all is not well at home: "She may be honest yet. Tell me but this: / Have you not sometimes seen a handkerchief / Spotted with strawberries in your wife's hand?" (3.3.438–40). The pattern's very inability to tell a coherent story—whether Desdemona's or Othello's or his mother's or the Egyptian sibyl's—reveals the extent to which Iago and Othello control the reading of domestic textiles in this play, in violation of the fact that in everyday European life, textiles usually lay within the purview of women, if always subject to the interpretation of men. Iago's question eventually informs Othello's language as he justifies to himself Desdemona's murder as covering their "lust-stain'd" bed with his imagined spots of lust (5.1.37). Although the murder as performed leaves no blood, the spots that Othello sees before him dictate his actions.

When Iago and Othello seize the meaning of the handkerchief, it speaks to them in the way that Desdemona once spoke to it: "It speaks against her with the other proofs" (3.3.446). By extension, they know what lies on the sheets as well: strawberry-like spots of illicit lust rather than the bloody spots resulting from Othello's rupturing of Desdemona's hymen, if in fact they have consummated their marriage.[37] The taking of interpretive control of these domestic textiles from Desdemona and Emilia coincides with the minimizing and invalidation of women's speech, including Iago's silencing of Emilia as she begins to discern his role in Desdemona's unhappiness (4.2.148), Othello's smothering of Desdemona (5.2.93), and Othello's attempt to silence Emilia's accurate explanation of the handkerchief's loss (5.2.169). As Eamon Grennan examines in more detail, only in the later acts do Emilia and Desdemona speak freely to one another, especially in the "Willow Scene," act 4, scene 3.[38] But unable to speak to Othello until a combination of their voices reveals the double murder plot, Emilia and Desdemona resort to the mute text of the wedding sheets at the moment when Othello's jealousy finally becomes apparent to his wife. Their appeal to the sheets, whether stained with Desdemona's virginal blood or evidence of her virginity, is an attempt to reassert women's relation to the household linens, linens that they frequently hemmed, washed, and managed as part of the household store.

An idealized expression of women's relation to household linens is available in Pieter de Hooch's *Interior with Two Women at a Linen Chest* (1663) (Figure 27). The interior domesticity of the scene is established by a child playing in the background before a series of doors that finally open to the distant street. A shallow wooden tub resting against a wicker laundry basket, placed forward and at the center of the composition, suggests the cleanliness and order of laundry day. Within this wealthy merchant home with its painting of a Madonna and Child, its tessellated floors, needlework cushion on a chair, and statue of Mercury with a bag of money over the doorway,[39] two women stand before an inlaid linen press, one weighed down by a stack of folded linens, the other, whom we might expect would be helping her to transfer them to the press, rests her right hand on the top sheet, as if caressing it. The two women, associated through the linens, are yet portrayed without the implicit sense of communication of Geertruid Roghman's engraving because they gaze in two different directions,

Figure 27. Pieter de Hooch, *Interior with Two Women at a Linen Chest*, c. 1663. Rijksmuseum, Amsterdam.

both suggesting the import of the linens: one looks into the interior of the linen press, where they belong; the other looks down as she runs her hand along their surface. The relation between the clean linens, the orderliness of the household, and the chastity of the women is implicit, with a hint of sensuality in the touch of the top sheet. But the connections de Hooch makes between sheets and chastity in his painting may, as in *Othello*, work against a woman as well as for her. If clean sheets represent a woman's chastity, spotted sheets—even those spotted during the consummation of Othello and Desdemona's marriage—come to signify adultery when Iago can teach Othello to see all spots as stains of infidelity. Desdemona expresses her dawning awareness of her wedding sheets' inability to articulate her chastity when, immediately after Othello tells her to go to bed and Emilia tells her that the sheets are laid on it, Desdemona replies to her, "If I do die before thee, prithee shroud me / In one of these same sheets" (4.3.23–24), an image that connects the textiles of marital sex with those of death. Within the play, Iago and Othello control the reading of both handkerchief and sheets, despite the audience's knowledge of their domestic uses and Desdemona's attempts to contain these textiles within a local, feminized reading.

Still another textile, the purse, intimately connects cloth with the body and the meanings assigned its apertures. Many purses at the turn of the seventeenth century resembled that in Plate 20, which is linen with embroidered with a bunch of grapes whose vines intertwine a pansy, a carnation, a lily, and a rose as well as a bird, a caterpillar, and a caterpillar turning into a butterfly.[40] Such purses were frequently a woven or embroidered gift from women wishing to mark alliance and connection, the kind that in the historical world an Emilia might have given her husband. Iago controls the physical purses in the play as well as their meanings from the play's first lines, when Roderigo protests, "I take it much unkindly / That thou, Iago, who hast had my purse / As if the strings were thine, shouldst know of this" (1.1.1–3). Apparently Roderigo has been giving Iago so much money to gain Desdemona that when the play begins, Iago holds Roderigo's purse "As if the strings were thine." Roderigo is upset because handing over his purse strings to Iago has failed to provide insurance against "this"—Othello's and Desdemona's elopement. In effect, Roderigo's purse "opens" *Othello* to the audience.

Roderigo's corrupt purse derives from the medieval tradition in which vice figures are associated with purses, stolen money, and the anus. In the morality play *Mankind*, the devil Titivillus urges the vices New Guise, Nowadays, and Nought to fill their purses empty "as a bird's arse" with thievery. In Geoffrey Chaucer's "Summoner's Tale" the Summoner describes a trick played on the greedy Friar, in which one Thomas invites him to "put in thyn hand doun by my bak" "and grope wel bihynde / Bynethe my buttok there shaltow fynde / A thyng that I have hyd in pryvetee." As the Friar's hand gropes around Thomas's "tuwell" or anus for a "thyng" of treasure, Thomas rewards him with a great fart. At the beginning of the fifteenth century, the vices of John Skelton's interlude *Magnyfycence* relieve the Prince of his purse and also steal from each other, as when Foly persuades Fansy to exchange purses, and Fansy discovers that he has been robbed: "Torde, I say! What have do? / Here is nothynge but the bockyll of a sho, / And in my purse was twenty marke."[41]

From the beginning of *Othello*, as Iago metaphorically holds the strings of Roderigo's purse, Shakespeare develops the purse as connecting the two men.

In performance the purses' suggestiveness can be amplified if Iago's purse hangs from his belt like enlarged testicles, as in the 1995 Action Company production of *Othello*. In the ensuing four acts, Roderigo and Iago work to "fill" Iago in order putatively to fill Desdemona. By feeding Roderigo's desire for Desdemona with lies about her, Iago continues to convince Roderigo that paying *him* will actually "fill" Roderigo's purse: "It cannot be long that Desdemona should continue her love to the Moor—put money in thy purse—nor he his to her. It was a violent commencement in her, and thou shalt see an answerable seques-tration—put but money in thy purse. These Moors are changeable in their wills—fill thy purse with money. . . . She must change for youth. When she is sated with his body, she will find the error of her choice. Therefore put money in thy purse" (1.3.335–44). In this passage, Iago "fills" Roderigo's purse with empty promises of filling Desdemona. Meanwhile, the money to buy Desde-mona passes so continually from Roderigo's purse to Iago's that eventually Rod-erigo's purse is emptied of "jewels" enough to "half have corrupted a votarist" (4.2.191).

Because a cloth purse opens when fingers push through its opening, and "purses" shut when the strings are drawn tight, the purse lewdly suggests not only Iago's and Roderigo's body parts that "purse"—the forehead, lips, and anus—but also Desdemona's vagina. In their exchange about feeding Roderigo's purse Desdemona's female sexuality becomes conflated with its secret sale. Then in 3.3 Iago incites Othello to his first paroxysm of jealousy by contrasting Othel-lo's "good name" with the "purse" that any man may have: "Who steals my purse steals trash; 'tis something, nothing," Iago suggests, using the "nothing" of the purse as slang for her vagina: "'Twas mine, 'tis his, and has been slave to thousands." While relishing the thought of every man's Desdemona, he argues to an Othello now obsessed with recapturing his "purse" that the theft of a good name is the true violence of adultery, in terms that nevertheless emphasize possession of the female body: "he that filches from me my good name / Robs me of that which not enriches him, / And makes me poor indeed" (3.3.162–66). Iago is very much in charge of the play's represented textiles and its textile props. Desdemona's "purse" has not been stolen or passed among "thousands," and the only genuine theft is Iago's gulling of Roderigo by taking the contents of Roderigo's purse to fill his own. The handkerchief, the wedding sheets, and the purse mark the fault lines of heterosocial and homosocial relationships, mimicking and touching the physical body in ways that discern the staged social body without the benefit of female interpretations of their meaning.

In the staged world, in which textiles mark the disruption and disintegration of everyday domestic categories, the only inviolable "thing" is the thing that comes to mean so many things—the handkerchief itself. Unlike domestic textiles, whose patterns existed to be copied from spot samplers onto sheets, christening robes, purses, and handkerchiefs within the context of shared domestic labor, this handkerchief's strawberry pattern cannot be copied or erased. Aware that they will have the handkerchief for only a short time, both Emilia and Cassio are so drawn to this strawberry needlework that they must "take it out."[42] What does it mean, to "take out the work"? The *Oxford English Dictionary* provides an explicitly textual definition: "To make a copy from an original; to copy (a writing, design, etc.) especially to extract a passage from a writing or book." This definition is complicated by the contemporary visual examples that follow, which include two of its four appearances in *Othello* and a quotation from *The Art of Limning* (1573), whose use of the phrase "to take out" joins the copying of texts or "letters" with the copying of textiles or "knotts": "A pretie devise *to take out* the true forme & proporcion of any letter, knott, flower, Image, or other worke" (my emphasis). "To take the work out" then means not only to copy, but to copy in some precise fashion both word and image, according to the "forme & proporcion" of the original. This meaning calls attention not only to the handkerchief as the text that Iago and Othello make it, but to the strawberry pattern itself. Like historical women who copied one another's stitches and patterns within a framework of communal talk and trade, both Emilia and Cassio are seized with a desire to possess their own version of its fruitful domesticity, the small red drops like those we suppose are on the wedding sheets. But unlike historical women, the characters in *Othello* handle the strawberry pattern as if they were disconnected from its source. They fail to "take out" or "copy" the pattern because to do so implies connection and communication. Nor can they "take out" the work in the sense of "undo" or "erase" it—a meaning also evoked by these lines. The handkerchief, removed from the processes of production and exchange, has become part of the phallogocentric discourse that Valerie Wayne has identified as central to the play's misogyny.[43] So situated, the strawberries on the handkerchief can be neither copied nor erased any more than the stains on a wedding sheet. Desdemona's body, marked indelibly as unfaithful, must be wrung to death, as Iago urges: "strangle her in her bed, even the bed she hath contaminated" (4.1.206–7).

Cymbeline *and the Architecture of Female Space*

Like *Othello*, the story of *Cymbeline* may be told in terms of its textiles but in the more elaborate terms of the genre identified as *dramatic romance*. Because textiles function differently in tragedy and romance, genre has gendered consequences. The murders of Desdemona and Emilia and the suicide of Othello proceed by collapsing time and space in ways that accelerate the equation of

Desdemona's body with handkerchief, purse, and sheets. The romance of *Cymbeline* proceeds by expanding the time and space in which the action occurs, consequently enlarging the number, kind, and meanings of the textiles that enable Innogen to skirt the violence that the play directs against her.

Although Edward Dowden first used the term *romance* to describe Shakespeare's late comedies in 1877, the term has considerable merit in that it connects early modern plays with the prose and verse romances from which they often derived. As in *The Countess of Pembroke's Arcadia* or *The Countess of Montgomery's Urania*, discussed in the next chapter, textiles not only clothe romance with opulent furnishings and the trappings of chivalry, but significant items of clothing, cross-dressing, and disguise are often integral to romance narratives. As Mary Ellen Lamb and Valerie Wayne have recently argued, "Appreciating the larger history associated with dramatic romance makes it more possible for us to see the historical continuities between prose fiction" and "Stuart plays."[44] One of the continuities between prose romance and *Cymbeline* is a wealth of textiles.

In *Cymbeline*, textiles are so integral to the play's interpretation of gender that the set of the 1997 Royal Shakespeare Company's production at Stratford consisted of a stage overhung with a great piece of white cloth rising like a wave of a giant handkerchief, a sheet, or a sail. Some of *Cymbeline*'s textiles recall the earlier *Othello* and some allow Innogen to express her identity and exercise agency. *Cymbeline* opens with the interrupted marriage of Posthumus and Innogen, daughter of Cymbeline, the king of Britain. As Posthumus departs England for Italy—a departure marked by a description of his receding handkerchief—he leaves Innogen at a court where her father the king is ineffectual, her stepmother the wicked queen enjoys playing with poisons (although the physician who supplies her has substituted a sleeping potion), and her self-important oaf of a stepbrother, Cloten, relentlessly woos her. Once in Italy, Giacomo and Posthumus enter a wager about Innogen's chastity, so that Giacomo proceeds in haste to England to test her. Having ascertained that she is chaste, Giacomo has himself smuggled inside a chest into Innogen's bedchamber for the night. This bedchamber, like those of many privileged women of the early modern period, is constructed through a compelling description of its interior design, as well as a related written text. These Giacomo notes as "proof" that he has successfully assailed Innogen's virtue, and, returning to Italy, provides Posthumus with a detailed description of the bedroom and gives him Innogen's "manacle," or bracelet, which he slipped from her arm while she lay sleeping. As a result, Posthumus in a fit of jealousy orders his servant Pisanio (who has stayed behind in England) to kill Innogen. Pisanio instead sends a bloody cloth to Posthumus as proof of Innogen's death, which Posthumus addresses as his wife in a fit of remorse. Meanwhile, in obedience to her husband's command that she come to Milford-Haven where she is to be murdered, Innogen makes her own use of textiles, dressing first as a franklin's wife, then, on learning of her husband's violent intentions, as a boy. So attired, she heads into the wilds of Wales, where she spends time in a cave with two men who will turn out to be her brothers, lost since early childhood. Cloten, who has pursued her dressed in Posthumus's clothing with the intent to rape and possess her, runs into one of these brothers and is beheaded in the ensuing fight—about his clothing. When Innogen feels unwell and takes the queen's potion, she falls into a sleep like death, from which she awakens beside the headless body of Cloten dressed as Posthumus, whom she takes to be her dead husband. Reconciliation and reunion occur at the end of the play when, with the Romans invading Britain, the brothers and a disguised Posthumus fight to save the country and are reunited with Cymbeline, who acknowledges his sons and heir in part because of the appearance of the royal mantle in which one prince was wrapped, and restores the British connection to Rome by paying the Romans their tribute.

Among the many textiles integral to the unfolding of narrative in *Cymbeline*, the handkerchief is the first to appear—and disappear. In act 1, scene 4, the handkerchief represents the increasing gulf between Posthumus Leonatus and Innogen as he sails away to Italy—a gulf that will result in the wager of her chastity, his jealousy when he believes her to have been unfaithful to him, and ultimately his attempt to murder her. As Pisanio describes Posthumus's leaving to Innogen, his report both connects Innogen to the scene and emblematizes the growing disconnection of the two newly married characters through the reported handkerchief. Innogen envies the handkerchief when Pisanio tells her that Posthumus kissed it on shore while sighing for her—"senseless linen, happier than I!" she cries; but it gradually fades from sight in Pisanio's description, as Posthumus continues to wave with "glove, or hat, or handkerchief" (1.3.7, 11) until it and Posthumus disappear. Posthumus's hold on the handkerchief both links and separates Posthumus and Innogen, signaling in this farewell the play's turn to the processes of interpretation that will eventually reduce Innogen's body to the "bloody cloth" of act 5.

Like the handkerchief and bedsheets in *Othello*, the textiles in *Cymbeline* ask us to consider the extent to which the male appropriation and interpretation of women's textiles silence the female characters of the plays and allow male characters violent access to the female bodies that they seek to possess. At the same time, these textiles are sometimes located within Innogen's control and so function as emblems of her identity and agency. In Innogen's bedroom the play stages the way in which privileged women surrounded themselves with texts and textiles as the means to articulate their identity both for themselves and for the intimate audience of those who might enter these interior spaces. Innogen's bedroom encloses her within three gynocentric narratives frequently embraced by educated women in the early modern period: Cleopatra meeting Antony, Philomel's rape with its whisper of Progne's revenge, and Diana and Actaeon. The play nevertheless attempts to erase the more complex sense of Innogen's subjectivity evoked by these narratives by translating textiles into metaphors and stage props that serve to objectify her female body and thus make it vulnerable to such male possessive acts as rape and murder.

In providing an ekphrastic description of Innogen's chamber, Shakespeare is adding to his source in the *Decameron*, which Boccaccio describes as containing unspecified "paintings, pictures, and beautiful hangings."[45] Innogen's room, as Georgianna Ziegler says of the Sala di Penelope designed for Eleonora of Toledo in the Palazzo Vecchio, encapsulates a way of thinking that grew out of the medieval practice of mingling allegorical self-representation with mythic and religious narratives in order to assert and validate identity. Although not yet completed at Eleonora's death of plague in 1562, the Sala de Penelope presents a rich interaction of "the discursive modes of impresa, heraldry and allegory with that of history painting to create a unified programme which invites reading(s) and both defines and breaks its architectural space" in its friezes of "Ulysses travels" and "four Cardinal Virtues," "personifications of four Italian rivers" alternating "with the Medici impresa and Medici/Toledo coats of arms." The whole is surmounted by a painting of Penelope, who simultaneously defines a woman's body as her husband's and who "asserts power over her own body with her conscious decision to remain chaste by repulsing the advances to her by men."[46] For still another aristocratic *salle*, that which Isabella d'Este, Duchess of Mantua, commissioned, Andrea Mantegna produced several Judiths, some in grisaille, as well as pictures of other mythic Worthy Women like Dido.[47] In both aristocratic rooms, the aim was to produce a *gesamtkunstwerk*, a complete environment from the architectural interplay of the discursive systems through which privileged women constructed their identity.

Textiles were included in such multimedia emblems of women's identities, for women had been defined through textiles through both Penelope and the ideal wife of Proverbs 31.[48] Textiles represented prominent women through their rooms in three ways. First, the production of textiles—whether represented by Penelope's loom or made visible by displaying the handiwork of its occupant—demonstrated female chastity as inseparable from approved female activity. Second, in such rooms, the architectural elements are so densely structured that they *look* like embroidery and so suggest the chastity of the room's inhabitant at the level of architectural design. And third, the choice of subjects for tapestry and the narratives and patterns of domestic needlework amplify the identity of the rooms' occupants through their association with the history of powerful women.

During the Renaissance, exceptional women frequently surrounded themselves with textiles that were chosen as the means to express identity. Elizabeth Tudor, whose inventory as "The Lady Elizabeth" included "6 pieces of Tapestry of the *City of Ladies*,"[49] may well have clothed one of her rooms with scenes from the text by Christine de Pizan. As discussed in Chapter 1, Mary Queen of Scots spent her imprisonment under the eyes of the Earl and Countess of Shrewsbury performing needlework that hung in her rooms and on her state bed as the expression of her identity as Scottish queen, widow of King Francis II, and heir to the throne of England. Bess of Hardwick collaborated with Mary in producing a number of emblematic pieces as well as large hangings of figures, which included Penelope and Lucrecia (Plates 3 and 4) that she hung in her Withdrawing Chamber at New Hardwick Hall.

Women like Eleonora de Toledo, Isabella d'Este, Elizabeth Tudor, Mary Stuart, and Bess of Hardwick lived within representations of their perceived identities and so, apparently, does Innogen. As Janet Adelman points out, "Initially, Imogen is a wonderfully vivid presence, shrewd, impetuous, passionate, and very much the proprietress of her own will."[50] Innogen's decision to marry Posthumus Leonatus against her father's wishes, her knowledge of the queen's sinister nature, and the fact that she is the heir apparent to her father's throne— which is why Posthumus calls her "queen"—give her considerable substance as a courageous if subsequently vulnerable female character, her formidable identity iterated in the symbolic architecture of her bedroom.[51] Innogen's chamber combines Cleopatra meeting Antony in one tapestry; a "chimney piece" features Diana and Actaeon—a myth of male voyeurism but also female revenge—while her book is turned down at the point where Tereus rapes Philomel (2.4.66–91, 81). Innogen sleeps her virgin sleep enshrined within this architecture of female identity—if indeed she and Posthumus have not yet consummated their marriage, as both the narrative and textile imagery suggest,[52] for Cleopatra is just meeting Antony, Diana is bathing and has not yet spied Actaeon, and Tereus's rape of Philomel is suspended in the telling because Innogen has put Ovid's *Metamorphoses* down at this point. All three females present in Innogen's room are worthy associations for the young heir to the throne. Cleopatra, in inhabiting the edge of the Roman world, inhabits also a realm in which chastity is not so highly valued as sexuality and the exercise of power, so, although Cleopatra has an undeniable appeal for male authors in the period, she does for women as well. That in the end she is silenced by suicide was perceived as a mark of strength and was typical of many strong female figures available to Renaissance women. The translation by Mary Sidney Herbert, Countess of Pembroke, of

Robert Garnier's *Antoinie* (1590) as the companion piece to her commissioned *Cleopatra* by Samuel Daniel makes strong claims for Cleopatra's intelligence, voice, and political activity. When Eras asks Cleopatra, "Are you therefore cause of his [Antonius's] overthrow?" Cleopatra answers in language that claims her agency in words that anticipate Desdemona's dying defense of Othello: "I am sole cause: I did it, only I." Diomede, Cleopatra's secretary, admiringly describes her "training speach" and "forcing voice," her "hearing sceptred kings embassadors" to whom she, like Elizabeth I, can "Answere to each in his owne language make."[53] In providing Innogen with a tapestry of Cleopatra, Shakespeare evokes both the male tradition of viewing Cleopatra and the female perception of Cleopatra as a desirable and an eloquent ruler.

The story of Diana and Actaeon in what Shakespeare called the "chimneypiece," which could refer to a tapestry, a painted panel, or a design in plaster, depicts a myth retold by Bess of Hardwick in the large needlework hanging that pictures the moment when Diana turns Actaeon into the stag (Plate 5). The textual reference to Philomel's rape is also a reference to a tapestry that again tells the story of a silenced but powerful female. Although Philomel's story is more disturbing than Cleopatra's, it consists in far more than the suspended rape on the page turned down next to Innogen. Philomel's narrative includes her weaving a tapestry to communicate her rape to other women through what E. Jane Burns, writing about the medieval French romance *Philomena*, calls "an alternate economy of seeing and knowing cast in terms of women's work." The tapestry through which Philomel tells her story, Burns concludes, "does more than make the silent woman speak. It also transfers the terms of embodiment and beauty from the lovely woman to the newly found woven 'speech,' a speech that is now embodied within an object, a speech given material form in fabric. This significant shift allows Philomena to write the body instead of being the body, to act upon a body of writing rather than having her body acted upon by others."[54] Like Bess of Hardwick's appliquéd embroidery of Lucrecia with a muscular arm and determined expression (Plate 4), Innogen's reading of Philomel's rape suggests early modern women's rereading of the narratives of violence toward women available to them, including Dido and Mariam as well as Philomel, Cleopatra, and Lucrece. Bess's Lucrecia, like Artemesia Gentileschi's painting, explores the moment before her suicide, with Lucrecia's bared arm suggesting the physical strength and determination necessary for a victim of rape to commit suicide.[55] Diana's transformation of Actaeon asserts the possibility of revenge when she, like Innogen, is violated by the male gaze. The chamber's architecture of Innogen's identity is borne out at the play's conclusion, when, like a virginal Cleopatra, she is united with her Roman, Posthumus Leonatus, amid the spectacle appropriate to the joining of bodies and empires.

Although we need to acknowledge the extent to which Innogen's self-perceived identity is located in the visual and textual tapestries in her room, the representations of gynocentric narratives that I have just discussed are contaminated in the telling because it is Giacomo who provides both descriptions of the bedroom he has violated. The first description comes when he is in the room talking to himself about the necessity to note its details in order to prove that Innogen has lain with him, a project that consumes him as much as observing Innogen, because by noticing each detail he is also taking in the visual forms of her identity: "But my design. / To note the chamber: I will write all down: / Such and such pictures . . . the arras . . . and *the contents of th' story* (2.2.23–27, my emphasis). If Giacomo were only interested in later redescribing the room, he would not make such a point of noting the story of Tereus's rape of Philomel, which in fact he never tells Posthumus about. Giacomo notes the rape narrative in order to place himself within it, although he chooses to call himself Tarquin instead of Tereus, fusing the identity of his victim into both Philomel and Lucrece. Giacomo is committing a metaphoric if unmistakable rape of Innogen's person by entering her chamber: "For Iachimo," writes Georgianna Ziegler, "a woman's body is part and parcel of her room and can be similarly violated. Though he does not physically rape Imogen, we feel that a rape has been committed in his voyeuristic intrusion on her privacy."[56] In recounting the room as Innogen's emblematic identity, Giacomo further assaults Innogen because he must appropriate her bedroom's expression of her identity in order to prove that she is unchaste. The Philomel rape narrative for example forms part of the architecture of Innogen's subjectivity that Giacomo takes in with such attention that he can later boast to Posthumus that he has "brought / The knowledge of your mistress home" (2.4.50–51)—a phrase that connects what a man may see and know with what he may possess.

The second description occurs when Giacomo describes the room in order to prove to Posthumus that he has had sex with Innogen. It is this description that provides our "knowledge" of the room on which I base my analysis, including the "tapestry of silk and silver, the story / Proud Cleopatra, when she met her Roman" (2.4.69–70); "the chimney-piece, / Chaste Dian, bathing" (81–82); the ornate ceiling "fretted" with "golden cherubins," and the "winking" Cupid andirons "of silver, each on one foot standing" (88–91). A double way of reading emerges from these two descriptions associated with and told through a male who threatens at least a metaphoric rape and prepares to recount a willing surrender. The first way of reading this scene, which I have teased out with the help of historical information about women's architectural expressions of identity, is to see how the play at least opens the possibility that women may express identity through the resources available to them in both verbal and visual media. The second way of reading this scene is that even the most chaste female is vulnerable to male violation, a vulnerability expressed by the female figures with whom Innogen is surrounded. Tereus, who rapes Philomel, and Actaeon, who violates Diana with his gaze, may be punished in their different bizarre ways—Tereus, when Progne cooks up their son for his dinner; Actaeon, by being turned into the stag that Bess of Hardwick so vividly portrays in the moment before he is torn apart by his dogs. Despite their punishments, these violators of the female body cannot be contained. Both Tereus and Actaeon violate a female body, just as Giacomo has succeeded in violating Innogen's, down to noting the unusually shaped, "cinque-spotted" (2.2.38) mole on her breast. The opportunity that exists to imagine Innogen's perception of her own subjectivity through her bedroom's texts and textiles, or for the audience to imagine one for her, is largely overwritten by the violation through which it comes to us. This violation is in turn overwritten by the fact that the rape remains metaphoric and thus easily denied, while preserving Innogen's physical chastity. Paying attention to the violence that occurs in Innogen's bedroom even as it is avoided reminds us of how much the play revolves around threats to Innogen.[57] Violence that threatens Innogen, but that she nevertheless avoids, constitutes the metanarrative of the play. Innogen's relation to textiles repeatedly conveys these threats and saves her from them.

Skirting Rape in *Cymbeline*

If the tapestries momentarily open up Innogen's royal, even mythic identity, many of *Cymbeline*'s other textiles—the handkerchief, sheets, and especially the bloody cloth—serve to objectify her body in ways that make the issue of its possession visual and immediate. Yet Innogen continues to assert her identity, even when it is reduced to cloth, and, by occupying two different disguises, survives the attempts by Giacomo, Cloten, and Posthumus to possess and annihilate her. *Cymbeline* presents a number of textiles whose richness and variety help to create—and are created by—the romance in which they appear. Although the possibility that Innogen wants to rule England is written out of the play when the disguises that she dons to preserve her virginity and life also lead to her missing brothers, she, unlike Desdemona, survives the play's insistence that cloth is metonymic of her body by asserting a decided if limited control over the play's textiles. In particular, as the textiles increasingly signify her violent end, moving from handkerchief to sheet to bloody cloth, Innogen demonstrates with the help of Pisanio that her ability to use cloth for her own purposes is not limited to her bedroom but includes using costumes to disguise her identity.

Shakespeare's audience might well have felt comfortable with the extent to which *Cymbeline*'s different textiles connect with one another because its members were familiar with the everyday practice whereby cloth moved from one form to another. In the sixteenth century, valuable textiles were reused, cut down, and reshaped in a process called "translating." Bess of Hardwick cut up medieval priests' copes acquired by her husband, William St. Loe, during the dissolution of the monasteries, in order to create her hangings of worthy ancient women. Anne Clifford records the practice of translating cloth in her diary of 1618: "About this time the Gallery was hung with all my Lords Caparasons which Edwards the upholsterer made up" so that even the fancy clothing of horses from tournaments or other court entertainment was reused to make hangings.[58] Rich cloth was also reused for costumes. In court performances, writes Jean MacIntyre, crimson satin "that first dressed cardinals, bishops, and then clowns was cut down repeatedly to be used as new costumes, then parts of costumes, and at last ever more exiguous trimmings." Thus one warrant from the Revels Office orders that "the guarding of vi compassed garments for women" become "Jerkins and half Sleeves of the astronomers' [costumes]. 20 of which were again *translated* into barbarians and thereof Into guarding of the nether lace & false sleeves of vi moors' garments." Costumes for Elizabeth I were likewise "*translated* and new made" to entertain marital ambassadors from France in 1564 (my emphasis).[59]

The historical process of "translating" textiles from bishop's robe to clown's motley to trimmings proves a useful contemporary term for what happens onstage to the textiles in *Cymbeline*, which have a strong tendency to mutate or "translate" from one form or meaning to another. To a lesser extent we are familiar with the process of a staged textile translation from *Othello*, which has us follow the strawberry-spotted handkerchief as it moves from hand to hand and then metaphorically becomes the wedding sheets on the bed where Othello strangles Desdemona.[60] In *Cymbeline*, the handkerchief evokes the interconnection of female chastity and male honor in the first act; in the second act, the handkerchief's associations move to Innogen's sheets, whose whiteness Giacomo notes as he approaches the sleeping Innogen, muttering, "Our Tarquin thus / Did softly press the rushes, ere he waken'd / The chastity he wounded" (2.2.12–14), and "fresh lily! / and whiter than the sheets! That I might touch! / But kiss, one kiss!" (2.2.15–17). As Giacomo casts himself in the role of Tarquin and Innogen as Lucrece, the Italian moves silently toward her to reenact the moment before Tarquin wakened "The chastity he wounded." In that moment, Giacomo/Tarquin sees Innogen/Lucrece as chastity itself, the "fresh lily . . . whiter than the sheets," a series of associations in which woman, chastity, lily, and sheets become the means by which Giacomo equates her body with her chastity, and that chastity with cloth.

Innogen's own language picks up on the extent to which textiles have become metonymic of her body when Pisanio shows her the letter in which Posthumus orders her murdered for her infidelity. But Innogen envisions herself as a complexly worked garment rather than the blank sheet of chastity on which a man might write. Before she begs Pisanio to carry out her husband's order, she castigates herself for having lost Posthumus's faith in her, calling herself "a garment out of fashion," which, too "rich" to be translated into a wall hanging, must be reduced to rags: "And, for I am richer than to hang by th' walls, / I must be ripp'd:—to pieces with me!" (3.4.50–53). As a garment too elaborately made—too complete in its own identity to be cut up and translated into a wall hanging—Innogen must be ritually destroyed, ripped to pieces. To Giacomo, she may be the blank white of the sheet, but Innogen sees herself in terms of luxurious, colorful textiles, even as she imagines herself as that rich cloth ripped to pieces.

At this moment, when Innogen's personal narrative connects with the interpretation of textiles that would enable her possession and murder, she has a powerful helper in the form of Pisanio. Like Iago, Pisanio understands the importance of reading cloth. But he also has access to the play's wardrobe in ways that help Innogen stay alive long enough to regain her ability to make cloth work for her. Pisanio knows that the best way to convince Posthumus of Innogen's death at his hands is not to send such an elaborate piece of cloth as she imagines herself to be but a simple piece stained with blood. As a chilling echo of *Othello*'s strawberry-spotted handkerchief and blood-spotted sheets, as well as the fatal version of Posthumus and Innogen's future wedding sheets, the bloody cloth provides Posthumus with the ocular proof of Innogen's murder. Act 5 opens with Posthumus sorrowfully addressing the bloody cloth as if it were Innogen, as he acknowledges her supposed death at his command: "Yea, bloody cloth, I'll keep thee: for I wish'd / Thou shouldst be colour'd thus" (5.1.1–2). The "Thou" he addresses is both Innogen and the cloth, which have become indistinguishable to him.[61]

The bloody cloth, which we assume to be some remnant of her clothing that Posthumus believes to be drenched with her blood, may have reminded Shakespeare's audience as well of the bloody cloths that women used during menstruation. Michael Drayton provides a rare mention of "a filthy menstreous cloth" in his *Harmonie of the Church* (1591), following the apocryphal continuation of Esther in which, praying to God for courage, she says of the royal crown on her head, "I abhorre it as a menstruous ragge." The significance of Posthumus holding the bloody cloth—and, as Valerie Wayne points out, Posthumus wearing it as well[62]—could easily trigger such associations for both Innogen's husband and Shakespeare's audience, providing a reminder of the fertility lost with Innogen's death. As Posthumus holds Innogen's own "mean'st garment," he holds a stage prop that recalls the full significance of his loss, an analog of Desdemona's bloodied wedding sheets and yet a more devastatingly ordinary memento mori. By giving him this bloody cloth, Pisanio, who knows so much about cloth and costume, successfully uses the logic of Iago, Othello, and Giacomo to make Posthumus confront the consequences of equating his wife with her chastity and that chastity with cloth. In mourning the bloody cloth as Innogen, Posthumus comes to realize the price of his jealousy and even questions whether her fidelity is more important than her life as he asks poignantly, "how many / Must murder wives much better than themselves / For wrying but a little?" (5.1.3–5).

A second group of textiles, the costume disguises, also undergoes translation within the play, taking on a life beyond costuming the actors in order to costume the characters. These alterations or "translations," like Bottom's "translation" in the woods of *A Midsummer Night's Dream*, reveal how much this theater relies on metaphoric translations made literal through costume change. Innogen crosses class as a franklin's wife to flee the court and (she thinks) rejoin Posthumus Leonatus, and then crosses gender as Fidele on hearing of Posthumus's order to have her murdered. Like Jessica in *The Merchant of Venice*, Innogen is a reluctant appropriator of male clothing and behavior. As a boy she is without the architectural subjectivity within which she usually sleeps. Her comment when she first enters in boy's clothing bewails her translation: "I see a man's life is a tedious one, / I have tir'd myself: and for two nights together / Have made the ground my bed. I should be sick, / But that my resolution helps me" (3.6.1–4). "Tiring" herself as a boy means being "tired" by rough living and incommodious sleeping arrangements.

However reluctant Innogen is to wear the cloth that thinly veils her gender, the disguise that she has obtained from the wardrober Pisanio preserves her virginity and her life. Pisanio also (rather surprisingly) happens to have the clothes that Posthumus wore when bidding his farewell to Innogen, which he gives to Cloten, who is obsessed with transforming into revenge Innogen's statement that she prefers Posthumus's "mean'st garment, / That ever hath but clipp'd his body" to him (2.3.128–30). But because they both left the court in disguise, the closest Cloten gets to her is when she awakens next to his dead body. Cloten's need to translate Innogen's love for Posthumus's "mean'st garment" into her rape derives from the fury with which he absorbs the news of her preference for Posthumus in act 2, scene 3. This scene combines Cloten's expressions of rage—"'His garment!' Now the devil . . . 'His garment!'"

(2.4.132) and "'His meanest garment!'" (144)—with Innogen's agitated attempt to find the bracelet stolen from her arm by Giacomo during his intrusion. This combining of Cloten's emerging violence with Innogen's search for the missing object is reminiscent of Desdemona's search for the missing handkerchief as Innogen directs her maid, whose name, Helen, is yet another reminder of mythic rape: "I do think / I saw't this morning: confident I am . . . go and search" (139–41). Cloten's increasing obsession with Posthumus's clothing combined with Innogen's search for her "manacle," juxtaposes the issue of Innogen's chastity and the possession of that chastity within rape. After Innogen exits, Cloten finishes the scene by vowing, "I'll be reveng'd: / 'His mean'st garment!' Well" (150–51). Cloten, who has earlier tried to "penetrate" Innogen's chamber with the song "Hark, hark the lark" in the hope that if the musicians can "penetrate her with your fingering, so: we'll try with tongue too . . . I'll never give o'er" (2.3.12–13), takes Innogen's statement as the insult that will justify her rape and possession: "With [Posthumus's] suit upon my back will I ravish her; first kill him, and in her eyes . . . and when my lust hath dined (which, as I say to vex her I will execute in the clothes that she so prais'd) to the court I'll knock her back" (3.5.134–40). But because Innogen is safely disguised and because Cloten has become obsessed with wearing Posthumus's clothing, he dies ridiculously in an argument with Innogen's older brother, Guiderius, about his tailor (4.2.73–113).[63] Instead of robbing Innogen of her maidenhead, Cloten is himself literally beheaded. This violent death both preserves Innogen's "head" and reverses the common image of the "headless" woman whose beheading conveys her lost virginity. But because Cloten remains dressed in Posthumus's clothing, Innogen must still experience the shock of awakening beside the headless body of the man she believes to be her husband.

Even Posthumus's disguise, which Posthumus adopts the moment he is through addressing the bloody cloth as Innogen, becomes a means to preserve her. Posthumus determines to change his clothes because "'tis enough / That, Britain, I have kill'd thy mistress" (5.1.19–20), "I'll disrobe me / Of these Italian weeds, and suit myself / As does Briton peasant: so I'll fight" (5.1.22–24). By dressing across class as a Briton peasant, Posthumus finally wins his place at Innogen's side after defending the narrow passageway from Milford-Haven. As Linda Woodbridge points out, the attack of this "lane" (5.3.2; 5.5.7, 13, 18) signifies a corporeal image of invasion: "When the Romans invade . . . [they] try to penetrate through a lane whose narrowness is repeatedly emphasized. A stand being made at the cervix of this lane, British society, direly endangered, is saved."[64] Posthumus's disguised appearance at the crucial moment at the port of Milford-Haven prevents still another kind of rape, the invasion of Britain as embodied in its queen-apparent, Innogen. Thus the disguises in the play, like the other textiles, circulate around issues of sexual possession and violence with all their political implications, including Posthumus's intent to have Innogen murdered, Cloten's intent to rape Innogen, and Posthumus's defense of a Britain whose "body" is, like England under threat from the Armada, feminized and thus conflated with the body of Innogen as heir. Still other disguises are revealed when the runaway courtier, Belarius, produces the "most curious mantle, wrought by th' hand / Of his queen mother" that had once wrapped Arviragus (5.6.362–63), and so proves the identity of Guiderius and Arviragus, Cymbeline's sons, whom he has raised in Wales far from such courtly textiles. Although this final revelation of disguise takes the throne from Innogen, she remains a royal bride. The textiles that represent, disguise, and aid her delimit her married, political identity, but she remains a viable political entity, like James I's daughter, Elizabeth, who became not only Electress of Palatine and Queen of Bohemia, but ultimately genetrix of the Hanover royal line when her grandson, George I, became King of England.

As part of the structures of everyday life, textiles enter Shakespeare's tragedy and dramatic romance as the means to recover and to violate the subjectivity of their female characters. In contrast with the structures of everyday life, however, textiles as staged and interpreted in the tragedy of *Othello* and the dramatic romance of *Cymbeline* enable the plays' violence against their female characters even when, as in *Cymbeline*, no lasting physical harm is done. In *Othello*, the reading of textiles is so overdetermined by Iago and Othello that the promise of Desdemona's and Emilia's agency is violently repressed. In the dramatic romance of *Cymbeline*, the textiles are so various and translatable that they themselves come to represent the multivalent interpretations residing in cloth. The emblematic architecture of Innogen's chamber, the contingencies presented by disguise and Pisanio's repeated interventions allow Innogen the time and material necessary to survive intact, as well as to open alternative if limited readings of a privileged woman's mind and body. As a result, at the play's conclusion Innogen and Posthumus live to unite handkerchief with bloody cloth, disguise with disguise. The path toward marital murder in *Othello* is paved with a purse, a handkerchief, and bedsheets; in *Cymbeline*, the path to marital consummation is paved with a handkerchief, the textualities of Innogen's bedroom, Innogen's sheets, the bloody cloth, and the escapes, misapprehensions, and recognitions occasioned by disguise, as well as the mantel "wrought" by her dead mother, an evocation of a historic queen who is otherwise missing from the stage. As in *Othello*, the textiles of *Cymbeline* allow the objectification of the central female character, demonstrating that the body of a male actor dressed as a woman is the possession of men. At the same time, however, these textiles allow at least the possibility of female self-possession. If at the play's conclusion Innogen finds herself both dispossessed of the throne and at last firmly affianced to Posthumus by her father's consent, Posthumus has finally acknowledged that her body is her own.

When *Othello* and *Cymbeline* stage women's relations to textiles, they proceed by simultaneously recalling and reinterpreting the historic relation of women to these objects and to the connections and social processes that they embody. On stage, the textiles become connected with violence because the plays evoke but disrupt the historical relation between women and their domestic textualities. This disruption in turn provides access to staged women's lives—to their forms of constructing identity, to their sexuality, and thus to their bodies. As disturbing as this process is, *Othello* and *Cymbeline* impersonate the importance of women's historical relations to textiles, the situation of these textiles within networks of kinship and domestic alliance, and their visual impact when worn on the body or used to create domestic space. In reinterpreting women's historical relations to textiles, these plays enact the centrality of textiles in early modern life as objects whose production offered to make the lives of women meaningful and safe. At the same time, these plays demonstrate that when women's worth rested on household materials and labor, their lives remained vulnerable to erotic and misogynist interpretation.

CHAPTER FIVE

Mary Sidney Wroth: Clothing Romance

In *Othello* and *Cymbeline*, the everyday, erotic, and theatrical properties of cloth locate Desdemona and Innogen in the genres of tragedy and dramatic romance. In these plays, as the meanings of cloth curtail and enable female agency, those meanings are realized in genre: the pace of events, the interaction of characters within narrative, and the play's outcome depend on the significance of handkerchiefs, an embroidered strawberry pattern, sheets, a bloody cloth, cross-dressing, and disguise. This chapter takes the discussion about textiles and female agency from male-authored drama to female-authored prose romance, from the compact structure of the plays to the 590,000 words forming the two volumes of Mary Sidney Wroth's *The Countess of Montgomery's Urania*.[1] For Wroth, who approaches her genre as a self-conscious explorer of women's personal, political, and authorial agency, cloth becomes central to writing romance.

In order to discuss Wroth's use of cloth in creating *Urania*, I consider four connected ways in which *Urania* relies on textiles for its impressive form, its creation of characters, and its awareness of itself as a romance of female authorship. I begin by discussing the relation of the "dilated" body of romance to women's bodies, which are in turn connected to cloth. Patricia Parker has discussed how dilation is crucial to romance because its exegetical and rhetorical meanings derive from figurations of the ample female body, from the positive—Rahab as figure of the church spreading out across the globe—to the monstrously feminine figure that threatens to disrupt the "masculine" desire to bring about conclusions to the narrative.[2] Several of the female figures that sixteenth-century readers of romance saw as blocking the conclusion of works like *The Odyssey* were associated with cloth. As Parker points out, one character who delays the story's conclusion is Calypso, whose name "means 'covering'" (Parker, 12). This meaning connects her with Penelope, who weaves and unravels her shroud for Laertes, creating a silent tale that nevertheless parallels Odysseus's own. As if in response to fears of feminine dilation, in *Urania* Wroth embraces dilation and the female figures who make it possible.

The second way in which cloth is central to Wroth's construction of *Urania* derives from the everyday material practices of the Sidney family. Like Innogen in her imagined royal bedroom, Eleonora of Toledo at the Palazzo Vecchio, and Bess of Hardwick at New Hardwick Hall, the Sidneys lived within carefully constructed architectures of identity, whose gardens, exteriors, and interior design were echoed in their elaborately wrought tapestries and embroidery. For both men and women in the Sidney family, the production and consumption, the giving and display of luxury textiles formed activities central to their politics. Wroth had lived the ways in which luxury defined privileged people and their spaces. Accordingly, she both idealized and satirized these practices in her romance.

The third way in which cloth is central to Wroth's creation of *Urania* derives from early modern rhetorical practice expressed as cloth. In addition to the Sidneys' use of textiles in their everyday life, as writers, courtiers, and public figures, they participated in that central Renaissance intellectual activity, the interpretation of rhetoric as expounded in classical texts. Sidneyan appropriations of classical rhetoric helped to redefine the English aesthetics of drama, verse, and prose over fifty years, in Philip's widely circulated letter protesting Elizabeth's proposed French marriage, in his *Defense of Poesy*, in the psalms that he and his sister Mary Sidney Herbert translated into English meters, in Philip's and Mary Sidney Wroth's experimental sonnet sequences, in Philip's court entertainment, and in Wroth's play, *Love's Victory*, as well as in the family's explorations of the pastoral romance as courtly aesthetic. Like Philip Sidney, Mary Sidney Wroth plays brilliantly and incessantly with the rhetorical structure of the sentence. She also uses the classical association of rhetoric with cloth to designate her characters through colors and fabrics that both reveal and disguise their interiority. And, like her aunt, Mary Sidney Herbert, who represented the poetic collaboration with her brother Philip as weaving and cloth, Wroth used the rhetorical power implicit in the semiotic interrelations of texts and textiles.

Although Wroth connects cloth and authorship in ways that resemble her aunt's and uncle's use of metaphor based in aristocratic practice, *Urania* emphasizes different practices than one might perhaps expect. Wroth inhabited a world in which women were still taught skilled needlework but in which the wealthiest families commissioned far more textiles than they produced domestically, even as the practice of embroidery was becoming well-established among the middling classes. Although Wroth describes the luxurious textiles prevalent at the royal court, for the most part she excludes domestic textile practice from her romance. In particular, the production of needlework is largely absent from both her narrative and her figural language. One exception points to Pamphilia's practice of needlework, which may possibly figure Wroth's own. It comes when Amphilanthus sees a miniature portrait of Pamphilia in her closet, "drawne by the best hand of her time." Her hair down, the sitter holds her right hand against her heart, and against "a wastecoate shee had of needle worke, wrought those flowers she loved in the field" (U1, 321). A waistcoat of one's favorite flowers is the kind of clothing that a woman of Wroth's time, place, and status might well have produced and had herself painted wearing by the best hand of her time. In fact, Isaac Oliver produced a portrait of an unidentified woman around 1605–15 who wears a dress heavily embroidered with flowers, with her right hand held against her heart in the same gesture that Wroth describes.[3] This reference to domestic needlework, however, stands alone within her brief description of a miniature.

Wroth's mingling of verbal with visual media, of written text and described textiles, is the fourth and final route through which cloth becomes a force in *Urania*. Wroth is the self-conscious mistress of a landscape in which the writing of ciphers, initials, and stanzas of poetry may take place on paper, on trees, as embroidery, in the pastoral landscape, and within architectural design. Such connections are implicit in the early modern conviction that the verbal and visual are versions of one another, as well as the belief that combining verbal and visual texts stimulates signification that is more meaningful than the sum of its parts. From the smallest details of characterization and mise-en-scène to metafictional commentary, Wroth creates a landscape of female textualities, pausing from time to time to comment on the process of composing her romance through connections between writing and clothing, narrative and tapestry, text and textile.

The Feminine, Cloth, and Western Narratival Tradition

Wroth's *Urania* confronts the English nervousness about the feminine qualities assigned to romance by taking the rhetorical concept of *dilatio* to an extreme in its two volumes. Wroth's lengthy romance both embodies Patricia Parker's discussion of the historical identification of romance's dilation with the female body in *Literary Fat Ladies* (1987) and suggests ways to further Parker's observations by considering Wroth's particular forms of amplification. Parker famously demonstrated the philological identification of romance with the feminine as it derives from biblical, rhetorical, and obstetrical sources, in which the injunction to "increase and multiply" connects the creation and interpretation of texts to the female body. She summarizes her argument: "Dilation as the 'opening' of a closed text to make it 'increase and multiply' and to transform its brevity into a discourse 'at large' . . . joins dilation as both sexual and obstetrical 'opening' and the production of generational increase" (Parker, 15, 236n.14). Helen Hackett further points out that women's reproduction combines with the orality of women's tale telling that is visible in romance: "The idea of these stories as unstructured, boundless and indeed oral, conceptualises them almost like a biological flow—something which just pours out."[4] Because dilation was connected to the capacity of the female body to reproduce, it suggested not just childbearing but the threat of uncontrollable production, of excess. Moreover, the dilation of any narrative, especially those produced by the "indulgence of romance," was widely perceived as dangerous because dilatory and leisurely (Parker, 11), and so formed part of the English anxiety that leisure, excess, and immorality were one and the same.

The figure *dilatio* was a key factor in gendering as feminine that most dilated of written genres, the prose romance, and in assuming that its readership was female—designations that, however negative, allowed avid male readers of romance the pleasures of occupying a feminine subject position while reading.[5] Parker points out that for the early modern thinkers who wrote about the processes—and dangers—of amplification in the epic romance, what mattered was the success of the male hero in returning home or founding Rome, while the obstacles that Odysseus or Aeneas met were female figures blocking closure, whether Circe, Calypso, or Dido. Parker notes that for Erasmus, who equates masculine prose with the control of the rhetorical amplification needed to create a text, ending a text meant "mastering or controlling the implicitly female, and perhaps hence wayward, body of the text itself."[6]

In *The Countess of Montgomery's Urania*, Wroth's primary innovation is the transformation of the female blocking figures used to amplify narrative into a single, monumental female—the author herself—who, by blocking the conclusion of the romance as a whole, exchanges the mastery of conclusion for the pleasures of a dilation so expanded and so leisurely that they challenge the limits of patriarchal discourse. This is in part why both the published and manuscript volumes of *Urania* end in mid-sentence, forbidding the reader closure.[7] And it is why, in Wroth's rewriting of romance, more than three hundred male and female figures replace Circe, Calypso, the Sirens, and Dido as opportunities to expand the narrative. Through the experiences of Wroth's plethora of characters and their stories, usually internested within still other narratives, Wroth produces the multiple scenarios comprising her two ample volumes of text. If the stories of slander surrounding her character Elyna, become "little Sluses, that but opened, let in Rivers, and Oceans of discourses" (*U1*, 599), Wroth's prose floods outward, from the female body generating her text.

To dilate her romance, Wroth appropriates the textualities of the strongest female figures from classical epic and romance, figures whose own forms are implicitly associated with cloth, from the Three Fates who twist and eventually cut the thread of each life to Helen's weaving of the story of Troy and Penelope's weaving of Laertes's shroud.[8] One of *Urania*'s poems in particular connects the textile production of classical female figures with Wroth's insistence on leisurely dilation. When the gentlewoman Doralina, a character afflicted with an inconstant lover, appears with both a tale to tell and a poem to recite, the Queen of Naples grants her all the time that she needs. Josephine Roberts notes that in "The Queen of Naples rare in Poetry" Wroth shadows her aunt, Mary Sidney Herbert.[9] In this scene, in Naples's capacity as monarch of both poetry and pastoral romance, she commands Doralina to recite her verses, "and the story too." Time is not an issue: "We have time enough for both, and no time being able to be better spent, we can affoord the evening into the bargaine, rather than misse such a relation" (*U1*, 492). The hundred-line poem that Doralina then recites to the Queen of Naples is directed at her absent male lover. Its first half describes women associated with thread and cloth in classical narratives about inconstant men: "Dido, one whose misery was had / By Love, for which she in Deathes robes was clad"; Ariadne, whose "thrid," or thread, the speaker has studied as the means to draw her lover "from harme"; and "Phillis," who made "a Cord the end / Of her affections." These threads not only create and end life but also compose narrative, as Wroth's lines make Ariadne's cord both a story in itself and a link to Phyllis's cord, with which she ended "her affections" by hanging herself (*U1*, 493). Wroth's recurring image of the labyrinth as the indecipherable mores of her time haunts passages in *Urania* and concludes her sonnet sequence, reminding her readers that Ariadne's thread brought Theseus out of the maze, although it eventually led to Ariadne's abandonment.[10]

The second half of Doralina's poem focuses on Penelope as a more hopeful figure associated with cloth, as the speaker compares her wait for her inconstant lover to Penelope's wait for Ulysses, while he dawdled with Circe and Calypso, as "Against his will, he oft his will enjoyed." Even as she speaks wryly of her inconstant lover's delays, Doralina uses Penelope's narrative to represent the hope that her lover may reappear. As she explains in an apostrophe to him, "I like Penelope have all this time / Of your absenting, let no thought to clime / In me of change, though courted, and pursu'd / By love, perswasions, and even fashons rude / Almost to force extending." The speaker ends her story by addressing her own knightly wanderer: "Come, I say, come againe, and with Ulisses / Enjoy the blessings of your best blisses" in a "chaste bed" (*U1*, 492–95). As Doralina recites her poem to the Queen of Naples, Wroth provides no conclusion for her and no homecoming for her Ulysses. The open-endedness of her story is very much the point in a romance whose two volumes each end in mid-sentence. As typified in this scene, the amplitude of *Urania* offers the reader its most elaborate fiction—the fiction of extended leisure.

A far shorter example of Wroth's prose, a letter that she wrote to her father, Robert Sidney as Viscount Lisle, shortly after the death of her husband, Robert Wroth, offers a stark contrast to this leisurely scene. In this letter written from Penshurst on 17 October 1614,[11] Wroth wrote for help in blocking her brother-in-law's attempt to gain the wardship of her infant son, James, her first and only legitimate child. If John Wroth had acquired his nephew's wardship, he would have had the use of the child's inherited lands and revenues until James came of age. With both her child's future and her own finances at stake, Mary Sidney Wroth wrote her father that without his help, "the poore child will have an ill account." As she replays the two sides of the argument between herself and her husband's family, she explains that "they say directly that they have, and must have the lease of the land till hee come of yeeres, I trust as your Lo[rdship]: hath correctly, and lovingly begun that so you will be pleased to proceed, for it is now your part to be his father being left both ways in blood." Wroth closes by explaining that she has written briefly at her father's request about this situation. As she concludes respectfully, referring to herself in the third person: "She hopes shortly now to see you the time growing on to leave this place, and [withal] for the other business which hath troubled her; and longs to have an end, yett non butt such as may best like you, and bee fittest for your honour, and house." The letter's shift to the third person together with Wroth's longing "to have an end" to this business, one "fittest for your honour, and house," allows her to narrate the story of a woman caught in the exigencies of battling with her husband's relatives for wardship of her son and for her own financial future, a woman who "longs to have an end" to these matters.

In the world of the everyday, resolution is the point, although it may lie in the power of others or, sadly, in the death of her son at age two. In the world of Wroth's romance, which she alone controls, delaying resolution means perpetrating the illusion of leisure as the means to explore connections between the desire for closure and the desire for the never-ending story. When Urania and Pamphilia stand before "a round building like a Theater," Pamphilia expresses a desire to see this portion of their tale conclude, "to see the end of it." But Urania reminds her of the overarching principle of this romance: "All adventures were not framed for you to finish" (*U1*, 372). In Wroth's romance, all outcomes exist for Wroth to end. Or not, as she chooses.

Sidney Women and the Politics of Cloth

The Sidneys had gained their lands, wealth, and public responsibility through their attendance at court and by handling consequent public appointments with a fair degree of effectiveness and honesty. Like all upwardly mobile families, their rise was closely connected to the signifying weight that their culture placed on textiles. A letter written 22 July 1573 from Wroth's grandmother, Mary Dudley Sidney, to the family retainer, John Cochrame, records the political importance of cloth in gaining and retaining favor at court. In 1573, the Sidneys were hoping that Henry Sidney would be reposted Governor of Ireland.[12] I quote it at length because its reiterated urgency conveys how important a gift of velvet to Queen Elizabeth could be to the family's political position, especially at the "sorest time for my Lord for diverse considerations": "Cockrame her majesty likes so well of the velvet that my Lord gave me last for a gown as she lately very earnestly willed me to send her so much of it as will make her a loose gown. I understand my Lord had his at Coopers or Cookes. I pray you fail not to inquire severally of whom and what is least of it. If there be 12 yards it is enough."[13] Elizabeth, who likes Mary Dudley Sidney's new clothing made of velvet, has asked for enough of the same cloth for a "loose gown." Sidney immediately writes to find out where her husband had acquired this velvet, and to get "12 yards" immediately. She points out that we "may not slack the care hereof for she will take it ill. And it is now the sorest time for my Lord for diverse considerations to dislike her for such a trifle. Wherefore I once again earnestly require this forthwith without all delays to go or send about it for there is no remedy but it must be had." She points out also that she will pay for this purchase herself from her stipend as lady-in-waiting: "I know my Lord will be well enough content withal for his Lordship shall be paid for it out of my Michaelmas stipend." Mary Sidney returns again to the speed with which Cochrame must act in order to press her husband's suit: "Otherwise if she conjecture we stand waiting her so small a matter it may presently hinder a greater matter towards my Lord in whom the fault would be laid and not to me because it is well known his Lordship hath the painage for all such things belonging to me." Wroth's grandmother connects the velvet for Elizabeth to the family hopes once more at the letter's conclusion, when she repeats, "I leave you with charge yet again for this velvet." Another, slightly later, accounting of a gift of velvet from Mary Sidney to Elizabeth, "14 yards of velvet for the Queen's Majesty" at a cost of "£14.12s.6d.," demonstrates that such gifts formed an ongoing requirement of her position as lady-in-waiting, courtier, and activist for her family's ambitions. During the same period, she paid just over £4 for a banquet in honor of the queen at Lambeth House, a presumably elaborate affair that nevertheless cost a pittance compared to twelve yards of velvet.[14]

As the Sidneys' political position spurred them to purchase luxury textiles in England and on the continent, their correspondence reveals how deeply engaged the men of the family also were with fine textiles while providing insight into how scarce and valuable such textiles were until later in the seventeenth century.[15] As Governor of Flushing from 1590 to 1616, Robert Sidney had an inside track to the tapestries, lace, and fine linen available in the Netherlands, although even across the Channel such commodities could be difficult to locate. Like Henry VIII decades before and like their older contemporary, Bess of Hardwick, the Sidneys participated in the trade in secondhand luxuries. In 1595, Rowland Whyte reported to his employer, Robert Sidney at Flushing, that "Lady Rich desires that if the hangings you write of are not gone, she would like a piece or two of the story of Cyrus," perhaps because the Emperor Cyrus's successes as a general suggested the military rise of Penelope Rich's brother, Robert Devereux, Earl of Essex. Robert Sidney is often involved with seeking tapestries for himself. In 1612, William Trumbull writes from the Netherlands to Sidney, by then Viscount Lisle, concerning his request for hangings "of five Flemish ells deep, and 100 in circumference," as well as lace. Trumbull has found some "old" tapestries of the "late Duke of Arschott" that are the right size, unless Sidney prefers new tapestries. Here the subject matter of the tapestries is not as important as their size, as they must have been intended for a particularly large room at Penshurst or Baynard's Castle, with each piece ten feet wide. Trumbull was less successful finding the lace, or "cutworks," because they were simply too dear to purchase: "These people," he writes, "will not part with them but at great and extraordinary rates" (*HMC Penshurst* 5:63–64). The Sidney correspondence from 1590 to 1620 contains brief mentions of waiting for hangings to be made, the transportation of professional embroiderers from the Netherlands to England, and the presentation by Robert Sidney's representative, Rowland Whyte, of suitable textile gifts at court, including a suite of hangings that Robert Sidney gave Robert Cecil, because in imparting "my suit to him," Whyte had promised, "I would bestow a fair set of hangings to have it effected."[16]

Still other textiles from the Sidneys' everyday world accessorize *Urania*, where Wroth's detailed descriptions of the textiles echo family inventories, as when Elyna gives Peryneus a scarf as a favor, "a marvellous rich one of Crimson Tafaty, embroidered with gold, silver, and dainty coloured Silkes" (*U1*, 597). Inventories, like the 1583 inventory of items at Kenilworth, list needlework pieces that were probably professional in origin, including the bed "tester, ceiler double valance and valances of crimson velvet richly embroidered with cinque-foils of cloth of silver, with my Lord's arms very richly embroidered in the midst of the ceiler and tester, supported with the white lion and bear, silver, lined through with red buckram" (*HMC Penshurst* 1:279). Large textiles emblazoned with heraldic identity, like the pastoral tapestry featuring the Earl of Leicester's arms at the center flanked by enclosed gardens (Plate 21), while professionally produced, contain elements frequently found in pastoral needlework designs created in the household. Also recorded are "cushions and stools of needle-work," their size suggesting that they were produced domestically. Such items include "a large cushion of needlework, the ground crimson silk wrought with flowers, etc., of gold, silver, and green silk, fringed with gold and silk, lined with crimson satin, with four buttons and tassels," together with "a cushion of silk needlework, with letters E.K. in gold in the midst, fringed and tasseled with gold, silver and silk of sundry colours, lined with crimson satin, striped with gold and silver" (1:289).

In the seventeenth century, the Sidney women continued to be givers of velvet and textiles, as when Wroth's mother gave Robert Cecil a fine piece of Holland linen "to make him shirts" in order to "put him in mind of her suit" for her husband's return from Flushing.[17] They likewise participated in the general imperative to perform needlework. The accounts of the Sidney family of 1573 for the future Mary Sidney Herbert include "Silk and thread for Mrs. Mary, to make her smocks, 3s"; and "knitting pins and needles for her" (*HMC Penshurst,* 1:267, 268). In time Herbert was praised among the queens and aristocrats whom John Taylor holds up as examples in *The Needles Excellency*. Although Taylor acknowledges Herbert's writing and scholarship, he suggests that it is her needlework that will ensure that her writing is remembered: "She wrought so well in Needlework, that she, / Nor yet her works, shall ere forgotten be." At Christmas in 1577 Herbert gave Elizabeth "a doublet of lawn embroidered all over with gold, silver, and silk of diverse colours, and lined with yellow taffeta," which was probably the work of her own hands.[18] When it came to fine needle-work, though, Herbert and Wroth were members of different generations. Although wealthy, even royal, women sewed in the sixteenth century, by the turn of the seventeenth century women as privileged as Wroth often supple-mented or replaced domestic output by commissioning professionally produced textiles. For example, the Sidneys, and perhaps Wroth specifically, presented Anne of Denmark with a pair of gloves professionally produced by a glover named Shepharde,[19] a very different kind of gift than the needlework that Eliza-beth had once prized as made by the hands of the giver.

Another factor in the decline of needlework in elite families was the trend toward interior rooms with matching decor. Instead of being furnished with the bed testers, cushion covers, and turkey work produced by a household of needleworkers led by its mistress, bedrooms and their related spaces were increasingly clothed in professionally produced fabrics whose patterns were woven in silk and silk blends instead of embroidered domestically. The Penshurst inventory of 1623 records that the suite of rooms called the "king's lodging" featured decor unified by gold and "russet," or reddish-brown. Its six "pieces of new Tapestry hangings of imagery work" were probably "bordered and striped" to accord with the gilt bedstead's "Tester of uncut Russet velvet garnished with gold and Russet lace with single Valance suitable to the same and deep fringe with gold," five curtains in the same color scheme, the whole topped with "gilt cups" and "feathers." "Leicester's Lodging" was decorated in "crimson and silver"; "Gloucester's Lodging" in "crimson and gold."[20] It seems likely that since these changes took place while Wroth was writing her volumes of *Urania*, they influenced not only domestic needlework practice but also the extent to which that everyday practice entered her romance. However, Wroth never loses sight of her heritage or the prestige that her family had accumulated through the favor of Queen Elizabeth and King James, aided in part by gifts of cloth. Although needlework practice is largely missing from her romance, Wroth employs a wealth of textiles to clothe her characters, to represent their interiority, and to dilate her narrative.

Two engravings by Simon de Passe take descriptions of the Sidney lifestyle into the visual dimension. His portrait of Wroth's famous aunt, Mary Sidney Herbert, of 1618 (Figure 28) closely connects her aristocratically clothed body, her identity as a Sidney, and her authorship. For this image Herbert chose to hold the book that she had co-authored with her brother Philip, labeled *Davids Psalms*, her major unpublished work, instead of the books that she had seen through press, including the *Arcadias* of 1593 and 1598, her own translations of Robert Garnier's *Antonie* in 1595, and Philippe de Mornay's *A Discourse of Life and Death*, which went through five editions.[21] Set at the top of the oval surrounding this portrait is the Sidney crest of the pheon, an arrow slicing through an obstacle; Herbert retained the use of this crest throughout her life, as did her niece, Mary Wroth.[22] The portrait overtly connects Herbert's social status with her translation of the psalms through her aristocratic clothing. Her gown of pinked satin is worn over a bodice and sleeves embroidered with flowering plants, recalling the needleworked waistcoat described in the *Urania* miniature. Her elaborate ruff is open and slightly flattened to cover her shoulders and frame her head. The ruff is a marvel of reticello lacemaking even in an age of intricate lace. Composed of a three-tiered design, the first two tiers are attached to one another. These consist of an inner border of squares with stars worked within them, then a series of partial ovals, with the design forming a lacey

Figure 28. Simon de Passe, *Portrait of Mary Sidney Herbert, Countess of Pembroke*, 1618. Engraving. Department of Prints and Drawings. © Trustees of the British Museum.

version of the Sidney crest. The third tier of lace, set on a wire frame separate from that holding the squares and pheons, features even larger ovals, each of which contains a swimming swan. Herbert's Vermeer-sized pearl earrings complement the double necklace of large pearls that lead the eye from her face to the book in her hand. The doubled row of pearls at her wrist, hanging just below the lace cuff, emphasizes the connection between her hand and the book it helped create. The weight of this aristocratic personage rests on the cartouche beneath it that reads, "The Right Honorable and most vertuous Lady Mary Sidney, wife to the late deceased Henry Herbert Earle of Pembroke etc."

Simon de Passe's title page for *The Countesse of Mountgomeries Urania* (Figure 29) also advertises a book as a Sidneyan achievement. Instead of the more common combination of a title page and an interior engraved portrait, the engraver and, very likely, Wroth herself opted for an elaborate title page with a cartouche similar to that of her renowned aunt. Wroth's lineage and connections appear as part of the book's title in the cartouche suspended at the top of the engraving's first arch, which forms the upper frame of a pastoral landscape: "The Countesse of Mountgomeries Urania. Written by the right honorable the Lady Mary Wroath. Daughter to the right Noble Robert Earle of Leicester. And Neece to the ever famous, and resnowned Sr Phillipe Sidney knight. And to the most excelent Lady Mary Countesse of Pembroke late deceased." Wroth's title demonstrates Ben Jonson's observation about Mary Wroth, that the name of Sidney was itself an "imprese of the great."[23] It also forms a verbal portrait, with the detailed picture of a pastoral landscape illustrating not her physical likeness but the luxurious pastoral landscape that her head and hand had created. Its central archways or monuments resemble those of James I's entry into London in 1604;[24] its dwellings and verdure, embroidered with gardens, hills, and trees, combines an idealized view of Penshurst with the pastoral and courtly landscape of the Sidneys' romances.

The audience of this title page gains access to its landscape by looking through the first of three elaborate "arches," as such triumphal monuments were called. Two dwarfed figures in pastoral dress, at the lower left, stand just within the first arch, liminal beings advancing on this landscape only slightly ahead of the viewer. Maureen Quilligan convincingly identifies them as "Pamphilia and Amphilanthus (both poets), coming to free the lovers trapped in the Palace of Love."[25] In *Urania*, Pamphilia at this moment is "apparreld in a Gowne of light Tawny or Murrey, embroidered with the richest, and perfectest Pearle for roundnesse and whitenes, the work contrived into knots and Garlands." Amphilanthus is "in Ashcolour, witnessing his repentance, yet was his cloake, and the rest of his suite so sumptuously embroidred with gold, as spake for him, that his repentance was most glorious" (*U1*, 169). With them, the

The
Countesse
of Mountgomeries
URANIA.
Written by the right honorable the Lady
MARY WROATH.
Daughter to the right Noble Robert
Earle of Leicester.
And Neece to the ever famous, and re-
nowned St Phillips Sidney knight. And to
ye most excellt Lady Mary Countesse of
Pembroke late deceased.

LONDON
Printed for IOH: MARRIOTT
and IOHN GRISMAND And
are to bee sould at theire shoppes in St Dunstons. Church
yard in Fleetstreet and in
Poules Ally at ye signe of
the Gunn.

Simō: Passæus sculp:

Figure 29. Simon de Passe, title page, *The Countess of Montgomery's Urania*, 1621. Engraving. © British Library.

viewer glimpses walled gardens to the right and left, of the kind evident in Leicester's pastoral tapestry bearing his arms (Plate 21). One garden is connected to a banqueting house set within its knot gardens, a manor house and small fortress or castle, a windmill—a common feature in the visual pastoral tradition, but also a possible allusion to the recently translated *Don Quixote*—and a countryside dotted with trees planted in rows, in the middle of which rises a promontory with another arch or monument at its top. The pastoral landscape joins *Urania* with Penshurst, where Wroth's mother, Barbara Gamage Sidney, kept a banqueting house. Although the family letters reveal the constant expense and attention required to produce the grapes, cherries, apricots, peaches, and boar meat that Barbara frequently sent to court, like Ben Jonson's "To Penshurst," this title page produces the family seat, like its fictional works, as the picture of abundance.[26]

Both Herbert's portrait and Wroth's title page mark for sale the Sidney likeness and the Sidneyan pastoral landscape as authorized by Sidney genealogies, building projects, and literary texts. The engraver signed the Herbert portrait as "sculpsit L Simon Passeus" and the *Urania* title page as "Simon Passeus, sculp." The portrait is labeled, "to be sold by Io[n] Sudbury and Geo[rge] Humble in Popeshed"; the title page declares, "Printed for Iohn Marriott and Iohn Grismand And are to bee sould at their shoppes in St. Dunstons Churchyard Fleetstreet and in Poules Alley at the signe of the Gunn," because de Passe was, like any engraver of the period, attached to the publishers who marketed his work.[27] These trade inscriptions are reminders that de Passe created likenesses of patrons for the Sidney women and Queen Anne of Denmark, while John Marriott and John Grismand have a clear claim to selling the book. The de Passe connection between the portrait and the title page, like Herbert's own connections to the book trade, makes it highly questionable that *Urania* was printed entirely without Wroth's knowledge.[28] The title page alone supports Helen Hackett's contention that Wroth envisaged that her literary production would gain her the notice of the court. The detail and ambition of the title page also suggests that Wroth wished this book to be the first of two or more volumes, because she had already begun the second volume before the first was published.[29] Evidence of further engagement with print appears in Wroth's second volume, when *Urania*'s only character involved in trade, Cordelius, appears, "master" of "a great booke sellers shop of bookes." Although Wroth successfully weaves this bookseller into her romance—it turns out that he's really Drusio, a Florentine knight—for a moment, Wroth diverts her narrative to the bookseller, whose "great shop" not only suggests the pleasures of the print marketplace but inserts the book as printed commodity into Wroth's second, unpublished, volume (*U2*, 290–91, 376). Herbert's portrait and Wroth's title page, together with Wroth's digression to Cordelius's bookshop, chart their business associations with London artisans, printers, and booksellers, contacts that underwrote their identity as authors.

Materializing Rhetorical Practice: Amplification Through Clothing, Color, and Disguise

Wroth's prose romance founds its characters and narratives not only on the display of fanciful clothing and architecture but also on rhetorical practices that rely on analogies between ornament and eloquence, metaphor and cloth, argument and color that were no less a part of the Sidney family repertoire. Wroth follows Sidneyan practice in creating her romance through artful and elaborate sentences that follow these rhetorical conventions. Like her Uncle Philip, Wroth crafted her prose according to English interpretations of Cicero's assertion that "the highest distinction of eloquence consists in amplification by means of ornament."[30] Just how much amplification was appropriate was a topic debated throughout the early modern period as part of the ongoing discussion about the appropriateness of a more amplified, Latinate (and dilated) style as opposed to the plain style. This discussion made frequent use of the metaphors of clothing, color, and disguise that were part of everyday expression among the educated in the early modern period. Cicero's discussion of the rhetoric of amplification includes an analogy between metaphor and clothing that explains metaphor itself as part of the advance of civilization: "For just as clothes were first invented to protect us against cold and afterwards began to be used for the sake of adornment and dignity as well, so the metaphorical employment of words was begun because of poverty, but was brought into common use for the sake of entertainment."[31] Following Cicero, clothing one's words came to mean amplifying them with rhetorical ornament, although such clothing also carried the possibility of deceit or disguise, as in Cicero's own example of a person who "employs a cloak of words, a fence of guilefulness" (125). In the *Defense of Poesy* Philip Sidney voiced a similar suspicion of rhetoric-as-disguise when he called his figure of excessively artful language, "that honey-flowing Matrone Eloquence, apparelled, or rather disguised, in a Courtisanlike painted affection."[32]

George Puttenham transmitted Cicero's connections among rhetorical amplification, textiles, and disguise in terms of the Elizabethan court in *The Art of English Poesy* (1589). According to Puttenham, in "disguising" "the ordinary and accustomed" English language, the poet makes the language more decent, "more agreeable to any civil ear and understanding." This statement takes Puttenham to an analogy between rhetoric and female courtiers, "these great mad-ams of honor," who understand the importance of dressing appropriately for their role. If they found themselves without "courtly habiliments" to "cover their naked bodies," they "would be half ashamed or greatly out of countenance to be seen in that sort." Puttenham uses this imagined reaction to assert that women at court "then think themselves more amiable in every man's eye, when they be in their richest attire, suppose of silks or tissues or costly embroideries," than "when they go in cloth or in other plain and simple apparel." Just as ladies of the court must dress luxuriously, in poetry, if "any limb be left naked and bare and not clad in his kindly clothes and colors, such as may convey them somewhat out of sight," then the poet has failed to provide the proper degree to which language must be "artificially handled" in order to "yield it much more beauty and commendation." Puttenham continues his analogy between poetry and courtly clothing in terms that unite poetry, embroidery, and portraiture when he states that this "ornament" or amplification "we speak of is given to it by figures and figurative speeches, which be the flowers as it were and colors that a poet setteth upon his language of art, as the embroiderer doth his stone and pearl or passements of gold upon the stuff of a princely garment, or as the excellent painter bestoweth the rich Orient colors upon his table of portrait."[33] The sense of "colors" as "rhetorical modes or figures; ornaments of style or diction, embellishments"[34] corresponds to the jewels and "passements," the borders usually made by a professional male embroiderer, and to the colors that the painter grinds from precious stones from the East in order to paint a portrait.

"Colors" as a rhetorical term is implicitly connected with textiles, because "colors" as an ornamented version of the truth shades into the meaning of "colors" as disguise as well as into the heraldic meaning of "colors" as the flag of a particular faction. Appearing under a "color" or "colors" on the battlefield or in romance announces which side one is on and so proclaims intention, even though such an announcement may be part of a ruse. Wroth is alert to the instabilities of the meanings of "color," as when Pamphilia asks Amphilanthus, "What colour shall wee have next: the last I saw was Crimson, now Watchet [light blue] and White; do you adde to your inconstancy, as fast as your colours?" (U1, 138). For Wroth as for many early moderns, the rhetorical meanings of "color" not only signaled the ability to paint one's intentions figuratively but merged with the material practices of heraldry and livery, in which people appeared under the banner of a cause, dressed alike for a mourners' procession, or wore livery announcing one's patron or profession.

In *Urania*, Mary Sidney Wroth uses all of these associations between rhetoric and clothing, cloth and color to articulate the emotions of her central characters and even to call her minor characters into existence. Her continual use of cloth and color to identify characters at times calls attention to the primacy of romance structure over characterization in *Urania*, even when the characters themselves choose their own outfits. In the first volume alone, Wroth assigns to more than eighty named characters the costumes and colors that declare their roles in Wroth's unfolding narratives. At times, characters "furnish" "themselves according to their humors," as when three knights prepare for a joust. The first, Amphilanthus, dresses "in Tawny, embroidred with Black and Silver," a combination that, as Josephine Roberts explains in her notes so vital to tracing Wroth's use of color, expresses mourning in a poem by Edward de Vere. The second knight, Ollorandus, chooses "Grasse-greene, and Gold," colors that Henry Peacham records as meaning "rejoycing, youth, or youthfulnesse." The third, Dolorindus, dresses "in Haire colour, or a kind of dead leafe colour, and Gold," which resembles a similar description in Philip Sidney's *New Arcadia* signifying "the straw-covered livery of ruin."[35] Even characters who are barely mentioned choose the color of their garments and so externalize their emotions: Sildurino, a shepherd who tells a tale to Pamphilia and Amphilanthus, describes taking refuge in a house whose mistress changes after hunting into "a garment of blacke Damaske, which reached to her knees, and another below that, that came to the small of her leg, of Sattin, buskins she had of the finest leather laced and tyed with pretty knots of ribbin, but al blacke, and so had she gone ever since her love left her" (*U1*, 575).

Wroth's narrator assigns many characters the colors that they wear as their defining characteristic. In her edition of the first volume of *Urania*, Roberts glosses over forty different colors that Wroth uses, which usually explain the significance of the characters' textiles as well: "green and gold" signify "a noble lover"; "murry," or "mulberry," means "constancy in love"; "russet," despite the redecoration of the "king's lodgings" at Penshurst in russet velvet and silk, signifies the color and cloth of "the peasant class." Several of the names of Wroth's characters even derive from the names of cloth with distinctive colors; the name Melasinda translates as the "black mourning cloth" that she wears, and the name Clorinus means "pale green," signifying "changeableness."[36] Such clothing of character makes certain that Puttenham's rhetorical "lymme" is not "left naked and bare" but "clad in his kindly clothes and colours." Yet when "color" comes to mean the significance of dressing an argument or character, nakedness can seem desirable, as the only means to represent some kind of unvarnished truth—to use a phrase that stems from the same rhetorical tradition.

In government documents, on stage, and in correspondence, Puttenham's positive sense of "colors" as rhetorical "embellishments" often gives way to Quintilian's use of the word "color" to mean "the particular slant or gloss one seeks to give an argument or a sequence of events."[37] In the thick records concerning Mary Queen of Scots, "nakedness" or honesty as opposed to "color" are recurring terms to which all sides resort in the attempt to protect themselves from deceit as they protest their own honesty. Mary insists on her desire to speak without pretense when she writes Elizabeth from Scotland on 5 January 1561/62, affirming that she has shown her "the bottom of our mynde nakedly." William Cecil's exhaustive "Articles delivered to the Queen of Scots" of 5 October 1570 attempts to exclude Mary from the succession regardless of "any Colour" she "ought or could make for her own Person, to be an Heir in Succession."[38] In other words, no spin that Mary puts on treasonous behavior would allow her to become the English queen. Because color took on this sense of "slant or gloss" it could also be a synonym for "pretense," as when William Cecil questioned why a visitor planned to visit Mary under the "colour" of visiting a female relative in the employ of "my Lady Shrewsbury." Prospero's language in *The Tempest* also connects "colours" to treason when he explains to Miranda how they managed to escape his brother's coup. Instead of being killed outright, the rebels "With colours fairer painted their foul ends," putting them to sea in "A rotten carcass of a butt, not rigged" (1.2.143,146).[39]

Wroth's attitude toward nakedness varies between Puttenham's sense of its impropriety and Quintilian's sense that nakedness is desirable because it signifies the opposite of the deceit implicit in colors. But Wroth is a composer of narrative first and rhetoric second in that she uses these variant meanings to create erotic scenes that feature women stripped by forceful males. Nereana, for example, meets the madman Alanius in the wood, who ties her to a tree and makes of her an emblem of pastoral "nature." He "undress'd her, pulling her haire downe to full length; cloathes hee left her none, save onely one little petticoate of carnation tafatie; her greene silke stockings hee turn'd, or row'ld a little downe, making them serve for buskins." Having transformed her into his pastoral fantasy, a scene ensues of the kind that Barbara Hodgdon describes as straight out of "classic pornography," a "scenario of lust-and-chase violence," as Alanius chases Nereana through the woods like Apollo chasing Daphne.[40]

Limena's ongoing torture at the hands of her jealous husband, Philargus, requires nudity that is unwanted, emblematic of an inner purity, and still unmistakably erotic. She is rescued from her torment by the knight Parselius, who finds her naked and bound at the hands of her husband in a ritual that begins the same way every day: "Then pulled hee off a mantle which she wore, leaving her from the girdle upwards al naked, her soft, daintie white hands hee fastened behind her, with a cord about both wrists, in manner of a crosse, as testimony of her cruellest Martyrdome." Parselius mortally wounds Philargus, who then sees the error of his ways and begs forgiveness for torturing his innocent wife. But this episode is not so much about vice and virtue as it is about sadomasochistic stripping presented as fantasy (*U1*, 197–98).[41]

Wroth considers the propriety of male nudity when two knights wrestle in a scene that, in reversing the clothing of chivalric combat, creates a moment of authorial self-consciousness in which she names her genre, the first known English use of the word "romance"—here, spelled "romancie." When Leonius fights the Castle Lord for his liberty, the Lord throws "his Gowne off," and the two of them, clad only in their shirts, fight in a "naked" fashion that the narrator claims is more authentic than the elaborate tournament descriptions of "discourses or Romancies." There "never was any combat like it," "naked men gravely performing, what discourses or Romancies strive with excellentest witty descriptions, to expresse in Knights armed, curious in their arming, and carefull. Here is no defence but vallour, and good fortune; armour, but delicate shirts, and more delicate skinnes; sheilds, but noble breasts of steele sufficient, being strong in worth" (*U1*, 475). In this scene, Wroth momentarily abandons her elaborate schemes of color and clothing to claim the validity of these men fighting in the shirts that functioned as underwear, in the process explaining her departure from the usual expectations of romance, "what discourses or Romancies strive with excellentest witty descriptions" to tell.[42] Two pages later, she returns to the signifying complexities of colored clothing when a prince signals that he no longer loves a woman by donning a color that she has forbidden him to wear (*U1*, 477).

Wroth's constant evocation of color, especially the color of textiles throughout *Urania*, playfully literalizes the rhetorical language of amplification, while using color and cloth to encode her characters' social and ethical status also furthers their stories. Puttenham's warning about the power of "the same colors in our art of Poesy," that if they "be not well tempered, or not well laid, or be used in excess, or never so little disordered or misplaced," might "disfigure the stuff and spoil the whole workmanship" (222), while repeating the concern of classical rhetoricians like Cicero and Quintilian that amplification can be taken to dangerous extremes, reinscribes the courtly connections among language, painting, embroidery, color, and cloth. The anxiety expressed in Spenser's proem to Book III of *The Faerie Queene* at presenting Elizabeth with versions of herself finds similar expression: "sith that choicest wit / Cannot your glorious pourtraict figure plaine / That I in colourd showes may shadow it, / And antique praises unto present persons fit."[43] Because the queen cannot be figured plainly even by the "choicest wit," Spenser's poet has no choice but to "shadow" her "in colourd showes," an image that brings together not just the visual and the verbal, portraiture and poetry, but extends the rhetorical sense of "color" to describe the genre of romance itself as "colourd showes."

The final rhetorical association between language and cloth that I will discuss as part of Wroth's familial heritage is the metaphoric relation between text and textile. Mary Sidney Herbert, who at Christmas in 1577 gave Elizabeth the doublet of embroidered lawn, made the giving of luxury textiles to her queen into an extended metaphor for presenting *Davids Psalms* in her poem, "Even Now That Care." Wroth would have known this poem, which apparently existed only in the copy of the Sidney Psalter at Wilton. This dedicatory poem to the manuscript of David's Psalms was prepared for presentation to Queen Elizabeth during an anticipated visit to the dowager countess's remarkable house at Wilton in 1599, although the visit never took place, making it unlikely that Elizabeth saw the poem.

In the first three stanzas of "Even Now That Care," Herbert situates Elizabeth within her political cares and power, while expressing the poet's fear that "my Muse offends" the queen. Herbert quickly turns to textile metaphors to describe the production and presentation of the psalms that she and her brother had translated. Although she doesn't name Philip, Herbert describes their collaboration on the psalms' translation in terms of weaving: "but hee did warpe, I weav'd this webb to end; / the stuffe not ours, our worke no curious thing," where "stuffe not ours" refers to the translation of biblical text, and "curious" means "unduly subtle" (OED)—disclaimers about the politics implicit in this psaltery and her dedication. After her image of their collaborative writing as weaving, Herbert presents their product, the psalms, "Theise holy garments," as she calls them later in the poem:

And I the Cloth in both our names present,
A liverie robe to bee bestowed by thee:
small parcell of that undischarged rent,
from which our paines, nor paiments can us free.
And yet enough to cause our neighbors see
wee will our best, though scanted in our will:
and those nighe feelds where sow's thy favors bee
unwalthy doo, no elce unworthie till. (my emphasis)[44]

The "stuffe" that Mary and Philip Sidney wove becomes the "cloth" that Mary presents to Elizabeth "in both our names."

The difficulty of unraveling the syntax of this "livery robe" stanza derives from the poem's obfuscation of whether the Sidneys owe the queen her due, or whether she owes their cause of militant Protestantism more support. The most obvious reading of the stanza's presentation of "livery" makes Herbert's presentation of the manuscript into an entirely dutiful act. Because "liverie" can mean "due, tribute," or, in the stanza's contractual language of rent due and paid, "the legal delivery of property into the corporeal possession of a person,"[45] Herbert is presenting her woven psalms as the queen's due. Because the preposition "by" could mean "in the presence of," Herbert's line, "A liverie robe to bee bestowed by thee," may be paraphrased as "a robe presented as tribute duly paid in the presence of the queen." According to this reading, the "liverie robe" that the Sidneys have fashioned is tribute "bestowed" on her. The stanza goes on to state that it is a small repayment, when no amount would be enough to pay their debt for the privileges granted the Dudley-Sidney-Herbert family, together described as "those nighe feelds where sow's thy favors bee"—the lands bestowed on them where Elizabeth has further sewn her favors.

Herbert's careful choice of words also undercuts this reading of her poem as wholly dutiful because its wording confuses who is giving and who is receiving the "liverie robe." However much the "liverie robe" means "tribute," "livery" was also given to those who shared one's point of view. According to this reading, presenting the queen with their "liverie robe" announces that she is—or should be—on the side of the Sidneys, who with Robert Dudley, Earl of Leicester, argued that England should more actively support Protestants when they were attacked by Catholics. Philip Sidney had died fighting for this cause in the Netherlands. His sister's question at the beginning of the next stanza, "For in our worke what bring wee but thine owne?" suggests that Elizabeth is both the source of their "worke"—the translation of the psalms into English by two embodiments of militant Protestantism—and their recipient, a person who agrees with their position. In this second reading, the stanza's final lines suggest that Elizabeth not only agrees with the siblings but also needs to affirm their cause. Herbert's lines gesture to the fields of Wilton and to a familial history of distinction by representing the Psalms as inadequate repayment to the queen for lives of privilege. But the modesty of the weaving and robe imagery cannot disguise the bold avowal of the Protestant cause, the "livery" situated in the living memory of Philip Sidney. To the extent that "wee will our best, though scanted in our will," suggests that the "will" of the Protestant cause has been "scanted" by the queen, the poem functions as a criticism of Elizabeth, who scants the Sidney cause represented in their woven "webb" and "liverie robe." Regardless of how dutiful the poem may be, Mary Sidney Herbert refers to politics, writing, and cloth production as interrelated activities, locating their figural language in the material, everyday practices that the *textus* of the psalms associated with convictions both religious and political.

The Visual and Verbal Textualities of Romance:
From "Character" to Metafiction

Under James I, militant Protestantism took on different forms, but the idea of figuring a written text as cloth remained a family tradition. Wroth's self-consciousness about writing "romancies" extends from her first naming of the genre in the passage about the naked knights, to figuring her writing as itself a textile. Wroth's female predecessors who had produced translations of romance, Margaret Tyler and Anne Dowriche, also saw a relationship among writing, cloth, and "working," meaning both domestic sewing and writing. In her dedication to *The First Part of the Mirror of Knighthood* (1580), Tyler calls her romance "a peece of work" as well as "a woman's work," while explaining that its "invention, disposition," and "trimming" are due to its original author. Dowriche's dedication to her brother in *The French Historie* (1589) states the hope that he will read past her romance's "simple attire of this outward form."[46] While Wroth may have been aware of these and similar remarks about composing romance, her own use of textile metaphors to describe her romance as a whole seems more to acknowledge Philip Sidney's influence. In the final ten pages of *Urania*'s first volume, Celina describes their movement through the narrative to a shepherdess in terms that describe the entire romance as a tapestry: "We are all picturd in that piece . . . a large cloth, and full of much worke" (*U1*, 595). Wroth's use of a tapestry metaphor to describe the intricate, artificial detail so central to Sidneyan romance, evokes her uncle's assertion that "Nature never set forth the earth in so rich tapestry as divers poets have done; neither with so pleasant rivers, fruitful trees, sweet-smelling flowers, nor whatsover else may make the too much loved earth more lovely. Her world is brazen, the poets only deliver a golden."[47] Wroth's shorter statement registers her awareness of her role as an author working within Philip's tapestry metaphor for the writing of poetry. Both tapestry metaphors are also reminiscent of Wroth's title page, featuring the golden world of the pastoral, however disturbed by the passage of its characters.

The inherent connection among tapestries, needlework with pastoral themes, and the pastoral as written genre lies at the heart of both Philip Sidney's and Wroth's analogies. From at least the Middle Ages, pastoral textiles and pastoral modes of writing, often linked with romance, existed as versions of one another. Wroth's description of the pastoral setting that her character, Antissius II, King of Romania, encounters resembles pastoral needlework as well as Wroth's title page. The King of Romania inhabits "a large and auncient house belonging to an Noble-man, built square of stone, standing rather upon a flat then a Hill." The pastoral landscape surrounds and enfolds this dwelling:

"There ranne behind the Garden, and Orchard wall, a sweete Brooke, on each side whereof fine and enamiled Meadowes lay, shewing their finenesses to each eye" (*U1*, 514). A detail of the border of the professionally embroidered Bradford carpet echoes this same pastoral landscape, with a moated great house combining Jacobean brick chimneys with classical domes and columns in the midst of a fertile pastoral landscape (Figure 30).[48] In the embroidery, trees, including two outsized fruit trees, a leaping stag, crouching rabbit, flying bird, and windmill recall as well the combination of great house architecture and pastoral elements visible in Wroth's title page (Figure 29).

For Wroth, the preferred method of encoding the world was through writing it, but throughout *Urania* she often represents writing itself as enciphered,[49] embroidered, carved, or, as in Romania, "enamiled" text as the means to imbue her descriptions with the splendor and apparent stability of visual objects. A similar ebullient sense of the relations between written text and pastoral landscape informs *As You Like It*, when Orlando seeks to learn of love from the trees, and then to record it there. As he says, hanging his poem about Rosalind on a tree,

> O Rosalind, these trees shall be my books,
> And in their barks my thoughts I'll character
> That every eye which in this forest looks
> Shall see thy virtue witnessed everywhere.
> Run, run Orlando: carve on every tree
> The fair, the chaste, and unexpressive she.[50]

Wroth transports this kind of scene to her prose romance by describing women's writing as textile production. Antissia carves her grief "in the trunke of that tree, till she had imbroiderd it all over with characters of her sorrow" (328); Pamphilia "tooke she a knife, and in the rine of an Oake insculpted a sypher, which contained the letters, or rather the Anagram of his name shee most and only lov'd" (325); wandering in the woods, the Queen of Naples and Perissus "found many knots, and names ingraven upon the trees, which they understood not perfectly, because when they had decipher'd some of them, they then found they were names fained and so knew them not. But Perissus remembered one of the Ciphers, yet because it was Pamphilias hee would not knowe it" (490).

In *Urania*, characters themselves become embodiments of the emblematic perception so common in Renaissance design, as when Amphilanthus assumes the identity of the Knight of the Cipher, "his Device only a Cipher, which was of all the letters of his Mistrisses name, delicately composed within the compasse of one" (339). When Pamphilia asks the significance of his device, the

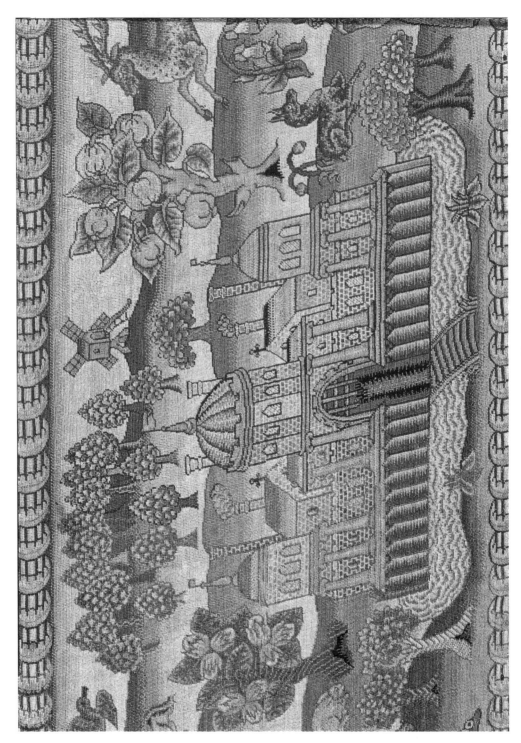

Figure 30. Professional embroidery, the Bradford Table Carpet, 1600–1615 (detail). Linen canvas, silk thread in tent stitch, T. 143-1928. © the Board of Trustees of the Victoria and Albert Museum.

Knight of the Cipher "made her answere, that although a Cipher were nothing in it selfe, yet joyned to the figures of her worth, whose name was therein, it was made above the valew of her selfe or Country" (339). Part of the construction and sprucing up of Penshurst in 1607 included a decision not to put the heraldic "lione and griffine upon every joint" of the "nether gallery" but instead to paint the "letters there R. B. and L," for Robert and Barbara Lisle (*HMC Penshurst* 3:374), doubtless within another Sidney cipher. Wroth's described ciphers derive from the immense significance of embroidered initials and ciphers of the early modern period like the young Elizabeth Tudor's cipher of her initials with her family's on the cover of manuscripts presented as New Year's gifts in 1545 (see Figure 5). In her self-portrait in miniature, the aristocratic Italian Sophonisba Anguissola (Figure 31) holds a similar letter cipher comprising her family initials within the inscription, "the maiden Sophonisba Anguissola painted this from a mirror held in her hand, Cremona." The value of Anguissola's cipher lies in its being "joyned to the figures of her worth";[51] that is, in its connections to her family members, a statement encircled by the inscription about her skilled hand as its creator.

In *Urania*, the ciphers and anagrams from needlework and painting traditions cross into writing when, for example, magic letters lead to the opening of the theater in which the book of *Urania* rests (*U1*, 373). Other crossovers from the visual tradition to Wroth's prose include the descriptive names assigned her human figures through anagram: Limena represents a figure characterized as a "Woman of home or threshold" (*U1*, 716); Philargus means "Love of Argus" and "Love of idleness," a name of particular significance because Wroth develops Argus as a figure of jealousy (716). Lucenia is "Shining one" (719); and Polarchus is "War lord" (735). Such anagrams sometimes have a basis in Wroth's biography: Josephine Roberts notes that within *Love's Victory*, two characters, Philisses and his sister Simena, "appear to be anagrams for Sir Philip Sidney and his sister, Mary Sidney, Countess of Pembroke" (38). In *Urania*, Roberts glosses over eighty of Wroth's anagrams that demonstrate the extent to which Wroth amplified the cipher and anagram, whose pleasure lies simultaneously in their ability to reveal and conceal the identity encoded in letters or "characters." Like Timothy Bright's system of shorthand "charactery," whose uses, Bright says, "are diverse: Short, that a swift hand may therewith write Orations, or public actions of speech," while "Secret, as no kind of writing like,"[52] ciphers and anagrams, which offer ways to reconfigure names in order to claim connection, simultaneously reveal and conceal that connection. Similarly a person's signature—the verbal name made visual—could carry great personal significance: Mary Queen of Scots modeled her signature, "marie," in lower-case Roman letters on that of her mother, Mary of Guise, while Mary

Figure 31. Sophonisba Anguissola, *Autoritrato in miniatura*, c. 1556. Oil on parchment, 8.3 x 6.4 cm (3 1/4 x 2 1/2 in.), enlarged. Museum of Fine Arts, Boston, Emma F. Munroe Fund, 60.155. Photograph © 2010 Museum of Fine Arts, Boston.

Sidney Wroth modeled her signature on that of her aunt and mentor, Mary Sidney Herbert. Mary Sidney Herbert, writes Margaret P. Hannay, also drew "identifying decorations, a form of personal cipher, consisting of an S with a diagonal slash, also used by Mary Wroth."[53] In this way, both Mary Stuart and Mary Wroth chose to transcend marital connection, signaling their affiliation with female kin who were mentors and role models as well as signifiers of social standing.

In Wroth's literary works, ciphers amplify the association between Wroth's personal desires and her writing, a textual encoding that represents connection to her lived experience as well as to the characters that derive from that experience. The ciphers that she created for herself register her identity as joined with but destabilized by her relations with her first cousin, William Herbert, whom she partly shadows as Amphilanthus in her sonnets and *Urania*. In her discussion of Wroth's sonnet sequence, *Pamphilia to Amphilanthus*, Roberts discusses the extent to which Pamphilia represents Wroth and Amphilanthus represents William Herbert. Although the connections are necessarily vexed and to insist on one-to-one connections between historical people and her fiction reductive, at one point Wroth signed the poem with which she ends her first section of sonnets, "Pamphilia," enticing the reader to make a direct connection between Wroth and Pamphilia. Moreover, as Josephine Roberts found, Wroth designed a cipher for the cover of the Penshurst manuscript of *Love's Victory* "consisting of the letters of the name AMPHILANTHVS," the letters all "arranged within the letter A," even though Amphilanthus and Pamphilia are not characters in this play."[54] This cipher is a real-life reversal of the cipher of Amphilanthus in *Urania*, formed using "all the letters of his Mistrisses name, delicately composed within the compasse of one" (*U1*, 339). For Wroth as early modern author, ciphers, anagrams, and initials connect her historical life to her creations by expressing the instabilities inherent in these relations.

In *Urania*'s second volume, largely about the adventures of the next generation of Wroth's characters, the Knight of the Cipher appears in a far different iteration, removed from the first volume's clarity that Amphilanthus is the Knight of the Cipher and that Pamphilia is the source of his cipher. In the second volume, a young man becomes the Knight of the Faire Design, a designation that hints that he is the natural son of Amphilanthus. As Mary Ellen Lamb observes, "Faire Design not only wears a cipher; as his name suggests, he is himself a cipher."[55] Neither the young man nor the reader discovers his rightful name, as Wroth's narrator explains only that all will be revealed when he eventually helps the woman who can inform him of his identity. Consequently, the Knight of the Faire Design can only introduce himself to Amphilanthus by saying, "I knowe noe parents, nor have I a name more then the unknowne. I have a sipher on my hart, which is said to bee her name whom I must by many hard adventures att last gaine, and knowe her by having a sipher likewise, which shall discover my name, and then I shalbee knowne." When Amphilanthus knights him, the youth's sword, "curious rich armour and horse reddy armed and furnisht in field furniture" appear in a cloud. Because "On the shield was represented the like sipher hee had on his brest," he is called the Knight of the Faire Designe, "for noe name hee must have till that sipher were desiphered, and that can nott bee dunn butt by one onely Creature who yett hee had nott mett with" (*U2*, 297–98). Although surrounded by a sense of destiny backed by the supernatural, the young man's narrative peters out in the second volume and the woman who could reveal his true identity never appears. A mysterious figure, the youth who shadows William Herbert's and Mary Wroth's illegitimate son, whom Herbert failed to acknowledge, has no clear present or future, much less a name on which to found his identity in time and space. As a result, he remains an unresolved cipher of an illegitimate child whose existence—and future—can scarcely be acknowledged, a "fair design" who embodies Wroth's unwillingness or inability to resolve the *Urania*'s narratives in its second volume. Whereas the ciphers of Elizabeth Tudor, Sofinisba Anguissola, and Mary Stuart are constructed from the initials of actual people, and Wroth created a cipher for Amphilanthus as well as Amphilanthus's cipher for Pamphilia, the figure for the young William Herbert, the Knight of Faire Designe, has no referent for the imprinted cipher on his shield and breast. In creating him, Wroth uses the expectation that ciphers announce the connections of past, present, and future through the visual design of their letters. The Knight of Faire Designe displays his lack of identity as the source of his unknown future.

Urania: The Distance from Everyday Practice

Although Wroth used such anagrams and ciphers as points of connection between the everyday and her literary works, like Shakespeare in *Othello* and *Cymbeline*, she leaves behind the everyday in *Urania*'s near-erasure of the processes of giving textiles and skilled sewing, two of the practices by which women in the Sidney family had earlier marked their political identities. Although in *Urania* the giving of clothing is one important way in which Wroth's characters become reclothed or step out of disguise, the politics of gift-giving so visible in Mary Sidney's letter of 1573 and Mary Sidney Herbert's dedication to the *Psalms* exist in *Urania* only as a rueful simile in which a Gentlewoman tells the Queen of Naples about how her gifts of "Verse and prose" to a man went unrecognized, in a possible dig at King James: "Hee remembered my kindnesses and thank'd me, but yet rewarded them no further, like a King that takes a Present and likes it, but thinks it was his Subjects due to present it, and so meanes not to reward the bringer, scarse the giver" (*U1*, 492). In marked contrast with the diaries of her contemporaries, Anne Clifford, Margaret Hoby, and Elizabeth Isham, Wroth's romance makes little reference to the perpetual mending and sewing that went on in all households, and that in literate households was accompanied by reading—often of romances. Anne Clifford's *Great Picture* (see Figure 2) includes volumes of romance that would have been typically read to the sewing members of her household, including the *Arcadia*, *The Faerie Queene*, *Don Quixote*, *Gerusalemme Liberata*, and *Argenis*.[56] Elizabeth Isham's brother loaned her "Sir Philip Sidney's Book (& after spencer)." Although Isham had heard people "discommend" "such Books of love," she affirms that "I found no such hurt." Isham finds that "these books of human learning" are "not worthy to be counted excellent unless they show forth the virtues of the mind as well as the perfections of the body which they both do."[57] As needleworkers like Anne Clifford and Elizabeth Isham listened to romance narratives read aloud while they worked, they brought to English households the shepherds, hunters, flowers, and trees that are the long-standing motifs of pastoral textiles.

The single example of women's "work" in the accepted sense of "needlework" in *Urania* appears in the first volume in a scene set in opulent royal chambers, in which the room's privileged owner has been reading a book to her ladies as they perform needlework. Parselius, elder son of the King and Queen of Morea, enters this "brave roome richly hang'd with hangings of Needleworke, all in Silke and Gold," and a tapestry, like that owned by a member of Wroth's family, "the Story being of Paris his Love, and rape of Helen."[58] In the next room he finds "Dalinea sitting under a Clothe of Estate, of Carnation Velvet, curiously and richly set with Stones, all over being Embrodered with purle of Silver, and Gold, the Gold made in Sunnes, the Silver in Starres." It becomes clear as the reader traverses the room with Parselius that Dalinea has just moved under the cloth of state upon hearing of his arrival. Before that, she was reading, seated in a now-vacant chair among her women. Because "In that Chaire lay a Booke" and "the Ladies were all at worke," it becomes clear that Parselius has just missed the moment in which "she read while they wrought" (*U1*, 124). Ann Rosalind Jones and Peter Stallybrass see this moment as one that preserves the mingled pleasures for women of reading and needlework, to which I would add that this is the only moment in which actual sewing is mentioned in an entire two-volume romance replete with textiles. Moreover, the scene in which the women perform needlework while Dalinea reads to them is over when Parselius arrives. For Wroth, it may be that skilled sewing lay too much in the past for England's most privileged women, or that because of her love affair with her cousin and their children, the performance of virtue through everyday activities—or their verbal description—held no appeal. Needlework did tend to be associated with the sharp distinctions between male and female roles that *Urania* so often seeks to blur. In her description of one "great" and "richly" clothed Lady, for example, Wroth plays with the fact that a woman may have a reputation as an equestrian and a hunter in defiance of some people's assumptions. In much the same way that a man may have a reputation as a "Needle-man," "she was . . . an excellent hors-woman, and hunts-woman she was, though these be no properer commendations, as some have said, then to say, a man is a fine Semster, or Needle-man, yet qualities they were, and are commended at this day, allowed of, and admired" (*U1*, 554). Or perhaps the domestic scene of women working while listening to a book was too everyday to deserve more than a mention within the story of the bonding of Parselius and Dalinea. The emphasis on this scene is not on courtly needlework but on Dalinea's spaces as defined by the grandeur of her tapestries and cloth of state, a grandeur that admits Parselius to her intimate interior.[59]

Elsewhere in *Urania*, Wroth gives away her practical knowledge of textiles in similes, which we may track backward from figural language to the everyday acts that they record. Pamphilia's dwelling on the inconstancy of Amphilanthus remains "like to a woman spinning," who "stops but to fasten the thread to begin againe to turne, and twine her sorrows" (*U1*, 303). A three-year-old love match gives way, as "other passions have crept in like Mothes into good stuffe" (*U1*, 517). Dorolina fails to speak of her "continual passions, which not utter'd did weare her spirits and waste them, as rich imbroyderies will spoyle one another, if laid without papers betweene them, fretting each other" (*U1*, 499). Except for such examples, Wroth banishes scenes of spinning, sewing, or caring for textiles and the metaphors that came so readily to Philip and Mary Sidney, in favor of invoking the use of costly textiles and the magical appearance of magnificent furnishings.

In Wroth's romance, the most important spaces tend to be under female control or gendered female. The theater, marked by mysterious letters on the pillars of the entrance, features a throne and "fowre rich chayers of Marble, in which were most delicate, and sumptuous imbroider'd cushions, a Carpet of rich embroidery lying before, and under them." "This richnes," which "*like women*" "must be neerer beheld," entices its female audience into the theater itself (*U1*, 373, my emphasis), where they remain until Leonia reopens it. At that moment, as their enchantment ends, "the Chaires were vanished, and a Pillar of Gold stood in their stead, on which hung a Booke . . . the whole story of Urania," which only Urania is allowed to take (*U1*, 455). Within this magical, feminized theater, the furniture and embroidered covers that spring from Wroth's prose are in turn translated into a book, as within *The Countess of*

Montgomery's Urania another *Urania* appears. This book-within-a-book is a *Urania* in the most precise sense because it is about one of the characters, Urania, who shadows the Countess of Montgomery. The second *Urania* appears in this scene created by Wroth as writing enchantress for her work's dedicatee, the Countess of Montgomery, the woman who may have been her most receptive audience.

Wroth's representations of a visual culture in which spaces and individual bodies alike are defined through what they wear produces descriptions of gorgeous textiles that would be radically impractical in everyday life. The narratives' silks, satins, lawns, embroidered braids, and taffetas, suitable for court masques and pastoral wear only, mark Wroth's metafictional comments about how the romance is structured. The young woman known only as the angling maid wears for her fishing expedition a "Gowne" "of greene Satten, with long sleeves to the ground; they, and her gowne buttoned to the bottom, with buttons of Diamonds, so were her wearing sleeves; but by reason the weather was warme, they were left open in spaces, through which her cut-worke Smock appeared, and here and there, her delicate skin was seene; shee held her angle as neglectively, as love the ill causer of her paine held her, when the poor little fish did plaie with the baite . . . 'So,' would she say 'doth Love with me'" (*U1*, 289). The fishing maid's gown, her "wearing" sleeves, also called "hanging or pendant sleeves,"[60] gathered in order to create ventilation, allow her skin to appear through the holes of her "cut-worke Smock," in something like the occasional and painfully playful fashion in which she glimpses the fish and—turn-about—in which Love glimpses her. As Ann Rosalind Jones and Peter Stallybrass observe about clothing in this period, "Renaissance clothes were piecemeal assemblages of parts."[61] In Wroth's complex sentence linking the maid's pieced-together clothing with the glimpse of love's narrative afforded the maid by her fishing, the relations among the different textiles that she wears function like the pieced-together narratives and viewpoints of romance. As the gown is to the sewn-in sleeves, the sleeves to their openings, the openings to the cut-work smock through which her skin enticingly appears, so the pieced-together narratives of Wroth's romance offer an occasional glimpse of the female body whose desires they both reveal and clothe, and often reveal by clothing, even as her entire text resembles the piecework assemblages of early modern clothing—and here calls attention to itself as such.

The clothing of narrative itself becomes a possibility in one of the romance's most self-referential passages, recalling the moment when the book called *Urania* appears within Wroth's theater. In both descriptions, the narrator considers the authority of the author to recode everyday experience within romance. When Pamphilia sends away her servants and follows a path "into a delicate thicke wood," she begins to read the book she has with her, of which "the subject was Love, and the story she then was reading, the affection of a Lady to a brave Gentleman, who equally loved, but being a man, it was necessary for him to exceede a woman in all things, so much as inconstancie was found fit for him to excel her in, hee left her for a new." As a result of her Thomas Wyatt-like conclusion about the competition between the sexes for inconstancy,[62] Pamphilia comes to the following conclusion about how writing love narratives amounts to clothing the personification, Love:

> "Poore love," said the Queene, "how doth all storyes, and every writer use thee at their pleasure, apparrelling thee according to their various fancies? canst thou suffer thy selfe to be thus put in cloathes, nay raggs instead of virtuous habits? punish such Traytors, and cherrish mee thy loyall subject who will not so much as keepe thy injuries neere me."
>
> Then threw she away the book, and walked up and downe, her hand on her heart, to feele if there were but the emotion left in the place of that shee had so freely given. (*U1*, 317)

In a sophisticated elaboration of Anne Dowriche's modest description of her romance as the "simple attire of this outward form," Wroth's Love is the figure whom stories—and writers—clothe according to the language of rhetorical dilation, usually in the rags of inconstancy "instead of virtuous habits." When the narrator describes the book that Pamphilia throws away, that narrator herself clothes Love in rags by disparaging the Gentleman who exceeds the woman's own inconstancy.

In commenting on romance as clothing Love, Wroth uses Pamphilia's apostrophe and book toss to call attention to her own authorship by asking who controls the narratives of romance. Is it Love, the personification of *Urania*'s most prominent emotion, that punishes writers who misclothe it and cherishes readers who know the difference? Or is it "every writer," "apparelling" Love "according to their fancies" who controls the interlocking narratives? Or is it the reader pictured in this scene who, bringing her own emotions and experience to romance, controls the book at the site of reception, interrogating its forms and capable of simply throwing the book aside? The implied questions of this passage call attention to the declared author of the title page, "the right honorable the Lady Mary Wroath." Like Mary Sidney Herbert before her, Wroth weaves language to clothe her romance according to feminine associations with cloth, as well as according to Sidneyan political and rhetorical strategies suspended among the early modern connections between the verbal and visual, text and textile, the wellspring of early modern English women's textualities.

Notes

INTRODUCTION

1. George Ballard, *Memoirs of Several Ladies of Great Britain*, 83–84. For a discussion of the care with which Ballard should be used as a source, see Margaret J. M. Ezell, *Writing Women's Literary History*, 88. Ballard's date of 1537 may be correct because the inscription's term for arithmetic, "algorisme," was used in the titles of printed texts published around 1537 (for an example see notes below), but the epitaph's description of Lucar's education is more consistent with what we know of girls' education in 1637.

Crooked Lane and St. Michael's Church are no longer extant; see Fran Chalfant, *Ben Jonson's London*, 61–62.

2. Heather Wolfe kindly identified what Lucar's three "Hands" would have included, and supplied in advance of publication her essay that discusses women's early modern hands, "Women's Writing in Early Modern England." See also Jonathan Goldberg, *Writing Matter: From the Hands of the English Renaissance*.

3. Early modern English social classes are difficult to describe accurately. Over half of men and women at mid-seventeenth century were of the "laboring class" that worked for wages (Keith Wrightson, *Earthly Necessities: Economic Lives in Early Modern Britain*, 197). At the upper end of the social scale, I rely on the discussion of "elite" in Sara Mendelson and Patricia Crawford, *Women in Early Modern England*, "in which 'elite' is used as shorthand for the wealthiest and most educated members of society, from the nobility to the minor gentry" (5). Members of the "merchant" class were often powerful members of English society who intermarried with the aristocracy and gentry and so qualify as members of the elite, but some merchants were more of the "middling" classes. Following William Harrison's useful term, the "middling sort," I use *middling* to designate those with incomes in the middle range of their society, including shop owners, shopkeepers, and farmers, from freeholders to successful tenants (*The Description of England: The Classic Contemporary Account of Tudor Social Life*, 94). On the "middling" classes or the "middle sort" in the context of early modern economic changes, see Wrightson, *Earthly Necessities*, 3–8, 200. For the class called "artisan," see Chapter 2, n.1.

4. Definitions, the *Oxford English Dictionary* (hereafter cited as OED).

The OED lists the contemporary use of "pen" as "a stylus, an instrument for cutting or pricking designs or letters." Pens were also used to perform arithmetic, as in *An introduction for to lerne to recken with the pen or with the counters accordynge to the trewe cast of algorysme* (1539). For a discussion of the pen, pencil, brush, and stylus in this period, see Peter Stallybrass, Roger Chartier, Franklin Mowery, and Heather Wolfe, "Hamlet's Tables and the Technologies of Writing in Renaissance England."

5. Wendy Wall, *Staging Domesticity: Household Work and English Identity in Early Modern Drama*, discusses how early modern plays "locate domesticity, in a deep structural way, as at the core of national identity" (6).

6. Ballard, *Memoirs of Several Ladies of Great Britain*, 84. This was not the only early modern epitaph that conflates writing, needlework, and nation. A century later, the verses commemorating Dorothy Selby of Ipswich praise her embroidery of political events like the discovery of the Gunpowder Plot. Selby's epitaph describes how her "Pen of Steele and silken ink" "turn's the abused Stage / Of this leud world into the Golden Age." Quoted in John L. Nevinson, "English Domestic Embroidery Patterns," 10; discussed in relation to women's embroidered intercessions in politics by Ann Rosalind Jones and Peter Stallybrass, *Renaissance Clothing and the Materials of Memory*, 162–65 (hereafter cited as Jones and Stallybrass).

7. Elizabeth I, *Collected Works*, 1:7, 11. On Elizabeth's embroidery-covered translations, see Chapter 1.

8. Lady Grace Mildmay, "The Autobiography of Grace, Lady Mildmay," 33–81; quotation, 60. On Mildmay, see Linda Pollock, *With Faith and Physic: The Life of a Tudor Gentlewoman Lady Grace Mildmay*. Jones and Stallybrass discuss this quotation from Mildmay and the quotation I cite below in the text from the biography of Elizabeth Cary as evidence of the ways in which "good stitchery" was "evidence of quick understanding and aesthetic intelligence" (145).

9. On the practice of *imitatio* as the principle underlying early modern education, see Joan Simon, *Education and Society in Tudor England*, 107–14.

10. Elizabeth Cary, *Lady Falkland: Life and Letters*, 186.

11. Rayna Kalas, *Frame, Glass, Verse: The Technology of Poetic Invention in the English Renaissance*, xii–xiii.

12. Juliet Fleming, *Graffiti and the Writing Arts of Early Modern England*, 13. Fleming discusses how the early modern English "lacked a systemic bifurcation between real and thought objects, and consequently apprehended matter not as that which is deprived of meaning but as a principle of structure that underpins all meaning" (21). Fleming's discussion of "Foucault's Renaissance episteme" is also useful in understanding how it is that for early moderns, "a word is a thing and is therefore only partly legible as a word, while things bear hidden signatures and appear, to those who can rightly read them, as words" (23).

Emblem studies provide another mode of analysis of early modern connections between word and picture. As useful as emblem studies are, emphasizing as they do contemporary analyses, I see women's textualities as participating in a larger sense of verbal and visual connection, even when women wrought emblems. See Michael Bath, *Speaking Pictures: English Emblem Books and Renaissance Culture*, and Peter Daly, *Literature in the Light of the Emblem*.

13. Thomas Elyot, *The Boke Named the Governour*, 2:25–26.

14. George Puttenham, *The Art of English Poesy*, 190–91.

15. Thomas Elyot, *The Boke Named the Governour*, 2:23–24.

16. Juliet Fleming, "Graffiti, Grammatology, and the Age of Shakespeare," 315–22.

17. Harrison, *The Description of England*, 200, 197.

18. Tessa Watt, *Cheap Print and Popular Piety 1550–1640*, 183, 196; see also 188, 192–95, 209. Michael Bath considers the many late sixteenth-century emblematic ceilings and rooms preserved in Scotland in *Speaking Pictures*.

19. Juan Vives, *The Instruction of a Christen Woman*, Sig. C3(v).

20. For examples of writing on walls and other surfaces, see Fleming, *Graffiti and the Writing Arts*, 29–72. Other examples include Anne Clifford's memoralizing tablets on the outside of her restored castles and Anne Bacon Drury's painted closet with sayings, emblems, and a visual herbal, around 1595–1605, Hawstead Panels, Christchurch Mansion, Ipswich.

21. Patricia Phillippy points out that "the Elizabethan understanding of painting as essentially an art of coloring meant that it was associated with the problematic practices of cosmetics and rhetoric." *Painting Women: Cosmetics, Canvases, and Early Modern Culture*, 141.

22. Richard Mulcaster, *Richard Mulcaster's Positions*, 133; hereafter cited as Mulcaster. Chapter 38 addresses the education of girls. Mulcaster wrote the account of Elizabeth's progress into London the day before her coronation, *The Queen's Majesty's Passage*, and wrote and directed entertainments for the court, including an entertainment at Kenilworth in 1575. See Richard L. De Molen, "Richard Mulcaster and Elizabethan Pageantry"; Susan Frye, *Elizabeth I: The Competition for Representation*, 13–14, 24–26, 31–54.

23. Although, as Jonathan Goldberg points out, Mulcaster fails to fulfill the promise in the *Positions* that he will explain his "elementary principles" in his later *The First Part of the Elementarie* (*Writing Matter*, 29).

24. William Shakespeare, *Pericles, Prince of Tyre*, 5.0.2–6; Richard Brome, *The Queen and Concubine*, 2:87–88. "Servant" is the name given this character in the list of "Drammatis Personae."

25. Bruce Smith alerted me to the existence of Constance Aston Fowler's commonplace book (Huntingdon Library MS 904) and graciously provided a copy of his unpublished paper, "On Pens and Needles: Seventeenth-Century Manuscripts as Gendered Objects," delivered at the 1996 Conference of the Modern Language Association. See Constance Aston Fowler, *The Verse Miscellany of Constance Aston Fowler*.

26. Esther Inglis, *Un Livret contenant diverses sorte de lettres* (no dedication); *Cinquante Emblemes Chrestiens premierement inventez par la noble damoiselle Georgette de Montenay en France* (dedicated to Prince Charles). See A. H. Scott-Elliot and Elspeth Yeo, "Calligraphic Manuscripts of Esther Inglis (1571–1624): A Catalogue," 80–84.

27. In my use of the terms *agency* and *identity*, I interpret for the study of the early modern period Judith Butler's discussion of these terms in *Gender Trouble: Feminism and the Subversion of Identity*. Her aim is "to affirm the local possibilities of intervention through participating in precisely those practices of repetition that constitute identity and, therefore, present the immanent possibility of contesting them" (147).

Butler espouses the formulation of "agency" as "a question of how signification and resignification work" (144) with the recognition that "identity" is a "signifying" "*practice*" (145). Identity as an "*effect*" must be conceptualized outside the "binarism of free will and determinism" (145–47). In Butler as in my own discussion, *identity* and *agency* do not exist in a cause-and-effect relationship but as versions of one another. *Identity* is the product of *agency*, at the same time that an always-evolving sense of *identity* itself results in *agency* within the culturally produced field of meaning. As Butler writes, cultural "construction is not opposed to agency; it is the necessary scene of agency, the very terms in which agency is articulated and becomes culturally intelligible" (147).

28. On the interior decoration of inns and "private houses and cottages," see Watt, *Cheap Print and Popular Piety*, 183–253.

29. Philip Sidney, sonnet 45, line 14, "Astrophil and Stella," *The Poems of Sir Philip Sidney*, 187.

30. Rowland Whyte to Robert Sidney, London, 29 November 1595, *Historical Manuscripts Commission Report on the Manuscripts of Lord de L'Isle and Dudley*, 2:193. Unfortunately, Barbara Sidney's correspondence was not preserved, but both Whyte and Robert Sidney frequently refer to her speech and letters, as well as to her activities as estate manager in her husband's absence. See Margaret P. Hannay, "'High Housewifery': The Duties and Letters of Barbara Gamage Sidney, Countess of Leicester."

31. Michel de Certeau, *The Practice of Everyday Life*, xi.

32. Patricia Fumerton, "Introduction: A New New Historicism," *Renaissance Culture and the Everyday*, 5. Writing on the meaning of the term *everyday*, as Fumerton further notes, the common or everyday has become an important focus of what she calls "social" new historicism, an extension of the "political" new historicism first practiced by Stephen Greenblatt, Louis Montrose, and Steven Mullaney. Instead of concentrating on masculinist, dominant structures, the "social" new historicism, writes Fumerton, "focuses primarily on the common, the common in both a class and cultural sense: the low (common people), the ordinary (common speech, common wares, common sense), the familiar (commonly known), the customary or typical or taken-for-granted (common law, commonplace, communal), etc. A new new historicism cites particular clusters of such myriad commonality within the context of the manifold details of cultural practice and representation—what we might call, evoking Michel de Certeau and Henri Lefebvre, the 'everyday'" (3–4).

33. Certeau, *The Practice of Everyday Life*, xiii–xiv.

34. One type of literacy that Heidi Brayman Hackel suggests is central to the history of early modern reading is "abecedarian literacy," based in the spelling out of words; see "Rhetorics and Practices of Illiteracy or The Marketing of Illiteracy," 171. For Margaret Ferguson's full consideration of "literacy as a site of social contest in the present" and also "in the European past," see *Dido's Daughters: Literacy, Gender, and Empire in Early Modern England and France*, 5.

35. Wall, *Staging Domesticity*, 5, 6.

36. The word count is from Suzanne Gossett and Janel Mueller, "Textual Introduction," *The Second Part of the Countess of Montgomery's Urania*, xviii.

37. Peter Beal, *In Praise of Scribes: Manuscripts and Their Makers in Seventeenth-Century England*, v.

38. Elyot, *The Boke Named the Governour*, 43.

39. Andrea Pearson, "Introduction," in *Women and Portraits in Early Modern England: Gender, Agency, Identity*, 1–2.

40. On needlework within early modern gift practice, see Lisa M. Klein, "Your Humble Handmaid: Elizabethan Gifts of Needlework," 459–93; Mendelson and Crawford, *Women in Early Modern England*, 223, 229.

41. "The Praise of the Needle" is John Taylor's verse introduction to *The Needles Excellency*, first published in 1631; I quote the edition of 1634, 4. Thomas Deloney, "Salomon's good housewife, in the 31 of his Proverbs," in *Strange Histories* (1607), Sig. A4(v).

42. Jane Schneider and Annette B. Weiner, "Introduction," in *Cloth and Human Experience*, 1.

43. Linda Woodbridge, "Patchwork: Piecing the Early Modern Mind in England's First Century of Print Culture," 36. Similarly, in Persian, "*Tar~z*," which "textile specialists use to mean either embroidered fabric generally, or the embroidered border on a fabric in particular" "means weave, to adorn, or to compose poetry." Jerome W. Clinton, "Image and Metaphor: Textiles in Persian Poetry," 7–11; quotation, 8.

44. William Shakespeare, *Titus Andronicus*, in *The Norton Shakespeare*.

45. Artist Manuel Vega on National Public Radio, April 7, 1999.

46. On the significance of the abstract patterns produced in Gee's Bend, Alabama, see *Gee's Bend: The Architecture of the Quilt*, ed. Paul Arnett, Joanne Cubbs, Eugene W. Metcalf, Jr.

Quilts are the subject of books too numerous to list. One of the most remarkable quilts of our time deserves mention, however: the AIDS quilt organized by the Names Project Foundation. Begun in 1985 and first exhibited on the Washington, D.C., mall in 1987, the quilt has grown to more than 44,000 3 x 6 foot squares.

47. In their chapter on needlework, "The Needle and the Pen: Needlework and the Appropriation of Printed Texts," Jones and Stallybrass acknowledge the problem of the pen-needle split, concluding that for needleworkers, the "needle could *be* a pen" (134–71; quotation, 144). Maureen Quilligan also points out in discussing Elizabeth Tudor's first embroidery-covered manuscript, "We usually understand the pen and needle to be opposed in the protofeminist discourse of the Renaissance," but in Elizabeth's work, "the pen and needle go together." Maureen Quilligan, "Elizabeth's Embroidery," 212. See also Wendy Wall's discussion of the cultural significance of the needle in *Staging Domesticity*, 65–67.

48. The Berger Collection contains what Roy Strong has called the largest collection of early English artwork outside the Tate and the National Portrait Gallery. Roy Strong, "Introduction," in *600 Years of British Painting*, viii; see also http://www.thebergercollection.org.

49. Lena Cowen Orlin, *Locating Privacy in Tudor London*; see also Lena Cowen Orlin, "Working the Early Modern Archive: The Search for Lady Ingram." Orlin's impressive scholarship discovered the identities of the painting's sitters. The Portrait, then called *Lady Ingram and her Two Sons, Martin and Steven* was first exhibited at the Denver Art Museum in 1998. Thanks to Orlin, the museum has now officially retitled the painting *Alice Barnham and her Sons, Martin and Steven*. Although Orlin and I have reached some of the same conclusions about the portrait itself, my emphasis is on the portrait as evidence of female agency represented by the pen and its written texts, and therefore on such paintings as a form of life writing.

50. The version quoted in the painting is from Edward VI's First Book of Common Prayer (1549), Church of England, *The First and Second Prayer-Books of Edward VI*, 212.

51. Anne Askew, *The lattre examinatyon of Anne Askew*, ed. Elaine V. Beilin, 88–89.

52. The metrical version of Proverbs by John Hall, which also contains metrical psalms and a long advice ballad, was published as *Certayne Chapters of the Proverbes of Salomon drawen into metre by T. Sterneholde, late grome of the Kynges Majesties Robes* (1549–50). The metrical version paraphrases the opening of Proverbs book 1, chapter 2, "My sonne, if thou wylt receive my woordes . . . applye thyne hearte then to understanding." *The Byble in Englishe* (1549). I have chosen this Bible as one that could have been familiar to the Barnham family in 1557. On the publication of the Bible during the reign of Edward VI, see David Daniell, *The Bible in English*, 245–46.

I provide the chapter and verse equivalents from the Geneva Bible because the Great Bible numbers chapters but not verses.

53. Bathsua Makin, *An Essay to Revive the Antient Education of Gentlewomen*, 35. Makin argues, "To buy Wooll and Flax, to die Scarlet and Purple, requires skill in Natural Philosophy. To consider a Field, the quantity and quality requires knowledge in Geometry. To plant a Vineyard, requires understanding in Husbandry: She could not Merchandize, without knowledge in Arithmetick: She could not govern so great a Family well, without knowledge in Politicks and Occonomicks: She could not look well to the wayes of her Household, except she understand Physick and Chirurgery: She could not open her Mouth with Wisdom, and have in Tonge the Law of kindness, unless she understood Grammar, Rhetorick and Logick" (35).

54. Karen Hearn, private communication. The two paintings by Gheeraerts are included in Karen Hearn, *Marcus Gheeraerts II*, 50–51. Still another British painting exists of an unknown woman and two girls, the woman with a domestically worked, proudly displayed bodice embroidered with cherries so that domestic fertility seems very much its point.

55. Orlin, "Working the Early Modern Archive," 742–46.

56. Michelle Dowd and Julie Eckerle, "Introduction," in *Genre and Women's Life Writing in Early Modern England*, 1.

57. On Anne Clifford's *Great Picture*, see Richard Spence, *Lady Anne Clifford Countess of Pembroke, Dorset and Montgomery*, 181–99; see also Edith Snook, *Women, Reading, and the Cultural Politics of Early Modern England*, 1–3.

58. Jonathan Goldberg discusses the instability of early modern gender binaries in *Desiring Women Writing: English Renaissance Examples*, 3–15, 42–72. See also Jonathan Goldberg, "The Female Pen: Writing as a Woman."

59. Guilliam Brallot is listed in the accounts of Katherine Parr included in *The Inventory of King Henry VIII: The Transcript*, items 17752 and 17760, page 437; because Brallot embroidered for Elizabeth as well, it is probable that he also served Mary. On Elizabeth's embroiderers, see Janet Arnold, *Queen Elizabeth's Wardrobe Unlock'd*, 189–92. On Edmund Harrison, see Patricia Wardle, "The King's Embroiderer: Edmund Harrison (1590–1667)": "Part I: The Man and His Milieu" and "Part II: His Work."

60. *The International Dictionary of Women Workers in the Decorative Arts*, ed. Alice Prather-Moses, 71.

61. John Lyly, *Gallathea*, 33.

62. On the internal evidence suggesting that *The Tenth Muse* was produced from manuscript pages meant for circulation rather than print, as John Woodbridge claims in his introduction to her book, see Joseph R. McElrath, Jr. and Allan P. Robb, "Introduction," in *The Complete Works of Anne Bradstreet*, xx, xxxi. This movement of Bradstreet's manuscript into print fits a pattern described by Margaret J. M. Ezell in "From Manuscript to Print: A Volume of Their Own?"

John Woodbridge quoted in McElrath and Robb, *Complete Works of Bradstreet*, xxxi.

63. On Bradstreet's stanza 5 of "The Prologue," see also Laurel Ulrich, "Pens and Needles: Documents and Artifacts in Women's History." Ulrich's essay makes the case that Puritan New England did not see a split between pen and needle, although she assumes that Renaissance women necessarily did.

64. Margaret Ferguson aptly summarizes Bradstreet's inhabiting of the roles represented by the needle and the pen as "reproducing the ideological injunction against female public expression and querying it by the very fact that she *is* writing and imagining public criticism, even in works that disclaim her intent to publish" ("A Room Not Their Own: Renaissance Women as Readers and Writers," 103). Bradstreet's reference to "carping tongues" has been a point of discussion. See Tamara Harvey on its context within the *querelle des femmes*, " 'Now Sisters . . . Impart Your Usefulnesse, and Force': Anne Bradstreet's Feminist Functionalism in *The Tenth Muse*," 7–8.

65. Bradstreet combines the plucked-feather imagery of the "Fift song" from *Astrophil and Stella*, in which the grieving Astrophil reflects on the failure of his writing: "See now those feathers pluckt, wherewith thou flewst most high" (Sidney, ed. Ringler, 213, l. 22;) and Sonnet 90, in which Sidney uses the connection among quills as pens / plumes and the writing or "wings" of other poets to protest that Stella is the only source of his inspiration for writing, as the poet refuses to "take" "my plumes from other's wings" (224, line 11).

66. Anne Bradstreet, *The Complete Works of Anne Bradstreet*, 7–8.

67. Margaret Cavendish (Lucas), Duchess of Newcastle, *Poems and Fancies*, 2–3.

68. Besides Jones and Stallybrass, discussed above, studies that complicate the pen-needle dichotomy include Kathryn R. King, "Of Needles and Pens and Women's Work"; and Carol Shiner Wilson, "Understanding Cultural Contexts: The Politics of Needlework in Taylor, Barbauld, Lamb, and Wordsworth."

69. Kate Millett, in *Sexual Politics*, admirably set out to prove that "sex is a status category with political implications" but assumed the existence of "well-defined and coherent groups: races, castes, classes, and sexes" (24). See Gerda Lerner, *The Creation of Feminist*

Consciousness from the Middle Ages to Eighteen-Seventy; Rozsika Parker, *The Subversive Stitch: Embroidery and the Making of the Feminine*, 103. Other feminist scholars whose specialty was more particularly the Renaissance avoided the pitfall of the transhistorical narrative—i.e., Linda Woodbridge, *Women and the English Renaissance: Literature and the Nature of Womankind, 1540–1620*.

70. Mary Lamb, "On Needle-work," in *The Works of Charles and Mary Lamb*, 1:176. Jeffrey Robinson first informed me of Lamb's article. Some scholars once accepted the existence of the pen-needle dichotomy at Lamb's word. See for example Elaine Hedges, "The Needle or the Pen," 343. For the biographical context of Lamb's essay, see Jane Aaron, *A Double Singleness: Gender and the Writing of Charles and Mary Lamb*, 68–79.

71. The Brontë sisters explored the interconnections among verbal and visual textualities at Haworth; Anne Brontë embroidered a piece of needlework signed and dated January 23, 1830, in which she stitched selections from Proverbs, including the "worthy wife" passage implied in the *Alice Barnham* portrait, in Juliet Barker, *Sixty Treasures: The Brontë Parsonage Museum*, plate 27. Louisa May Alcott, *The Journals of Louisa May Alcott*, 78. Elizabeth Barrett Browning, *Aura Leigh* (1856), 255–56. Gertrude Stein quotation from *How to Write*, 119, discussed in Wolfgang Karrer, "Gertrude Stein's Poetry: From Cubism to Embroidery, 1914–1933." Gertrude Stein and Alice B. Toklas embroidered Picasso's designs for the seats of their Louis XVI chairs. In "The Applicant," Sylvia Plath impatiently and distantly writes of the wife, "It can sew, it can cook, / It can talk, talk, talk," but in other poems like "Finisterre" and "The Princess and the Goblins," embroidery and thread form central images of connection and loss. *The Collected Poems: Sylvia Plath*, 182, 169, 133.

72. As Nicholas Penny writes of paintings on canvas in her introduction to the *Renaissance Studies* issue, "The Biography of the Object in Late Medieval and Renaissance Italy," "Our keen interest in the display of easel paintings is itself an anachronistic priority, reflecting the huge prestige that such works of art now possess and the high proportion of academic attention that they now receive." Sixteenth-century Venetian inventories demonstrate that in households "such pictures were not established, as they would be in the seventeenth century, as a usual form of display in affluent houses" ("Toothpicks and Green Hangings," 586).

73. Ezell, *Writing Women's Literary History*, 164.

74. I am indebted to Bruce Smith's development of the idea of "historical phenomenology" in several sources, including his "Introduction" to "Forum: Body Work," *Shakespeare Studies*; his book, *The Acoustic World of Early Modern England*, and the Shakespeare Association Seminar that he organized, "Knowing Bodies," in 1999, in which I participated.

75. On feathers, see Margaret Ferguson, "Feathers and Flies: Aphra Behn and the Seventeenth-Century Trade in Exotica"; on sugar, see Kim Hall, "Culinary Spaces, Colonial Spaces: The Gendering of Sugar in the Seventeenth Century"; on sound in the Renaissance, see Smith, *Acoustic World*; on handkerchiefs, codpieces, and beards, see Will Fisher, *Materializing Gender in Early Modern English Literature and Culture*.

76. Margreta de Grazia, Maureen Quilligan, and Peter Stallybrass, "Introduction," in *Subject and Object in Renaissance Culture*, 2.

77. Peter Stallybrass, "Material Culture: Introduction," 123.

78. Maurice Merleau-Ponty, *The Visible and the Invisible*, 135.

79. According to Merleau-Ponty, the thickness separating the body from the thing is not that of René Descartes's *Cogito*, with its claims to an objectivity based on the imagined division of mind and body, but that of "a knowing body," which may not necessarily find immediate expression in language, and which, like language, is based in the "signs" that are "the transparent envelope within which [one] might live." Maurice Merleau-Ponty, *Phenomenology of Perception*, 408, 133. Historical phenomenology posits the physical body as never

separate from the cultural formations through which we conceptualize its workings. See Smith, "Forum: Body Work, Introduction," 23.

Phenomenological descriptions of how the body "knows" the external world suggest ways to revise poststructuralism while still using discursive analysis. In *Bodies That Matter*, Judith Butler recasts Merleau-Ponty's analysis into a contemporary semiotic and poststructuralist idiom as the means to examine the category of "sex." The body's perception of objects via "the thickness of the body" she calls the "materiality" of the body, finding that "every effort to refer to materiality takes place through a signifying process which, in its phenomenality, is always already material." Butler's marking of the reciprocal relation between the material body and the signifying process provides a useful way to conceptualize the knowing body's reaction to extant objects, whether standing before the portrait of an unknown woman once called "Ingram" in Denver, Colorado, or walking through New Hardwick Hall in Derbyshire. If we can conceptualize the signified both as language and as a set of culturally shaped sensations and interrelations, then the twenty-first century subject may be said to experience the *Alice Barnham* portrait or New Hardwick Hall in terms that are always located within cultural discourse even when not fully articulated, especially because these objects have been reordered according to evolving theories of what the past should look like.

80. Simon J. Bronner, "The Idea of the Folk Artifact," 1.

81. de Grazia, Quilligan, and Stallybrass, "Introduction," in *Subject and Object in Renaissance Culture*, 5.

82. Smith, *Acoustic World*, 29.

CHAPTER ONE

1. The woman who began her life as Elizabeth Hardwick continues to be referred to as "Bess of Hardwick." Calling her "Bess" makes her seem more familiar than she can ever be, although it is a convenient handle for a woman who married four times and whose personal iconography stresses her identity as a St. Loe, a Cavendish, and a Talbot. Referred to in letters as "Lady Shrewsbury," she is fond of the initials ES for Elizabeth, Countess of Shrewsbury. Recent scholars refer to her as Bess; see Stephen Orgel, *Impersonations: The Performance of Gender in Shakespeare's England*, 134–38; and Maureen Quilligan, "Elizabeth's Embroidery," 213.

2. Lady Zouche had served both Anne Boleyn and Jane Seymour as lady-in-waiting. Mary Lovell, *Bess of Hardwick: Empire Builder*, 18–21, 28–30 (hereafter cited as Lovell).

3. On Bess's position within news-sharing networks, see James Daybell, "'Such Newes as on the Quenes Hye Wayes We Have Mett': The News and Intelligence Networks of Elizabeth Talbot, Countess of Shrewsbury (c. 1527–1608)." On Bess's needlework, see Santina Levey's monumental *The Embroideries at Hardwick Hall: A Catalogue*; see also Santina Levey, *Elizabethan Treasures: The Hardwick Hall Textiles*.

4. Annette B. Weiner, *Inalienable Possessions: The Paradox of Keeping-While-Giving*, 3. Weiner's project is to examine the largely unquestioned assumptions of reciprocal exchange theory and to enlarge it by recognizing the place of women's wealth, particularly as produced through cloth.

5. *Literary Remains of King Edward the Sixth*, ed. J. B. Nichols, 1:cclxii, cclxv.

6. *Oxford English Dictionary* (hereafter cited as OED).

7. See this point discussed in the Introduction. Juan Vives, *The Instruction of a Christen Woman*, Sig. K1(r). In this period a "shirt," according to Maria Hayward, was "an undergarment worn next to the skin, with a neck band and small upright collar" (*Dress at the Court of King Henry VIII*, 435). Hayward concurs that Elizabeth's second gift was a "bracer" (211).

8. John Bale, *A Godly Meditation of the Christen Sowle* (1548). Maureen Quilligan, *Incest and Agency in Elizabeth's England*, 34, 36–51, 51–75.

9. Elizabeth's three extant calligraphic manuscripts are (1) *The Glass of the Sinful Soul* (1544), her English translation of Marguerite de Navarre's *Le Miroir de l'âme pécheresse*, Bodleian Library, Oxford, MS Cherry 36, reprinted in Marc Shell, *Elizabeth's Glass*, 111–44; (2) Elizabeth's English translation of John Calvin's *Institution Chrétienne* (1545), MS #R.H. 13/78, Scottish Record Office; and (3) her translation into Latin, French, and Italian of Katherine Parr's *Prayers, or Meditations* (1545) titled "Precationes sev meditationes," BL, MS Royal 7.D.X.MS. Margaret Swain first noted that the three extant manuscripts point to a missing fourth, "A New Year's Gift from Princess Elizabeth." Another early translation produced by Elizabeth is her gift in 1552 to her brother, King Edward VI, of a translation from Italian into Latin, of Bernardino Ochino's "Sermon on the Nature of Christ" (O: Bodl. MS 6). For the *Diologus Fidei*, see later in the chapter.

10. See Lisa M. Klein, "Your Humble Handmaid: Elizabethan Gifts of Needlework," 462. Klein, who also discusses these gifts as "inalienable objects" but focuses on their immediate function as courtly gifts, also discusses Elizabeth's choice of the pansy for their covers, 476–85. Maureen Quilligan considers *The Glass* as a gift of cloth between women in "Elizabeth's Embroidery"; Patricia Fumerton also discusses—and expands—the concept of gift exchange in *Cultural Aesthetics: Renaissance Literature and the Practice of Social Ornament*, 29–66. See also Jane Donawerth, "Women's Poetry and the Tudor-Stuart System of Gift Exchange." The germinal anthropological work on the meaning of gift-giving is Marcel Mauss, *The Gift*.

On the concept of gift-exchange, see David Cheal, *The Gift Economy*; Joel Rosenthal, *The Purchase of Paradise: Gift Giving and the Aristocracy, 1307–1485*. For the intellectual origins of reciprocal exchange theory and a revision of Marcel Mauss, see Weiner, *Inalienable Possessions*, 44–65. In *Incest and Agency*, Quilligan goes on to argue in relation to Weiner's revision, that "female agency empowers and is empowered by an endogamous assertion of family prestige" (22–28).

11. Weiner, *Inalienable Possessions*, 11, 17. Weiner summarizes the problem of accepting the standard idea of exchange relations. Her own "cases from Australia and New Guinea" "demonstrate the narrowness imposed on kinship and gender analyses when the norm of reciprocity is considered the primary feature of exchange relations. Then, all objects, including women, remain signs of the transactional relations between men rather than signs of the reproductive imperatives surrounding keeping-while-giving that involve women as central actors in their own right" (126). I import Weiner's analysis to my discussion of early modern English women because it counters the dominant, male-oriented sense of gift exchange derived from earlier anthropological analysis, and because it offers a way out of thinking of inalienable objects as mere gifts of the moment.

Maureen Quilligan concludes that Elizabeth's first embroidery-covered manuscript "results in a gesture that looks oddly like the trade in woven heirlooms" that Weiner describes as requiring "us to revise our sense of the 'traffic in women' outlined by Lévi-Strauss and Marcel Mauss" ("Elizabeth's Embroidery," 211–12). In this chapter, I extend this portion of Quilligan's argument to include the textualities of Mary Stuart and Bess of Hardwick as producing "inalienable possessions."

12. Weiner, *Inalienable Possessions*, 1–15; quotation, 6.

13. Karen Hearn, *Dynasties: Painting in Tudor and Jacobean England*, 47.

14. On Parr's prayers, see Janel Mueller, "Devotion as Difference: Intertextuality in Queen Katherine Parr's *Prayers and Meditations* (1545)"; Elaine V. Beilin, *Redeeming Eve: Women Writers of the English Renaissance*; and John N. King, "Patronage and Piety: The Influence of Catherine Parr."

15. Elizabeth I, *Collected Works*, 1:6–7. Further citations of this edition appear by volume and page. Elizabeth's teachers, who included the English master of the italic, Roger Ascham, must be regarded as her collaborators, to the extent that all schoolwork is collaborative. But Elizabeth took full responsibility for her translation's scribal publication.

16. Lady Margaret Beaufort, Henry VII's mother, was descended from John of Gaunt, Duke of Lancaster and his third wife, Katherine Swynton. On Anne Boleyn's copy of *Glass*, see Shell, 3; Quilligan assumes that Elizabeth was working from this edition: *Incest and Agency*, 47. But see Anne Lake Prescott's argument that Elizabeth was working from the Geneva edition of 1539 ("The Pearl of the Valois and Elizabeth I: Marguerite de Navarre's *Miroir* and Tudor England," 66–67). On connections between this translation and the religious agenda of Henry VIII, see Louis Adrian Montrose, *The Subject of Elizabeth: Authority, Gender, and Representation*, 33–36.

17. Margaret Beaufort, *The Mirroure of Golde of the Synfall Soule* (1506). This book of fifty-five pages was printed to resemble an illuminated manuscript. Each page's margins are decorated with a repeating keyhole image that suggests both an eye and a vagina; included are miniaturist woodcuts of Jeremiah, Saint John, Death with his Dart, and Souls in Paradise. On Margaret Beaufort and print culture, see Jennifer Summit, "William Caxton, Margaret Beaufort and the Romance of Female Patronage."

18. Elizabeth may also have been asserting her membership in the group of intellectual women headed by Katherine Parr that John King discusses in "Patronage and Piety." According to King, this group included Parr, Anne Seymour, Catherine Brandon, and Mary Fitzroy (49).

19. Conversation with Bruce Barker Benfield, Duke of Humphreys Library, 1994; Susan James, *Kateryn Parr: The Making of a Queen*, 162–63, 408–9, 443.

20. Margaret Swain in conversation, Edinburgh, 1994. Swain had examined the manuscript and concluded that the "KP" and pansies were embroidered but that the knots were created by sewing braid to the cover. Elizabeth probably sewed on the "braid," as well as the "guard," a form of braid, around the edge of the cover, held in place by a double column of running stitch in red thread, which can be seen where the braid is now missing. In "A New Year's Gift from Princess Elizabeth," Margaret Swain pointed out that this book was not professionally bound. Instead, in the manner in which "nuns in convents cover their missals," Elizabeth's embroidered covers were produced as slipcovers (266).

21. For more on braid, see Chapter 3, where I discuss two seventeenth-century manuscripts detailing how to make intricately woven braids and cords at home and how Elizabeth Isham, author of lifewritings, seems to have enjoyed making "breadstitch" or braid. Elizabeth Langton is listed in Henry VIII's accounts as "the king's silkwoman." She supplied Edward and Elizabeth with "bonnets, buttons, frontlets, girdles, lacing ribbon, round silk ribbon, silk laces, silk points, sipers and tassels." Maria Hayward, *Dress at the Court of King Henry VIII*, 327.

22. Susan Foister, *Holbein and England*, 1. Holbein's designs have their origin in both continental and English traditions of ciphers formed from initials. See John Rowlands, *The Age of Dürer and Holbein: German Drawings 1400–1550*, 239, 247; quotation, 239; discussion of "HISA," 245. For examples of Holbein's ciphers joining from five to ten letters, see 244–46; for their history, 247.

23. Rowlands points out that "the initials are joined with a lovers' knot," *The Age of Dürer and Holbein*, 239.

24. See the Introduction for a discussion of Elizabeth Lucar's epitaph, which praised her "Pictures artificiall. / Curious Knots, or Trailes, what fancie could devise."

25. The letter is British Library, Cotton MSS Vespasian, F iii; Elizabeth I, *Collected Works*, 1:35 (Figure 6). Its first two paragraphs read:

Like as the rich man that daily gathereth riches to riches, and to one bag of money layeth a great sort till it come to infinite, so methinks your Majesty, not being sufficed with many benefits and gentleness showed to me afore this time, doth now increase them in asking and desiring where you may bid and command, requiring a thing not worthy the desiring for itself but made worthy for your Highness's request. My picture, I mean, in which if the inward good mind toward your grace might as well be declared as the outward face and countenance shall be seen, I would not have tarried the commandment but prevent it, nor have been the last to grant but the first to offer it. For the face, I grant, I might well blush to offer, but the mind I shall never be ashamed to present. For though from the grace of the picture the colors may fade by time, may give by weather, may be spotted by chance, yet the other nor time with her swift wings shall overtake, nor the misty clouds with their lowerings may darken, nor chance with her slippery foot may overthrow. Of this, although yet the proof could not be great because the occasions hath been but small, notwithstanding (as a dog hath a day) so may I perchance have time to declare it in deeds, where now I do write them but in words.

And further, I shall most humbly beseech your Majesty that when you shall look on my picture you will witsafe to think that as you have but the outward shadow of the body afore you, so my inward mind wisheth that the body itself were oftener in your presence. Howbeit because both my so being (I think) could do your majesty little pleasure, though myself great good, and again because I see as yet not the time agreeing thereunto, I shall learn to follow this saying of Orace, *Feras non culpes quod vitari non potest* ["May you not blame what cannot be avoided," Horace, Ode 1:24, "Lament for Quintilius"]. (my edition)

On the portrait *Elizabeth When a Princess* and this letter to Edward, see Susan Frye, "Elizabeth When a Princess: Early Self-Representations in a Portrait and a Letter"; on the portrait, see Louis Adrian Montrose, *The Subject of Elizabeth*, 28–33.

26. See Klein, "Your Humble Handmaid," figures 5 and 6, comparing the signatures of Henry and Elizabeth, although she does not compare them as penned knots.

27. Elsebeth Lavold, *Viking Patterns for Knitting*, 11–15; on the Frode symbol, 30–33; on the infinity sign, 14. John Wallis first used it in the lemniscate in *De sectionibus conicus*, in *Operum Mathematicorum* (1656).

28. Baron von Waldstein, *The Diary of Baron Waldstein*, 51; William Brenchley Rye, *England as Seen by Foreigners in the Days of Elizabeth and James the First*, 165, 171, 266n.122, 282n.153. See also Rye, 133. Erasmus's colloquy is reformist in that it argues that the men composing the church may become corrupt. Desiderius Erasmus, "Concerning Faith," 173.

29. Examples of Elizabeth's insistence on the connection between word and meaning include the letter to her brother as Edward VI reproduced in my Figure 6, and in the note above, also *Elizabeth I: Collected Works*, 1:35–36; the 1554 "Tide Letter" to Mary Tudor, 1:41–42; Elizabeth's reply to Parliament in 1563 on the question of her marriage, 1:79–80; a letter of 1583 to James VI, 261–62; and Elizabeth to James in Harrison, *The Letters of Queen Elizabeth*, 159. On this trope in Elizabeth's writing, see Susan Frye, *Elizabeth I: The Competition for Representation*, 4–5. Portraits that Elizabeth seems to have commissioned or collaborated in producing include *Elizabeth When a Princess*, portraits by Levina Teerlinc (see Chapter 2), and the androgynous portrait that she sent to Eric of Sweden about 1560.

30. David Starkey, *Elizabeth: The Struggle for the Throne*, 50–53, stresses that what mattered to Elizabeth was her relationship with her father.

31. *The Inventory of King Henry VIII*, number 10719.

32. Andrea Pearson, "Introduction," in *Women and Portraits in Early Modern England*, 6–7.

33. This is the same letter whose knots I discuss above.

34. Ann Rosalind Jones and Peter Stallybrass, *Renaissance Clothing and the Materials of Memory*, 34 (hereafter cited as Jones and Stallybrass).

35. Mary Tudor received an equal amount of financial support. See David Starkey, *Elizabeth: The Struggle for the Throne*, 65; 335n1. On Elizabeth's finances after her father's death, see David Loades, *Elizabeth I*, 63, 71, 76–78. *Acts of the Privy Council* 1547–50, 2:86.

36. W. K. Jordan, *Edward VI: The Young King: The Protectorship of the Duke of Somerset*, 66.

37. Janet Arnold, *Queen Elizabeth's Wardrobe Unlock'd*, 303.

38. Nicholas Hilliard, *Nicholas Hilliard's Art of Limning: A New Edition of a Treatise Concerning the Arte of Limning*, 29, 45; James, *Kateryn Parr*, 419–22.

39. When Karen Hearn viewed the painting with infrared equipment she saw the inscription "Elizabetha / [. . .] or Regis," which suggests that it read "Elizabetha soror Regis." Private communication, 1995.

40. Antonia Fraser, *Mary Queen of Scots*, 50, 57. On Mary's education, see Mary Burke, "Queen, Lover, Poet: A Question of Balance in the Sonnets of Mary, Queen of Scots," 102–4 and Michael Lynch, "Introduction," in *Mary Stewart: Queen in Three Kingdoms*, ed. Michael Lynch, 10; see also John Durkan, "The Library of Mary, Queen of Scots," 74.

41. Pierre de Ronsard, "A La Royne de France," *Oeuvres Complètes*, 6:337, discussed in J. E. Phillips, *Images of a Queen: Mary Stuart in Sixteenth-Century Literature*, 19 and 241n. 41.

42. On the English reaction to the new French coat of arms after the death of Mary Tudor in 1557, see *Calendar of State Papers, Foreign, of the Reign of Elizabeth*, 1558–59: 347, 314 cited in Marcus Merriman, *The Rough Wooings: Mary Queen of Scots, 1542–1551*, 45, 51n.56.

43. Roger Ascham, letter from Augsburg of 5 October 1550 to Mr. Raven, quoted in Lawrence V. Ryan, *Roger Ascham*, 123.

44. Herbert Norris, *Tudor Costume and Fashion*, 107, 455; for illustrated discussions of the "barbe," see 107, 455–56; figure 149, 551–54. Mary Tudor, sister of Henry VIII and briefly wife of Louis XII, wore the *deuil blanc* in seclusion for six weeks, following the death of her husband. See Walter C. Richardson, *Mary Tudor: The White Queen*, 130.

45. It is not clear from this exchange whether Mary had already sent Elizabeth a copy of her portrait in white mourning. When imprisoned in England, Mary ordered copies of her portrait to be given as gifts to supporters—a lesson learned at the French court. See *Calendar of State Papers Relating to Scotland and Mary, Queen of Scots, 1547–1603* (hereafter cited as *CSP Scotland*), 2:488–89; Lionel Cust, *Notes on the Authentic Portraits of Mary Queen of Scots*, 68 (hereafter cited as Cust).

46. Roy Strong, *Tudor and Jacobean Portraits*, 1:219–20. Strong dates the first *deuil blanc* portrait before the death of Francis II and lists Mary's portraits of that type, including "the miniature in the Uffizi," "a second miniature in the Maruitshuis," and its reverse visible in a double portrait of her with Darnley at Hardwick Hall (220). On Charles I's copies, see Cust, 52; on the derivation of this portrait's copies, see Helen Smailes and Duncan Thomson, *The Queen's Image: A Celebration of Mary Queen of Scots*, 31 (hereafter cited as Smailes and Thomson).

47. Mary Queen of Scots, "Ode on the Death of Her Husband, King Francis II, When He Was Sixteen and She Was Seventeen Years Old. 1560," in *Bittersweet Within My Heart: The Collected Poems of Mary, Queen of Scots*, 18–20; quotation, 19 (hereafter cited as Bell). I translate the French in order to keep the form of Mary's poetry and a more literal sense of her wordplay. See also Peter C. Herman, "'mes subjectz, mon ame assubjectie': the Problematic (of) Subjectivity in Mary Stuart's Sonnets," 19.

48. Helen Smailes, trans., Smailes and Thomson, 33.

49. Quoted in Cust, 48, my translation.

50. Inventory of Mary Stuart's wardrobe of 1562, summarized in Susan Watkins, *Mary Queen of Scots*, 105.

51. Thomas Randolph to Leicester, July 1565, Cott. Lib. Cal. b.ix.fol 216; reprinted in Thomas Wright, *Queen Elizabeth and Her Times: A Series of Original Letters*, 1:199–204. I am grateful for Retha Warnicke's help in locating this document, which does not specify that Mary wore *white* mourning.

52. Cust also notes the extent to which Mary Stuart's portrait in white mourning becomes the prototype for most of her portraiture (48–78).

53. *CSP Scotland*, 2:237.

54. Retha Warnicke, *Mary Queen of Scots*, 188.

55. See Michael Bath, *Emblems for a Queen: The Needlework of Mary Queen of Scots*. On Mary's needlework, partly in relation to Bess of Hardwick's, see Margaret Swain, *The Needle-work of Mary Queen of Scots*. On both needleworkers, see George Wingfield Digby, *Elizabethan Embroidery*, 53–66; Susan Frye, "Sewing Connections: Elizabeth Tudor, Mary Stuart, Elizabeth Talbot, and Seventeenth-Century Anonymous Needleworkers," 165–82.

56. Jayne Lewis, *The Trial of Mary Queen of Scots: A Brief History with Documents*, 84.

57. Margaret Swain, *The Needlework of Mary Queen of Scots*, 75. Joanne Gaudio studied this needlework as evidence against Norfolk at his trial in a seminar paper published as "A Message in Tent Stitch and a Reply: The Politics of Mary, Queen of Scots, and Elizabeth I of England." "Veriscit Vulnere Veritas" is used in many ways during the early modern period. Anne Dowriche's *French Historie* (1589) begins and ends with an emblem featuring this motto. Bath discusses it with reference to John 15:1–5 and other contemporary examples in *Emblems for a Queen*, 62–66. See also Margaret Ferguson, who reaches similar conclusions to mine through different routes and who also discusses this emblem's classical derivation and its relation to Elizabeth Cary, *Dido's Daughters: Literacy, Gender, and Empire in Early Modern England and France*, 306–7. See also Jennifer Summit, *Lost Property: The Woman Writer and English Literary History*, 199–201.

58. *CSP Scotland*, 2:56–57. Durkan, "The Library of Mary, Queen of Scots," notes that this volume, "Composed perhaps in the 1570s," was *"Tetrasticha ou Quatrains* addressed to her son, given to Edinburgh University after James's death by Drummond of Hawthornden but now missing" (77). Montague quoted in Swain, *Needlework of Mary Queen of Scots*, 86.

59. Bath discusses Mary's bed of state in *Emblems for a Queen*, 17–21; see also Michael Bath, "Embroidered Emblems: Mary Stuart's Bed of State."

60. William Drummond of Hawthornden to Ben Jonson, 1 July 1619, printed in Margaret Swain, *Historical Needlework*, 114–16. Bath discusses discovering the three other descriptions of Mary's bed of state in *Emblems for a Queen*, 17–21.

61. For the phoenix octagon, see Swain, *Needlework of Mary Queen of Scots*, 70.

62. John Guy, *Queen of Scots: The True Life of Mary Stuart*, 267 (hereafter cited as Guy).

63. Bath, *Emblems for a Queen*, 20. Cust describes the miniature as part of a full-length portrait of Mary at New Hardwick Hall, probably painted at the beginning of the seventeenth century from an earlier Hilliard miniature. Cust is quoting George Scharf, his predecessor as "Keeper and Secretary of the National Portrait Gallery," 71–73, 156. On James IV's book of hours, see Chapter 2.

64. Nicholas White to William Cecil, 26 February 1568, of which a full transcript is printed in Historical Manuscript Commission, *Calendar of the Manuscripts of the Marquis of Salisbury*, 1:509–12.

65. Elizabeth's ciphered letter to Moray printed in Alan Haynes, *Invisible Power: The Elizabethan Secret Services 1570–1603*, 20–21.

66. R. W. Maslen observes about the prose fiction writers of the 1570s that early moderns "delight in manufacturing and accumulating secrets" while "they also seem unusually susceptible to giving them away. They are vulnerable as well as devious," and so open to "exploitation by the cunning orchestrators of the better-organized and less penetrable policies of the state" (*Elizabethan Fictions: Espionage, Counter-Espionage, and the Duplicity of Fiction in Early Elizabethan Prose Narratives*, 14–15).

67. Lady Brilliana Harley, *The Letters of The Lady Brilliana Harley*, 186, 191–94. Women in other places and times have resorted to textile-based codes. For example, in nineteenth-century America, quilts were used to communicate with slaves escaping on the Underground Railroad. See Jaqueline L. Tobin and Raymond G. Dobard, *Hidden in Plain View: The Secret Story of Quilts and the Underground Railroad*. Chinese women in Jiangyong Prefecture, Hunan Province, developed the secret alphabet "nu shu," a "syllabic script" that "they embroidered into cloth and wrote" in "books and on paper fans." Nu shu was especially used to create small books given as gifts among women, often upon marriage. See http://homepage3.nifty.com/nushu/symposium.htm. Janice Harris drew my attention to this practice. On women's codes, see Joan Newlon Radner, *Feminist Messages: Coding in Women's Folk Culture*.

68. On Mary's letter ciphers, see Simon Singh, *The Code Book: The Evolution of Secrecy from Mary Queen of Scots to Quantum Cryptography*, 1–44.

69. David N. Durant, *Bess of Hardwick: Portrait of an Elizabethan Dynast*, 19, 55 (hereafter cited as Durant). Lovell discusses the Cavendishes' building of a new home at Chatsworth, 73.

70. Levey uses this title to describe this series of hangings, replacing its inaccurate earlier title, the "Four Virtues" (*The Embroideries at Hardwick Hall*, 58).

71. Ralph Sadler to William Cecil, January 21, 1571–2, paraphrased in *CSP Scotland*, 93. In October 1571, George Talbot wrote William Cecil to defend his wife's intimacy with Mary, explaining that he had asked her to spy on her "in such sort that she might the better learn the Queen's intentions," and testifying that "my wife is utterly ignorant" "touching any letters, tokens, or intelligence . . . between her and the Duke of Norfolk" (*CSP Scotland*, 2:16).

72. John Guy also estimates that Bess and Mary "continued to sew together" until about 1577 (435); quotations: *CSP Scotland*, 2:93, 109. On the books owned by Mary Queen of Scots and shared with Bess of Hardwick as the source of their needlework pictures, see Margaret Swain, *Figures on Fabric: Embroidery Design Sources and Their Application*, 26–37; on Mary's library, see Durkan, "The Library of Mary, Queen of Scots."

73. Swain, *Needlework of Mary Queen of Scots*, 30, 102.

74. Durant, 52.

75. *CSP Scotland*, 2:657; Durant, 98.

76. Durant discusses how the marriage between Bess's daughter and Charles Stuart may have been manipulated, although the details will probably never be known (80–88); on Arbella Stuart, see 89–103 and especially Sara Jayne Steen, "Introduction," in *Arbella Stuart, The Letters of Arbella Stuart*, 68–70. Stephen Orgel discusses Arbella's escape attempt in *Impersonations*, 114–15.

77. Steen, "Introduction," 14.

78. On Mary's "scandal letter," see Guy, 441. On the question of whether Bess spread rumors that Mary was having an affair with Shrewsbury, see Guy, 440; Durant, 119–20, 129–34; Lovell, 262–63.

79. In this sentence I have summarized years of legal battles fought between the Earl and Countess of Shrewsbury; see Durant, 136–43. See also Warnicke's description of the Shrewsburys' affairs and Mary's transfer to Sadler's custody in *Mary Queen of Scots*, 216–18.

80. Steen, "Introduction," 14–16.

81. Durant, 72–73, 80–81, 100–101; Guy, 429, 440, 453.

82. See Santina M. Levey, "References to Dress in the Earliest Account Book of Bess of Hardwick," 22. George Digby points out Nicholas Hilliard's designation of the "broderer" as one who was a "skilled draughtsman" trained to "cull the many sources of current design and adapt them" (*Elizabethan Embroidery*, 51, 30).

Other names surface in Mary's accounts as artisans and tapissiers. In May 1571 Mary lists among her household a "Jacques de Senlis, groom of the wardrobe," and the "tailor William Blak, 'who serves in absence of Forent, the tapissier'" (*CSP Scotland*, 2:565).

83. Jane Roberts notes that while imprisoned at Lochleven in 1567–68, Mary "had to petition the Scottish lords for 'an embroiderer to draw forthe such work as she could be about,'" *Royal Artists from Mary Queen of Scots to the Present Day*, 38. Bess paid "Webb the imbroderer" "18s 4d a quarter" according to the accounts of 1598; see also Durant, 65; Mark Girouard, *Hardwick Hall*, 24.

84. On *taillure*, see Charles Germain de Saint-Aubin, *Art of the Embroiderer* (1770), 111. On appliqué as a technique for making tents and other large textiles, see Levey, *Elizabethan Treasures*, 69; Swain, *Needlework of Mary Queen of Scots*, 80.

85. Given her oration in defense of the education of women, Mary might well have owned a *City of Ladies* manuscript. The *City* includes lengthy accounts of Penelope, Lucrecia, and Zenobia, with Arthemisia's story immediately following Zenobia's. Christine did not include Cleopatra in her descriptions of worthy women, but Petrarch, in addition to mentioning in his *Triumphs* Penelope, Lucrecia, Zenobia, and Arthemisia, also mentions Cleopatra as one of the "warrior women," with Zenobia, in "The Triumph of Fame." Boccaccio's *Concerning Famous Women* is still another possible source (on Boccaccio as a source, see Chapter 2). Bess's interest in these particular exemplars connects her with similar tastes among elite women, visible in Elizabeth's *City of Ladies* tapestries as well as Mary Sidney Herbert's translation of the *Triumph of Death* and the play *Antonie*. Christine de Pizan, *The Book of the City of Ladies*, 52–57, 158, 160–62. Petrarch, *The Triumphs of Petrarch*, 22, 44, 83. On Elizabeth's ownership of a suite of City of Ladies tapestries, see Susan Groag Bell, *The Lost Tapestries of the City of Ladies*.

86. Levey, *The Embroideries at Hardwick Hall*, 86–109. Levey, 108, identifies Faith as a portrait of Queen Elizabeth. Levey, 98–99, concludes that the virtues-vices series was begun in the 1570s but completed in the 1590s. See also Durant, 17, 28.

87. Levey, *The Embroideries at Hardwick Hall*, 110–79.

88. Historical Manuscript Commission, *Calendar of the Manuscripts of the Marquis of Salisbury* 3:158–61; discussed by Levey, *Elizabethan Treasures*, 15.

89. *Hardwick Hall Inventories of 1601*, ed. Lindsay Boynton, 28. Anthony Wells-Cole notes that although Virgil Solis was the "most prolific print designer in Southern Germany" from about 1540 to 1562, very few of his prints were adapted for English interiors (*Art and Decoration in Elizabethan and Jacobean England: The Influence of Continental Prints, 1558–1625*, 23–25).

90. See *Hardwick Hall Inventories of 1601*, 48–49, for the contents of the Long Gallery. Bess relied on a Solis woodcut for the design of "Europa and the Bull," another long cushion. Levey reproduces both woodcut and cushion of Europa in *Elizabethan Treasures*, 51, but does not list Solis as a source of "Diana and Actaeon," probably because Solis's design has been so altered. See *Embroideries at Hardwick Hall*, 396.

91. Amias Paulet to Queen Elizabeth I, Tutbury, 27 April 1585, Amias Poulet [Paulet], *The Letter-Books of Sir Amias Poulet Keeper of Mary Queen of Scots*, 11–14.

92. *Accounts and Papers Relating to Mary Queen of Scots*, "Charges of the Funeral of Mary Queen of Scots," 28–42.

93. On the collaboration of Bess and Smythson, see Mark Girouard, *Robert Smythson and the Elizabethan Country House*, 146. Alice T. Friedman, "Architecture, Authority, and the Female Gaze: Planning and Representation in the Early Modern Country House," 50. Also on New Hardwick Hall's architecture, see Lena Cowen Orlin, *Locating Privacy in Tudor London*, 78–90, 88–93, 243–47.

94. On the design of New Hardwick, see Girouard, *Robert Smythson*, 156–60; Friedman, "Architecture, Authority, and the Female Gaze," 54; and Girouard, *Hardwick Hall*, 47–80.

95. Patrick Collinson also remarks on the intrusion of Bess's initials in Elizabeth's motto in *The English Captivity of Mary Queen of Scots*, 17–18.

96. Attributed to John Balechouse, *The Return of Ulysses to Penelope*, perhaps 1570s but before 1601. Hearn, *Dynasties*, 101; *Hardwick Hall Inventories of 1601*, 47.

97. I am grateful to Bradin Cormack for suggesting this line of inquiry. Kurt W. Forster, "Introduction," in Aby Warburg, *The Renewal of Pagan Antiquity*, 13; Leon Battista Alberti, *Libro della Pittura*, quoted in Aby Warburg, "Sandro Botticelli's *Birth of Venus and Spring*: An Examination of Concepts of Antiquity in the Italian Early Renaissance (1893)," 96. Levey acknowledges that the *Chastity* figure "resembles the white mourning worn by Mary Queen of Scots in a painting of about 1559, now in the Royal Collection" but also describes her wearing "a close-fitting wimple extending down onto her shoulders," a kind of "out-of-date fashion." *The Embroideries at Hardwick Hall*, 75.

98. Guy, 49. Mary's hearse and funeral standard is described in *Est natura hominum nouitatis anida: The Scottish queens buriall at Peterborough*, Sig. 2(v) and 2(r); 3(v). The funeral standard with unicorn is reproduced in *Accounts and Papers Relating to Mary Queen of Scots*, on a pull-out insert "copied from a drawing" taken from "William Dethicke, Garter King of Arms" (vii). On James IV's motto, see Duncan Macmillan, *Scottish Art 1460–2000*, 26.

99. The inventory of 1601 records that the room's paintings included "pictures of the Queen of Scots, the same Queen and the King of Scots with their Arms both in one, the King and Queen of Scots her father & mother in an other" (*Hardwick Hall Inventories of 1601*, 47). Roy Strong points out that in this picture with Darnley, Mary is pictured according to the profile type used in her *deuil blanc* pictures, although she is wearing an Italian cap rather than the shaped cap of mourning (Strong, *Tudor and Jacobean Portraits*, 220). Caroline McCracken-Flesher informed me that a version of this painting showing only Mary's head and this cap has recently been declared a contemporary painting and is on view at the National Portrait Gallery, London.

100. Tapestries often include portraits. Catherine de Medici is portrayed in black mourning in the tapestry series *Festivities at the Valois Court* about 1582–85. Florence, Galleria degli Uffizi, inv. Arazzi n. 495, 384 x 605 cm. Infanta Dona Maria and Don Alvaro de Castro are portrayed in a tapestry of 1557 (Guy Delmarcel, *Flemish Tapestry*, 125). My thanks to Peter Davidson for pointing out the reference to an embroidered Mary Stuart portrait in Digby, *Elizabethan Embroidery*, 87.

101. Nicholas Hilliard, *Art of Limning*, 16.

102. Karen Robertson and J.-A. George, "Introduction," in *Horestes*, 3; George Buchanan, *Ane Detection of the Doings of Mary Queen of Scots* (1571), excerpted in Lewis, *The Trial of Mary Queen of Scots*, 65–67. See also Edmund Spenser, *The Faerie Queene*, V.ix.48. For James's protests, see *CSP Scotland*, 12:359. On Duessa's trial and the historical record, see Lowell Gallagher, *Medusa's Gaze: Casuistry and Conscience in the Renaissance*, 215–61.

This discussion of the conflation of Mary's supposed murder of Darnley and adultery with Bothwell provides only a small taste of the sexual invective directed against her. See Phillips, *Images of a Queen*, on the character attacks of ballads, manuscripts, and printed materials, 41–51.

1. The category of *artisan* was assigned to people who made things, regardless of their social standing, from dressers of wool cloth to goldsmiths and painters. Cockeram's dictionary defines *artisan* simply as "A hand-craftsman." Henry Cockeram, *The English Dictionarie*. William Harrison has difficulty assigning a social position to artisans or, as he calls them, "artificers." See *The Description of England*, 94, 94n.2.

2. E. Sambo, "Giulio Clovio," in Giulio Bora, *I Campi* (Electa, 1985), cited in Liana De Girolami Cheney, Alicia Craig Faxon, and Kathleen Lucey Russo, *Self-Portraits by Women Painters*, 220n.45 (hereafter cited as Cheney, Faxon, and Russo).

3. On this Latin original, published as Filipo Barbieri, *Sibyllaru de Christo Vaticinia* (Venice, 1510) but which first circulated in the late fourteenth century, see Jessica Malay, "Jane Seager's Maidenly Negotiation Through Elizabethan Gift Exchange."

4. Jane Segar, *The Prophecies of the Ten Sibills upon the Birth of Christ*, BL MS Add. 10037. I quote my transcript of this manuscript throughout. Despite searches by me and by the helpful staff of the Manuscript Student's Room, no information about the provenance of the manuscript exists aside from its purchase for the British Library collections in 1836. The full text is available in Werner Kraner, "Zür Englischen Kurzschrift in Zeitalter Shakespeares: Das Jane-Seager Manusckript. (The Divine Prophecies of the Ten Sibyls)." Jill Seal Millman and Gillian Wright print Segar's dedication, three sibylline poems, and her concluding poem in *Early Modern Women's Manuscript Poetry*, 15–19. Jane Stevenson and Peter Davidson print Segar's dedication, and "Lybica," in *Early Modern Women Poets: An Anthology*, 115–16.

5. On women and medieval manuscript production, see Cheney, Faxon, and Russo, 17–19; on Christine de Pizan and the question of who illuminated her manuscripts, see 23–26. On Christine as scrivener, see Charity Canon Willard, *Christine de Pizan: Her Life and Works*, 45–47.

A woman artist has been identified working in the workshop of Jean le Noir in Paris in the fourteenth century. In January 2008 the Cloisters Museum labeled the *Psalter and Hours of Bonne of Luxembourg, Duchess of Normandy* as "probably" the work of "Jean le Noir, his daughter, and his workshop," "France, Paris, before 1349." In Italy, convents produced illuminated manuscripts throughout the Renaissance (Cheney, Faxon, and Russo, 31–34).

6. My thanks to Susan Foister, curator of Northern European Art, National Gallery of Art, London, for our conversations that helped me to visualize how such studios or workshops worked, and how women might have collaborated in the family business conducted there.

7. Gower was himself Sergeant Painter in 1581. Erna Auerbach, *Tudor Artists*, 108, 114.

8. See Susan Foister, *Holbein and England*, 127, for a book manuscript Holbein helped to produce, *Canones Horoptri*; for designs of cups, table fountains, and clocksalt, 138–39, 142–43; for a bookcover, 145; for a chimneypiece, 146.

9. Roy Strong, *The English Renaissance Miniature*, 8.

10. *The Inventory of King Henry VIII*, 237.

11. *The Inventory of King Henry VIII*, 232, 400.

12. The particulars that follow about Susanna Horenbout derive from Lorne Campbell and Susan Foister, "Gerard, Lucas and Susanna Horenbout." See also Strong, *English Renaissance Miniature*, 12–44.

13. Strong, *English Renaissance Miniature*, 41.

14. Jessica Wolfe, *Humanism, Machinery, and Renaissance Literature*, 163.

15. Strong stresses as well the "exclusive," royal aspects of the miniature over its origins in religious texts, and the secrecy surrounding the miniaturist's craft, *English Renaissance Miniature*, 9.

16. Duncan Macmillan, *Scottish Art 1460–2000*, 24–27. For a description of the *Book of Hours of James IV and Margaret Tudor* in the Osterreiches Staatsbibliothek, see Leslie Macfarlane, "The Book of Hours of James IV and Margaret Tudor," 3–20.

17. For an overview of Levina Teerlinc's life and attributions, see Ann Sutherland Harris and Linda Nochlin, *Women Artists 1550–1950*, 102–6; Roy Strong, *Artists of the Tudor Court: The Portrait Miniature Rediscovered 1520–1620*, 48–57; and Strong, *English Renaissance Miniature*, 54–64. See also Mary Edmond, *Hilliard and Oliver: The Lives and Works of Two Great Miniaturists*, 20, 301; Auerbach, *Tudor Artists*, 103–6; chronology of Teerlinc's life, 187–88.

18. Giorgio Vasari, *La vite de'piùeccellenti pittori* (1550/1568), VI: 217, quoted in Clare Robertson, "*Phoenix Romanus*: Rome, 1534–1565," 209. *The Farnese Book of Hours*, Pierpont Morgan Library and Museum, MS M.69, fols. 72v–73r. On Clovio and tapestries, see Robertson, "*Phoenix Romanus*," 204, and John Henry, *Illuminated Manuscripts in Classical and Medieval Times*, 202.

19. Strong argues that Teerlinc was recruited into Henry VIII's service as one of several miniaturists needed to fill court demand after the deaths of Holbein in 1543 and Lucas Hornebout in 1544, *English Renaissance Miniature*, 54. See also Auerbach, *Tudor Artists*, 51, 104; Campbell and Foister, "Gerard, Lucas, and Susanna Horenbout," 722.

20. On the Gentlemen Pensioners, see Stephen May, "Chapter 1: The Social Organization of the Court," *The Elizabethan Courtier Poets: The Poems and Their Contexts*, 14–16. See also Maria Hayward, who points out that Henry VIII created this group and that its members paid for the privilege of belonging (*Dress at the Court of King Henry VIII*, 45, 290–91).

21. Auerbach, *Tudor Artists*, 51. Susan James discusses the Parrs' patronage of the Teerlincs in *Kateryn Parr: The Making of a Queen*, 159. On Katherine Parr's payments for portraits to Lucas Hornebout's wife, Margaret, "for making of the Queen's picture and the king's" and to Margaret's second husband "for drawing of the king's pictures & the Queen's," see Campbell and Foister, "Gerard, Lucas, and Susanna Horenbout," 724–25.

22. This portrait of Elizabeth (c. 1551) may be the one Elizabeth mentions to her brother in the letter from Hatfield discussed in Chapter 1. Auerbach, *Tudor Artists*, 76; Strong, *English Renaissance Miniature*, 55. Three Teerlinc portraits of Elizabeth have been identified, one at the Yale Center for British Art and two in the Royal Collections. Both Auerbach and Strong note, without explanation, that the amount of £10 in the warrant is large.

23. For Teerlinc's annuity, see Auerbach, *Tudor Artists*, 103–4. For the document confirming her death, see Auerbach, *Tudor Artists*, 105.

24. Charlotte Isabelle Merton, *The Women Who Served Queen Mary and Queen Elizabeth: Ladies, Gentlewomen and Maids of the Privy Chamber, 1553–1603*, 31–32.

25. For these lists of New Year's gifts, see Auerbach, *Tudor Artists*, 188, and Strong, *English Renaissance Miniature*, 55.

26. Strong, *English Renaissance Miniature*, 57.

27. Strong, *English Renaissance Miniature*, 57–64. Susan Foister casts doubt on the strength of some of Strong's attributions, especially the woodcut hunting scenes featuring Elizabeth in George Tuberville's *Book of Hunting* (1575), "Tudor Miniaturists at the V&A."

28. Quoted in Gillian Perry, *Gender and Art*, 46.

29. On dating Elizabeth's pictures using the style of her ruffs, see Janet Arnold, *Queen Elizabeth's Wardrobe Unlock'd*, 25–35. Cheney, Faxon, and Russo, figure III.3, 35–36.

30. Carole Levin, "Levina Teerlinc," in *Extraordinary Women of the Medieval and Renaissance World*, ed. Carole Levin et al., 280. Elsa H. Fine notes dice among the dress pleats in a woman's portrait at the Victoria and Albert Museum in *Women Artists: An Illuminated History*, 26.

31. Levina Teerlinc, "The Ceremonye for the healing of them that be diseased with the

kynges Evill," in *Queen Mary's Manual for blessing cramp rings and touching for the evil: the rituals of the royal healing ceremonies* (Titled on the manuscript *Certain Prayers to be used by the quenes heignes in the consecration of the crampe rynges*), no sig.

32. Carole Levin, "'Would I Could Give You Help and Succour': Elizabeth I and the Politics of Touch," 10–38. See also Carole Levin, *The Heart and Stomach of a King: Elizabeth I and the Politics of Sex and Power,* on the Maundy's history and the practice of specific ceremonies by Mary and Elizabeth, 23–25, 33–35. Levin notes the importance of creating such ceremonies, as "For queens ruling instead of kings, this aspect of power through ritual and spectacle could be particularly important" (*Heart and Stomach of a King,* 24).

33. See Levin, *Heart and Stomach of a King,* 34. In 1536, Henry VIII refused Catherine of Aragon the right to perform her Maundy ceremony (Peter A. Wright, *The Pictorial History of the Royal Maundy,* 4).

34. Strong points out that the picture was probably once a rectangle, cut down to its present oval shape. Although he prefers to think that this is a New Year's miniature, he admits that "it is conceivable that this has been cut from an illuminated page" (Strong, *Artists of the Tudor Court,* 55).

35. Brian Robinson, *The Royal Maundy,* 41.

36. Thomas Lambarde, in *The Progresses and Processions of Queen Elizabeth,* ed. John Nichols, 1:325–37; see also Levin, *Heart and Stomach of a King,* 33–34. Strong identifies several participants in the painting and comments on its composition (*Artists of the Tudor Court,* 55).

37. On Hilliard, see Erna Auerbach, *Nicholas Hilliard;* Auerbach, *Tudor Artists;* Edmond, *Hilliard and Oliver;* and Nicholas Hilliard, *Nicholas Hilliard's Art of Limning: A New Edition of A Treatise Concerning the Arte of Limning.*

38. See Malay's discussion of the European tradition of the Sibyl, "Jane Seager's Maidenly Negotiation," 177–79.

39. Alan Stewart, "The Early Modern Closet Discovered," 92, 98n.30.

40. Richard York, Archivist at the College of Arms, led me to William Segar's draft of the Segar genealogy in July 1993. The genealogy is in College of Arms MS H14, the Suffolk Visitation of 1561 and 1577, fol. 13. Millman and Wright also conclude that William Segar is Jane's brother (*Early Modern Women's Manuscript Poetry,* 17). Roy Strong, in *The English Icon: Elizabethan and Jacobean Portraiture,* summarizes Segar's life and provides a catalog of his artwork, 17–19, 215–24.

41. Francis Meres, *Palladius Tumia,* fol. 287. Auerbach, *Tudor Artists,* 121, 122.

42. Francis Segar merits two mentions in the Sidney correspondence, Historical Manuscripts Commission, *Report on the Manuscripts of Lord de L'Isle and Dudley HMC Penshurst* 5:78, 237; editors William Shaw and G. Dyfnallt Owen note that Francis not only acted as Landgrave's agent at James's court, but that he was "said to have been a favourite" (5:78n.). Roy Strong disagrees that Francis could have been active in the Segar studio, suggesting that "Francis possibly only aided his brother in maintaining some sort of studio" (*English Icon,* 17). David Piper, however, had earlier concluded that "Any attempt to disentangle their work one from the other would at present be futile . . . they may well have worked in partnership" "The 1590 Lumley Inventory: Hilliard, Segar and the Earl of Essex–II," 303).

43. Definitions, *Oxford English Dictionary,* hereafter cited as OED.

44. Paul Hentzner, in 1598 a visitor to England from Brandenberg, described Elizabeth's library at Whitehall Palace, where "All these books are bound in velvet of different colours, though chiefly red, with clasps of gold and silver; some have pearls and precious stones set in their bindings." Quoted in William Brenchley Rye, *England as Seen by Foreigners in the Days of Elizabeth and James the First,* 103, 282.

Margaret Swain examined an enlarged color photo of Segar's back cover with me and determined that, although the lacy trim appears to be needlework, it is in fact a kind of braid lace, a trimming, or *passement*, of the kind often supplied by a silk woman but possibly the product of Segar's own hand. Sewing braid lace to the manuscript book's red velvet cover would have approximated embroidery. On braid lace and *passement*, see Hayward, *Dress at the Court of King Henry VIII*, 359.

45. OED lists 1907 as the first use of the term *verre églomisé*. Miss R. Stockdale, Curator of the British Library Manuscript Collections, examined the Segar manuscript under a microscope and determined that Segar had painted the reverse side of the inset glass covers. Miss Stockdale added, "In 1956 the fragments were secured and the front and back glass replaced with unplasticised perspex, so [that] the protective surface is modern." Segar's techniques were highly unusual; Stockdale wrote, "I have not found any other manuscript binding described in our catalogues in the same way, and I am not aware of any other examples in our collections" (letter dated 20 June 1991).

46. Jill Finsten, *Isaac Oliver: Art at the Courts of Elizabeth I and James I* (New York: Garland Publishing, 1981), 9, 90. In 1598, Paul Hentzner mentions seeing at Whitehall *Christ's passion, in painted glass* (Rye, *England as Seen by Foreigners*, 165, 283n.153).

47. Stephen Orgel discussed the volume's back cover with me and made valuable suggestions about its iconography.

48. On Britain founded by the offspring of Aeneas, Brut or Brutus, see Geoffrey of Monmouth, *Histories of the Kings of Britain*. On the relation between Elizabeth's virginal and imperial iconography, see Frances Yates, *Astraea: The Imperial Theme in the Sixteenth Century*; Roy Strong, *The Cult of Elizabeth: Elizabethan Portraiture and Pageantry*; Louis Adrian Montrose, "The Elizabethan Subject and the Spenserian Text"; Louis Adrian Montrose, "'Eliza, Queen of Shepheardes,' and the Pastoral of Power"; Susan Frye, *Elizabeth I: The Competition for Representation*, 20–22, 101–4.

49. Timothy Bright, Dedication to Elizabeth, *Characterie: An Art of Swift and Secret Writing* (1588), n.p.

50. William J. Carlton, *Timothe Bright Doctor of Phisicke: A Memoir of "The Father of Modern Shorthand,"* 60–63.

Bright's patent failed to preclude competing systems. In *The Writing Schoolemaster* (1590), Peter Bales presented a system based on an "Alphabet of Roman or Italian letters" (B2V). Quoted in Jonathan Goldberg, *Writing Matter: From the Hands of the English Renaissance*, 204. Simon Forman records in 1600 that he "copied out also the 4 bookes of Steganno-graphia," presumably to compare and learn the existing forms of shorthand (*The Autobiography and Personal Diary of Dr. Simon Forman*, 30). J. Willis's *Art of Stenographie* (1602) went through fourteen editions by 1647. On shorthand in the seventeenth century and Bathsua Makin's creation of her own system of "radiography," see Frances Teague, *Bathsua Makin: Woman of Learning*, 30, 35–38.

51. Bright, "Dedication," *Characterie*, n.p. Bright's system not only recommended itself as a convenient cipher to the Cecils and Elizabeth, it fulfilled its promise to make possible the recording of public events, like Anthony Tyrrell's *A fruitfull sermon . . . taken by charactrye* (1589).

52. J. Westby Gibson, *The Shorthand Society*, 135. Carlton, Bright's biographer, found that the "unlimited time" Segar needed to produce her manuscript allowed its relative perfection: "Had the nymph written under the stress of *verbatim* reporting . . . her notes must have been infinitely more obscure," *Timothe Bright Doctor of Physicke*, 97–98. Charles Dickens, *David Copperfield*, 418.

53. On the Latin original, see Malay, "Jane Seager's Maidenly Negotiation." Margaret

Arnold made this point to me about facing-page editions during a seminar held at the University of Kansas. On whether translation was considered a "denigrated" form of writing in the sixteenth century, see Jonathan Goldberg, *Desiring Women Writing: English Renaissance Examples*, 75–90. On the "perception of the cultural and ontological mobility of translation" that appears "to underlie the malleable notions of gender that attach to translation," see Margaret Ferguson, *Dido's Daughters: Literacy, Gender, and Empire in Early Modern England and France*, 8.

54. Giovanni Boccaccio, *Concerning Famous Women*, 41–42, 50–51. As Maureen Quilligan notes, Boccaccio's book in Latin was written for men: "Its purpose is not to praise women but to spur men on to humanist achievements by goading them with the examples of heroic pagan women" (*The Allegory of Female Authority: Christine de Pizan's Cité des Dames*, 39).

55. Christine de Pizan, *The Book of the City of Ladies*, 30.

56. Alexandre de Pontaymeri, *A Woman's Woorth* (1599), 18.

57. [Christine de Pizan], *The boke of the cyte of ladyes*, anonymously translated. On the loss of Christine's name in relation to *The City of Ladies*, see Christina Malcomson, "Christine de Pizan's City of Ladies in Early Modern England," 15–35, and Jennifer Summit *Lost Property: The Woman Writer and English Literary History*, 61–108.

58. George Gascoigne, *The Princely Pleasures of Kenelwoorth Castle*, 486–87. On Sibylla's welcome, see Frye, *Elizabeth I*, 65–69.

59. Diane Watt, *Secretaries of God: Women Prophets in Late Medieval and Early Modern Europe*, 55; see also Diane Watt, "Reconstructing the Word: The Political Prophecies of Elizabeth Barton (1506–1534)." The language of the statute outlawing prophecy is from *The Statutes of the Realm* (1819; rpt., London: Dawsons, 1963), vol. 4, part 1, 445. Quoted in Howard Dobin, *Merlin's Disciples: Prophecy, Poetry, and Power in Renaissance England*, 110.

60. Edward Topsell, *Times Lamentation* (London: Edm. Bollifant, 1599), 63, quoted in George Wingfield Dobin, *Merlin's Disciples: Prophecy, Poetry, and Power in Renaissance England*, 110.

61. On women prophets, see Crawford, *Women and Religion in England 1500–1720*, especially 98–115. See also Matchinske, "Holy Hatred"; Smith, "Jane Lead's Wisdom"; Berg and Berry, "'Spiritual Whoredom'"; Diane Purkiss, "Invasions: Prophecy and Bewitchment in the Case of Margaret Muschamp"; Eleanor Davies, *Prophetic Writings of Lady Eleanor Davies*.

62. *Elizabeth*, engraving by Crispin de Passe (1596), in Roy Strong, *Portraits of Queen Elizabeth I*, 113, 115.

63. Edmund Spenser, *The Faerie Queene*.

64. *Calendar of State Papers, Domestic Series, Elizabeth*, 2:560.

65. William Segar, "Justs at the Tilt-yard, 1590," from *Honors Military and Civil* (1602), excerpted in *Progresses and Processions of Queen Elizabeth*, ed. John Nichols, 3:49.

66. "Speeches to the Queen at Sudeley, 1592," 3:139. The sibyl's speech is a paraphrase of Stephen Gosson's dedication to Philip Sidney from *The Schoole of Abuse*: "The whole world is drawen in a mappe, Homers Iliades in a nutteshell; a Kings picture in a pennie; Little Chestes may holde great Treasure; a fewe Cyphers contayne the substa[n]ce of a rich Merchant; . . . and the harshest penne maye sette down somewhat woorth the reading." Perhaps Gosson, author of plays and romances as well as antitheatrical polemics, in 1592 a lecturer at St. Dunstan's in London, was an author of these entertainments; alternatively, someone copied Gosson. Stephen Gosson, *The Schoole of Abuse* (1579), 3–4. On the trope of "a copy of the *Iliad* inscribed in a nutshell or on a grain of rice," see Wolfe, *Humanism, Machinery, and Renaissance Literature*, 171–72.

67. Millman and Wright, *Early Modern Women's Manuscript Poetry*, 15.

68. Millman and Wright speculate that Lionel Plumtree, or Plumptree, could have been

a member of a prosperous Nottingham merchant family, *Early Modern Women's Manuscript Poetry*, 17. But see "The fift voiage into Persia made by M. Thomas Banister, and master Geofrey Ducket, Agents from the Moscovie companie . . . Written by P. I. from the mouth of M. Lionel Plumtree," in Richard Hakluyt, *The Principal Navigations Voyages Trafiques & Discoveries of the English Nation* (1599), 3:150–57. It is possible that this is the Lionel Plumtree whom Segar married, if he were a young man at the time of the voyage, 1568–74. Otherwise, Segar married his son or other relative of the same name, another member of the Muskovy Company who accompanied her to Russia in 1603.

69. See, for example, the French printed books copied by scribes to produce "a *de luxe* manuscript" as discussed in James Carley, "'Her moost lovyng and fryndely brother sendeth gretyng': Anne Boleyn's Manuscripts and Their Sources," 267. On printing, see Elizabeth L. Eisenstein, *The Printing Revolution in Early Modern Europe*, and Margaret J. M. Ezell, *Social Authorship and the Advent of Print*. On manuscript culture in England, see Harold Love, *Scribal Publication in Seventeenth-Century England*. On both print and manuscripts, see Wendy Wall, *The Imprint of Gender: Authorship and Publication in the English Renaissance* and Arthur F. Marotti, *Manuscript, Print, and the English Renaissance Lyric*.

70. Esther Inglis, *Argumenta Psalmoru Davidis per tetrasticha manu Estherae Inglis exarata, strenai nomine Illus: Principi Henrico oblate*, Cat. 65; Folger Shakespeare Library V.a.94.

71. This biographical account is my summary of A. H. Scott-Elliot and Elspeth Yeo, "Calligraphic Manuscripts of Esther Inglis (1571–1624): A Catalogue," 12–14 (hereafter cited as Cat.), based on David Laing, "Notes Relating to Mrs Esther (Langlois or) Inglis, the Celebrated Calligraphist." My thanks to Elspeth Yeo for giving me an offprint of this article and for the illuminating conversation about Esther Inglis as I first sought out Inglis's books, and to Georgianna Ziegler for sharing her knowledge of and publications on Inglis. For a discussion of the extent to which Inglis might be considered an "author," see Susan Frye, "Materializing Authorship in Esther Inglis's Books." See also Georgianna Ziegler, "'More than Feminine Boldness': The Gift Books of Esther Inglis," 19–37; and Georgianna Ziegler, "Hand-Ma[i]de Books: The Manuscripts of Esther Inglis, Early-Modern Precursors of the Artists' Book"; Tricia Bracher, "Esther Inglis and the English Succession Crisis of 1599"; Anneke Tjan Bakker, "Dame Flora's Blossoms: Esther Inglis's Flower-Illustrated Manuscripts."

72. *Registrum Secreti Sigilli*, VIII, No. 591, quoted in Cat., 12. Marie Presot, Newberry Library Manuscript, dated "Edimbourg le 24. d'aoust, 1574."

73. Richard Mulcaster, *The First Part of the Elementarie* (1582; rpt. Menston: Scolar Press, 1970, 56), quoted in Goldberg, *Writing Matter*, 55.

74. Cat. no. 3, 28. *Discours de la Foy*, Huntingdon Library, HM 26068; Dedicated to Queen Elizabeth, dated 1 January 1591 (Cat., 15). Georgianna Ziegler's translation from the French of this dedication, "Gift Books," 20.

75. See Laing, "Notes Relating to Mrs. Esther (Langlois or) Inglis," 288. Scott-Elliot and Yeo point out that this document has since disappeared, along with other items from Laing's archive on Inglis, some of which, like Inglis's portrait, have since resurfaced (Cat., 13).

76. On Kello's activities, see Frye, "Materializing Authorship," 472–74, and Bracher, "Esther Inglis and the English Succession Crisis," 132–46.

77. On Inglis's patterns of dedication, see Ziegler, "Gift Books," esp. 23–27.

78. National Library of Scotland, Adv. MS. 33.1.6, vol. 20, no. 21, quoted in Laing, "Notes Relating to Mrs Esther (Langlois or) Inglis," 307–8.

79. Ziegler, "Hand-Ma[i]de Books," 79.

80. *Ce Livre contenant cinquante Emblemes Chrestiens premierement inventez par la noble damoiselle Georgette de Montenay* (1624), British Library, Royal MS. Cat. no. 54.

81. Ziegler, "Hand-Ma[i]de Books," 79; Cat. no. 36. Scott-Elliot and Yeo note that the self-portraits in Cat. nos. 12, 53–55 are modeled on the Montenay portrait (Cat., 18).

82. Cat. no. 36, my transcription.

83. Elaine Beilin provides a detailed description of Lanyer's nine dedicatees in *Redeeming Eve: Women Writers of the English Renaissance*, 182–91; see also Sharon Cadmun Seelig, "'To all vertuous Ladies in generall': Aemilia Lanyer's Community of Strong Women"; Leeds Barroll, "Looking for Patrons in Amelia Lanyer: Gender, Genre, and the Canon."

84. The passage reads, "Ton saint Esprit tousiours / en ce sentier humain / Asseure, ouvre, redresse, / illumine, conduise, / Mon coeur, mon oeil, mon pied, / mon esprit et ma main." Esther Inglis, Dedication, *Le Livre des pseaumes ecrites en diverswes sortes de letters par Esther Anglois Francoise* 1599. Christ Church College, Oxford (Cat. no. 7). Transcription, Cat. 34–35, my translation.

85. See Cat. no. 10, p. 40. Several other books contain a similar self-portrait, which Scott-Elliott and Yeo classify as "Type 1," complete with inkpot, pen, music, and lute back. See Cat. nos. 7, 8, and 9; pp. 33–39; and nos. 16, 17, 18, and 19; pp. 45–49.

86. See Cheney, Faxon, and Russo, figures IV.2, IV.8, and IV.12.

87. Joseph Moxon, *The Mechanick Exercises on the Whole Art of Printing*, ed. Herbert Davis and Harry Carter (1683–84; rpt. London: Oxford University Press, 1978), 181, quoted in Margreta de Grazia, "Imprints: Shakespeare, Gutenberg and Descartes," 83.

88. De Grazia, "Imprints," 82–83. Wendy Wall has argued that "the page is encoded as feminine while the machinery of the press, the writer, and the ink are depicted as masculine" (*Imprint of Gender*, 220). For additional seventeenth century examples, see Love's discussion of the "procreative pen" metaphor, *Scribal Publication*, 148–57.

89. On the interaction of print and calligraphy, see Goldberg, *Writing Matter*, 136. On women and calligraphy, see 137–45, and on Inglis, 146–53. Goldberg writes that Inglis was "a copyist with a hand like a machine, virtually indistinguishable from print" (153).

90. Cat. no. 27, 21. Scott-Elliot and Yeo point out that Inglis's crossed-pen designs derive from "Jacobus Houthusius, *Exemplaria sive formulae scripturae ornatioris xxxvi* (Aachen, 1591)"; it recurs in numbers 22–27 with variations in the motto" (Cat., 50).

91. Wall, *Imprint of Gender*, 219–20.

92. Laing, "Notes Relating to Mrs Esther (Langlois or) Inglis," 284.

93. This is my translation of the French, "Ce qui m'a induitte avec plus grande confidence, quoy que ie sois femme, et de petite condition, d'esperer que ce petit present, escrit de ma main, au pais estranger, pourra obtenir place en quelque coing retiré de vostre cabinet...." *Le Livre des Pseaumes 1599*, College of Christ Church Library, Oxford; Cat. no. 7.

94. Patricia Fumerton, *Cultural Aesthetics: Renaissance Literature and the Practice of Social Ornament*, 70–71. Ziegler discusses Inglis's books as miniatures, "The small size of many of Inglis's books also points to the very personal nature of their use" ("Gift Books," 32).

95. Ann Rosalind Jones and Peter Stallybrass, *Renaissance Clothing and the Materials of Memory*, 44.

96. See Quilligan, *Allegory of Female Authority*, 1–10, 11–68.

CHAPTER THREE

1. I use the term *domestic needlework* to differentiate needlework produced by women for gifts and the "household store" from the professional needlework of men and women produced for wages. As Mark Overton, Jane Whittle, Darron Dean, and Andrew Hann point out, both men and women worked from the home for wages in the early modern period (*Production and Consumption in English Households, 1600–1750*, 5).

2. Michel de Certeau, *The Practice of Everyday Life*, xiii. Certeau is discussing the Native Americans colonized by the Spanish: "Submissive, and even consenting to their subjection,

the Indians nevertheless often *made* of the rituals, representations, and laws imposed on them something quite different from what their conquerors had in mind; they subverted them not by rejecting or altering them, but by using them with respect to ends and references foreign to the system they had no choice but to accept" (xiii). Although wary of the analogy between early modern women and colonized Native Americans, I find that recognizing how oppressed groups might use dominant language and social practice toward their own ends helps to explain women's household practice as the activity of (limited) agents rather than as victims.

3. See Introduction for Lady Grace Mildmay's description of her drawings for embroidery. See Chapter 1 for Bess of Hardwick's textiles.

4. Keith Wrightson summarizes these changes as occurring in "population and prices, in the distribution of land and agrarian social relations, in commerce and the enhancement of commercial motivation, in the enjoyment of some of new wealth and the endurance by others of greater poverty" (*Earthly Necessities: Economic Lives in Early Modern Britain*, 4).

5. Liz Arthur, *Embroidery 1600–1700 at the Burrell Collection*, 59 (hereafter cited as Arthur).

6. Ann Rosalind Jones and Peter Stallybrass, *Renaissance Clothing and the Materials of Memory*, 156–71; quotation, 171 (hereafter cited as Jones and Stallybrass).

A few scholars began studying women's early modern needlework from the mid-1980s, all with different but complementary points of view. My own emphasis was on the continuum of women's textualities from needle and textile work through the writing of domestic texts and the kinds of writing that we now call literature.

In 1997 I participated in the Shakespeare Association Seminar organized by Ann Jones and Peter Stallybrass, "Borrowed Robes," for which I began working on the idea of Hebrew samplers. Their *Renaissance Clothing and the Materials of Memory* appeared in 2000; my article outlining many of the directions taken in Chapters 1 and 3 of this book appeared in 1999, as they were completing their chapter on needlework. I found on publication of their book that, in addition to discovering a great deal of material that was new to me, we were using some of the same sources to discuss our different emphases, although some of our conclusions are similar. As a result, I direct anyone interested in this subject to their book and other publications. See Susan Frye, "Sewing Connections: Elizabeth Tudor, Mary Stuart, Elizabeth Talbot, and Seventeenth-Century Anonymous Needleworkers."

7. Jones and Stallybrass concentrate on the extent to which individual women and their embroidery participated in questions of national policy, especially the Civil War as "They turned the habit of domestic stitchery into a public practice" (158–71; quotation, 170).

8. John Skelton, "Here after foloweth the boke of Phyllyp Sparowe compyled by Mayster Skelton, poete laureate," *John Skelton: The Complete English Poems*, ed. John Scattergood, 77, lines 210–17.

9. William Shakespeare, *Titus Andronicus* 2.4.138–39, in *The Norton Shakespeare*. The pathetic point that Lavinia cannot work her *sampler* is replayed in "Titus Andronics complaint" (Richard Johnson, *The Golden Garland* (1620), Sig. f(v)).

10. Elizabeth Isham, "A single folio page inscribed with lists and short jottings," Northamptonshire County Record Office IL3365, panel 2, quoted in Margaret Ezell, "Elizabeth Isham's Books of Remembrance and Forgetting," par. 21. Isham's life writings include this summation of her life inscribed in minute writing on a single folio page. I am grateful to Rebecca Laroche for calling my attention to Elizabeth Isham.

11. Henry Chettle, *The Tragedy of Hoffman*, Act IV (Sig. G(v)). Nicholas Hookes, "To Mr. John Mors, Merchant in Kings Lynne, on the death of Mrs. A. Mors His Wife," in *Amanda* (1653), 117. In her samplers, Mrs. Mors also worked "Birds feather'd with her silk

you'd swear did flie, / Camels have past too through her needles eye." He also notes that her classical subjects included the Muses, Venus and Cupid, Diana, and the Three Graces.

12. Jessica Wolfe, *Humanism, Machinery, and Renaissance Literature*, 183.

13. Randle Cotgrave, *Dictionarie of the French and English Tongues* (1611). Discussed in François Rigolot, "The Renaissance Crisis of Exemplarity," 558.

14. See Karlheinz Stierle, "Three Moments in the Crisis of Exemplarity: Boccaccio-Petrarch, Montaigne, and Cervantes," 584.

15. Jasper Mayne, *The City Match*, 2.2. Written from the royalist point of view, the play makes fun of a maid who has learned needlework from her Puritan mistress, with the implication that the study of ancient languages like Hebrew is included. The term *Hebrew sampler* also contains the early modern sense that women from the Bible themselves wrought needlework pictures. Thus Dubartas's Judith in his *Historie of Judith* embroiders a range of biblical narratives, including Lot's wife, Susanna and the Elders, Joseph and Potipher's wife, and Jeptha and his daughter. The last three are known subjects for seventeenth-century embroidery. Guillaume Salluste Dubartas, *The Historie of Judith*, 55–56.

16. As Jones and Stallybrass write, "More often than needlewomen chose Ovid as a source for subjects" they "worked episodes from the Old Testament" where it is possible "to read resistance to repressive contemporary lessons in femininity" (158). On Ovidian motifs, see Jones and Stallybrass, 146–59; see also Margaret Swain, *Figures on Fabric: Embroidery Design Sources and Their Application*, 52–65.

17. N. H. Keeble, *The Literary Culture of Nonconformity in Later Seventeenth-Century England*, 264–65.

18. Elizabeth Isham, *My Book of Remembrance*, online edition edited by Isaac Stephens, http://www.history.ucr.edu/people/grad_students/index.html (hereafter cited as Isham). Quotations from Isham, passage written about 1630, 31, 47, 72. I have modernized Isham's spelling and expanded abbreviations. On her "Adam and Eve," Isham, NCRL IL3365, panel 9, quoted in Ezell, "Elizabeth Isham's Books," par. 21. See also the more recent edition of *My Book of Remembrance*, ed. Elizabeth Clarke and Erica Longfellow, which at this writing is under construction.

19. Gerard de Jode, *Thesaurus Sacrarum Historiarum Veteris Testamenti* (Antwerp: 1585); for comparisons of seventeenth-century needlework and de Jode sources, see Arthur, *Embroidery 1600–1700*, 79–103. See also Ann Rosalind Jones, "Needle, Scepter, Sovereignty: The Queen of Sheba in Englishwomen's Amateur Needlework."

20. For examples of Stuart royalty in needlework, see "The Royal Image," in *English Embroidery from the Metropolitan Museum of Art, 1580–1700*, ed. Andrew Morrall and Melinda Watt, 109–43. See also Ruth Geuter, "Embroidered Biblical Narratives and Their Social Context," 57–77, published after I had completed this chapter.

21. On spot samplers, see Arthur, *Embroidery 1600–1700*, 61–62.

22. Historical women were valued within the economic and social structures that women themselves helped to create and perpetuate, and which afforded them no small degree of identity and agency (where, again, *identity* describes the consciously or unconsciously constructed "self" of the interpellated subject through the discursive systems at hand, and *agency* describes the actual choosing of forms of representation from within those discursive systems as the means to construct identity). For a longer explanation of the derivation of my definition of the interdependent concepts of *identity* and *agency* based on Judith Butler, see Introduction, notes.

23. On the Lee and Corbet animal patterns, see Pamela Clabburn, *The Shire Book: Samplers*, 8–9. On the significance of knots, see Chapter 1; on strawberry patterns, Chapter 4. See also Jones and Stallybrass, 156–58.

24. Liz Arthur affirms, "At a time when books were rare, samplers must have been an invaluable source of reference for patterns and stitches and were considered important enough by embroiderers to be mentioned in wills" (60).

25. *Essex Review* 18 (1908): 147; cited in the OED, "sampler," 1.II.9.

26. Skelton, "XXI Garlande or Chapelet of Laurell," *Complete English Poems*, 334.

27. Lady Margaret Hoby, *The Private Life of an Elizabethan Lady: The Diary of Lady Margaret Hoby 1599–1605*, ed. Joanna Moody, 41, 145, 167, 22, 24, 151, 28, 96, 15, 16, 39, 40, 48, 89, 110, 143.

28. Anne Clifford, *The Diary of Anne Clifford 1616–1619*, 60 (hereafter cited as Clifford).

29. Richard T. Spence, *Lady Anne Clifford Countess of Pembroke, Dorset and Montgomery (1590–1676)*, 3 (hereafter cited as Spence).

30. On the pillow cushion in Figure 19, see http://collections.vam.ac.uk/objectid/O46183. John Aubrey describing the view of Nicholas and Francis Bacon's plantings at Gorhamby (*Aubrey's Brief Lives*, 13).

31. On the French fashion for unified suites, see Peter Thornton, *Seventeenth-Century Interior Decoration in England, France and Holland*, 103–4; Clifford, 53, 59, 69 (1616–17). On Clifford's library, see Heidi Brayman Hackel, *Reading Material in Early Modern England: Print, Gender, and Literacy*, 222–40.

32. Isham, 47. Isham's father kept "play books" from her as harmful (75, 61).

33. Isham, 20, 45, 49, 61, 73. For the ways in which braid work was accomplished, using one, two, and three hands, see "Manuscript describing how to make purse strings, with samplers" (1625–50). See also a strikingly similar manuscript book also with samples of appended braids, Lady Bindloss, *A transcription of the Lady Bindloss braid manuscript*.

34. Thomas Trevelyon, *The Trevelyon Miscellany of 1608: A Facsimile Edition of Folger Shakespeare Library* MS V.b.232.

35. On band samplers, see Arthur, 59–61; Betty Wing, *Girlhood Embroidery: American Samplers & Pictorial Needlework 1650–1850*; Clare Brown and Jennifer Wearden, *Samplers from the Victoria and Albert Museum*. The Textile Collection of the Victoria and Albert Museum contains about 700 samplers. See also Clabburn, *The Shire Book*; Jane Toller, *British Samplers: A Concise History*; *The Goodhard Samplers: 300 Years of Embroidered Samplers—A Superb Collection 26 October–30 November 1985*; Carol Humphrey, *Samplers*, Fitzwilliam Museum Handbooks.

36. Wrightson, *Earthly Necessities*, 165. Despite the growth of markets, "prices continued to rise, real wages fell, and the period echoed to complaints of poverty and distress" (181).

37. Catherine Richardson, "Introduction," in *Clothing Culture*, 13. See also Jonathan Barry and Christopher Brook, *The Middling Sort of People: Culture, Society and Politics in England, 1550–1800*.

38. On the Sidneys' hunt for luxury textiles, see Chapter 5. On the shift toward upholstered furniture amid the move toward designing rooms en suite, see Peter Thornton, *Seventeenth-Century Interior Decoration*, 97–106; on oriental carpets and turkey work, see 109–11. On domestic imitations of turkey work through knotted textiles, see Lanto Synge, *Antique Needlework*, 45, 88.

39. Thorsten Veblen, *The Theory of the Leisure Class* (1899), 51, 53, 58.

40. Hoby, *Private Life of an Elizabethan Lady*, 70. Anne Halkett, *Lady Anne Halkett: Selected Self-Writings*, 55. Patricia Crawford has also engaged the question of women's leisure, concluding, "For the majority of women—and for men—in the past, the concept of leisure is meaningless. The tasks involved in the maintenance of life occupied all of the adults' time." Patricia Crawford, "'The Only Ornament in a Woman': Needlework in Early Modern England," 9.

41. On the shift in the amount of textiles available through trade from around 1600 to 1660 and the consequential "development of an intricate network of shops" and "evidence of rising comfort in the possessions of the middling sections of society by the 1680s," see Ronald M. Berger, *The Most Necessary Luxuries: The Mercers' Company of Coventry, 1550–1680*, 1–12, 15–57; quotations, 6. See also Elizabeth Kowaleski-Wallace, *Consuming Subjects: Women, Shopping, and Business in the Eighteenth Century*; Beverly Lemire, "Peddling Fashion: Salesmen, Pawnbrokers, Taylors, Thieves and the Second-hand Clothes Trade in England, c. 1700–1800"; Beverly Lemire, *Fashion's Favourite: The Cotton Trade and the Consumer in Britain 1660–1800*; Lorna Weatherill, *Consumer Behavior and Material Culture in Britain, 1660–1760*; Carole Shammas, *The Pre-Industrial Consumer in England and America*; Fiona Kerlogue, "The Early English Textile Trade in South-East Asia: The East India Company Factory and the Textile Trade in Jambi, Sumatra, 1615–1682"; Peter Earle, *The Making of the English Middle Class: Business Society and Family Life in London, 1660–1730*; N. B. Harte, "The Economics of Clothing in the Late Seventeenth Century." Furthermore, account books like Grisell Baillie, *The Household Book of Lady Grisell Baillie 1692–1733*, make clear that large households toward the end of the seventeenth century were no longer producing their own textiles but purchasing them instead.

42. Donald F. Bond, "Introduction," in *The Spectator*, 1:lxxxiii, 5:71.

43. *Spanish stitch* was another name for *blackstitch*, a popular form of embroidery through the late sixteenth century. Arthur, 61. See also Swain, *Figures on Fabric*, 79. Juliet Fleming points out that the patterns in these books could also be transferred to wood or glass for other forms of home decoration. Juliet Fleming, "Hannah Woolley and the Death of the Book" unpublished paper, Renaissance Society of America Conference, 2007, cited with her permission.

44. John Taylor, *The Needles Excellency* (London: 1631), STC 23775.5; 1634, STC 23776; 1640, STC 23777; quotations are from the 1634 edition. As Swain points out, Taylor's book is copied "from various editions of Sibmacher's *Mödelbuch*" (*Figures on Fabric*, 80). See Jones and Stallybrass on Taylor, 135–44.

45. See Lunger Knoppers, "Opening the Queen's Closet: Henrietta Maria, Elizabeth Cromwell, and the Politics of Cookery." Another example of the titles offering this kind of transference is W. M.'s *The Queen's Closet Opened, Incomparable Secrets in Physick, Chirurgery, Preserving, Candying, and Cookery* (London, 1668).

46. There were several Elizabeth Dormers in this period. Taylor's Elizabeth Dormer may be the mother-in-law of Henry Howard, sixth Duke of Norfolk, as she was part of the earlier generation whom Taylor is lauding. On pattern books' offer of social mobility, see Jones and Stallybrass, 140.

47. Rozsika Parker, *The Subversive Stitch: Embroidery and the Making of the Feminine*, her figure 51. Parker erroneously concludes that spot samplers gave way to band samplers, 85, when the forms continued to coexist. See Arthur, 61.

48. Raised or padded work has also been called *stumpwork*. See Jane Nicholas, *Stumpwork Embroidery*, for how this effect was created.

49. See, for example, T.178-1925, Donald King and Santina Levey, *The Victoria and Albert's Textile Collection: Embroidery in Britain from 1200 to 1750*, 108.

50. Anon., "When I Was Young I Little Thought," from a sampler at the Victoria & Albert Museum, no. 480–1894, late seventeenth century, in Jane Stevenson and Peter Davidson, *Early Modern Women Poets: An Anthology*, 468. The sampler also exhibits a wide variety of stitches, including "cross-stitch, two-sided Italian cross-stitch, satin stitch, double running stitch, herringbone, Algerian eye, and decorated buttonhole stitches." On Mary Lamb, see Introduction.

51. *Advice to the Women and Maidens of London* (London, 1678). Like so many apparent disparagements of the needle, however, the pamphlet, apparently written by a woman, lauds the importance of household needlework.

52. Liz Arthur notes that in the Burrell Collection, the twenty-six samplers "have between eight and twenty-three rows of pattern" (61).

53. Heidi Brayman Hackel, "Rhetorics and Practices of Illiteracy or The Marketing of Illiteracy," 169–83; quotation, 171.

54. Certeau, *The Practice of Everyday Life*, 21.

55. André Mollet, *The garden of pleasure containing several draughts of gardens, both embroyder'd-ground-works, knot-works of grass.*

56. Lucy Hutchinson, *Memoirs of the Life of Colonel Hutchinson with the fragment of an autobiography of Mrs. Hutchinson*, 288; Isham, 24.

57. I am grateful to the Curators of Textiles at the Victoria and Albert Museum for allowing me to examine a large number and variety of sixteenth- and seventeenth-century domestic textiles. Margaret Swain pointed out to me that the red and green samplers are the most common because red and green thread was least expensive. For an overview of early modern needlework, I am indebted to many fruitful hours of conversation with Margaret Swain in Edinburgh, August 1994. Caroline Bowles, "The Birthday," in *British Women Poets of the 19th Century*, ed. Margaret Randolph Higonnet, 210, lines 522–29.

58. Jones and Stallybrass observe that women who sewed names and initials "sewed themselves into a different memory system [from the genealogy of father-to-son inheritance], a subculture recorded in physical objects that were nearly always transmitted among women" (156).

59. Lanto Synge, *Art of Embroidery: History of Style and Technique*, 128–29. I have modernized the spelling of these samplers slightly, changing "thee" to "the" and "frut" to "fruit."

60. On the *Alice Barnham* painting, Proverbs, and Anne Brontë's sampler, see Introduction.

61. In this chapter, quotations from the Authorized / King James Version of the Bible (1611) are from *The English Bible Translated Out of the Original Tongues by the Commandment of King James the First*.

62. Carol Humphrey likewise notes, "Typical of work of the late seventeenth century is the dominance of lettering over pattern bands. Literacy had become increasingly important for young females, and the stitching of name, date, alphabets, and improving verses was seen as a means of instilling basic secular and moral education" (*Samplers*, 34). On school-related groups of band samplers, see Humphrey, 34, and Mary M. Brooks, *English Embroideries of the Sixteenth and Seventeenth Centuries in the Collection of the Ashmolean Museum*, 68.

63. The number of printed works by women increased throughout the seventeenth century, with an unmistakable jump taking place between the late 1630s and 1640 (first editions, 5; total editions, 11) and 1641 and 1645 (first editions, 43; total editions, 57). From there, the upward trend continues. See Richard Bell and Patricia Crawford, "Appendix 2: Statistical Analysis of Women's Printed Writings 1600–1700," 265.

64. Early examinations of the relation between embroidery design and prints included J. L. Nevinson, "English Domestic Embroidery Patterns of the Sixteenth and Seventeenth Centuries"; and Nancy Graves Cabot, "Pattern Sources of Scriptural Subjects in Tudor-Stuart Embroideries"; see also Swain, *Figures on Fabric*, 38–65. See Jones and Stallybrass on the economic and gendered relations between pattern book and needlework, 134–71.

Brilliana Harley refers to her needlework throughout her letters to her son. On Brilliana Harley's use of a pattern-drawer located in London, see Kathleen Staples, "Embroidered Furnishings," in *English Embroidery from the Metropolitan Museum of Art, 1580–1700*, 28. Mr.

Nelham is mentioned only once in Harley's letters, however, so that assuming that all her drawn patterns on cloth derive from him may be a stretch. Brilliana Harley, *The Letters of The Lady Brilliana Harley*, 86.

65. On slips, see Synge, *Antique Needlework*, 49. For a bibliography and examples, see Meg Andrews, "Late 16th / Early 17th Century Embroidery: Slips." On the derivation of the slip from *opus anglicanum*, see Nevinson, "English Domestic Embroidery Patterns," 1–2.

66. Alexander Globe, *Peter Stent, London Printseller circa 1642–1665*, vii and facing-page illustration, "A Catalogue of Plates and Pictures that are printed and sould by Peter Stent, dwelling at the Signe of the White Horse in Guilt-spur Street betwixt Newgate and Pycorner"; see also 114. Although the practice of transferring print to cloth in a printshop was relatively new, many of the prints themselves were sixteenth century in origin. About a third of Stent's prints dated from the reign of Queen Elizabeth. Also on print sources for needlework, see J. L. Nevinson, "Peter Stent and John Overton, Publishers of Embroidery Designs"; Swain, *Figures on Fabric*, 25–51, and Rozsika Parker, *The Subversive Stitch: Embroidery and the Making of the Feminine*, 96–97.

67. Alexander Browne, *Ars Pictoria* (1675), Department of Prints and Drawings, British Museum, 167.C.1.

68. As Rozsika Parker comments about women's preferences for certain stories in *Subversive Stitch*, "Among those [prints] available from Peter Stent, 'Susanna and the Elders' and 'The Sacrifice of Isaac' were often embroidered, but no embroidery survives of 'Moses Lifting the Serpent'" (97).

69. Female figures from the Old Testament and Apocrypha are not the only repeating designs: Tobias, Jacob's Dream, and Jeptha's Daughter are just a few of the narratives women frequently embroidered, but I have focused on the most common themes.

70. On how amateur embroiderers transferred designs, see Swain, *Figures on Fabric*, 104–7. Art historian Jason Flora provided the information about the pouncing of frescoes. On pouncing and drawing in a professional workshop, see Charles Germain de Saint-Aubin, *Art of the Embroiderer* (1770), 20–21. For the information on raised work kits, I am indebted to Margaret Swain, private conversation.

71. Jones and Stallybrass, 135. Ann Rosalind Jones also discusses the lack of concern about perspective in early modern needlework pictures, determining that such images "which often juxtapose an immense butterfly or flower with smaller human figures" resulted when "Englishwomen often combined designs from different pattern books, mixing different scales in a single piece of embroidery" ("Dematerializations: Textile and Textual Properties in Ovid, Sandys, and Spenser," 201).

72. The four versions of *David and Bathsheba* deriving from similar transfers from combined de Jode prints are at the Ashmolean Museum (my Plate 14), the Burrell Collection (Arthur, figure 73), and the Metropolitan Museum of Art (Andrew Morrall and Melinda Watt, *English Embroidery from the Metropolitan Museum of Art, 1580–1700*, figure 237). Lanto Synge, *Art of Embroidery*, reproduces a partially worked version that reverses the composition (Synge, figure 108). For the four de Jode prints combined into a single design for *David and Bathsheba*, see Brooks, *English Embroideries*, 44–47. Many other versions of this story exist; *David and Abigail* was also popular for needlework.

73. The phrase "densely packed spaces" is Jessica Wolfe's, part of her discussion of the modes of thinking that drew people in the Renaissance to the metaphor of "Homer in a nutshell" (*Humanism, Machinery, and Renaissance Literature*, 163).

74. Mary D. Garrard writing about Susanna and the Elders, *Artemisia Gentileschi: The Image of the Female Hero in Italian Baroque Art*, 191.

75. Svetlana Alpers, *The Art of Describing: Dutch Art in the Seventeenth Century*, 206.

76. Liz Arthur notes that there are five scenes in this panel "based on four engravings from Gerard de Jode's *Thesaurus Sacrarum Historiarum Veteris Testamenti*, Antwerp 1585," 96.

77. Also on the choice of Susanna for needlework, see Geuter, "Embroidered Biblical Narratives," 59–63.

78. Lionel Cust, *Notes on the Authentic Portraits of Mary Queen of Scots*, 72. Cust uses a description of a portrait of Mary Stuart at New Hardwick Hall that is probably an early seventeenth-century copy of the earlier, missing Hilliard miniature. In this copy, the details of Mary's motto, and the miniature within her crucifix suggest this is a faithful copy of a portrait made from life.

79. The fifth of the twelve sonnets that Mary Queen of Scots supposedly addressed to her third husband, the Earl of Bothwell, states that "he took my body and made it his own / Although my heart was not yet won" (lines 2–3). See Mary Queen of Scots, *Bittersweet Within My Heart: The Collected Poems of Mary, Queen of Scots*, 39. The authorship of the sonnets, which appeared as part of the casket letters in June 1567, has long been in dispute.

The story of Susanna is not the only common needlework picture that contains the threat of rape. In the story of Esther, her husband, Ahasueras, seeing a drunken Haman on Esther's bed, thinks that Haman is about to "force the Queene before me in the house" (Esther 7). Holofernes intends to "deceive" Judith in his tent (Judeth 12), although, as her song of triumph relates, it was she who "took a linen garment to deceive *him*" (Judeth 16; my emphasis).

80. Susanna Parr, *Susanna's Apologie Against the Elders* (1659). Placing this case within the context of the Susanna narrative, Patricia Crawford concludes, "Most interesting of all is that Susanna Parr claimed the right to define the quarrel as one about sexual power" (*Women and Religion in England 1500–1720*, on Parr, 152–59; quotation, 158).

81. A more literal reading of the the Latin is "With the boy Ishmael, Hagar was sent far away, whom Sarah was not willing to be his concubine." The Latin reads, "Cum puero Ismieil procul, dimmititur Hagar, Quem Sarah haeredem noluit esse suum." As my colleague Carolyn Anderson points out, "*Dimmititur* is passive of the perfect tense, and matches the tense but not the mood of *noluit* which is also perfect tense, but active. The Imperfect of *nolere* would make it a process rather than a decision on Sarah's part."

82. http://collections.vam.ac.uk/objectid/078859. See also Arthur, figure 56, and Brooks, *English Embroideries*, 34–35, 40–44.

83. On the legal issues involved in Clifford's separation from Margaret, see Spence, 59–66, 70–71. Suzanne Gossett, "Resistant Mothers and Hidden Children." On Wroth's fear of her son's wardship, see Chapter 5.

84. This panel may have been worked for a cabinet. See http://collections.vam.ac.uk/objectid/046183.

85. For the popularity of Esther and Ahasueras also noted by Parker, *Subversive Stitch*, 96, and backed by my personal observation, see Jones and Stallybrass, 158, 308n.70. Ruth Geuter reaches the same conclusion based on her survey, "Embroidered Biblical Narratives," 74n.40. See also Geuter on Esther, 64–68, published after I had completed this chapter.

86. The two parts of the Esther story tend to become conflated. The book in the Apocrypha, "The rest of the Chapters of the Booke of Esther," contains Esther's famous and lengthy prayer of Chapter 14, beginning "O my Lord, thou onely art our king: helpe me desolate woman, which have no helper but thee: for my danger is in mine hand." The apocryphal continuation is the source for Esther's three-day fasting and prayer and her fainting before Ahasueras (Chapter 15).

87. Mary Garrard points out that the fainting Esther is a common type in Italian and

indeed Catholic art, in which Esther figures Mary as the intermediary between sinners and God (*Artemisia Gentileschi*, 76).

88. I am indebted to Suzanne Trill, who generously supplied this quotation from Lady Anne Halkett's unpublished NLS Ms 6501, 186–200. Although, as Trill pointed out to me, the majority of Halkett's meditation is on Ahasueras's male authority.

89. *Queen Mary I When Princess* by Hans Eworth, oil on panel, c. 1550–55, Fitzwilliam Museum, Cambridge, CPC 81. Bergit Franke discusses the Esther and Ahasueras medallion in Eworth's portrait of Mary I and its likely connection to *The Interlude of Queen Hester* in *Assurerus und Esther am Burgunderhof: Zür Reception des Buches Esther in den Niederlanden (1450 bis 1530)*, 114–15, plates 72–73.

90. Margaret Swain, *The Needlework of Mary Queen of Scots*, 91.

91. Jones and Stallybrass, 159; Arthur, 92 and figure 65.

92. Brilliana Harley, 19 March 1640, *The Letters of The Lady Brilliana Harley*, 119.

93. See Christine de Pizan, *The Book of the City of Ladies*, 146–47; and see Jennifer Summit on Christine in the sixteenth century, *Lost Property: The Woman Writer and English Literary History, 1380–1589*, 61–108, and on the *Monument of Matrons* and "the Recovery of Women's Prayer," 157–62. Alexandre de Pontaymeri, *A Womans Woorth, defended against all the men in the world*. Francis Quarles, *Hadassa: or the History of Queen Esther: with Meditations thereupon, Divine and Morall* (1621). On the narratival and linguistic complexities of the Esther texts, see Timothy K. Beal, *Esther*. For still other contemporary references to Esther, see Saralynn Ellen Summer, "Like Another Esther: Literary Representations of Queen Esther in Early Modern England."

94. On James I's misogyny and the debate on women, see Josephine Roberts, "Introduction," in Lady Mary Wroth, *The First Part of the Countess of Montgomery's Urania*, xv–xvi. Aemilia Lanyer, *The Poems of Aemilia Lanyer: Salve Deus Rex Judaeorum*, 48–49. Further citations of Lanyer appear parenthetically.

95. Barbara Kiefer Lewalski writes that Lanyer's volume "as a whole is conceived as a Book of Good Women," in "Old Renaissance Canons, New Women's Texts: Some Jacobean Examples," 397–406; quotation, 401. Susanne Woods calls *Salve Deus Rex Judaeorum* an "unapologetic creation of a community of good women for whom another woman is the spokesperson and commentator." "Introduction," in *The Poems of Aemilia Lanyer: Salve Deus Rex Judaeorum*, xxxi.

96. Thomas Swetnam, *The Arraignment of Lewd, Idle, Froward, and Unconstant Women*, STC 23533; Esther Sowernam, *Esther hath hang'd Haman: or an answere to a lewd Pamphlet, entituled, The Arraignment of Women*. Discussions of the pamphlet wars on the nature of women include Linda Woodbridge's pathbreaking *Women and the English Renaissance: Literature and the Nature of Womankind, 1540–1620*. Valerie Wayne discusses the relation of a dramatic text to the Swetnam controversy in "The Dearth of the Author: Anonymity's Allies and *Swetnam the Woman-hater*." See also Gwynne Kennedy, *Just Anger: Representing Women's Anger in Early Modern England*, 23–50; Ann Rosalind Jones, "Counterattacks on 'the Bayter of Women': Three Pamphleteers of the Early Seventeenth Century"; and Diane Purkiss, "Material Girls: The Seventeenth-Century Woman Debate." Julie Campbell has extended the debate to the genre of romance in *Literary Circles and Gender in Early Modern Europe: A Cross-Cultural Approach*.

97. Within *Esther hath hang'd Haman* there is only one mention of Esther, at Chapter 3 (Sowernam, 112). The pseudonymous Constantia Munda's response to Swetnam begins with a dedicatory poem to her mother, in which Munda explains that the publication of Esther's pamphlet delayed her own. Here, Munda uses the phrase "*Hester hanged / Haman*" to mean that the tract accomplished its purpose in silencing Swetnam. Constantia Munda, from *The*

Worming of a Mad Dog, in *Early Modern Women Poets: An Anthology*, ed. Jane Stevenson and Peter Davidson, 197–98.

98. *Unto every individual Member of Parliament: The humble Representations of divers afflicted Women-Petitioners to the Parliament, on behalf of Mr. John Lilburn.* Elizabeth Lilburne proved an irrepressible advocate for her husband. See Andrew Sharp, "Lilburne, John," in *Oxford Dictionary of National Biography*, http://www.oxforddnb.com/view/article/16654. On Elizabeth Lilburne's role, see T. P. Connor, "Malignant Reading: John Squier's Newgate Prison Diary 1642–46."

99. Hester Pulter, "Poems Breathed forth By The Nobel Hadassas," in Jill Seal Millman and Gillian Wright, *Early Modern Women's Manuscript Poetry*, 111–27. On why so many of "the seventeenth-century women whom we think of as the forerunners and founders of feminism were, almost without exception, Tories," see Catherine Gallagher, "Embracing the Absolute: The Politics of the Female Subject in Seventeenth-Century England."

100. On Hannah Smith's cabinet, also called a "casket," see also Jones and Stallybrass, 159. Details of the needlework courtesy of Frances Pritchard, Curator of Textiles at the Whitworth Art Gallery. The cabinet has often been reproduced with the images on the doors reversed. Pritchard confirms that on the original cabinet, Deborah and Barak are on the left and Jael and Sisera are on the right.

101. Margaret P. Hannay, "'So May I with the *Psalmist* Truly Say': Early Modern Englishwomen's Psalm Discourse," 116–17.

102. Lady Anne Halkett, unpublished manuscript courtesy of Suzanne Trill's transcription, NLS Ms 6499, 327, 332.

103. Philip Sidney, *Sir Philip Sidney's Defense of Poesy*, 11.

104. Michael Drayton, *Harmonie of the Church Containing The Spirituall Songes and Holy Hymnes, of Godly men, patriarkes and Prophetes* (1591). Despite the title, Drayton's dedication to Jane Devereux stresses that the female poets he is translating are prophets ("Dedication," page 1 of 2).

105. Margaret Askew Fell, *Women's Speaking Justified, Proved and Allowed by the Scriptures* (1666), B4r15 and B4v16.

106. Richard Mulcaster, *The Quene's Majestie's passage*, 31–33. Elizabeth I, *Collected Works*, 1:157; further quotations cited parenthetically. For additional connections between Elizabeth and Deborah, see Alexandra Walsham, "'A Very Deborah?': The Myth of Elizabeth I as a Providential Monarch."

107. Bathsua Makin, *An Essay to Revive the Antient Education of Gentlewomen*, 6, 10.

108. Anne Finch, Countess of Winchelsea, "The Introduction," in *Selected Poems*, 26–28. On Finch's calculated position as author, see Marta Straznicky, "Restoration Women Playwrights and the Limits of Professionalism"; see also Carol Barash, *English Women's Poetry, 1649–1714: Politics, Community, and Linguistic Authority*.

109. Geuter, "Embroidered Biblical Narratives," 74n.40. Margarita Stocker, *Judith, Sexual Warrior*.

110. On Gentileschi's *Judith Slaying Holofernes* (Uffizi Gallery) and *Judith and Her Maid Carrying the Head of Holofernes* (Pitti Palace), see Patricia Phillippy, *Painting Women: Cosmetics, Canvases, and Early Modern Culture*, 75–83.

111. In emphasizing Judith's authorization by God, Lanyer also invokes the common allegory that Judith's beheading of Holofernes is the beheading of sin: "For that one head that *Judeth* bare away, / Thou [Margaret, Countess of Cumberland] tak'st from Sinne a hundred heads a day" (115).

I am grateful to Clark Hulse, to his assistant Elli Shellist, and to Valerie Wayne, Karen Robertson, and Peter Parolin for their valuable comments on the article that was the foundation for this chapter, "Staging Women's Relations to Textiles in Shakespeare's *Othello* and *Cymbeline*," in *Early Modern Visual Culture: Representation, Race, and Empire in Renaissance England*. More recently, David Riggs read and commented on this revision.

Othello, *Titus Andronicus*, and *Cymbeline* quotations are from *The Norton Shakespeare*, ed. Stephen Greenblatt, Walter Cohen, Jean E. Howard, and Katherine Eisaman Maus (New York: W. W. Norton, 1997). The Oxford edition on which the *Norton Shakespeare* is based prints "Innogen" for other editions' "Imogen" and "Giacomo" for "Iachimo."

1. As Mariët Westermann concludes of Roghman's series, *Two Women Sewing*; *Women Reading*; *Woman Cooking*; *Woman Spinning, with Girl*; and *Woman Cleaning Kitchen Utensils*, "There is no suggestion of the moral ambiguity imputed to so many women in thematically related paintings," especially in that "conventional signs of moral obligation such as the distaff, skull, and clock underscore the utter seriousness with which these women take their duties." Unusually, Roghman was both the "inventor and engraver" of these pictures. Mariët Westermann, *Art and Home: Dutch Interiors in the Age of Rembrandt*, 193. See also Martha M. Peacock, "Geertruydt Roghman and the Female Perspective in Seventeenth-Century Dutch Genre Imagery," 3–10. For Dutch interiors with moral ambiguities, read on.

2. The similarities between English and Dutch domestic culture are especially visible in places like Great Yarmouth, where Dutch influence was a fact of life. Extant Yarmouth merchant houses are modeled on the Dutch pattern and were even built of brick laid in the "Flemish bond" pattern and imported from Holland. See Christopher Hanson-Smith, *The Flemish Bond: East Anglia and the Netherlands—Close and Ancient Neighbors*, 4–73. Many more Dutch homes featured paintings than needlework pictures on the walls, yet paintings frequently feature women's textile production as emblematic of the producers' combined overt sexuality and demure femininity. See Wayne E. Franits, *Paragons of Virtue: Women and Domesticity in Seventeenth-Century Dutch Art*, and Whitney Chadwick, *Women, Art, and Society*, 104–19. On Holland linens, see Peter Thornton, *Seventeenth-Century Interior Decoration in England, France and Holland*, 178.

3. On women's relationships of exchange, see Sara Mendelson and Patricia Crawford, *Women in Early Modern England 1550–1720*, 221 (hereafter cited as Mendelson and Crawford). Alice Clark's chapter, "Textiles," in *Working Life of Women in the Seventeenth Century*, 93–149, remains the most comprehensive discussion of English women and textile labor. As Clark points out, "There can be no doubt that the Woollen Trade depended chiefly upon women and children for its labour supply" (98). See also the discussions of women and textiles in Mendelson and Crawford, including 219–24, 307–9, 331–33, 341–42.

On women's connections as forming a distinct female culture, see Mendelson and Crawford, 13, 202–55. See also the forms of women's association detailed in Susan Frye and Karen Robertson, *Maids and Mistresses, Cousins and Queens: Women's Alliances in Early Modern England*.

4. Diarist and landholder Margaret Hoby records that on a trip to London in November 1600 she bought "a little spinning wheel, and span of that til prayers' time." Margaret Hoby, *The Private Life of an Elizabethan Lady: The Diary of Lady Margaret Hoby 1599–1605*, 125.

Ann Rosalind Jones and Peter Stallybrass discuss the skill, ideology, and cultural significance of spinning in "The Fate of Spinning: Penelope and the Three Fates," *Renaissance Clothing and the Materials of Memory*, 104–33.

5. On the attempted prohibition of "any maiden, damsel, or other women" from weaving, see Steve Rappaport, *Worlds Within Worlds: Structures of Life in Sixteenth-Century London*, 37–40; see also Alice Clark, *Working Life of Women*, 103–4. On women continuing to weave during the early modern period, see Clark, *Working Life of Women*, 104–5; Alfred P. Wadsworth and Julia De Lacy Mann, *The Cotton Trade and Industrial Lancashire 1600–1780*, 333–37; and J. de L. Mann, *The Cloth Industry in the West of England from 1640 to 1880*, 228.

6. bell hooks, *Art on My Mind: Visual Politics*, 3.

7. Jakob Burckhardt, *The Civilisation of the Renaissance in Italy*, 308, 398. In fairness to Burckhardt, he was aware that "to each eye, perhaps, the outlines of a given civilisation present a different picture" ("Introduction," 3).

8. Mary Ann Calo, *Bernard Berenson and the Twentieth Century*, 32. Bernard Berenson, "Decline and Recovery in the Figure Arts," 25.

9. See for example Miriam Schapiro, *Wonderland*, a sampler tacked onto canvas, and *Barcelona Fan*, in Norma Broude and Mary D. Garrard, *The Power of Feminist Art: The American Movement of the 1970s, History and Impact*, figures 217 and 84. For African American artist Emma Amos, cloth borders around her paintings point to historic connections to Africa and the Civil War. See *The Overseer*, *Mrs. Gaughin's Shirt*, and *Malcolm X, Morley, Matisse & Me*, reproduced in color inserts in bell hooks, *Art on My Mind*, n.p. See also Norma Broude and Mary D. Garrard, "Conversations with Judy Chicago and Miriam Schapiro." Judy Chicago's 1979 *Dinner Party*, now on display at the Brooklyn Museum of Art, remains an eloquent statement about women's place in history and the relation of needlework to that place. The two books about *The Dinner Party*, one of which is specifically about its embroidery, explore this relationship in detail and in the process offer a history of women's relation to textiles. See Judy Chicago, *The Dinner Party*, and Judy Chicago, *Embroidering Our Heritage: The Dinner Party Needlework*. For a reassessment of *The Dinner Party* from a 1990s perspective, see Josephine Wither, "Judy Chicago's Dinner Party."

Male artists also turned to textiles in the twentieth century, though usually with a less overt sense of their historical significance. Robert Rauschenberg's *Bed 1955* at the New York Museum of Modern Art, for example, is a collage for which he may have used his own bedclothes. In the words of the museum's posted description, the work consists of "a well-worn pillow, sheet, and quilt, scribbled on with a pencil and splashed with paint."

10. Dinah Prentice, "Sewn Constructions," 182.

11. On clothes as receiving "the human imprint," see Peter Stallybrass, "Worn Worlds: Clothes, Mourning, and the Life of Things," 37. See also the later version of his essay, "Worn Worlds: Clothes and Identity on the Renaissance Stage," in *Subject and Object in Renaissance Culture*.

12. Jane Schneider and Annette B. Weiner, "Introduction," in *Cloth and Human Experience*, 3.

13. For an overview of the ways in which the early modern stage pictured women sewing, see Lena Cowen Orlin, "Three Ways to Be Invisible in the Renaissance: Sex, Reputation, and Stitchery," 183–203.

14. William Barley, *A Book of Curious and Strange Inventions, Called the First Parte of Needleworks* (1596), A1(v). The book is dedicated to "Lady Isabel, Douwager of Rutlind," whom Barley cites as known for her "excellent skill in curious Needleworks" (A1).

15. Richard Brome, *The Queen and Concubine* (1659), 87–88.

16. Thomas Dekker, *The Shoemakers' Holiday*, 3.4.13–17. Further references appear in the text.

17. Mario DiGangi notes that this question is also Mistress Openwork's more self-consciously suggestive line in *The Roaring Girl*: "Gentlemen, what is't you lack?" (2.1.1), and that

this is a version of the usual London sales pitch. "Sexual Slander and Working Women in *The Roaring Girl*," 153.

18. In the unpublished paper that led to his article "Sexual Slander and Working Women in *The Roaring Girl*," Mario DiGangi considers the extent to which women's domestic labor was—and often still is—perceived as "natural" rather than as the skilled labor ascribed to men, a perceptive approach that further explains the semiotic mechanism by which sewing and the material sewn come to represent women's sexualized body. Mario DiGangi, "Pricking Out a Living: Eroticizing Women's Work in Early Modern England," paper for the seminar, "Domesticities / Sexualities / Work" organized by Wendy Wall, Shakespeare Association of America, 1998.

19. Whereas the maker of needle or bobbin lace produces its characteristic holes and patterns by winding and twisting threads about one another to create a finished piece of cloth, the maker of open or cut work uses stitches and cutouts to shape a preexisting piece of cloth into lacy patterns. In "Sexual Slander and Working Women in *The Roaring Girl*," DiGangi points out that "Mistress Openwork's attempt to lure gentlemen customers by announcing the desirability of her openwork stitchery likewise activates the pun on sexual openness in her name" ("Sexual Slander and Working Women in *The Roaring Girl*," 154).

20. On the symbolism of the partridge, see David R. Smith, "Irony and Civility: Notes on the Convergence of Genre and Portraiture in Seventeenth-Century Dutch Painting," 415.

21. Jacob Cats, *Sinn-en Minne-Beelden & Emblemata Amores Morelqüe spectantia* (Amsterdam: Willem Iansz Blaeuw, 1622), quoted in Linda Stone-Ferrier, "Spun Virtue, the Lacework of Folly, and World Wound Upside-Down: Seventeenth-Century Dutch Depictions of Female Handwork," 222.

22. *The Wisdome of Doctor Dodypoll* (1600), Sig. A3(r).

23. Henry Cockeram, *The English Dictionarie: or, An interpreter of hard English words*.

24. Karl Marx, *Grundrisse*, 92. For a discussion of this passage with reference to feminist art history, see Griselda Pollock, *Vision and Difference: Femininity, Feminism, and Histories of Art*, 2–5.

25. Margreta de Grazia, Maureen Quilligan, and Peter Stallybrass, "Introduction," in *Subject and Object in Renaissance Culture*, 5.

26. Peter Stallybrass, "Patriarchal Territories: The Body Enclosed," 139.

27. On the relation between paper and cloth that enhances the idea of Othello "reading" his wedding sheets, see Peter Stallybrass, "Worn Worlds: Clothes and Identity on the Renaissance Stage," 306–7.

28. Peter Parolin made this point to me. Edward Snow has also discussed the difference between Othello's sibyl speech and the explanation for the handkerchief's existence as male-centered. See Edward Snow, "Sexual Anxiety and the Male Order of Things in *Othello*," 404–5. See also Valerie Wayne's discussion of Snow regarding this point in "Historical Differences: Misogyny and *Othello*," 170–71.

29. On Iago's ability to twist both Othello's and Desdemona's origins to explain why she might prefer Cassio, see Michael Neill, "Unproper Beds: Race, Adultery, and the Hideous in *Othello*," 410.

30. Patricia Parker, *Literary Fat Ladies: Rhetoric, Gender, Property*, 71.

31. As Stephen Greenblatt writes, Othello's "identity depends upon a constant performance . . . of his story, a loss of his own origins, an embrace and perpetual reiteration of the norms of another culture." *Renaissance Self-fashioning from More to Shakespeare*, 245.

32. John Gerard, *The Herball or Generall Historie of Plantes* (1633), 997–98.

33. On the handkerchiefs produced for sale and as part of the drama of English courtship, see Juana Green, "The Sempter's Wares: Merchandising and Marrying in *The Fair Maid*

of the Exchange (1607)." See also Will Fisher, *Materializing Gender in Early Modern English Literature and Culture*, 36–58.

34. Textiles around the globe embody a variety of cultural, discursive experiences that support the significance of early modern needlework patterns. For example, in Ghana, the kente cloth has a wide variety of patterns, each of which has a symbolic meaning, such as "Toku's soul cloth," named for "Toku, a queen mother and warrior" who was "defeated in battle" but still "greatly admired for her courage." In the Kente cloth tradition, colors, too, are as precisely indicative of emotion as the colors of early modern English romance. In addition, many Kente patterns encode wise sayings. "Ewe" cloth, also from Ghana, has representational motifs with specific meanings like the pineapple pattern, which means "you cannot get to the pineapple without being pricked by its thorns (meaning no pain, no gain)." Doran H. Ross, *Wrapped in Pride: Ghanaian Kente and African American Identity*, 113, 138.

35. Holland Cotter, "Polyphony for the Eye: The Many Splendors of Islamic Art," E25.

36. On the strawberry as signifying the Virgin Mary and hence virginity, see Linda Boose, "Othello's Handkerchief: 'The Recognizance and Pledge of Love,'" 56.

37. On the custom of displaying the wedding sheet as ocular proof of a bride's virginity, see Boose, "Othello's Handkerchief," 57. Boose points out that the handkerchief is "a visually recognizable reduction of Othello and Desdemona's wedding-bed sheets, the visual proof of their consummated marriage, the emblem of the symbolical act of generation so important to our understanding of the measure of this tragedy" (56).

38. See Eamon Grennan, "The Women's Voices in *Othello:* Speech, Song, Silence."

39. On Mercury, "the guardian deity of commerce" in this painting, see Simon Schama, *The Embarrassment of Riches: An Interpretation of Dutch Culture in the Golden Age*, 393.

40. This purse is worked in silver, gold, and silk thread in tent, Gobelin, and laited braid stitches (http://collections.vam.ac.uk/objectid/046183).

41. "Mankind," 269; Geoffrey Chaucer, "The Summoner's Tale," 128–36; quotation, 134; Chaucer's use of this convention is part of the conflict between the Summoner and the Friar as pilgrims; John Skelton, "Magnyfycence," 376. On Chaucer and the iconographic association of purses with Judas, see Laura F. Hodges, *Chaucer and Clothing: Clerical and Academic Costume in the General Prologue to The Canterbury Tales*, 139n.22.

42. Emilia says when she picks up the handkerchief that Desdemona has carelessly let drop, "I'll have the work ta'en out, / And give't Iago" (3.3.300–301). When he receives the handkerchief, Cassio gives it to Bianca, saying, "Sweet Bianca / Take me this work out" (3.4.179–80); when Bianca questions him about the source of the handkerchief, Cassio replies, "I found it in my chamber. / I like the work well. Ere it be demanded—/ As like enough it will—I would have it copied" (3.4.183–85). In the next scene, however, Bianca rejects Cassio along with the handkerchief: "I must take out the work? . . . This is some minx's token, and I must take out the work. . . . Wheresoever you had it, I'll take out no work on't" (4.1.145–50).

43. See Wayne, "Historical Differences," 153–75. Wayne discusses the problem of "taking the work out" on page 172, concluding, "Because the handkerchief serves as proof of married chastity, it cannot be copied by Emilia and Bianca."

44. Edward Dowden, *Shakespere*, 55–56. Mary Ellen Lamb and Valerie Wayne, "Introduction," in *Staging Early Modern Romance, Prose Fiction, Dramatic Romance, and Shakespeare*, 1.

45. Boccaccio, *Decameron*, "The Second Day: the ninth Novell (1620)," in Geoffrey Bullough, *Narrative and Dramatic Sources of Shakespeare*, 8:55. The other source for Giacomo's bedroom visitation is *Frederyke of Jennen*, which does not describe the chamber (Bullough, *Narrative and Dramatic Sources of Shakespeare*, 69).

46. Georgianna Ziegler, "Penelope and the Politics of Woman's Place in the Renais-

sance," 26. After walking through the Palazzo Vecchio room featuring Penelope, the next of Eleonora's rooms is painted with scenes of Esther and Ahasueras.

47. See Mauro Lucco, *Mantegna a Mantova 1460–1506*, 108–9, on the timing of this chamber that strongly suggests that Isabella d'Este worked with Mantegna on this room. My thanks to Sarah Cockram for confirming this point over e-mail.

48. *The English Bible Translated Out of the Original Tongues by the Commandment of King James the First.* Proverbs, vol. 3.

49. W. G. Thomson, *Tapestry Weaving in England from the Earliest Times to the End of the Eighteenth Century*, 41. On Elizabeth's *City of Ladies* tapestries, see Susan Bell, *The Lost Tapestries of the City of Ladies.*

50. Janet Adelman, *Suffocating Mothers: Fantasies of Maternal Origin in Shakespeare's Plays, Hamlet to the Tempest*, 209.

51. On Innogen's bedchamber, see also Peggy Muñoz Simonds, *Myth, Emblem, and Music in Shakespeare's* Cymbeline: *An Iconographic Reconstruction*, 95–134. Posthumus Leonatus calls Innogen his queen at 1.1.93, 100; 5.6.226.

52. On the question of whether Innogen and Posthumus have consummated the marriage, see David Bevington, "Sexuality in *Cymbeline*," 160.

53. See Margaret P. Hannay, *Philip's Phoenix: Mary Sidney, Countess of Pembroke*, 223. In *Othello* Shakespeare may convert this statement into Desdemona's dying words to Emilia. When Emilia asks, "O, who hath done this deed?" Desdemona responds, "Nobody, I myself. Farewell" (5.2.133–34), an acceptance of responsibility that Othello interprets as an attempt to shield him" (5.2.138). Mary Sidney Herbert, *The Tragedie of Antonie Doone into English by the Countesse of Pembroke*, Sig. 12(v), H1(v).

54. E. Jane Burns, *Bodytalk: When Women Speak in Old French Literature*, 131.

55. On Artemisia Gentileschi's treatment of Lucrece, see Mary D. Garrard, *Artemisia Gentileschi: The Image of the Female Hero in Italian Baroque Art*, 210–44; on Cleopatra, see 210–16, 241–77. Santina Levey discusses the sources for Lucrecia's pose in *The Embroideries at Hardwick Hall: A Catalogue*, 74–75.

56. Georgianna Ziegler, "My Lady's Chamber: Female Space, Female Chastity in Shakespeare," 82. Patricia Parker noted that "Iachimo's inventory becomes a substitute . . . for an actual act of rape" (*Literary Fat Ladies*, 136).

57. See Linda Woodbridge, "Palisading the Elizabethan Body Politic," 334–35.

58. On Bess of Hardwick's hangings, see Chapter 1. Anne Clifford, *The Diary of Anne Clifford 1616–1619*, 118.

59. R. O. Elizabeth, 25, quoted in Jean MacIntyre, *Costumes and Scripts in the Elizabethan Theatres*, 55–56, 65.

60. Linda Boose, "Othello's Handkerchief," 65.

61. Compare Janet Adelman's reading of the cloth in *Suffocating Mothers*, 214. See also Stallybrass, "Worn Worlds," 310. Valerie Wayne argues that during Posthumus's speech opening act 5, he puts on the bloody cloth. This action signifies his reconnecting himself to, and acceptance of, Innogen's body ("The Woman's Parts of *Cymbeline*," 298–300, 313–14).

62. As Valerie Wayne points out, "The supposed stain of Innogen's blood is designed to confirm her murder, but it also evokes the bloodstained sheets of a marriage bed" as well as having "associations with menstruation" ("The Woman's Parts of *Cymbeline*," 298). Michael Drayton, *Harmonie of the Church Containing The Spirituall Songes and Holy Hymnes, of godly men, patriarkes and Prophetes* (1591), Sig. F2(r). "The Rest of the Chapters of The Booke of Esther," (chapter 14), Apocrypha, *The English Bible* 5:113.

63. On the costumes in *Cymbeline*, see Stallybrass, "Worn Worlds: Clothes and Identity on the Renaissance Stage," 308–10. As Stallybrass points out, because "in the Renaissance

clothes could be imagined as retaining the identity and the form of the wearer," for Innogen, Posthumus's clothing "bears quite literally the trace and the memory of its owner" (310), with the result that "For Cloten, as much as for Imogen, Posthumus's clothes come to embody memory": "It is as if the clothes will keep Posthumus, imagined as dead, alive so that he, in the remaining form of his suit, can witness Imogen's rape, while, simultaneously, the suit, and thus Posthumus, will be both defiled and appropriated by Cloten" (309).

64. Woodbridge, "Palisading the Elizabethan Body Politic," 334.

CHAPTER FIVE

My thanks to Margaret P. Hannay and Naomi Miller for their comments on an early form of this chapter, presented at the Sixteenth Century Conference, and to Valerie Wayne and Mary Ellen Lamb, whose 2004 Shakespeare Association seminar on women and romance brought together so many points of view on romance, especially those on Wroth of Lori Newcomb and Julie Crawford. Mary Ellen Lamb also provided helpful suggestions regarding a later draft.

1. Mary Sidney Wroth produced *Urania* in two parts, the first of which was published in 1621, of which twenty-nine copies are known to survive, and the second of which is in manuscript at the Newberry Library, published for the first time in 1999. The scholarship informing this chapter begins with Josephine Roberts, "Introduction," Lady Mary Wroth, *The First Part of the Countess of Montgomery's Urania* (quotations from Wroth's first volume will be cited as *U1*). Mary Ellen Lamb, *Gender and Authorship in the Sidney Circle*; Helen Hackett, *Women and Romance Fiction in the English Renaissance*; Mary Ellen Lamb, "Wroth, Lady Mary (1587?–1651/53)," *Oxford Dictionary of National Biography*, http://www.oxforddnb.com/view/article/30082; Patricia Parker, *Literary Fat Ladies: Rhetoric, Gender, Property* (hereafter cited as Parker).

The word count is from Suzanne Gossett and Janel Mueller, "Textual Introduction," Lady Mary Wroth, *The Second Part of the Countess of Montgomery's Urania*, xviii (quotations from Wroth's second volume will be cited as *U2*).

2. Parker, 8–35. In Parker's discussion, romance is associated with the female body because the rhetorical figure of "dilatio" derives from the patristic interpretation of Rahab, whose name in Hebrew means "wide" or "broad" (Parker, 9–10). Mary Ellen Lamb discusses "Wroth's vast romance" in terms of its "complex and open-ended structure" (*Gender and Authorship in the Sidney Circle*, 143–48).

3. This miniature was formerly identified as Lucy, Countess of Bedford. See the Fitzwilliam Museum, Cambridge University, Museum Accession number 3902. Aileen Ribeiro comments that "After the mid-1620s," privileged women were no longer eager to display their needlework skills in portraits "except for provincial and middle-class images" (*Fashion and Fiction: Dress in Art and Literature in Stuart England*, 77).

4. Hackett, *Women and Romance Fiction*, 15.

5. On the supposed female readership of romance, see Helen Hackett, "Lady Mary Wroth's *Urania* and the 'Femininity' of Romance," 45–69; see also Hackett, *Women and Romance Fiction*. Lori Newcomb provides several male-authored addresses to romance readers as a female readership and discusses the complexity of gendering the readers of romance as female in *Reading Popular Romance in Early Modern England*, 37–47. Joan Pong Linton discusses the English history of feminizing the romance reader and its implications for women in *The Romance of the New World*, 17–18.

6. Parker, 11, 13–15; Parker is discussing Erasmus's *De Copia* and *Ciceronianus*, Roger Ascham's *Schoolmaster*, and Augustine's *Confessions*.

7. The fact that Philip Sidney's *The Countess of Pembroke's Arcadia* stops in mid-sentence

in Book 3 no doubt also influenced Wroth. For an interpretation of this break as a deliberate move by Philip Sidney instead of an accidental consequence of the countess's edition, see Steve Mentz, *Romance for Sale*, 102.

8. George Chapman, trans., *The Whole Works of Homer in his Iliads and Odysses*, 40, lines 148–52. Richmond Lattimore's twentieth-century translation acknowledges, as do others, that Helen is weaving a "robe" to be worn: "a great web, / a red folding robe, and working into it the numerous struggles / of Trojans, breakers of horses, and bronze-armoured Achaians, / struggles that they endured for her sake at the hands of the war god." Homer, *The Iliad of Homer*, trans. Richmond Lattimore, 103; Book 3, lines 125–28. Elizabeth Hacker pointed out this passage to me. See also Ann Rosalind Jones and Peter Stallybrass, *Renaissance Clothing and the Materials of Memory*, 113.

9. I follow Roberts in using Edmund Spenser's verb, "shadow," to describe how Wroth's characters, like Spenser's allegorical figures, signify a variety of meanings, often simultaneously (*U1*, xxxvii).

10. In *The Aeneid*, Dido is implicitly connected to Aeneas via clothing, linens, and other luxury items; her funeral pyre consists of Aeneas's arms, clothing, and their marriage bed. For Wroth's last sonnet, see Mary Sidney Wroth, *The Poems of Lady Mary Wroth*, 134. On the labyrinth as an image related to "the overlapping gardening, needlework, and writing images" in Wroth's sonnet sequence, see Jennifer Munroe, "'In This Strang Labourinth, How Shall I Turne?': Needlework, Gardens, and Writing in Mary Wroth's *Pamphilia to Amphilanthus*," 36. In the early modern period, *The Iliad* and *The Odyssey* were in part considered romances. Parker points out that *The Aeneid* negotiates "Odyssean or romance dilatoriness with Iliadic or epic haste" to become "the progenitor of so many Renaissance hybrids, or epic-romances" (Parker, 13), while during the Renaissance, *The Odyssey* was referred to as a "romance or *romanzo*" (Parker, 235n.8).

11. Letter of Mary Sidney Wroth to Robert Sidney, Viscount Lisle, from Penshurst, 17 October 1614. De L'Isle Papers, U1475 C81/184, Centre for Kentish Studies, Maidstone, reproduced with the permission of Lord De L'Isle. On Wroth's widowhood, see Gary Waller, *The Sidney Family Romance: Mary Wroth, William Herbert, and the Early Modern Construction of Gender*, 119–28.

12. On Henry Sidney's political position in 1573, see Wallace T. MacCaffrey, "Sidney, Sir Henry (1529–1586)," in *Oxford Dictionary of National Biography*, http://www.oxforddnb.com/view/article/25520; see also Margaret P. Hannay, *Philip's Phoenix: Mary Sidney, Countess of Pembroke*, 29–30.

13. De L'Isle papers, U1475 C52, Centre for Kentish Studies, reproduced with the permission of Lord De L'Isle. The quotations that follow are from this letter.

14. See 29 April 1574 and "1572–1573, Account of William Bluntt, from 1st May, 1572, to 1st May, 1573," in Historical Manuscripts Commission, *Report on the Manuscripts of Lord de L'Isle and Dudley Preserved at Penshurst Place* (hereafter cited as *HMC Penshurst*), 1:249.

15. On the increase in textiles available through trade in the seventeenth century, see Chapter 3 and notes.

16. *HMC Penshurst*, 3:19; 2:264.

17. Rowland Whyte to Robert Sidney, 23 June 1600, *HMC Penshurst* 2:470.

18. John Taylor, *The Needles Excellency*, 1634 edition, 7. Margaret P. Hannay, *Philip's Phoenix*, discusses Taylor's encomium, 129–30. *Progresses of Queen Elizabeth*, ed. John Nichols, 2:66–68, 82–83, cited in Hannay, *Philip's Phoenix*, 42. As Hannay discusses, Elizabeth reciprocated with a "silver and gilt" bowl weighing twenty-four ounces (42).

19. I have reached the tentative conclusion that Wroth obtained gloves as a gift for the queen by putting together two letters. The first is Robert Sidney to Barbara Gamage Sidney, 12

September 1604, in Robert Sidney, *Domestic Politics and Family Absence: The Correspondence (1588–1621) of Robert Sidney, First Earl of Leicester, and Barbara Gamage Sidney, Countess of Leicester*, 118–19; the second letter is William Browne to Lord Sidney, 19 October 1604, *HMC Penshurst*, 3:140.

20. "Penshurst Inventory, 1623," Centre for Kentish Studies in Maidstone, CKS U1, 500, quoted in Germaine Warkentin, "Jonson's Penshurst Reveal'd? A Penshurst Inventory of 1623," 10–11.

21. Margaret P. Hannay points out that in this portrait, Mary Sidney Herbert "stands in a liminal position between scribal publication and print" in "The Countess of Pembroke's Agency in Print and Scribal Culture," 18. See also Michael G. Brennan, "The Queen's Proposed Visit to Wilton House in 1599 and the 'Sidney Psalms,'" 29; on Herbert's portrait, 39–40. Herbert's translation of Philippe de Mornay's *Discourse of Life and Death* was published in 1592, 1600, 1606, 1607, and 1608.

22. Margaret P. Hannay, "'Your vertuous and learned Aunt': The Countess of Pembroke as a Mentor to Mary Wroth," 18.

23. Ben Jonson, Epigram 103, "To Mary, Lady Wroth," *Poems of Ben Jonson*, 261.

24. Stephen Harrison, *The Archs of Triumph Erected in honor of the High and mighty prince James* (1604).

25. Josephine Roberts identifies the second arch as fitting Wroth's description of the three towers of the bridge to the Palace or Throne of Love on Cyprus (*U1*, cvi, 47–48). See also Maureen Quilligan, *Incest and Agency in Elizabeth's England*, 185; on the title page or "frontispiece" as a whole, 179–91. Quilligan reads the title page in the light of its scholarly history and the different styles of architecture present there. She and I reach a similar conclusion about its picturing of Penshurst, although Quilligan, significantly, emphasizes the importance of its landed authorization of Wroth as a woman writer.

26. Barbara Sidney routinely sent gifts of meat and fruit from Penshurst (*HMC Penshurst* 2:423, 429; 5:63). The existence of Barbara Sidney's banqueting house may be surmised from the letters about its painting (*HMC Penshurst* 3:374). Goldying admires the end result, including the casting of "a marble colour upon the pillars of my Lady's Banqueting House," with the help of painters brought from Knole (3:386–87). One important feature of the rebuilding at Penshurst was connecting the gardens with the interior of the home through a "great window" under construction from the gallery onto "the garden" (3:147), as well as "dores about the gardens and that gallery" (3:374). For Robert Sidney's building at Penshurst and his holdings, see Millicent V. Hay, *The Life of Robert Sidney, Earl of Leicester (1563–1626)*, 186–91; Don Wayne, *Penshurst: The Semiotics of Place and the Poetics of History*.

27. See Antony Griffiths, *The Print in Stuart Britain 1603–1689*, 16–17. See also A. M. Hind, *Engraving in England in the Sixteenth and Seventeenth Centuries: A Descriptive Catalogue with Introductions*, volume 2.

28. On Mary Sidney Herbert's connections to London printers, see Michael Brennan, "The Queen's Proposed Visit to Wilton," 29. Simon de Passe only engraved five other known title pages, as Josephine Roberts points out (*U1*, cvi). Although Wroth asserted to George Villiers, Duke of Buckingham that her books "were solde against my minde I never purposing to have had them published," as Roberts discusses, this is a carefully worded response that does not preclude that she knew of *Urania*'s proposed publication (*U1*, cix). Likewise, there is no evidence that any copies were recalled from circulation (Wroth, *Poems* 35; Hackett, *Women and Romance Fiction*, 183).

29. Hackett, *Women and Romance Fiction*, 161. See Roberts on Wroth's beginning volume 2 as early as 1620 (*U1*, xvii).

30. I base this discussion of amplification and prose style on my interpretation of Wesley

Trimpi's courses on the transmission of classical literary theory, Stanford, 1983–84. Cicero, *De Oratore*, 3:83.

31. Cicero, *De Oratore*, 3:122–23.

32. Philip Sidney, *Sir Philip Sidney's Defense of Poesy*, 51.

33. George Puttenham, *The Art of English Poesy by George Puttenham*, 222.

34. Definitions, *Oxford English Dictionary* (hereafter cited as OED).

35. Roberts, *U1*, 726, glosses "Tawny, wrought all over with blacke" with Edward de Vere's line, "For Black and Taunie will I weare, which mournyng colours be," from "Compaint of a Lover," in Stephen W. May, *The Elizabethan Courtier Poets: The Poems and Their Contexts*, 12; on Ollorandus: Roberts, *U1*, 765, quotes Henry Peacham, *The Compleat Gentleman* (1661), 156. On Dolorindus: Roberts, *U1*, 396; Roberts, *U1*, 765, quotes Philip Sidney, *The Countess of Pembroke's Arcadia* (*The New Arcadia*), ed. Victor Skretkowica (Oxford: Oxford University Press, 1987), 367.

36. *U1*: 725, 726, 728. On Melasinda and Clorinus, 727, 729, 730.

37. Quintilian summarized by Richard A. Lanham, *A Handlist of Rhetorical Terms*, 25; see Quintilian, *Instituto Oratioria*, IX.

38. *Calendar of State Papers Relating to Scotland*, 1:586–87. "Articles delyvered to the Queene of Scots by Sir William Cecill Secretarie, and Sir Walter Myldmaye Chancellar of the Exchequer . . . 5 October, 1570," Historical Manuscript Commission, *Calendar of the Manuscripts of the Marquis of Salisbury*, 1:612.

39. *Calendar of State Papers Relating to Scotland*, 2:31; *The Tempest*, in *The Norton Shakespeare*.

40. Barbara Hodgdon, *The Shakespeare Trade: Performances and Appropriations*, 3. Hodgdon is describing versions of *The Taming of the Shrew*. *U1*, 197–98.

41. Hackett's discussion of the marriage of Limena and Philargus points out this episode's relationships to Wroth's with Robert Wroth and William Herbert, as well as its correspondence to medieval saints' lives (*Women and Romance Fiction*, 168–69).

42. *U1*, 475.9–10; 774n. Roberts notes the first OED citation for "romancy" in the singular in her note, *U1*, 794. The citation derives from the moment when Alarinus asks of the combat held to determine Myra's honor in another self-referential moment: "Must . . . shee be named as if in a Romancy, that relates of Knights, and distressed Damosells, the sad Adventures?" (*U1*, 595.25–26). Nevertheless, Wroth's first mention of "romancie" is in the plural as the two "naked" knights fight more than 100 pages earlier. Hackett points out that Wroth may have owed much of her knowledge of the romance genre to the library and connections of Susan Herbert, Countess of Montgomery (*Women and Romance Fiction*, 164).

43. Edmund Spenser, *The Faerie Queene*, 3.proem.iii:6–9.

44. Mary Sidney Herbert, "Even now that Care which on thy Crowne attends," from the Sidney Psalter, in Danielle Clarke, *Isabella Whitney, Mary Sidney and Aemilia Lanyer: Renaissance Women Poets*, 47–49, 303–6. As Danielle Clark glosses the line, "small parcell of that undischarged rent," "parcell" means "portion," and "undischarged rent" means "the gratitude, praise and faith owed to God" (304). I am indebted to Clark's gloss of "scanted in our will," since "the implication is that 'will,' namely support for Continental Protestantism, is not matched by action." Margaret P. Hannay discusses this poem in full as Mary Sidney Herbert's weaving "of a web of words to create a livery with which to adorn Elizabeth, a livery that would emphasize the queen's own position as servant to God and to the Protestant cause. The queen can then bestow this livery on others, those who serve her cause and God's" (*Philip's Phoenix*, 90–91). I agree with this reading but wish to stress more what it means to ask Elizabeth to wear this particular livery.

Maureen Quilligan, writing about this dedicatory poem in its entirety, concludes that

"This text, like Elizabeth's own embroidered gift of a translation to her stepmother Katherine Parr, works like the woven textiles circulating among women, articulating in the exchange the closely interlocked social hierarchies among interlocking families" (*Incest and Agency*, 113–16, quotation, 115). See also Patricia Demers on "web," "weaving," and "livery" as images that Philip and Mary Sidney share, "'Warpe' and 'Webb' in the Sidney Psalms: The 'Coupled Worke' of the Countess of Pembroke and Sir Philip Sidney," esp. 44–47.

45. All definitions in this discussion are from the OED.

46. Margaret Tyler, *The first part of the Mirror of princely deedes and knighthood* (1580), Sig. A2(r); Anne Dowriche, *The French Historie* (1589), Sig. Aii(r), Aiii(v).

47. Philip Sidney, *Defense of Poesy*, 9.

48. On the Bradford Table Carpet, see http://collections.vam.ac.uk/objectid/046183.

49. See Chapter 1 on Mary Queen of Scots's ciphering in needlework, and Chapter 2, on Jane Segar's use of Timothy Bright's shorthand. See also Reid Barbour, *Deciphering Elizabethan Fiction*.

Helen Hackett suggests that Wroth's "fictional, symbolic, or otherwise encoded forms" prove a connection to "her imagined ideal reader as an affectionate, female, romance-loving relative and friend." For Hackett, such encoding is part of a "discreet, very Sidneian game" in which she "expected her audience" to engage (*Women and Romance Fiction*, 161).

50. William Shakespeare, *As You Like It* in *The Norton Shakespeare*, 3.2.5–10.

51. For Elizabeth's books with embroidered ciphers, see Chapter 1.

The Latin inscription of Sofonisba Anguissola's *Autoritrato in miniatura* reads, "Sophonisba Anguissola Vir[ ] ipsus manu ex speculo depicta Cremonae." Ilya Sandra Perlingieri identifies the letters "E, R, A, C, K, Y, and M" and discusses them as relating to the names of Anguissola's sisters, their family name, and her mother's maiden name, as well as "C" for "Cremona and/or Camp with whom she began her artistic studies" (*Sofonisba Anguissola: The First Great Woman Artist of the Renaissance*, 63–64).

52. Bright, Dedication to Elizabeth, *Characterie: An Art of Swift and Secret Writing*, no sig.

53. Margaret P. Hannay, *Philip's Phoenix*, 193; Josephine Roberts, "Deciphering Women's Pastoral." See also Mary Ellen Lamb, "The Biopolitics of Romance in Mary Wroth's *The Countess of Montgomery's Urania*."

54. Wroth, *Poems*, 115, line 14n. Josephine Roberts, *U1*, 755n. Josephine Roberts points out that the cipher's appearance on the manuscript cover of *Love's Victory* "alerts readers of the manuscript to the presence of what Musella [a character in *Urania*] calls 'the secretts of the mind'" in "Deciphering Women's Pastoral," 165, 173.

55. See Mary Ellen Lamb on Wroth's second generation of characters and their relation to her illegimate children, whose father was William Herbert, who refused to acknowledge them legally. "The Biopolitics of Romance," 122–27.

56. Helen Hackett points out that *Argenis* is a "political *roman à clef* in romance form" (*Women and Romance Fiction*, 7). She also notes that in the Clifford triptych some of these romances appear on the far left, as "the reading matter of her youth," and others on "the other side" as "the reading of her maturity."

57. Elizabeth Isham, *My Book of Remembrance*, online edition edited by Isaac Stephens. See also the more recent edition of *My Book of Remembrance*, edited by Elizabeth Clarke and Erica Longfellow, which at this writing is under construction.

58. The Earl of Leicester's 1583 inventory at Kenilworth lists tapestries that Robert Sidney may have inherited on Dudley's death in 1588, although the crown seized Kenilworth at that time and many of his possessions went to the earl's son, Robert. These tapestries consisted of classical stories, including Paris and the rape of Helen, Hercules, Alexander the Great, and

Demophon and Achilles. Biblical narratives in these tapestries include Esther, Judith and Holofernes, the story of David, and the story of Abraham, as well as a suite of "gilt leather hangings" featuring the story of Susanna. *HMC Penshurst* 2:297.

59. Jones and Stallybrass, 145–46. As Lamb points out, one of the scene's most important aspects is that it demonstrates that reading a book—presumably, a romance—leads to an exchanged narrative that produces love, *Gender and Authorship in the Sidney Circle*, 178.

60. Josephine Roberts cites Janet Arnold for this definition of "wearing sleeves," *Queen Elizabeth's Wardrobe Unlock'd*, 127; *U1*, 750, note to 289.24–25. For a discussion of Shakespeare's pieced-together structures resembling quilts, see Linda Woodbridge, "Patchwork: Piecing the Early Modern Mind in England's First Century of Print Culture," in *English Literary Renaissance* 23 (1993): 36.

61. Jones and Stallybrass, 22.

62. Wroth knew her Wyatt. For example, in *Love's Victory*, she paraphrases "Whoso list to hunt"; Mary Sidney Wroth, *Love's Victory*, 88.

Selected Bibliography

PRE-1900 PRIMARY SOURCES

Accounts and Papers Relating to Mary Queen of Scots. Ed. Allan J. Crosby and John Bruce. 1867. Reprint. New York: AMS, 1968.

Acts of the Privy Council of England. 32 vols. Ed. J. R. Dasent. London: His Majesty's Stationers Office, 1890–1907.

Advice to the Women and Maidens of London shewing, that instead of their usual pastime and education in needlework . . . it were far more necessary [to learn] *the method of keeping books of account*. London: 1678. Wing A664.

Alcott, Louisa May. *The Journals of Louisa May Alcott*. Ed. Joel Myerson and Daniel Shealy. Athens: University of Georgia Press, 1997.

Ancient MS Poems, Ballads, Letters, Plays and Sonnets. MS Add. 22601. British Library.

Askew, Anne. *The lattre examinatyon of Anne Askew, latelye martyred in Smythfelde, by the wycked Synagoge of Antichrist, with the Elucydacyon of Johan Bale*. 1547. In *The Examinations of Anne Askew*, ed. Elaine V. Beilin. New York: Oxford University Press, 1996.

Aubrey, John. *Aubrey's Brief Lives*. Ed. Oliver Lawson Dick. 1949. Reprint. Ann Arbor: University of Michigan Press, 1957.

Baillie, Grisell. *The Household Book of Lady Grisell Baillie 1692–1733*. Ed. Robert Scott-Moncrieff. Edinburgh: Edinburgh University Press, 1911.

Bale, John. *A Godly Meditation of the Christen Sowle*. Marburg: Dirik van der Straten, 1548.

Bales, Peter. *The Writing Schoolemaster: brachygraphie, orthographie, calygraphie*. 1590. Reprint. New York: Da Capo Press, 1969.

Ballard, George. *Memoirs of Several Ladies of Great Britain Who Have Been Celebrated for Their Writings or Skill in the Learned Languages, Arts and Sciences*. Ed. Ruth Perry. Detroit, Mich.: Wayne State University Press, 1985.

Barley, William. *A Book of Curious and Strange Inventions, Called the First Parte of Needleworks*. London, 1596. STC 18418.

Beaufort, Margaret. *The Mirroure of Golde of the Synfall Soule*. London: Richard Pynson, 1506. STC 6894.5.

Bindloss, Lady. *A transcription of the Lady Bindloss braid manuscript*. Before 1660. Ed. Zoe Kuhn Williams. Wigan Council Heritage Archives. http://fingerloop.org/bindloss/.

Boccaccio, Giovanni. *Concerning Famous Women*. New Brunswick, N.J.: Rutgers University Press, 1963.

Bradstreet, Anne. *The Complete Works of Anne Bradstreet*. Ed. Joseph R. McElrath Jr. and Allan P. Robb. Boston: Twayne Publishers, 1981.

Bright, Timothy. *Characterie: An Art of Swift and Secret Writing*. London, 1588.

Brome, Richard. *The Queen and Concubine.* 1659. In *The Dramatic Works of Richard Brome Containing Fifteen Comedies Now First Collected in Three Volumes*, ed. John Pearson. Vol. 2.1873. Reprint. New York: AMS Press, 1966.

Browne, Alexander. *Ars Pictoria.* London, 1675.

Browning, Elizabeth Barrett. *Aura Leigh.* 1856. In *British Women Poets of the 19th Century*, ed. Margaret Randolph Higonnet. New York: Penguin Meridian, 1996. 255–56.

Buchanan, George. *Ane Detection of the Doings of Mary Queen of Scots.* London: 1571. STC 3981.

Bullough, Geoffrey, ed. *Narrative and Dramatic Sources of Shakespeare.* Vol. 8. London: Routledge and Kegan Paul, 1975.

The Byble in Englishe. London, 1549. STC 2070.

Calendar of State Papers, Domestic Series Elizabeth. 4 vols. Ed. Robert Lemon. 1865. Reprint. Nendeln: Liechtenstein, 1967.

Calendar of State Papers, Foreign, of the Reign of Elizabeth. 23 vols. Ed. Joseph Stevenson. London: Her Majesty's Public Record Office, 1863–1950.

Calendar of State Papers Relating to Scotland and Mary, Queen of Scots, 1547–1605. 12 vols. Ed. Markham John Thorpe. Edinburgh: His Majesty's General Register House, 1898–1969.

Cary, Elizabeth, Lady Falkland. *Elizabeth Cary, Lady Falkland: Life and Letters.* Ed. Heather Wolfe. Tempe: Arizona Center for Medieval and Renaissance Studies, 2001.

———. *The Tragedy of Mariam, the Fair Queen of Jewry.* Ed. Barry Weller and Margaret Ferguson. Berkeley: University of California Press, 1994.

Cavendish (Lucas), Margaret, Duchess of Newcastle. *Poems and Fancies.* London, 1653. Brown Women Writers Online.

Chaucer, Geoffrey. *The Canterbury Tales.* Ed. Larry Benson. 3rd ed. Boston: Houghton Mifflin, 1987.

Chettle, Henry. *The Tragedy of Hoffman Or A Revenge for a Father.* London, 1631. STC 5125.

Christine de Pizan. *The Book of the City of Ladies.* Trans. Earl Jeffrey Richards. New York: Persea Books, 1982.

[———.] *The boke of the cyte of ladyes.* Trans. Anon. London, 1521. STC 7271.

Church of England. *The First and Second Prayer-Books of Edward VI.* 1910. Reprint. New York: E. P. Dutton, 1927.

Cicero. *De Oratore.* 4 vols. Cambridge, Mass.: Harvard University Press, 1927.

Clarke, Danielle, ed. *Isabella Whitney, Mary Sidney and Aemilia Lanyer: Renaissance Women Poets.* New York: Penguin Putnam, 2000.

Clifford, Anne. *The Diary of Anne Clifford 1616–1619.* Ed. Katherine O. Acheson. New York: Garland Publishing, 1995.

Cockeram, Henry. *The English Dictionarie: or, An interpreter of hard English words.* London, 1623. STC 5461.2.

A Collection of State Papers Left by William Cecil Lord Burghley. Ed. Samuel Haynes. London: William Bowyer, 1740.

Cotgrave, Randle. *Dictionarie of the French and English Tongues.* London, 1611. STC 5830.

[Cynthia]. *The Tragical History of Almerin and Desdemona.* London, 1687. Wing C7710A.

Davies, Eleanor. *Prophetic Writings of Lady Eleanor Davies.* Ed. Esther S. Cope. New York: Oxford University Press, 1995.

Dekker, Thomas. *The Shoemakers' Holiday.* 1599. Reprint. Ed. Merritt E. Lawlis. Woodbury, N.Y.: Barron's Educational Series, 1979.

Deloney, Thomas. *Strange Histories.* London, 1607. STC 1349:05.

De L'Isle Papers. Centre for Kentish Studies, Maidstone. Mary Sidney Wroth to Robert Sidney, 17 October 1614. U1, 475 C81/184.

———. U 1475 C52.

———. Mary Sidney to John Cockrame, 22 July 1573. U1, 500 C 1/3.

Dickens, Charles. *David Copperfield*. 1849–50. Reprint. Ed. George H. Ford. Boston: Houghton Mifflin, 1958.

Dowriche, Anne. *The French Historie*. London, 1589. STC 7159.

Drayton, Michael. *Harmonie of the Church Containing The Spirituall Songes and Holy Hymnes, of Godly men, patriarkes and Prophetes*. London, 1591. STC 7199.

Drury, Anne Bacon. "Hawstead Panels." Ca. 1595–1605. Christchurch Mansion, Ipswich.

Dubartas, Guillaume Salluste. *The Historie of Judith*. Edinburgh, 1584. STC 21671.

Edward VI. *The Literary Remains of King Edward the Sixth*. Ed. J. G. Nichols. 1857. Reprint. New York: Burt Franklin, 1963.

Elizabeth I. *Collected Works*. 2 vols. Ed. Leah S. Marcus, Janel Mueller, and Mary Beth Rose. Chicago: University of Chicago Press, 2000.

———. Translation of John Calvin's *Institution Chrétienne*. 1545. Scottish Record Office. MS #R.H. 13/78.

———. *The Letters of Queen Elizabeth*. Ed. G. B. Harrison. 1935. Reprint. New York: Funk and Wagnalls, 1968.

———. *Le Miroir de l'âme pécheresse*. Bodleian Library MS Cherry 36.

———. "Precationes sev meditationes." 1545. British Library MS Royal 7.D.X.MS.

Elyot, Thomas. *The Boke Named the Gouernour*. 2 vols. 1531. Reprint. Ed. Henry Croft. New York: Burt Franklin, 1967.

The English Bible Translated Out of the Original Tongues by the Commandment of King James the First. 6 vols. Reprint. New York: AMS Press, 1967.

Erasmus, Desiderius. "Concerning Faith." In *The Whole Familiar Colloquies of Desiderius Erasmus of Rotterdam*. Trans. Nathan Bailey. 1733. Reprint. New York: Smith, Leton & Co., 1877. 168–75.

Est natura hominum nouitatis anida. The Scottish queens buriall at Peterborough, upon Tues being Lanmas Day, 1587. London, 1589. STC 17566.7.

Fell, Margaret Askew. *Women's Speaking Justified, Proved and Allowed by the Scriptures*. London, 1666. Wing F642. Brown Women Writers Online.

Finch, Anne, Countess of Winchelsea. *Selected Poems*. Ed. Denys Thompson. Manchester: Carcanet, 1987.

Forman, Simon. *The Autobiography and Personal Diary of Dr. Simon Forman*. Ed. James Orchard Halliwell. London: Halliwell, 1849.

Fowler, Constance Aston. *Commonplace Book*. 1630–60. Huntington Library. HM 904.

———. *The Verse Miscellany of Constance Aston Fowler*. Ed. Deborah Aldrich-Watson. Tempe, Ariz.: Renaissance Text Society, 2000.

Gascoigne, George. *The Princely Pleasures of Kenelwoorth Castle*. In *The Progresses of Queen Elizabeth*, ed. John Nichols. Reprint. New York: Burt Franklin, 1966. 1: 485–523.

Geoffrey of Monmouth. *Histories of the Kings of Britain*. Trans. Sebastian Evans. New York: E. P. Dutton, 1920.

Gerard, John. *The Herball or Generall Historie of Plantes*. London, 1633.

Gosson, Stephen. *The Schoole of Abuse*. 1579. Reprint. Ed. Arthur Freeman. New York: Garland Publishing, 1973.

Hakluyt, Richard. *The Principal Navigations Voyages Trafiques & Discoveries of the English Nation*. Vol. 3. 1599. Reprint. New York: Macmillan, 1903.

Halkett, Anne. *Lady Anne Halkett: Selected Self-Writings*. Ed. Suzanne Trill. Aldershot: Ashgate, 2007.

Hall, John. *Certayne Chapters of the Prouerbes of Salomon drawen into metre by T. Sterneholde, late grome of the Kynges Majesties Robes*. London, 1549–50. STC 2760.

Hardwick Hall Inventories of 1601. Ed. Lindsay Boynton. London: Furniture History Society, 1971.

Harley, Brilliana. *The Letters of The Lady Brilliana Harley, Wife of Sir Robert Harley, of Brampton Bryan, Knight of the Bath.* Ed. Thomas Taylor Lewis. London: Camden Society, 1854.

Harrison, Stephen. *The Archs of Triumph Erected in honor of the High and mighty prince James the first of that name King, of England, and the Sixt of Scotland.* London, 1604. STC 12863.

Harrison, William. *The Description of England: The Classic Contemporary Account of Tudor Social Life.* Ed. Georges Edelen. 1968. Reprint. Washington, D.C.: Folger Shakespeare Library, 1994.

Herbert, Mary Sidney. *The Tragedie of Antonie Doone into English by the Countesse of Pembroke.* London, 1595. STC 11623.

Heywood, Thomas. *The exemplary lives and memorable acts of the most worthy women in the World: Three Iewes, Three gentiles, Three Christians.* London, 1640. STC 13316.

Higonnet, Margaret Randolph, ed. *British Women Poets of the 19th Century.* New York: Meridian / Penguin Books, 1996.

Hilliard, Nicholas. *Nicholas Hilliard's Art of Limning: A New Edition of A Treatise Concerning the Arte of Limning.* Ed. Arthur F. Kinney. Boston: Northeastern University Press, 1983.

Historical Manuscript Commission. *Calendar of the Manuscripts of the Marquis of Salisbury.* 24 vols. London: His Majesty's Stationers Office, 1883.

Historical Manuscripts Commission. *Report on the Manuscripts of Lord de L'Isle and Dudley Preserved at Penshurst Place.* 5 vols. Ed. C. L. Kingsford. London: His Majesty's Stationers Office, 1934.

Hoby, Margaret. *The Private Life of an Elizabethan Lady: The Diary of Lady Margaret Hoby 1599–1605.* Ed. Joanna Moody. Phoenix Mill, England: Sutton Publishing, 1998.

Homer. *The Iliad of Homer.* Trans. Richmond Lattimore. Reprint. Chicago: University of Chicago Press, 1961.

———. *The Whole Works of Homer In his Iliads and Odysses.* Trans. George Chapman. London, 1634. STC 13624.5.

Hookes, Nicholas. *Amanda.* London, 1653. Wing H2665.

Horestes. Ed. Karen Robertson and J.-A. George. Dublin: Galway University Press, 1996.

Hutchinson, Lucy. *Memoirs of the Life of Colonel Hutchinson with the fragment of an autobiography of Mrs. Hutchinson.* Ed. James Sutherland. London: Oxford University Press, 1973.

Inglis, Esther. *Argument Psalmoru Davidis per tetrasticha manu Estherae Inglis exarata, strenai nomine Illus: Principi Henrico oblata*, 1608. Folger Shakespeare Library.V.a.94.

———. *Discours de la Foy.* Huntingdon Library. HM 26068.

———. *Ce Livre contenant cinquante Emblemes Chrestiens premierement inventez par la noble damoiselle Georgette de Montenay in France, forts plaisants & delectables a lire & voir lesquels sont, a present, ecrits, tirez, et tracez, par la main et plume de moy Esther Inglis l'an de mon age cinquante et trois. A Lislebourg en Escosse, l'an 1624.* British Library. Royal MS. 17.D.XVI.

———. *Le Livre de l'Ecclesiaste.* 1599. British Library. Add. MS 27927, f. 2.

———. *Le Livre des Pseaumes 1599.* College of Christ Church Library. Oxford. MS 180.

An introduction for to lerne to recken with the pen or with the counters accordynge to the trewe cast of algorysme. London, 1539. STC 14118.

The Inventory of King Henry VIII: The Transcript. Vol. 1. Ed. David Starkey. London: Harvey Miller Publishers, 1998.

Isham, Elizabeth. *My Book of Remembrance.* Online edition. Ed. Isaac Stephens. http://www.history.ucr.edu/people/grad_students/index.html.

———. *My Book of Remembrance.* Online edition. Ed. Elizabeth Clarke and Erica Longfellow. http://www2.warwick.ac.uk/fac/arts/ren/projects/isham/.

Jode, Gerard de. *Thesaurus Sacrarum Historiarum Veteris Testamenti.* Antwerp, 1585.

Johnson, Richard. *The Golden Garland.* London, 1620. STC 14674.

Jonson, Ben. *Poems of Ben Jonson.* Ed. Ian Donaldson. New York: Oxford University Press, 1985.

Lamb, Charles and Mary. *The Works of Charles and Mary Lamb.* 7 vols. Ed. E. V. Lucas. 1903. Reprint. New York: AMS Press, 1968.

Lanham, Richard A. *A Handlist of Rhetorical Terms.* 1968. Reprint. Berkeley: University of California Press, 1969.

Lanyer, Aemilia. *The Poems of Aemilia Lanyer: Salve Deus Rex Judaeorum.* Ed. Susanne Woods. New York: Oxford University Press, 1993.

Lyly, John. *Gallathea.* 1592. New York: Malone Society Reprints, 1998.

Makin, Bathsua. *An Essay to Revive the Antient Education of Gentlewomen, in Religion, Manners, Arts & Tongues: With an Answer to the Objections Against this Way of Education.* London, 1673. Wing 697:02. Brown Women Writers Online.

"Mankind." In *Medieval Drama: An Anthology,* ed. Greg Walker, Oxford: Blackwell Publishers, 2000. 258–79.

"Manuscript describing how to make purse strings, with samplers." 1625–50. Victoria and Albert Museum, T 313–1960. http://collectionsvam.ac.uk.objectid/011031.

Mary Queen of Scots. *Bittersweet Within My Heart: The Collected Poems of Mary, Queen of Scots.* Ed. and trans. Robin Bell. 1992. Reprint. London: Pavilion Books Limited, 1995.

Mayne, Jasper. *The City Match: A comoedye. Presented to the King and Queene at White-Hall.* Oxford: Leonard Lichfield, 1639. STC 17750.

Meres, Francis. *Palladius Tumia.* London, 1598. STC 17834.

Mildmay, Lady Grace. "The Autobiography of Grace, Lady Mildmay." Ed. Randall Martin. *Renaissance and Reformation / Renaissance et Réforme* 18:1 (1994): 33–81.

Millman, Jill Seal, and Gillian Wright, eds. *Early Modern Women's Manuscript Poetry.* Manchester: Manchester University Press, 2005.

Mollet, André. *The garden of pleasure containing several draughts of gardens, both embroyder'd-ground-works, knot-works of grass.* London, 1670. Wing M2392.

Mulcaster, Richard. *The Quene's Majestie's passage through the citie of London to westminster the daye before her coronacion.* In *Elizabethan Backgrounds: Historical Documents of the Age of Elizabeth I,* ed. Arthur F. Kinney. Hamden, Conn.: Archon Books, 1975. 7–39.

———. *Richard Mulcaster's Positions.* Ed. Richard L. DeMolen. 1581. Reprint. New York: Teachers College Press, 1971.

Nichols, John, ed. *The Progresses and Public Processions of Queen Elizabeth.* 3 vols. 1823. Reprint. New York: Burt Franklin, 1966.

Ostovich, Helen, and Elizabeth Sauer, ed. *Reading Early Modern Women: An Anthology of Texts in Manuscript and Print 1550–1700.* New York: Routledge, 2004.

Parr, Susanna. *Susanna's Apologie Against the Elders.* 1659. Reprinted in *The Early Modern Englishwoman: A Facsimile Library of Essential Works, Series II: Printed Writings, 1641–1700: Part I,* ed. Elizabeth Skerpan-Wheeler. Aldershot: Ashgate, 2001. 1:n.p.

Petrarch. *The Triumphs of Petrarch.* Trans. Ernest Hatch Wilkins. Chicago: University of Chicago Press, 1962.

Pontaymeri, Alexandre de. *A Woman's Woorth, defended against all the men in the world.* Trans. Anthony Gibson. London, 1599. STC 11831.

Poulet [Paulet], Amias. *The Letter-Books of Sir Amias Poulet Keeper of Mary Queen of Scots.* London: Burns and Oates, 1874.

Presot, Marie. Dated "Edimbourg le 24. d'aoust, 1574." Newberry Library. Wing MS.ZW 543.

Psalter and Hours of Bonne of Luxembourg, Duchess of Normandy. The Cloisters Collection, 1969 (59.86).

Puttenham, George. *The Art of English Poesy by George Puttenham: A Critical Edition*. Ed. Frank Whigham and Wayne A. Rebhorn. Ithaca, N.Y.: Cornell University Press, 2007.

Quarles, Francis. *Hadassa: or the History of Queen Esther: with Meditations thereupon, Diuine and Morall*. London, 1621. STC 20546.

Quintilian. *Instituto Oratoria IV, Books 9–10*. Trans. and ed. Donald A. Russell. Boston: Boston University Press, 2002.

Ronsard, Pierre de. *Oeuvres Complètes*. 20 vols. Ed. Paul Laumonier. Paris: Librairie Nizet, 1982.

Rye, William Brenchley, ed. *England as Seen by Foreigners in the Days of Elizabeth and James the First*. 1865. Reprint. New York: Benjamin Blom, 1967.

"The Saga of the People of Laxardal." Trans. Keneva Kunz. In *The Sagas of Icelanders: A Selection*. New York: Viking Penguin, 2000. 270–421.

Saint-Aubin, Charles Germain de. *Art of the Embroiderer*. 1770. Reprint. Trans. and ed. Nikki Scheuer. Boston: David R. Godine, 1983.

Segar, Jane. *The Prophecies of the Ten Sibills upon the Birth of Christ*. British Library. MS Add. 10037.

Segar, William. "Justs at the Tilt-yard, 1590." In *Progresses of Queen Elizabeth*, ed. John Nichols. Reprint. New York: Burt Franklin, 1966. 3:41–50.

Shakespeare, William. *The Norton Shakespeare Based on the Oxford Edition*. Ed. Stephen Greenblatt, Walter Cohen, Jean E. Howard, and Katharine Eisaman Maus. New York: W. W. Norton, 1997.

Shakespeare, William. *Pericles, Prince of Tyre*. Ed. Suzanne Gossett. London: Arden Shakespeare, 2004.

Sidney, Philip. *The Countess of Pembroke's Arcadia*. Ed. Maurice Evans. New York: Penguin Books, 1982.

———. *The Poems of Sir Philip Sidney*. Ed. William A. Ringler. Oxford: Clarendon Press, 1962.

———. *The Prose Works of Sir Philip Sidney*. 3 vols. Ed. Albert Feuillerat. Reprint. Cambridge: Cambridge University Press, 1962.

———. *Sir Philip Sidney's Defense of Poesy*. Ed. Lewis Soens. Lincoln: University of Nebraska Press, 1970.

Sidney, Robert. *Domestic Politics and Family Absence: The Correspondence (1588–1621) of Robert Sidney, First Earl of Leicester, and Barbara Gamage Sidney, Countess of Leicester*. Ed. Margaret P. Hannay, Noel J. Kinnamon, and Michael G. Brennan. Aldershot: Ashgate, 2005.

Skelton, John. *John Skelton: The Complete English Poems*. Ed. John Scattergood. New Haven, Conn.: Yale University Press, 1983.

———. "Magnyfycence." In *Medieval Drama: An Anthology*, ed. Greg Walker. Oxford: Blackwell Publishers, 2000. 349–408.

Sowernam, Esther [pseud.]. *Esther hath hang'd Haman: or an answere to a lewd Pamphlet, entituled, The Arraignment of Women*. 1617. In *The Woman's Sharp Revenge: Five Women's Pamphlets from the Renaissance*, ed. Simon Shepherd. New York: St. Martin's Press, 1985. 85–124.

The Spectator. 5 vols. Ed. Donald F. Bond. Oxford: Clarendon Press, 1965.

"Speeches to the Queen at Sudeley, 1592." In *Progresses of Elizabeth*, ed. John Nichols. Reprint. New York: Burt Franklin, 1966. 3:136–43.

Spenser, Edmund. *The Faerie Queene*. Ed. Thomas P. Roche. 1978. Reprint. New York: Penguin Books, 1987.

Stevenson, Jane, and Peter Davidson, eds. *Early Modern Women Poets: An Anthology*. Oxford: Oxford University Press, 2001.

Stuart, Arbella. *The Letters of Arbella Stuart*. Ed. Sara Jayne Steen. New York: Oxford University Press, 1994.

Swetnam, Thomas. *The Arraignment of Lewd, Idle, Froward, and Unconstant Women*. London, 1615. STC 23533.

Taylor, John. *The Needles Excellency*. 1631. Reprint. London, 1634.

Teerlinc, Levina (attrib.). *Queen Mary's Manual for blessing cramp rings and touching for the evil: the rituals of the royal healing ceremonies*. Westminster Cathedral Library.

Trevelyon, Thomas. *The Trevelyon Miscellany of 1608: A Facsimile Edition of Folger Shakespeare Library MS V.b.232*. Ed. Heather Wolfe. Washington, D.C.: Folger Shakespeare Library, 2007.

Tyler, Margaret. *The first part of the Mirror of princely deedes and knighthood*. London, 1580. STC 7159.

Tyrrell, Anthony. *A fruitfull sermon preached at Christs-Church taken by characterye*. London, 1589. STC 24474.

Unto every individual Member of Parliament: The humble Representations of divers afflicted Women-Petitioners to the Parliament, on behalf of Mr. John Lilburn. London, 1653. Wing U99.

Vives, Juan. *The Instruction of a Christen Woman*. Trans. Richard Hyrde. London, 1540. STC 24856.

Waldstein, Baron von (Zdenek Brtnick & z Valdtejna). *The Diary of Baron Waldstein: A Traveller in Elizabethan England*. Trans. G. W. Groos. London: Thames and Hudson, 1981.

Wallis, John. *De sectionibus conicus*, in *Operum Mathematicorum*. Oxford: 1656. Wing W598A.

The Wisdome of Doctor Dodypoll. 1600. Reprint. Oxford: Malone Society Reprints, 1964.

Wright, Thomas, ed. *Queen Elizabeth and Her Times: A Series of Original Letters*. 2 vols. London: Henry Colburn, 1838.

Wroth, Lady Mary. *The First Part of the Countess of Montgomery's Urania*. Ed. Josephine Roberts. Binghamton, N.Y.: Medieval and Renaissance Texts & Studies, 1995.

———. *Love's Victory*. In *Renaissance Drama by Women: Texts and Documents*, ed. S. P. Cerasano and Marion Wynne-Davies. New York: Routledge, 1996. 90–126.

———. *The Poems of Lady Mary Wroth*. Ed. Josephine Roberts. Baton Rouge: Louisiana State University Press, 1983.

———. *The Second Part of the Countess of Montgomery's Urania*. Ed. Josephine A. Roberts, Suzanne Gossett, and Janel Mueller. Tempe: Renaissance English Text no. 24, 1999.

SECONDARY SOURCES

Aaron, Jane. *A Double Singleness: Gender and the Writing of Charles and Mary Lamb*. Oxford: Clarendon Press, 1991.

Adelman, Janet. *Suffocating Mothers: Fantasies of Maternal Origin in Shakespeare's Plays, Hamlet to The Tempest*. New York: Routledge, 1992.

Alpers, Svetlana. *The Art of Describing: Dutch Art in the Seventeenth Century*. Chicago: University of Chicago Press, 1983.

Andrews, Meg. "Late 16th / Early 17th Century Embroidery: Slips." http://www.victoriana.com/shops/andrews/slips.htm.

Arnold, Janet. *Queen Elizabeth's Wardrobe Unlock'd*. 1988. Reprint. Westport, Conn.: Greenwood Press, 2000.

Arnett, Paul, Joanne Cubbs, and Eugene W. Metcalf Jr., eds. *Gee's Bend: The Architecture of the Quilt*. 2006. Reprint. Atlanta, Ga.: Tinwood Books, 2007.

Arthur, Liz. *Embroidery 1600–1700 at the Burrell Collection*. London: John Murray Publishers, 1995.

Auerbach, Erna. *Nicholas Hilliard*. London: Routledge & Kegan Paul, 1961.

———. *Tudor Artists: A Study of Painters in the Royal Service and of Portraiture on Illuminated Documents from the Accession of Henry VIII to the Death of Elizabeth I*. London: Athlone Press, 1954.

Bakker, Anneke Tjan. "Dame Flora's Blossoms: Esther Inglis's Flower-Illustrated Manuscripts." In *English Manuscript Studies 1100–1700*, ed. Peter Beal and Margaret J. M. Ezell. London: British Library, 2000. 9:49–71.

Barash, Carol. *English Women's Poetry, 1649–1714: Politics, Community, and Linguistic Authority*. Oxford: Clarendon Press, 1996.

Barbour, Reid. *Deciphering Elizabethan Fiction*. Newark: University of Delaware Press, 1993.

Barker, Juliet R. V. *Sixty Treasures: The Brontë Parsonage Museum*. Highgate, Kendal, Cumbria: Titus Wilson & Son, 1988.

Barroll, Leeds. "Looking for Patrons in Amelia Lanyer: Gender, Genre, and the Canon." In *Aemilia Lanyer: Gender, Genre, and the Canon*, ed. Marshall Grossman. Lexington: University Press of Kentucky, 1998. 29–48.

Barry, Jonathan, and Christopher Brooks, eds. *The Middling Sort of People: Culture, Society and Politics in England, 1550–1800*. Basingstoke: Macmillan, 1994.

Bath, Michael. *Emblems for a Queen: The Needlework of Mary Queen of Scots*. London: Archetype Publications, 2008.

———. "Embroidered Emblems: Mary Stuart's Bed of State." *Emblematica* 15 (2007): 5–32.

———. *Speaking Pictures: English Emblem Books and Renaissance Culture*. London: Longman, 1994.

Beal, Peter. *In Praise of Scribes: Manuscripts and Their Makers in Seventeenth-Century England*. Oxford: Clarendon Press, 1998.

Beal, Timothy K. *Esther*. Collegeville, Minn.: Liturgical Press, 1999.

Beilin, Elaine V. *Redeeming Eve: Women Writers of the English Renaissance*. Princeton, N.J.: Princeton University Press, 1987.

Bell, Richard, and Patricia Crawford. "Appendix 2: Statistical Analysis of Women's Printed Writings 1600–1700." In *Women in English Society 1500–1800*, ed. Mary Prior. London: Methuen, 1985. 265–82.

Bell, Susan Groag. *The Lost Tapestries of the City of Ladies*. Berkeley: University of California Press, 2004.

Berenson, Bernard. "Decline and Recovery in the Figure Arts." In *Studies in Art and Literature for Belle da Costa Greene*, ed. Dorothy Miner. Princeton, N.J.: Princeton University Press, 1954.

Berg, Christine, and Philippa Berry. "'Spiritual Whoredom': An Essay on Female Prophets in the Seventeenth Century." In *1642: Literature and Power in the Seventeenth Century*, ed. Francis Barker et al. Colchester: University of Essex, 1981. 37–54.

Berger, Ronald M. *The Most Necessary Luxuries: The Mercers' Company of Coventry, 1550–1680*. University Park: Pennsylvania State University Press, 1993.

Bevington, David. "Sexuality in *Cymbeline*." *Essays in Literature*. 10:2 (fall 1983): 159–68.

Bond, Donald F. "Introduction." *The Spectator*, ed. Donald F. Bond. Oxford: Clarendon Press, 1965. 1:xiii–cix.

Boose, Linda. "Othello's Handkerchief: 'The Recognizance and Pledge of Love.'" In *Critical Essays on Shakespeare's Othello*, ed. Anthony Barthelemy. New York: G. K. Hall, 1994. 55–67.

Bracher, Tricia. "Esther Inglis and the English Succession Crisis of 1599." In *Women and Politics in Early Modern England*, ed. James Daybell. Aldershot: Ashgate, 2004. 132–46.

Brennan, Michael G. "Creating Female Authorship in the Early Seventeenth Century: Ben Jonson and Lady Mary Wroth." In *Women's Writing and the Circulation of Ideas*, ed. George L. Justice and Nathan Tinker. Cambridge: Cambridge University Press. 2002. 73–93.

———. "The Queen's Proposed Visit to Wilton House in 1599 and the 'Sidney Psalms.'" *Sidney Journal* 20:1 (2002): 27–53.

Bronner, Simon J. "The Idea of the Folk Artifact." In *American Material Culture and Folklore: A Prologue and Dialogue*, ed. Simon J. Bronner. Ann Arbor, Mich.: UMI Research Press, 1985. 3–46.

Brooks, Mary M. *English Embroideries of the Sixteenth and Seventeenth Centuries in the Collection of the Ashmolean Museum*. London: Jonathan Horne, 2004.

Broude, Norma, and Mary D. Garrard. "Conversations with Judy Chicago and Miriam Schapiro." In *The Power of Feminist Art: The American Movement of the 1970s, History and Impact*, ed. Norma Broude and Mary D. Garrard. New York: Abrams, 1994. 66–87.

Broude, Norma, and Mary D. Garrard, eds. *The Power of Feminist Art: The American Movement of the 1970s, History and Impact*. New York: Abrams, 1994.

Brown, Clare, and Jennifer Wearden. *Samplers from the Victoria and Albert Museum*. London: V&A Publications, 1999.

Burckhardt, Jakob. *The Civilisation of the Renaissance in Italy*. Trans. S. G. C. Middlemore. London: Swan Sonnenschein & Co., 1898.

Burke, Mary. "Queen, Lover, Poet: A Question of Balance in the Sonnets of Mary, Queen of Scots." In *Women, Writing, and the Reproduction of Culture in Tudor and Stuart Britain*, ed. Mary E. Burke et al. Syracuse, N.Y.: Syracuse University Press, 2000. 101–18.

Burns, E. Jane. *Bodytalk: When Women Speak in Old French Literature*. Philadelphia: University of Pennsylvania Press, 1993.

———. *Courtly Love Undressed: Reading Through Clothes in Medieval French Culture*. Philadelphia: University of Pennsylvania Press, 2002.

Butler, Judith. *Bodies That Matter*. London: Routledge, 1993.

———. *Gender Trouble: Feminism and the Subversion of Identity*. New York: Routledge, 1990.

Cabot, Nancy Graves. "Pattern Sources of Scriptural Subjects in Tudor-Stuart Embroideries." *Bulletin of the Needle and Bobbin Club* 30:1–2 (1946): 3–17.

Calo, Mary Ann. *Bernard Berenson and the Twentieth Century*. Philadelphia: Temple University Press, 1994.

Campbell, Julie. *Literary Circles and Gender in Early Modern Europe: A Cross-Cultural Approach*. Aldershot: Ashgate, 2006.

Campbell, Lorne, and Susan Foister. "Gerard, Lucas and Susanna Horenbout." *Burlington Magazine* 128:1003 (October 1986): 719–27.

Carley, James P. "'Her moost lovyng and fryndely brother sendeth gretyng': Anne Boleyn's Manuscripts and Their Sources." In *Illuminating the Book, Makers and Interpreters: Essays in Honour of Janet Backhouse*, ed. Michelle P. Brown and Scot McKendrick. Toronto: University of Toronto Press, 1998. 261–80.

Carlton, William J. *Timothe Bright Doctor of Phisicke: A Memoir of "The Father of Modern Shorthand."* London: Elliot Stock, 1911.

Certeau, Michel de. *The Practice of Everyday Life*. Trans. Steven Rendall. 1984. Reprint. Berkeley: University of California Press, 1988.

Chadwick, Whitney. *Women, Art, and Society*. 1990. Reprint. London: Thames and Hudson, 1994.

Chalfant, Fran C. *Ben Jonson's London: A Jacobean Placename Dictionary*. Athens: University of Georgia Press, 1978.

Cheal, David. *The Gift Economy*. London: Routledge, 1988.

Cheney, Liana De Girolami, Alicia Craig Faxon, and Kathleen Lucey Russo. *Self-Portraits by Women Painters*. Aldershot: Ashgate, 2000.

Chicago, Judy. *The Dinner Party*. 1986. Reprint. New York: Penguin, 1996.

———. *Embroidering Our Heritage: The Dinner Party Needlework*. Garden City, N.Y.: Anchor Press/Doubleday, 1980.

Clabburn, Pamela. *The Shire Book: Samplers*. Princes Risborough, Buckinghamshire: Shire Publications, 1998.

Clark, Alice. *Working Life of Women in the Seventeenth Century*. 1919. Reprint. New York: Routledge, 1992.

Clinton, Jerome W. "Image and Metaphor: Textiles in Persian Poetry." In *Spun from the Heart: Textile Arts of Safavid and Qajar Iran 16th-19th Centuries*, ed. Carol Bier. Washington, D.C.: Textile Museum, 1987. 7–11.

Collinson, Patrick. *The English Captivity of Mary Queen of Scots*. Sheffield: Sheffield History Pamphlets, 1987.

Connor, T. P. "Malignant Reading: John Squier's Newgate Prison Diary 1642–46." *The Library: The Transactions of the Bibliographical Society* 7:2 (June 2006): 154–84.

Cotter, Holland. "Polyphony for the Eye: The Many Splendors of Islamic Art." *New York Times*, July 16, 2004:B23, 31.

Crane, Mary. *Framing Authority: Sayings, Self, and Society in Sixteenth-Century England*. Princeton, N.J.: Princeton University Press, 1993.

Crawford, Patricia. "'The Only Ornament in a Woman': Needlework in Early Modern England." In *All Her Labours Two: Embroidering the Framework*, ed. Jean Blackburn et al. Sydney, Australia: Hale & Iremonger, 1984. 7–20.

———. *Women and Religion in England 1500–1720*. London: Routledge, 1993.

Cust, Lionel. *Notes on the Authentic Portraits of Mary Queen of Scots*. London: John Murray, 1903.

Daly, Peter. *Literature in the Light of the Emblem: Structural Parallels Between the Emblem and Literature in the Sixteenth and Seventeenth Centuries*. 7th ed. Toronto: University of Toronto Press, 1998.

Damon, Maria. "'Independent Embroidery': Theorizing Improvising Textile Collaborations." In *Chain / 4: Procedures*, ed. Jena Osman, Juliana Spahr, and Janet Zweig. Buffalo, N.Y.: Leave Books, 1997. 37–41.

Daniell, David. *The Bible in English: Its History and Influence*. New Haven, Conn.: Yale University Press, 2003.

Daybell, James. "'Such Newes as on the Quenes Hye Wayes We Have Mett': The News and Intelligence Networks of Elizabeth Talbot, Countess of Shrewsbury (c. 1527–1608)." In *Women and Politics in Early Modern England 1450–1700*, ed. James Daybell. Aldershot: Ashgate, 2004. 114–31.

de Grazia, Margreta. "Imprints: Shakespeare, Gutenberg and Descartes." In *Alternative Shakespeares*. ed. Terence Hawkes. Vol. 2. London: Routledge, 1996. 65–96.

de Grazia, Margreta, Maureen Quilligan, and Peter Stallybrass. "Introduction." In *Subject and Object in Renaissance Culture*. Cambridge: Cambridge University Press, 1996. 1–16.

de Grazia, Margreta, Maureen Quilligan, and Peter Stallybrass, eds. *Subject and Object in Renaissance Culture*. Cambridge: Cambridge University Press, 1996.

Delmarcel, Guy. *Flemish Tapestry*. New York: Abrams, 2000.

Demers, Patricia. "'Warpe' and 'Webb' in the Sidney Psalms: The 'Coupled Worke' of the Countess of Pembroke and Sir Philip Sidney." In *Literary Couplings: Writing Couples, Collaborators, and the Construction of Authorship*, ed. Marjorie Stone. Madison: University of Wisconsin Press, 2007. 41–58.

De Molen, Richard L. "Richard Mulcaster and Elizabethan Pageantry." *Studies in English Literature* 14 (1974): 209–21.

DiGangi, Mario. "Sexual Slander and Working Women in *The Roaring Girl*." *Renaissance Drama* 32 (2003): 147–76.

Digby, George Wingfield. *Elizabethan Embroidery*. New York: Thomas Yoseloff, 1964.

Dobin, Howard. *Merlin's Disciples: Prophecy, Poetry, and Power in Renaissance England*. Stanford, Calif.: Stanford University Press, 1990.

Donawerth, Jane. "Women's Poetry and the Tudor-Stuart System of Gift Exchange." In *Women, Writing, and the Reproduction of Culture in Tudor and Stuart Britain*, ed. Mary E. Burke et al. Syracuse, N.Y.: Syracuse University Press, 2000. 3–18.

Dowd, Michelle M., and Julie A. Eckerlie, eds. *Genre and Women's Life Writing in Early Modern England*. Aldershot: Ashgate, 2007.

Dowden, Edward. *Shakespere*. London: Macmillan, 1877.

Duncan-Jones, Katherine. *Sir Philip Sidney, Courtier Poet*. New Haven, Conn.: Yale University Press, 1991.

Durant, David N. *Bess of Hardwick: Portrait of an Elizabethan Dynast*. 1977. Reprint. New York: Atheneum, 1978.

Durkan, John. "The Library of Mary, Queen of Scots." In *Mary Stewart: Queen in Three Kingdoms*, ed. Michael Lynch. Oxford: Basil Blackwell, 1988. 71–104.

Earle, Peter. *The Making of the English Middle Class: Business Society and Family Life in London, 1660–1730*. London: Methuen, 1989.

Edmond, Mary. *Hilliard and Oliver: The Lives and Works of Two Great Miniaturists*. London: Robert Hale, 1983.

Eisenstein, Elizabeth L. *The Printing Revolution in Early Modern Europe*. Cambridge: Cambridge University Press, 1983.

Ezell, Margaret J.M. "Elizabeth Isham's Books of Remembrance and Forgetting." http://www2.warwick.ac.uk/fac/arts/ren/projects/isham/workshop/ezell.

———. "From Manuscript to Print: A Volume of Their Own?" In *Women and Poetry, 1660–1750*, ed. Sarah Prescott and David Shuttleton. Basingstoke: Palgrave Macmillan, 2003. 140–60.

———. *Social Authorship and the Advent of Print*. Baltimore: Johns Hopkins University Press, 1999.

———. *Writing Women's Literary History*. Baltimore: Johns Hopkins University Press, 1993.

Ferguson, Margaret. *Dido's Daughters: Literacy, Gender, and Empire in Early Modern England and France*. Chicago: University of Chicago Press, 2003.

———. "Feathers and Flies: Aphra Behn and the Seventeenth-Century Trade in Exotica." In *Subject and Object in Renaissance Culture*. Cambridge: Cambridge University Press, 1996. 135–59.

———. "A Room Not Their Own: Renaissance Women as Readers and Writers." In *The Comparative Perspective on Literature: Approaches to Theory and Practice,* ed. Clayton Koelb and Susan Noakes. Ithaca, N.Y.: Cornell University Press, 1988. 93–116.

Fine, Elsa H. *Women Artists: An Illuminated History*. 3rd ed. New York: Abbeville Press Publishers, 1997.

Finsten, Jill. *Isaac Oliver: Art at the Courts of Elizabeth I and James I*. New York: Garland Publishing, 1981.

Fisher, Will. *Materializing Gender in Early Modern English Literature and Culture*. Cambridge: Cambridge University Press, 2006.

Fleming, Juliet. *Graffiti and the Writing Arts of Early Modern England*. London: Reaktion Books, 2001.

———. "Graffiti, Grammatology, and the Age of Shakespeare." In *Renaissance Culture and the Everyday,* ed. Patricia Fumerton and Simon Hunt. Philadelphia: University of Pennsylvania Press, 1999. 315–51.

Foister, Susan. *Holbein and England.* New Haven, Conn.: Yale University Press, 2004.

———. "Tudor Miniaturists at the V&A." *Burlington Magazine* 125 (1976): 635–36.

Forster, Kurt W. "Introduction." In Aby Warburg, *The Renewal of Pagan Antiquity: Contributions to the Cultural History of the European Renaissance.* Trans. David Britt. Los Angeles: Getty Research Institute, 1999. 1–75.

Franits, Wayne E. *Paragons of Virtue: Women and Domesticity in Seventeenth-Century Dutch Art.* Cambridge: Cambridge University Press, 1993.

Franke, Bergit. *Assurerus und Esther am Burgunderhof: Zur Reception des Buches Esther in den Niederlanden (1450 bis 1530).* Berlin: Gebr. Mann Verlag, 1998.

Fraser, Antonia. *Mary Queen of Scots.* 1971. Reprint. New York: Dell, 1972.

Friedman, Alice T. "Architecture, Authority, and the Female Gaze: Planning and Representation in the Early Modern Country House." *Assemblage* 18 (August 1992): 40–61.

Frye, Susan. *Elizabeth I: The Competition for Representation.* New York: Oxford University Press, 1993.

———. "Elizabeth When a Princess: Early Self-representations in a Portrait and a Letter." In *The Body of the Queen: Gender and Rule in the Courtly World, 1500–2000,* ed. Regina Schulte. New York: Berghahn Books, 2006. 43–60.

———. "Materializing Authorship in Esther Inglis's Books." *Journal of Medieval and Early Modern Studies* 32:3 (fall 2002): 469–92.

———. "Sewing Connections: Elizabeth Tudor, Mary Stuart, Elizabeth Talbot, and Seventeenth-Century Anonymous Needleworkers." In *Maids and Mistresses, Cousins and Queens: Women's Alliances in Early Modern England*, ed. Susan Frye and Karen Robertson. New York: Oxford University Press, 1999. 165–82.

———. "Staging Women's Relations to Textiles in *Othello* and *Cymbeline*." In *Early Modern Visual Culture: Representation, Race, and Empire in Renaissance England*, ed. Peter Erickson and Clark Hulse. Philadelphia: University of Pennsylvania Press, 2000. 215–250.

Frye, Susan, and Karen Robertson, eds. *Maids and Mistresses, Cousins and Queens: Women's Alliances in Early Modern England.* New York: Oxford University Press, 1999.

Fumerton, Patricia. *Cultural Aesthetics: Renaissance Literature and the Practice of Social Ornament.* Chicago: University of Chicago Press, 1991.

———. "Introduction: A New New Historicism." In *Renaissance Culture and the Everyday,* ed. Patricia Fumerton and Simon Hunt. Philadelphia: University of Pennsylvania Press, 1999. 1–17.

Fumerton, Patricia, and Simon Hunt, ed. *Renaissance Culture and the Everyday.* Philadelphia: University of Pennsylvania Press, 1999.

Gallagher, Catherine. "Embracing the Absolute: The Politics of the Female Subject in Seventeenth-Century England." *Genders* 1 (spring 1988): 24–39.

Gallagher, Lowell. *Medusa's Gaze: Casuistry and Conscience in the Renaissance.* Stanford, Calif.: Stanford University Press, 1991.

Garrard, Mary D. *Artemisia Gentileschi: The Image of the Female Hero in Italian Baroque Art.* Princeton, N.J.: Princeton University Press, 1989.

Gaudio, Joanne. "A Message in Tent Stitch and a Reply: The Politics of Mary, Queen of Scots, and Elizabeth I of England." *Piecework* 9:5 (September/October 2001): 36–40.

Geuter, Ruth. "Embroidered Biblical Narratives and Their Social Context." In *English Embroidery from the Metropolitan Museum of Art, 1580–1700,* ed. Andrew Morrall and Melinda Watt. New York: Bard Graduate Center, 2008. 57–78.

Gibson, J. Westby. "Manuscript Illustrations of Timothy Bright's Shorthand." *The Shorthand Society* (London) 2 (May, 1884): 132.

Girouard, Mark. *Hardwick Hall.* 1989. Reprint. London: National Trust, 1992.

———. *Robert Smythson and the Elizabethan Country House.* 2nd ed. Reprint. New Haven, Conn.: Yale University Press, 1985.

Globe, Alexander. *Peter Stent, London Printseller circa 1642–1665.* Vancouver: University of British Columbia Press, 1985.

Goldberg, Jonathan. *Desiring Women Writing: English Renaissance Examples.* Stanford, Calif.: Stanford University Press, 1997.

———. "The Female Pen: Writing as a Woman." In *Language Machines: Technologies of Literary and Cultural Production,* ed. Jeffrey Masten, Peter Stallybrass, and Nancy Vickers. New York: Routledge, 1997. 17–38.

———. *Writing Matter: From the Hands of the English Renaissance.* Stanford, Calif.: Stanford University Press, 1990.

The Goodhard Samplers: 300 Years of Embroidered Samplers—A Superb Collection 26 October–30 November 1985. Swansea: Glynn Vivian Art Gallery, 1985.

Gossett, Suzanne. "Resistant Mothers and Hidden Children." In *Pilgrimage for Love: Essays in Honor of Josephine A. Roberts,* ed. Sigrid King. Tempe: Arizona Center for Medieval and Renaissance Studies, 1999. 191–207.

Gossett, Suzanne, and Janel Mueller. "Textual Introduction." In Lady Mary Wroth, *The Second Part of the Countess of Montgomery's Urania,* ed. Josephine A. Roberts, Suzanne Gossett, and Janel Mueller. Tempe, Ariz.: Renaissance English Text Society, 1999. xvii–xliv.

Green, Juana. "The Sempter's Wares: Merchandising and Marrying in *The Fair Maid of the Exchange* (1607)." *Renaissance Quarterly* 53:4 (winter 2000): 1084–118.

Greenblatt, Stephen. *Renaissance Self-fashioning from More to Shakespeare.* Chicago: University of Chicago Press, 1980.

Grennan, Eamon. "The Women's Voices in *Othello*: Speech, Song, Silence." *Shakespeare Quarterly* 38:3 (autumn 1987): 275–92.

Griffiths, Antony. *The Print in Stuart Britain 1603–1689.* London: British Museum Press, 1998.

Grossman, Marshall, ed. *Amelia Lanyer: Gender, Genre, and the Canon.* Lexington: University Press of Kentucky, 1998.

Guy, John. *Queen of Scots: The True Life of Mary Stuart.* New York: Houghton Mifflin, 2004.

Hackel, Heidi Brayman. *Reading Material in Early Modern England*: *Print, Gender, and Literacy.* Cambridge: Cambridge University Press, 2005.

———. "Rhetorics and Practices of Illiteracy or The Marketing of Illiteracy." In *Reading and Literacy in the Middle Ages and Renaissance,* ed. Ian Frederick Moulton. Turnhout, Belgium: Brepols Publishers, 2004. 169–83.

Hackett, Helen. "Lady Mary Wroth's *Urania* and the 'Femininity' of Romance." In *Early Modern Women Writers: 1600–1720,* ed. Anita Pacheco. London: Longman, 1998.

———. *Women and Romance Fiction in the English Renaissance.* Cambridge: Cambridge University Press, 2000.

Hall, Kim. "Culinary Spaces, Colonial Spaces: The Gendering of Sugar in the Seventeenth Century." In *Feminist Readings of Early Modern Culture: Emerging Subjects,* ed. Valerie Traub, M. Lindsay Kaplan, and Dympna Callaghan. Cambridge: Cambridge University Press, 1996. 168–90.

Hannay, Margaret P. "The Countess of Pembroke's Agency in Print and Scribal Culture." In *Women's Writing and the Circulation of Ideas,* ed. George L. Justice and Nathan Tinker. Cambridge: Cambridge University Press, 2002. 17–49.

———. "'High Housewifery': The Duties and Letters of Barbara Gamage Sidney, Countess of Leicester." *Early Modern Women* 1 (2006): 7–35.

———. *Philip's Phoenix: Mary Sidney, Countess of Pembroke.* New York: Oxford University Press, 1990.

———. "'So May I with the *Psalmist* Truly Say': Early Modern Englishwomen's Psalm Discourse." In *Write or Be Written: Early Modern Women Poets and Cultural Constraints,* ed. Barbara Smith and Ursula Appelt. Aldershot: Ashgate, 2001. 105–34.

———. "'Your vertuous and learned Aunt': The Countess of Pembroke as a Mentor to Mary Wroth." In *Reading Mary Wroth: Representing Alternatives in Early Modern England,* ed. Naomi J. Miller and Gary Waller. Knoxville: University of Tennessee Press, 1991. 15–34.

Hanson-Smith, Christopher. *The Flemish Bond: East Anglia and the Netherlands—Close and Ancient Neighbors.* Diss, Norfolk: Groundnut Publishing, 2004.

Harris, Ann Sutherland, and Linda Nochlin, eds. *Women Artists 1550–1950.* New York: Alfred A. Knopf, 1977.

Harte, N. B. "The Economics of Clothing in the Late Seventeenth Century." *Textile History* 22:2 (1991): 277–96.

Harvey, Tamara. "'Now Sisters . . . Impart Your Usefulnesse, and Force': Anne Bradstreet's Feminist Functionalism in *The Tenth Muse* (1650)." *Early American Literature* 35:1 (2000): 5–28.

Hay, Millicent V. *The Life of Robert Sidney, Earl of Leicester (1563–1626).* Washington, D.C.: Folger Shakespeare Library, 1984.

Haynes, Alan. *Invisible Power: The Elizabethan Secret Services 1570–1603.* Wolfeboro Falls, N.H.: Alan Sutton Publishing, 1992.

Hayward, Maria. *Dress at the Court of King Henry VIII.* Leeds: Maney Publishing, 2007.

Hearn, Karen, ed. *Dynasties: Painting in Tudor and Jacobean England.* Peterborough: Tate, 1995.

———. *Marcus Gheeraerts II: Elizabethan Artist in Focus.* London: Tate Publishing, 2002.

Hedges, Elaine. "The Needle or the Pen: The Literary Rediscovery of Women's Textile Work." In *Tradition and the Talents of Women,* ed. Florence Howe. Urbana: University of Illinois Press, 1991. 338–64.

Heninger, S. K. "Speaking Pictures: Sidney's Rapprochement Between Poetry and Painting." In *Sir Philip Sidney and the Interpretation of Renaissance Culture,* ed. Gary F. Waller and Michael D. Moore. London: Croom Helm, 1984. 3–16.

Henry, John. *Illuminated Manuscripts in Classical and Medieval Times.* Cambridge: Cambridge University Press, 1892.

Herman, Peter C. "'mes subjectz, mon ame assubjectie': The Problematic (of) Subjectivity in Mary Stuart's Sonnets." In *The Poetry of Henry VIII, Mary Stuart, Elizabeth I, and James VI/I,* ed. Peter C. Herman. Tempe: Arizona Center for Medieval and Renaissance Studies, 2002. 51–78.

Hind, A. M. *Engraving in England in the Sixteenth and Seventeenth Centuries: A Descriptive Catalogue with Introductions.* 3 vols. Cambridge: Cambridge University Press, 1952–64.

Hodgdon, Barbara. *The Shakespeare Trade: Performances and Appropriations.* Philadelphia: University of Pennsylvania Press, 1998.

Hodges, Laura F. *Chaucer and Clothing: Clerical and Academic Costume in the General Prologue to The Canterbury Tales.* Cambridge: D. S. Brewer, 2005.

hooks, bell. *Art on My Mind: Visual Politics.* New York: New Press, 1995.

Hulse, Clark. *The Rule of Art: Literature and Painting in the Renaissance.* Chicago: University of Chicago Press, 1990.

Humphrey, Carol. *Samplers.* Cambridge: Cambridge University Press, 1997.

James, Susan. *Kateryn Parr: The Making of a Queen*. Aldershot: Ashgate, 1999.

Jones, Ann Rosalind. "Counterattacks on 'the Bayter of Women': Three Pamphleteers of the Early Seventeenth Century." In *The Renaissance Woman in Print: Counterbalancing the Canon,* ed. Anne Haselkorn and Betty Travitsky. Amherst: University of Massachusetts Press, 1990. 45–62.

———. "Dematerializations: Textile and Textual Properties in Ovid, Sandys, and Spenser." In *Subject and Object in Renaissance Culture,* ed. Margreta de Grazia, Maureen Quilligan, and Peter Stallybrass. Cambridge: Cambridge University Press, 1996. 189–212.

———. "Needle, Scepter, Sovereignty: The Queen of Sheba in Englishwomen's Amateur Needlework." *Early Modern Culture.* Vol. 2. http://emc.eserver.org/1–3/jones.html.

Jones, Ann Rosalind, and Peter Stallybrass. *Renaissance Clothing and the Materials of Memory.* Cambridge: Cambridge University Press, 2000.

Jordan, W.K. *Edward VI: The Young King: The Protectorship of the Duke of Somerset*. Cambridge: Harvard University Press, 1968.

Kalas, Rayna. *Frame, Glass, Verse: The Technology of Poetic Invention in the English Renaissance.* Ithaca, N.Y.: Cornell University Press, 2007.

Karrer, Wolfgang. "Gertrude Stein's Poetry: From Cubism to Embroidery, 1914–1933." In *Poetry and the Fine Arts: Papers from the Poetry Sessions of the European Association for American Studies Biennial Conference, Rome 1984,* ed. Roland Hagenbüchle and Jaqueline S. Ollier. Regensburg: Pustet, 1989. 124–37.

Keeble, N. H. *The Literary Culture of Nonconformity in Later Seventeenth-Century England.* Athens: University of Georgia Press, 1987.

Kennedy, Gwynne. *Just Anger: Representing Women's Anger in Early Modern England.* Carbondale: Southern Illinois University Press, 2000.

Kerlogue, Fiona. "The Early English Textile Trade in South-East Asia: The East India Company Factory and the Textile Trade in Jambi, Sumatra, 1615–1682." *Textile History* 28:2 (1997): 149–60.

King, Donald, and Santina Levey. *The Victoria and Albert's Textile Collection: Embroidery in Britain from 1200 to 1750.* London: Victoria and Albert Museum, 1995.

King, John N. "Patronage and Piety: The Influence of Catherine Parr." In *Silent But for the Word: Tudor Women as Patrons, Translators and Writers of Religious Works,* ed. Margaret Hannay. Kent, Ohio: Kent State University Press, 1985. 43–60.

King, Kathryn R. "Of Needles and Pens and Women's Work." *Tulsa Studies in Women's Literature* 14:1 (spring 1995): 77–93.

Knoppers, Lunger. "Opening the Queen's Closet: Henrietta Maria, Elizabeth Cromwell, and the Politics of Cookery." *Renaissance Quarterly* 60:2 (summer 2007): 464–99.

Klein, Lisa M. "Your Humble Handmaid: Elizabethan Gifts of Needlework." *Renaissance Quarterly* 50:2 (summer 1997): 459–93.

Kowaleski-Wallace, Elizabeth. *Consuming Subjects: Women, Shopping, and Business in the Eighteenth Century.* New York: Columbia University Press, 1996.

Kraner, Werner. "Zür Englischen Kurzschrift in Zeitalter Shakespeares: Das Jane-Seager Manusckript. (The Divine Prophecies of the Ten Sibyls)." *Shakespeare-Jahrbuch* 67 (1931): 26–61.

Laing, David. "Notes Relating to Mrs Esther (Langlois or) Inglis, the Celebrated Calligraphist." *Proceedings of the Antiquaries of Scotland* 6 (1865): 284–309.

Lamb, Mary Ellen. "The Biopolitics of Romance in Mary Wroth's *The Countess of Montgomery's Urania*." *English Literary Renaissance* 31:1 (2001): 107–30.

———. *Gender and Authorship in the Sidney Circle.* Madison: University of Wisconsin Press, 1990.

———. "Wroth, Lady Mary (1587?–1651/53)." *Oxford Dictionary of National Biography,* ed. H. C. G. Matthew and Brian Harrison. Oxford: Oxford University Press, 2004. Online edition. Ed. Lawrence Goldman. http://www.oxforddnb.com/view/article/30082.

Lamb, Mary Ellen, and Valerie Wayne. "Introduction." In *Staging Early Modern Romance, Prose Fiction, Dramatic Romance, and Shakespeare.* London: Routledge, 2008. 1–20.

Lamb, Mary Ellen and Valerie Wayned, eds. *Staging Early Modern Romance, Prose Fiction, Dramatic Romance, and Shakespeare.* London: Routledge, 2008.

Lavold, Elsebeth. *Viking Patterns for Knitting.* Trans. Robin Orm Hansen. 1998. Reprint. North Pomfret, Vt.: Trafalgar Square Books, 2000.

Lemire, Beverly. *Fashion's Favourite: The Cotton Trade and the Consumer in Britain 1660–1800.* Oxford: Oxford University Press, 1991.

———. "Peddling Fashion: Salesmen, Pawnbrokers, Taylors, Thieves and the Second-hand Clothes Trade in England, c. 1700–1800." *Textile History* 22:1 (1991): 67–82.

Lerner, Gerda. *The Creation of Feminist Consciousness from the Middle Ages to Eighteen-seventy.* Oxford: Oxford University Press, 1993.

Levey, Santina M. *The Embroideries at Hardwick Hall: A Catalogue.* 2007. Reprint. London: National Trust, 2008.

———. *Elizabethan Treasures: The Hardwick Hall Textiles.* London: National Trust Enterprises, 1998.

———. "References to Dress in the Earliest Account Book of Bess of Hardwick." *Costume* 34 (2000): 13–24.

Levin, Carole. *The Heart and Stomach of a King: Elizabeth I and the Politics of Sex and Power.* Philadelphia: University of Pennsylvania Press, 1994.

———. "'Would I Could Give You Help and Succour': Elizabeth I and the Politics of Touch." *Albion* 21 (1989): 191–205.

Levin, Carole, et al., eds. *Extraordinary Women of the Medieval and Renaissance World: A Biographical Dictionary.* Westport, Conn.: Greenwood Press, 2000.

Lewalski, Barbara Kiefer. "Old Renaissance Canons, New Women's Texts: Some Jacobean Examples." *Proceedings of the American Philosophical Society* 138:3 (1994): 397–406.

Lewis, Jayne, ed. *The Trial of Mary Queen of Scots: A Brief History with Documents.* Boston: Bedford/St. Martin's, 1999.

Linton, Joan Pong. *The Romance of the New World.* Cambridge: Cambridge University Press, 1998.

Loades, David. *Elizabeth I.* London: Hambledon and London, 2003.

Love, Harold. *Scribal Publication in Seventeenth-Century England.* London: Oxford University Press, 1993.

Lovell, Mary S. *Bess of Hardwick: Empire Builder.* London: W. W. Norton, 2005.

Lynch, Michael. "Introduction." In *Mary Stewart: Queen in Three Kingdoms,* ed. Michael Lynch. Oxford: Basil Blackwell, 1988. 1–29.

MacCaffrey, Wallace T. "Sidney, Sir Henry (1529–1586)." *Oxford Dictionary of National Biography,* ed. H. C. G. Matthew and Brian Harrison. Oxford: Oxford University Press, 2004. Online edition. Ed. Lawrence Goldman. http://www.oxforddnb.com/view/article/25520.

McElrath, Joseph R., Jr., and Allan P. Robb. "Introduction." *The Complete Works of Anne Bradstreet.* Boston: Twayne Publishers, 1981.

Macfarlane, Leslie. "The Book of Hours of James IV and Margaret Tudor." *Innes Review* 11 (1960): 3–20.

MacIntyre, Jean. *Costumes and Scripts in the Elizabethan Theatres.* Edmonton: University of Alberta Press, 1992.

Macmillan, Duncan. *Scottish Art 1460–2000.* 1990. Reprint. Edinburgh: Mainstream Publishing, 2000.

Malay, Jessica L. "Jane Seager's Maidenly Negotiation Through Elizabethan Gift Exchange." *English Literary Renaissance* 36:2 (April 2006): 173–88.

Malcomson, Christina. "Christine de Pizan's City of Ladies in Early Modern England." In *Debating Gender in Early Modern England, 1500–1700,* ed. Christina Malcomson and Mihoko Suzuki. New York: Palgrave Macmillan, 2002. 15–35.

Mann, J. de L. *The Cloth Industry in the West of England from 1640 to 1880.* Oxford: Clarendon Press, 1971.

Marotti, Arthur F. *Manuscript, Print, and the English Renaissance Lyric.* Ithaca, N.Y.: Cornell University Press, 1995.

Marx, Karl. *Grundrisse.* Trans. Martin Nocolaus. Harmondsworth: Penguin Books, 1973.

Maslen, R. W. *Elizabethan Fictions: Espionage, Counter-Espionage, and the Duplicity of Fiction in Early Elizabethan Prose Narratives.* Oxford: Clarendon Press, 1997.

Matchinske, Megan. "Holy Hatred: Formations of the Gendered Subject in English Apocalyptic Writing, 1625–1651." *ELH* 60:2 (summer 1993): 349–77.

Mauss, Marcel. *The Gift.* Trans. W. D. Halls. 1950. Reprint. New York: W. W. Norton, 1990.

May, Stephen W. *The Elizabethan Courtier Poets: The Poems and Their Contexts.* Columbia: University of Missouri Press, 1991.

Mendelson, Sara, and Patricia Crawford. *Women in Early Modern England 1550–1720.* Oxford: Clarendon Press, 1998.

Mentz, Steve. *Romance for Sale.* Aldershot: Ashgate, 2006.

Merleau-Ponty, Maurice. *Phenomenology of Perception.* Trans. Colin Smith. 1962. Reprint. London: Routledge, 1992.

———. *The Visible and the Invisible.* Trans. Alphonso Lingis. Evanston, Ill.: Northwestern University Press, 1968.

Merriman, Marcus. *The Rough Wooings: Mary Queen of Scots, 1542–1551.* East Linton: Tuckwell, 2000.

Merton, Charlotte Isabelle. "The Women Who Served Queen Mary and Queen Elizabeth: Ladies, Gentlewomen and Maids of the Privy Chamber, 1553–1603." Ph.D. diss., Cambridge University, 1992.

Miller, Naomi J., and Gary Waller, ed. *Reading Mary Wroth: Representing Alternatives in Early Modern England.* Knoxville: University of Tennessee Press, 1991.

Millett, Kate. *Sexual Politics.* New York: Doubleday, 1970.

Montrose, Louis Adrian. "'Eliza, Queen of Shepheardes,' and the Pastoral of Power." *English Literary Renaissance* 10 (1980): 153–82.

———. "The Elizabethan Subject and the Spenserian Text." In *Literary Theory/Renaissance Texts,* ed. Patricia Parker and David Quint. Baltimore: Johns Hopkins University Press, 1986. 303–40.

———. *The Subject of Elizabeth: Authority, Gender, and Representation.* Chicago: University of Chicago Press, 2006.

Morrall, Andrew, and Melinda Watt, eds. *English Embroidery from the Metropolitan Museum of Art, 1580–1700: 'Twixt Art and Nature.* New York: Bard Graduate Center, 2008.

Mueller, Janel. "Devotion as Difference: Intertextuality in Queen Katherine Parr's *Prayers and Meditations* (1545)." *Huntingdon Library Quarterly* 53 (1990): 171–97.

Munroe, Jennifer. "'In This Strang Labourinth, How Shall I Turne?': Needlework, Gardens, and Writing in Mary Wroth's *Pamphilia to Amphilanthus.*" *Tulsa Studies in Women's Literature* 24:1 (2005): 35–55.

Names Project Foundation. http://www.aidsquilt.org/history.html.

Neill, Michael. "Unproper Beds: Race, Adultery, and the Hideous in *Othello.*" *Shakespeare Quarterly* 40:4 (winter 1989): 383–412.

Nevinson, John L. "Embroidered by Queen and Countess." *Country Life* 22 (January 1976): 194–96.

———. "English Domestic Embroidery Patterns of the Sixteenth and Seventeenth Centuries." *Walpole Society* 28 (1939–40): 1–13.

———. "Peter Stent and John Overton, Publishers of Embroidery Designs." *Apollo* 24:143 (November 1936): 279–83.

Newcomb, Lori. *Reading Popular Romance in Early Modern England*. New York: Columbia University Press, 2002.

Nicholas, Jane. *Stumpwork Embroidery*. 1995. Reprint. Burra Creek, Australia: Sally Milner Publishing, 1996.

Norris, Herbert. *Tudor Costume and Fashion*. 1938. Reprint. Mineola, N.Y.: Dover Publications, 1997.

O'Malley, Susan Gushee. *"Custome Is an Idiot": Jacobean Pamphlet Literature on Women*. Urbana: University of Illinois Press, 2004.

Orgel, Stephen. *Impersonations: The Performance of Gender in Shakespeare's England*. Cambridge: Cambridge University Press, 1996.

Orlin, Lena Cowen. *Locating Privacy in Tudor London*. New York: Oxford University Press, 2008.

———. "Three Ways to be Invisible in the Renaissance: Sex, Reputation, and Stitchery." In *Renaissance Culture and the Everyday*, ed. Patricia Fumerton and Simon Hunt. Philadelphia: University of Pennsylvania Press, 1999. 183–203.

———. "Working the Early Modern Archive: The Search for Lady Ingram." *Literature Compass* 4:3 (2007): 737–50. 10.1111/j.174104113.2007.00425.x.

Overton, Mark, Jane Whittle, Darron Dean, and Andrew Hann. *Production and Consumption in English Households, 1600–1750*. London: Routledge, 2004.

Parker, Patricia. *Literary Fat Ladies: Rhetoric, Gender, Property*. New York: Methuen, 1987.

Parker, Rozsika. *The Subversive Stitch: Embroidery and the Making of the Feminine*. New York: Routledge, 1984.

Peacock, Martha M. "Geertruydt Roghman and the Female Perspective in Seventeenth-Century Dutch Genre Imagery." *Woman's Art Journal* 14:2 (1993): 3–10.

Pearson, Andrea. "Introduction." In *Women and Portraits in Early Modern England: Gender, Agency, Identity*, ed. Andrea Pearson. Aldershot: Ashgate, 2008. 1–14.

Penny, Nicholas. "Toothpicks and Green Hangings." *Renaissance Studies* 19:5 (November 2005): 581–90.

Perlingieri, Ilya Sandra. *Sofonisba Anguissola: The First Great Woman Artist of the Renaissance*. New York: Rizzoli International Publications, 1992.

Perry, Gillian. *Gender and Art*. New Haven, Conn.: Yale University Press, 1999.

Phillippy, Patricia. *Painting Women: Cosmetics, Canvases, and Early Modern Culture*. Baltimore: Johns Hopkins University Press, 2006.

Phillips, J. E. *Images of a Queen: Mary Stuart in Sixteenth-Century Literature*. Berkeley: University of California Press, 1964.

Piper, David. "The 1590 Lumley Inventory: Hilliard, Segar and the Earl of Essex–II." *Burlington Magazine* 99:654 (September 1957): 298–301.

Plath, Sylvia. *The Collected Poems: Sylvia Plath*. Ed. Ted Hughes. New York: Harper & Row, 1981.

Pollock, Griselda. *Vision and Difference: Femininity, Feminism, and Histories of Art*. New York: Routledge, 1988.

Pollock, Linda. *With Faith and Physic: The Life of a Tudor Gentlewoman Lady Grace Mildmay*. London: Collins & Brown Limited, 1993.

Prather-Moses, Alice, ed. *The International Dictionary of Women Workers in the Decorative Arts: A Historical Survey from the Distant Past to the Early Decades of the Twentieth Century*. Metuchen, N.J.: Scarecrow Press, 1981.

Prentice, Dinah. "Sewn Constructions." In *New Feminist Art Criticism: Critical Strategies*, ed. Katy Deepwell. Manchester: Manchester University Press, 1995. 182–87.

Prescott, Anne Lake. "The Pearl of the Valois and Elizabeth I: Marguerite de Navarre's Miroir and Tudor England." In *Silent But for the Word: Tudor Women as Patrons, Translators, and Writers of Religious Works*, ed. Margaret P. Hannay. Kent, Ohio: Kent State University Press, 1985. 61–76.

Purkiss, Diane. "Invasions: Prophecy and Bewitchment in the Case of Margaret Muschamp." *Tulsa Studies in Women's Literature* 17:2 (fall 1998): 235–53.

———. "Material Girls: The Seventeenth-Century Woman Debate." In *Women, Texts and Histories 1575–1760*, ed. Clare Brant and Diane Purkiss. London: Routledge, 1992. 69–101.

Quilligan, Maureen. *The Allegory of Female Authority: Christine de Pizan's Cité des Dames*. Ithaca, N.Y.: Cornell University Press, 1991.

———. "Elizabeth's Embroidery." *Shakespeare Studies* 28 (2000): 208–14.

———. *Incest and Agency in Elizabeth's England*. Philadelphia: University of Pennsylvania Press, 2005.

Radner, Joan Newton. *Feminist Messages: Coding in Women's Folk Culture*. Urbana: University of Illinois Press, 1993.

Rappaport, Steve. *Worlds Within Worlds: Structures of Life in Sixteenth-Century London*. Cambridge: Cambridge University Press, 1989.

Ribeiro, Aileen. *Fashion and Fiction: Dress in Art and Literature in Stuart England*. New Haven: Yale University Press, 2005.

Richardson, Catherine. *Clothing Culture*. Aldershot: Ashgate, 2004.

Richardson, Walter C. *Mary Tudor: The White Queen*. Seattle: University of Washington Press, 1970.

Rigolot, François. "The Renaissance Crisis of Exemplarity." *Journal of the History of Ideas* 59: 4 (October 1998): 557–63.

Roberts, Jane. *Royal Artists from Mary Queen of Scots to the Present Day*. London: Grafton Books, 1987.

Roberts, Josephine. "Deciphering Women's Pastoral." In *Representing Women in Renaissance England*, ed. Claude J. Summers and Ted-Larry Pebworth. Columbia: University of Missouri Press, 1997. 163–74.

———. "Introduction." Lady Mary Wroth. *The First Part of the Countess of Montgomery's Urania*, ed. Josephine Roberts. Binghamton, N.Y.: Medieval and Renaissance Texts & Studies, 1995. xv–cxx.

Robertson, Clare. "*Phoenix Romanus*: Rome, 1534–1565." In *Artistic Centers of the Italian Renaissance: Rome*, ed. Marcia B. Hall. Cambridge: Cambridge University Press, 2005. 184–245.

Robertson, Karen, and J.-A. George. "Introduction." In *Horestes*, ed. Karen Robertson and J.-A. George. Dublin: Galway University Press, 1996. 1–31.

Robinson, Brian. *The Royal Maundy*. London: Kaye & Ward, 1977.

Rosenthal, Joel. *The Purchase of Paradise: Gift Giving and the Aristocracy, 1307–1485*. London: Routledge & Kegan Paul, 1972.

Ross, Doran H. *Wrapped in Pride: Ghanaian Kente and African American Identity*. Los Angeles: UCLA Fowler Museum of Cultural History, 1998.

Rowlands, John. *The Age of Dürer and Holbein: German Drawings 1400–1550*. Cambridge: Cambridge University Press, 1988.

Ryan, Lawrence V. *Roger Ascham*. Stanford, Calif.: Stanford University Press, 1963.

Schama, Simon. *The Embarrassment of Riches: An Interpretation of Dutch Culture in the Golden Age*. New York: Knopf, 1987.

Schneider, Jane, and Annette B. Weiner. "Introduction." In *Cloth and Human Experience*, ed. Annette B. Weiner and Jane Schneider. Washington, D.C.: Smithsonian Institution Press, 1989. 1–27.

Scott-Elliot, A. H., and Elspeth Yeo. "Calligraphic Manuscripts of Esther Inglis (1571–1624): A Catalogue." *The Papers of the Bibliographic Society of America* 84 (March 1990): 10–86.

Seelig, Sharon Cadmun. "'To all vertuous Ladies in generall': Aemilia Lanyer's Community of Strong Women." In *Literary Circles and Cultural Communities in Renaissance England*, ed. Claude J. Summers and Ted-Larry Pebworth. Columbia: University of Missouri Press, 2000. 44–58.

Shammas, Carole. *The Pre-Industrial Consumer in England and America*. Oxford: Clarendon Press, 1990.

Shell, Marc. *Elizabeth's Glass*. Lincoln: University of Nebraska Press, 1993.

Simon, Joan. *Education and Society in Tudor England*. Cambridge: Cambridge University Press, 1967. 107–14.

Simonds, Peggy Muñoz. *Myth, Emblem, and Music in Shakespeare's* Cymbeline: *An Iconographic Reconstruction*. Newark: University of Delaware Press, 1992. 95–134.

Singh, Simon. *The Code Book: The Evolution of Secrecy from Mary Queen of Scots to Quantum Cryptography*. New York: Doubleday, 1999.

Smailes, Helen, and Duncan Thomson. *The Queen's Image: A Celebration of Mary Queen of Scots*. Edinburgh: Scottish National Portrait Gallery, 1987.

Smith, Bruce. *The Acoustic World of Early Modern England*. Chicago: University of Chicago Press, 1999.

———. "Forum: Body Work, Introduction." *Shakespeare Studies* 29 (2001): 19–26.

Smith, Catherine F. "Jane Lead's Wisdom: Women and Prophecy in Seventeenth-Century England." In *Poetic Prophecy in Western Literature*, ed. Jan Wojcik and Raymond Jean Frontain. Teaneck, N.J.: Fairleigh Dickinson University Press, 1984. 55–63.

Smith, David R. "Irony and Civility: Notes on the Convergence of Genre and Portraiture in Seventeenth-Century Dutch Painting." *Art Bulletin* 69:3 (1987): 407–30.

Snook, Edith. *Women, Reading, and the Cultural Politics of Early Modern England*. Aldershot: Ashgate, 2005.

Snow, Edward. "Sexual Anxiety and the Male Order of Things in *Othello*." *English Literary Renaissance* 10 (1980): 384–412.

Spence, Richard T. *Lady Anne Clifford Countess of Pembroke, Dorset and Montgomery (1590–1676)*. Frome, Somerset: Sutton Publishing, 1997.

Staples, Kathleen. "Embroidered Furnishings." In *English Embroidery from the Metropolitan Museum of Art, 1580–1700: 'Twixt Art and Nature*, ed. Andrew Morrall and Melinda Watt. New York: Bard Graduate Center, 2008. 23–38.

Stallybrass, Peter. "Material Culture: Introduction." *Shakespeare Studies*. 28 (2000): 123–29.

———. "Patriarchal Territories: The Body Enclosed." In *Rewriting the Renaissance: The Discourses of Sexual Difference in Early Modern Europe*, ed. Margaret W. Ferguson, Maureen Quilligan, and Nancy J. Vickers. Chicago: University of Chicago Press, 1986. 123–42.

———. "Worn Worlds: Clothes, Mourning, and the Life of Things." *Yale Review* 81:2 (1993): 35–50.

———. "Worn Worlds: Clothes and Identity on the Renaissance Stage." In *Subject and Object in Renaissance Culture*, ed. Margreta de Grazia, Maureen Quilligan, and Peter Stallybrass. Cambridge: Cambridge University Press, 1996. 289–320.

Stallybrass, Peter, Roger Chartier, Franklin Mowery, and Heather Wolfe. "Hamlet's Tables and the Technologies of Writing in Renaissance England." *Shakespeare Quarterly* 55:4 (winter 2004): 379–419.

Starkey, David. *Elizabeth: The Struggle for the Throne.* 2000. Reprint. New York: HarperCollins, 2001.

Steen, Sara Jayne. "Introduction." In *The Letters of Arbella Stuart*, ed. Sara Jayne Steen. New York: Oxford University Press, 1994. 1–105.

Stein, Gertrude. *How to Write.* 1931. Reprint. New York: Dover Publications, 1975.

Stierle, Karlheinz. "Three Moments in the Crisis of Exemplarity: Boccaccio-Petrarch, Montaigne, and Cervantes." *Journal of the History of Ideas* 59:4 (October 1998): 581–95.

Stewart, Alan. "The Early Modern Closet Discovered." *Representations* 50 (spring 1995): 76–100.

———. *Philip Sidney: A Double Life.* New York: St. Martin's Press, 2000.

Stocker, Margarita. *Judith, Sexual Warrior: Women and Power in Western Culture.* New Haven, Conn.: Yale University Press, 1998.

Stone-Ferrier, Linda. "Spun Virtue, the Lacework of Folly, and World Wound Upside-Down: Seventeenth-Century Dutch Depictions of Female Handwork." In *Cloth and Human Experience*, ed. Annette B. Weiner and Jane Schneider. Washington, D.C.: Smithsonian Institution Press, 1989. 215–42.

Straznicky, Marta. "Restoration Women Playwrights and the Limits of Professionalism." *ELH* 64 (1997): 703–26.

Strong, Roy. *Artists of the Tudor Court: The Portrait Miniature Rediscovered 1520–1620.* London: Victoria and Albert Museum, 1983.

———. *The Cult of Elizabeth: Elizabethan Portraiture and Pageantry.* London: Thames and Hudson, 1977.

———. *The English Icon: Elizabethan and Jacobean Portraiture.* London: Routledge, 1969.

———. *The English Renaissance Miniature.* London: Thames and Hudson, 1983.

———. "Introduction." *600 Years of British Painting: The Berger Collection at the Denver Art Museum.* Denver, Colo.: Denver Art Museum, 1998.

———. *Portraits of Queen Elizabeth I.* Oxford: Clarendon Press, 1963.

———. *Tudor and Jacobean Portraits.* London: Her Majesty's Stationers Office, 1969.

Summer, Saralynn Ellen. "Like Another Esther: Literary Representations of Queen Esther in Early Modern England." Ph.D. diss., Georgia State University, 2005.

Summit, Jennifer. *Lost Property: The Woman Writer and English Literary History, 1380–1589.* Chicago: University of Chicago Press, 2000.

———. "William Caxton, Margaret Beaufort and the Romance of Female Patronage." In *Women, the Book, and the Godly: Selected Proceedings of the St. Hilda's Conference*, ed. Lesley Smith and Jane H. M. Taylor. Woodbridge, Suffolk: D. S. Brewer, 1995. 151–65.

Swain, Margaret. *Embroidered Stuart Pictures.* Dyfed: Shire Publications Ltd., 1990.

———. *Figures on Fabric: Embroidery Design Sources and Their Application.* London: Adam & Charles Black, 1980.

———. *Historical Needlework.* London: Barrie and Jenkins, 1970.

———. *The Needlework of Mary Queen of Scots.* 1973. Reprint. Carlton, Bedford: Ruth Bean Publishers, 1986.

———. "A New Year's Gift from Princess Elizabeth." *The Connoisseur* 183:738 (August 1973): 258–66.

Synge, Lanto. *Antique Needlework.* Poole, Dorset: Blandford Press, 1982.

———. *Art of Embroidery: History of Style and Technique.* Woodbridge, England: Antique Collectors' Club, 2001.

Teague, Frances. *Bathsua Makin: Woman of Learning.* Lewisburg: Bucknell University Press, 1998.

Thomson, W.G. *Tapestry Weaving in England from the Earliest Times to the End of the Eighteenth Century.* London: B. T. Batsford, 1914.

Thornton, Peter. *Seventeenth-Century Interior Decoration in England, France and Holland.* New Haven, Conn.: Yale University Press, 1978.

Tobin, Jaqueline L., and Raymond G. Dobard. *Hidden in Plain View: The Secret Story of Quilts and the Underground Railroad.* New York: Doubleday, 1999.

Toller, Jane. *British Samplers: A Concise History.* Chichester, Sussex: Phillimore and Company, 1980.

Tomlinson, Gary. "Unlearning the Aztec *Cantares* (Preliminaries to a Postcolonial History)." In *Subject and Object in Renaissance Culture*, ed. Margreta de Grazia, Maureen Quilligan, and Peter Stallybrass. Cambridge: Cambridge University Press, 1996. 260–88.

Traub, Valerie. *The Renaissance of Lesbianism in Early Modern England.* Cambridge: Cambridge University Press, 2002.

Trill, Suzanne. "Early Modern Women's Writing in the Edinburgh Archives, c. 1550–1740: A Preliminary Checklist." In *Woman and the Feminine in Medieval and Early Modern Scottish Writing*, ed. Sarah M. Dunnigan, C. Marie Harker, and Evelyn S. Newlyn. Basingstoke: Palgrave Macmillan, 2004. 201–26.

Ulrich, Laurel. "Pens and Needles: Documents and Artifacts in Women's History." *Uncoverings: Research Papers of the American Quilt Study Group* 14 (1993): 200–207.

Veblen, Thorsten. *The Theory of the Leisure Class.* 1899. Reprint. New York: Augustus M. Kelley, 1965.

Wadsworth, Alfred P., and Julia De Lacy Mann. *The Cotton Trade and Industrial Lancashire 1600–1780.* New York: Augustus M. Kelley Publishers, 1968.

Wall, Wendy. *The Imprint of Gender: Authorship and Publication in the English Renaissance.* Ithaca, N.Y.: Cornell University Press, 1993.

———. *Staging Domesticity: Household Work and English Identity in Early Modern Drama.* Cambridge: Cambridge University Press, 2002.

Waller, Gary. *The Sidney Family Romance: Mary Wroth, William Herbert, and the Early Modern Construction of Gender.* Detroit, Mich.: Wayne State University Press, 1993.

Walsham, Alexandra. "'A Very Deborah?': The Myth of Elizabeth I as a Providential Monarch." In *The Myth of Elizabeth*, ed. Susan Doran and Thomas S. Freeman. Basingstoke: Palgrave Macmillan, 2003. 143–68.

Warburg, Aby. *The Renewal of Pagan Antiquity: Contributions to the Cultural History of the European Renaissance.* Trans. David Britt. Los Angeles: Getty Research Institute, 1999.

———. "Sandro Botticelli's *Birth of Venus* and *Spring*: An Examination of Concepts of Antiquity in the Italian Early Renaissance (1893)." In *The Renewal of Pagan Antiquity: Contributions to the Cultural History of the European Renaissance*, trans. David Britt. Los Angeles: Getty Research Institute, 1999. 88–163.

Wardle, Patricia. "The King's Embroiderer: Edmund Harrison (1590–1667)." *Textile History* 25:1 (1994): 29–59.

———. "The King's Embroiderer: Edmund Harrison (1590–1667). Part II. His Work." *Textile History* 26:2 (1995): 139–84.

Warkentin, Germaine. "Jonson's Penshurst Reveal'd? A Penshurst Inventory of 1623." *Sidney Journal* 20 (2002): 1–25.

Warnicke, Retha. *Mary Queen of Scots.* London: Routledge, 2006.

Watkins, Susan. *Mary Queen of Scots.* London: Thames and Hudson, 2001.

Watt, Diane. "Reconstructing the Word: The Political Prophecies of Elizabeth Barton (1506–1534)." *Renaissance Quarterly* 50:1 (spring 1997): 136–63.

————. *Secretaries of God: Women Prophets in Late Medieval and Early Modern Europe*. Rochester: D. S. Brewer, 1997.

Watt, Tessa. *Cheap Print and Popular Piety 1550–1640*. Cambridge: Cambridge University Press, 1991.

Wayne, Don. *Penshurst: The Semiotics of Place and the Poetics of History*. Madison: University of Wisconsin Press, 1984.

Wayne, Valerie. "The Dearth of the Author: Anonymity's Allies and *Swetnam the Woman-hater*." In *Maids and Mistresses, Cousins and Queens: Women's Alliances in Early Modern England*, ed. Susan Frye and Karen Robertson. New York: Oxford University Press, 1999. 221–40.

————. "Historical Differences: Misogyny and *Othello*." In *The Matter of Difference: Materialist Feminist Criticism of Shakespeare*, ed. Valerie Wayne. Ithaca, N.Y.: Cornell University Press, 1991. 153–79.

————. "The Woman's Parts of *Cymbeline*," In *Staged Properties in Early Modern English Drama*, ed. Jonathan Gil Harris and Natasha Korda. Cambridge: Cambridge University Press, 2002. 153–315.

Weatherill, Lorna. *Consumer Behavior and Material Culture in Britain, 1660–1760*. London: Routledge, 1988.

Weiner, Annette B. *Inalienable Possessions: The Paradox of Keeping-While-Giving*. Berkeley: University of California Press, 1992.

Weiner, Annette B., and Jane Schneider, ed. *Cloth and Human Experience*. Washington, D.C.: Smithsonian Institution Press, 1989.

Wells-Cole, Anthony. *Art and Decoration in Elizabethan and Jacobean England: The Influence of Continental Prints, 1558–1625*. New Haven: Yale University Press, 1997.

Westermann, Mariët. *Art and Home: Dutch Interiors in the Age of Rembrandt*. Zwole, Netherlands: Waanders Publishers, 2001.

Wiesner, Merry E. *Women and Gender in Early Modern Europe*. 1993. Reprint. Cambridge: Cambridge University Press, 1995.

Wilcox, Helen, ed. *Women and Literature in Britain, 1500–1700*. Cambridge: Cambridge University Press, 1996.

Willard, Charity Canon. *Christine de Pizan: Her Life and Works, A Biography*. New York: Persea Books, 1984.

Williams, Raymond. *The Sociology of Culture*. New York: Schocken Books, 1982.

Wilson, Carol Shiner. "Understanding Cultural Contexts: The Politics of Needlework in Taylor, Barbauld, Lamb, and Wordsworth." In *Approaches to Teaching British Women Poets of the Romantic Period*, ed. Stephen C. Behrendt and Harriet Kramer Linkin. New York: Modern Language Association, 1997. 80–84.

Wing, Betty. *Girlhood Embroidery: American Samplers & Pictorial Needlework 1650–1850*. 2 vols. New York: Knopf, 1993.

Wither, Josephine. "Judy Chicago's Dinner Party." In *The Expanding Discourse: Feminism and Art History*, ed. Norma Broude and Mary D. Garrard. New York: HarperCollins, 1992. 451–65.

Wolfe, Heather. "Women's Writing in Early Modern England." *The Cambridge Companion to Women's Writing*, ed. Laura Knoppers. Cambridge: Cambridge University Press. Forthcoming.

Wolfe, Heather, ed. *Elizabeth Cary, Lady Falkland: Life and Letters*. Tempe: Arizona Center for Medieval and Renaissance Studies, 2001.

Wolfe, Jessica. *Humanism, Machinery, and Renaissance Literature*. Cambridge: Cambridge University Press, 2004.

Woodbridge, Linda. "Palisading the Elizabethan Body Politic." *Texas Studies in Literature and Language* 33:3 (fall 1991): 327–54.

———. "Patchwork: Piecing the Early Modern Mind in England's First Century of Print Culture." *English Literary Renaissance* 23:1 (1993): 5–45.

———. *Women and the English Renaissance: Literature and the Nature of Womankind, 1540–1620*. Urbana: University of Illinois Press, 1984.

Woods, Susanne. "Introduction." In *The Poems of Aemilia Lanyer: Salve Deus Rex Judaeorum*, ed. Susanne Woods. New York: Oxford University Press, 1993. xv–xlii.

———. *Lanyer: A Renaissance Woman*. New York: Oxford University Press, 1999.

Wright, Peter A. *The Pictorial History of the Royal Maundy*. London: Pitkin Pictorials, 1973.

Wrightson, Keith. *Earthly Necessities: Economic Lives in Early Modern Britain*. New Haven, Conn.: Yale University Press, 2000.

Yates, Frances. *Astraea: The Imperial Theme in the Sixteenth Century*. London: Routledge & Kegan Paul, 1975.

Ziegler, Georgianna. "Hand-Ma[i]de Books: The Manuscripts of Esther Inglis, Early-Modern Precursors of the Artists' Book." In *English Manuscript Studies 1100–1700*, ed. Peter Beal and Margaret J. M. Ezell. London: British Library, 2000. 9: 73–87.

———. "'More Than Feminine Boldness': The Gift Books of Esther Inglis." In *Women, Writing, and the Reproduction of Culture in Tudor and Stuart Britain*, ed. Mary E. Burke, Jane Donawerth, Linda L. Dove, and Karen Nelson. Syracuse, N.Y.: Syracuse University Press, 2000. 19–37.

———. "My Lady's Chamber: Female Space, Female Chastity in Shakespeare." *Textual Practice* 4:1 (1990): 73–100.

———. "Penelope and the Politics of Woman's Place in the Renaissance." In *Gloriana's Face: Women, Public and Private in the English Renaissance*, ed. S. P. Cerasano and Marion Wynne-Davies. London: Harvester Wheatsheaf, 1992. 25–46.

Index

125–28, 130–35, 155, 223–25n, 227n, 234n, 237n, 250n

education in visual and verbal media, 30–31, 33, 35, 39–41, 55; emblems, 6, 21, 52–54, 56, 58, 73, 106–7, 111, 113, 119, 179, 208, 224n, 235n, 258–59n; letters of, 3, 39–41, 55, 58, 72; needle-work of, 31, 33, 34 (fig. 3), 35, 36 (fig. 5), 37, 45, 73, 230n; and portraiture, 42 (and fig. 7), 43–44, 46, 240n; prayers, 154; translations, 3, 32, 39, 224n, 231n

Edward VI of England, xvii, 16, 19, 38, 41–42, 75, 80–81, 84, 227n, 233–34n

Eisenstein, Elizabeth L., 244n

elite classes, definition of, xvii, 19, 223n

Elizabeth I of England (Elizabeth Tudor), 30–74, 76–92, 95–102, 107, 112–13, 118, 140, 149, 197, 199, 208–11, 228n, 232–35n, 241–43n, 253–64n

embroiderers, 23, 43, 60, 63, 110, 118–19, 139, 167, 237n, 248n, 251n. *See also* needleworkers

embroidery, xv, xviii–xix, 2, 6–7, 14, 26, 37, 43–44, 52–53, 56, 63, 86, 102, 108, 113, 117, 119, 123, 132–33, 137, 140, 162, 167, 180, 192–93, 206, 209, 213, 224, 229, 251n, 256n. *See also* needlework

engravers, 77, 110, 202, 204

epitaphs, xvi, 1–3, 13, 25, 223n, 224n

Esther (Hester), 117–18, 133, 136–37, 145, 147–52, 154, 156–57, 186, 244–45n, 252–53n, 259n, 265n

Europoea, 98–99

everyday, 2–3, 10–12, 28–29, 163, 172–73, 176, 191, 196, 218, 220, 226n

everyday life, xix, 11, 21, 31, 74, 153, 163, 168, 189, 192, 221, 226n, 245n, 250n

Eworth, Hans, 149, 253n

Ezell, Margaret J. M., 27, 223n, 228–29n, 244n, 246–47n

female body, xix, 61, 139, 165, 167, 169, 176, 179–80, 184, 191, 193–95, 221, 260n

the feminine, xviii, xx, 2, 6, 9–10, 18, 31, 107, 114, 128, 135, 167–68, 170, 193–94, 229n, 245n, 249n, 251n

Finch, Anne, Countess of Winchelsea, 115, 118, 155, 254n

flame stitch. *See* Irish stitch

Fleming, Juliet, 4, 12, 27, 224n, 249n

Foister, Susan, 232n, 239–40n

Fowler, Constance Aston, 8–9, 225n

French knots, 122

gardens, 37, 44, 124–27, 132, 192, 199, 202, 203 (fig. 29), 204, 213, 214 (fig. 30), 250n, 261–62n, plates 10, 21

garments, 4, 31, 50, 68, 156, 185–88, 206–7. *See also* clothing; costumes; disguise

Garrard, Mary D., 139, 251–52n, 256n, 259n

Gee's Bend, Alabama, 14, 226n

gender, 112, 226, 229–30, 232, 235, 240, 243–45, 248n, 257n, 260n, 265n, 273–74n

genre, xix, 21, 25, 121, 131, 136–37, 145, 159, 177, 191, 209, 212, 227n, 245n, 257n, 274n

Gentlemen Pensioners, 80, 240

gentlewomen, 7, 19, 76, 78–79, 81, 128, 136, 155, 218, 227n, 240n, 254n

gentry, 56, 57, 130, 161, 167, 223n

Gibson, Anthony, 95, 149

Goldberg, Jonathan, 27, 103–4, 223, 225, 228, 242–45n

Gossett, Suzanne, 226n, 231n, 252n, 260n

Hackel, Heidi Brayman, 131, 226n, 248n, 250n

Hackett, Helen, 194, 260n, 262–64n

handkerchiefs, 26, 121, 125, 162–63, 229n, 257–58n. *See also* Shakespeare, William

handwriting, 89, 104. *See also* calligraphy; letters, forming of

hangings, xviii, 5, 54–55, 58, 60, 61–63, 68–69, 71, 127–28, 182, 185–86, 195, 198, 202, 213, 219, 236n. *See also* painted cloths; tapestries

Hannay, Margaret P., 152, 217, 225n, 254n, 259–64n

Hardwick Hall. *See* Bess of Hardwick

Harley, Brilliana, Lady, 56, 136, 149, 236n, 250–51n, 253n

Harrison, Edmund, 23, 228n

Hearn, Karen, 227n, 231n, 234n, 238n

Henry II of France, 45–46, 54

Henry VIII of England, xvii, 4, 30–32, 39, 41, 44, 54, 59, 75–81, 84–85, 87, 95, 198, 232n, 234n, 240–41n, 274n

Hepburn, James, Earl of Bothwell, 45, 50, 72, 140, 252n

Herbert, Mary Sidney, Countess of Pembroke, 15, 107, 115, 129, 154–55, 181, 192, 195, 199, 200, 201 (fig. 28), 210–11, 215, 217, 220, 259n, 262–63n

Herbert, William, Earl of Pembroke, 217, 261n, 263–64n

Hilliard, Nicholas, 44, 72, 87

historical phenomenology, 27, 229n

Hoby, Margaret, Lady, xv, 123, 125, 128, 219, 248n, 255n

Holbein, Hans, 35 (and fig. 4), 37, 44, 80, 232n, 239–40n

Holofernes, 156, 252n, 254n, 265n

Homer, 102, 243n, 261n. *See also* Penelope; Ulysses

Hooch, Pieter de, 173–74 (and fig. 27)

Hookes, Nicholas, 120

Horenbout, Susanna, 78–81, 89, 102, 114, 239–40n

shorthand, 89, 92–93, 215, 223n, 242n. *See also* anagrams; codes; charactery; ciphers; initials

sibyls, 87–88, 91, 93–96, 99–100, 170, 239n, 241n

Sidney, Henry, 197, 261n

Sidney, Mary Dudley, 197, 218, 261n

Sidney, Philip, 11, 24–25, 154, 192, 207, 210–12, 215, 220, 225, 228n, 243n, 254n, 260–61n, 263–64n, 272n

Sidney, Robert, Viscount Lisle, Earl of Leicester, 20, 50, 127, 196, 198, 225n, 261–62n, 264n, 268n, 272n

Sidney name, 202

signature, 33, 37, 50, 215, 217, 233n

silk, 44, 49, 59–60, 70, 77, 137, 142, 148, 170, 183, 199–200, 206–7, 221, 246n

Skelton, John, 118–19, 123, 175, 246n, 248n, 258n

Smith, Bruce 27, 29, 225n, 229n

Smith, Hannah, x–xi, 133–34, 152, 254n

Solis, Virgil, 63–64 (and fig. 10), 237n

Solomon, x, xviii, 18, 107, 121, 125, 135, 139, 144–45, 154

song, 8, 10, 21, 85, 96, 101, 154–55, 188, 258n

Spain, 6, 51–52, 149

The Spectator, 128

speech, 3, 13, 40, 93, 117, 142, 147, 149, 151–55, 164, 168, 173, 182, 206, 215, 225–26n

speeches, 30, 41, 73, 102, 243n, 257n

spinning, xix, 10, 13, 21, 25, 220, 255n

spots, 98, 118, 130, 145, 164–65, 172–74

spot samplers, xviii, 116–17, 121–23, 126, 172, 177, 247n, 249n; Jane Bostocke's, 122, 172, plate 9

Stallybrass, Peter, 27–29, 118, 168–69, 229–30n, 256–57n, 259n. *See also* Jones, Ann

state bed, 53–54, 72, 181, 235n

Stein, Gertrude, 26–27, 229n

Stent, Peter, 136, 251n

stitches, 25, 58–59, 117, 119, 122–23, 126, 129, 131, 133, 145, 147, 166, 172, 177, 248–49n, 257n. *See also* beadwork; blackwork; buttonhole stitch; chain stitch; crewel work; cross stitch; French knots; Irish stitch; raised work; running stitch; satin stitch; tent stitch; true stitch

strawberry patterns, 122, 131–32, 148, 164, 170–72, 177, plate 9

Strong, Roy, 77, 81, 83, 227n, 234n, 238–43n

Stuart, Arbella, 59–60, 65–66

stumpwork. *See* raised work

subjectivity, xvi, 11, 21, 111, 118, 153, 162, 180, 183–84, 187, 189

subjects: and agency, 118, 122 (*see also* agency; identity); and attempt to define the "self," 11; and object, xvi, 27–29, 168, 229–20n, 257n; positions of, 12, 194; and social relations, 11

succession, 32, 39, 43, 45, 95, 208

suicide, xix, 177, 181–82

Susanna, xviii, 10, 78, 107, 135, 139–41, 145, 156, 247n, 251–52n, 265n

Swain, Margaret, 60, 231–32n, 235–37n, 242n, 247n, 249–51n, 253n

Talbot, George, Earl of Shrewsbury, xvii, 57, 62, 65, 73, 236n

tapestries, xi, 3, 5, 15, 57–59, 61, 66, 72, 77, 79–80, 86, 127, 135, 180–83, 192–93, 198, 212, 219–20, 238n, 240n, 264–65n. *See also* hangings; painted cloths

Tarquin, 183, 185

Taylor, John, 129–30, 199, 249, 287, 289

Teerlinc, George, 80

Teerlinc, Levina, vii, ix, xi, xv, xvii, 9, 75–115, 116, 233, 240

tent stitch, 51–52, 58, 70 (and fig. 13), 129, 133, 235n

Tereus, 183–84

textile metaphors, 210, 212

textiles, vii, xv, xviii–xix, 13–14, 19, 21, 23, 27, 29, 44, 61, 71, 80, 110, 116, 126–27, 135, 152, 160, 163, 167–68, 170–73, 175, 177–81, 184–87, 189–93, 197–99, 205–7, 209–10, 212, 218–22, 249–50n, 254–56n, 258n, 261n. *See also* cloth

texts, verbal. *See* band samplers; diaries; epitaphs; inscriptions; letters; life writing; *names of individual authors*; paintings, inscriptions in; poetry; prayers; psalms; romance; samplers; speech, speeches

texts, visual, xx, 3, 9, 15, 73, 75, 113, 135, 168. *See also* design; miniatures; *names of individual artists*; needlework; paintings

textualities, women's, xv–xx, 1–8, 9, 12, 15, 25–26, 30, 41, 51, 75, 88, 132, 135, 189–90, 193, 195, 212–18, 229n, 224n, 231n, 246n

thread, 13, 25, 117, 136–37, 140, 160, 165–66, 195, 199, 220; silver thread, 35, 39, 51, 113

Tickell, Thomas, 128

title page, 83, 101, 103, 111–14, 202–3 (and fig. 29), 204–5, 222, 262n

tradition, xv, xviii, 14, 54, 68, 75, 78, 82, 85, 92, 95, 108, 115, 120, 139, 153, 157, 159

translation, xvii–xviii, 2, 6, 12, 18, 30–33, 39–40, 43–44, 52, 73, 93, 95, 96, 98, 100, 110, 149, 181, 200, 210–12, 224n, 231–32n, 237n, 243n, 261n, 264n. *See also* cloth, translation of

true stitch, 119

turkey work, 5, 127, 200, 248n

Tyler, Margaret, 212, 264n

Ulysses, 66, 195–96, 238

Urania. See Wroth, Mary Sidney, *Countess of Montgomery's Urania*

Acknowledgments

This book was more than a decade in the making, and would not exist without the help of many people. Among its most recent supporters are Jerry Singerman of the University of Pennsylvania Press and his assistant, Caroline Winschel. Joan Pong Linton and David Riggs, as well as the press's readers, Ann Rosalind Jones and Maureen Quilligan, generously read the entire manuscript. Still others ready with encouragement and suggestions include Valerie Wayne, Georgianna Ziegler, Karen Hearn, Stephen Orgel, Bruce Smith, Lowell Gallagher, Valerie Traub, Heather Wolfe, Steven May, Sara Jayne Steen, James Daybell, Julie Crawford, Bradin Cormack, Patricia Parker, Barbara Hodgdon, and Lori Newcomb. Mary Ellen Lamb read a penultimate draft of the last chapter with characteristic care. James Brain, Elspeth Yeo, Susan Foister, Margaret Hannay, Hilarie Cash, Diana Lewton Brain, Naomi Miller, Rebecca Laroche, Elizabeth Robertson, Jeffrey Robinson, and Suzanne Trill helped with information at key moments. Peter Parolin helped me to unknot early drafts. As my co-editor of *Maids and Mistresses, Cousins and Queens: Women's Alliances in Early Modern England*, a precursor of this book, Karen Robertson was central to the formation of my argument and provided many helpful suggestions about the bibliography and organization. For more than a decade, many students contributed to this project's formation in seminar discussions, papers, theses, and publications including Heather Ackerman, Joanne Gaudio, Benjamin Casten, Amy Tigner, and Jennifer Munroe. Charity DuPrat proved an able research assistant, while Sandra Schwartzkopf, who left us far too young, was student, research assistant, and friend. During the crucial time that my research became a manuscript, Cathy Connelly, Lois Berry, Theresa Bogard, and Susanna Goodin provided emotional support in the form of a lively bridge group.

I thank my colleagues in the English Department at the University of Wyoming for their support, especially Susan Aronstein, Janice Harris, Cedric Reverand, Carolyn Anderson, Robert Torry, Jeanne Holland, Caroline McCracken Flesher, Duncan Harris, Vicky Lindner, Janet Constantinides, Sandy Clark, and

Harvey Hix, as well as staff members Keith Kanbe, Patricia Romero, and Plum Schultz. Also at the University of Wyoming, B. Oliver Walter, Dean of Arts and Sciences; Maggie Farrell, Dean of the Libraries; William Gern, Vice President for Research; and English Department heads Mark Booth, Janice Harris, and Peter Parolin provided key financial and logistical support.

As I worked on this book, I often found myself thinking about how fortunate I was in my teachers, who, in the 1970s and 1980s, sent me off on my trajectory of research, writing, and teaching. Accordingly, I would like to thank my professors at Smith College, especially Thomas Mendenhall, Klemens von Klemperer, Howard Nenner, Patricia Skarda, and Richard Young. My professors at the University of New Mexico, including Morris Eaves, Mary Bess Whidden, Hamlin Hill, and James Thorsten, offered me the chance to see further. At Stanford the faculty, including Mary Wack, Ronald Rebholz, John Bender, David Riggs, Wesley Trimpi, and Stephen Orgel, were both generous and rigorous. The seminars of visiting professors Louis Adrian Montrose and Morton Bloomfield were crucial in helping me to form an intellectual model of the early modern period that is always under construction.

In libraries and archives I have been fortunate to meet people who were not only professional but also kind about providing materials and sharing insights. I would have been lost without Elizabeth Bress, Digital Art Librarian at the University of Wyoming, whose technical expertise and organization were crucial in bringing together this volume's illustrations. Kaijsa Calkins, English Department Liaison, helped me find key texts. The Interlibrary Loan staff at the Coe Library—Dee Salo, Ellen Swingle, Emily Guier, and Lindsay Ross—have made it possible for me to conduct research on many early modern topics with goodwill and good cheer. In England, Robert York, archivist at the College of Arms, London, led me to Jane Segar's biographical details; Margaret Swain graciously answered my questions about early modern needlework for hours together in Edinburgh, August 1994; Frances Hartog and Koynia Marko of the National Trust Conservation Studio at Blickling allowed me to spend a day in close proximity to the needlework of Mary Queen of Scots; Carmella Gallea at the Great Yarmouth Old Merchants Houses explored with me the architectural and cultural connections between Yarmouth and the Dutch. Still others who made key materials available were Bruce Barker Benfield at the Duke of Humphreys Library; Janet McMullen at the Christ Church College Library, Oxford; Mrs. Hughes and Margaret Turley of Hardwick Hall; Joanna Linda Wooley at the Victoria and Albert Museum; Jill Ivy at the Durham Cathedral Library; and Helen Orme at the Maidstone Archive, Kent. I am also grateful to the helpful staff at the Huntington Library, the British Museum's Department of Prints and

Drawings, the British Library's Manuscripts Students' Room, and the National Library of Scotland.

Financial support of this project included a University of Wyoming Faculty Grant-in-Aid, Faculty Development Grants from the College of Arts and Sciences at Wyoming, and a National Endowment for the Humanities Fellowship. I would like to thank Mark Horowitz and Ed Hudson for the many ways they provided support for this endeavor. For subvention support for the color illustrations, I am grateful to the University of Pennsylvania Press and the University of Wyoming Research Office, the College of Arts and Sciences, and the English Department.

From the first moment of my life to this, my family has provided me with a sense of personal and intellectual connection. My father, Bruce Frye, who died in 2002, raised me as a historian's daughter. My brothers, Tom and Brad, are sources of joy and memory. My mother, Caroline Frye, started me off as a student of Shakespeare at the age of seven, when she gave me a used copy of *Romeo and Juliet* bound in blue leather. Over the years that I spent on this project, she provided many active forms of support, from looking after my young daughter during research trips and conferences, to sustaining us with delicious meals, to asking the right question because of her own interests in history and literature. Included in my family now is my daughter's fiancé, Hervé Picherit, who, as my friend and colleague, has provided unwavering support and many insights from the point of view of his specialty, French literature.

My daughter, Elizabeth Caroline Hacker, called "Lizzie," illuminates my life. Early in our relationship, she turned the tables on me, becoming my support as much as I was hers and teaching me how much we have to learn from our children. At various points during this project, she has acted as sounding board, research assistant, editor, and consultant on visual materials. As I finished this manuscript, she was finishing her English honors degree at Smith College, which included a year at the University of Edinburgh, experiences that are sending her off on her own path as intellect and author, seeking her own definitions of the feminine. In love, respect, and gratitude, I dedicate this book to her.

Lord de L'Isle graciously granted permission to use and publish materials from the Centre for Kentish Studies, Maidstone.

Some of the material in this book is based on earlier publications, with the permission of the publishers:

"Elizabeth When a Princess: Early Self-representations in a Portrait and a Letter." In *The Body of the Queen: Gender and Rule in the Courtly World, 1500–2000*, ed. Regina Schulte. New York: Berghahn Books, 2006. 43–60.
"Materializing Authorship in Esther Inglis's Books." *Journal of Medieval and*

Early Modern Studies 32:3 (fall 2002): 469–92 (published by Duke University Press).

"Sewing Connections: Elizabeth Tudor, Mary Stuart, Elizabeth Talbot, and Seventeenth-Century Anonymous Needleworkers." In *Maids and Mistresses, Cousins and Queens: Women's Alliances in Early Modern England*, ed. Susan Frye and Karen Robertson. New York: Oxford University Press, 1999. 165–82.

"Staging Women's Relations to Textiles in *Othello* and *Cymbeline*." In *Early Modern Visual Culture: Representation, Race, and Empire in Renaissance England*, ed. Peter Erickson and Clark Hulse. Philadelphia: University of Pennsylvania Press, 2000, 215–50.

Acknowledgments